OSSAN IDOL! 04

MANGA ◆ ICHIKA KINO
ORIGINAL STORY ◆
MOCHIKO MOCHIDA
CHARACTER DESIGN ◆
MIZUKI SAKAKIBARA

STORY

MIROKU, A 270 LB UNEMPLOYED SHUT-IN, WAS SPURRED ON BY THE POPULARITY OF HIS "LET'S TRY DANCING" VIDEO, JOINED A GYM, GOT IN SHAPE, AND TRANSFORMED INTO A MIDDLE-AGED HUNK IN NO TIME! ALONG WITH YOICHI AND SHIJU, HE CAUGHT THE EYE OF A FAMOUS PRODUCER, MR. LAVENDER, AND THE THREE MEN SUCCESSFULLY DEBUTED AS MIYOSHI! THE EVENTS THEY PARTICIPATED IN WERE ALL HUGE SUCCESSES, TOO. BUT A YOUNG MAN NAMED ONO HAS APPEARED, SAYING THAT HE LOVES MIROKU'S OLDER SISTER, MIHACHI!

CHARACTERS

be fore

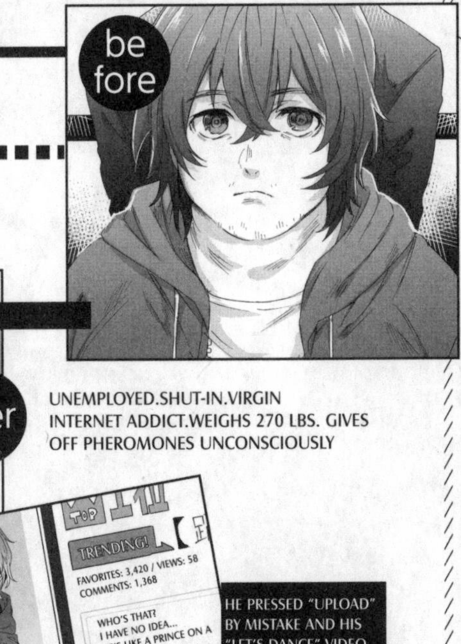

MIROKU (36)

MIROKU OSAKI

TURNED INTO A PRINCE!♥

after

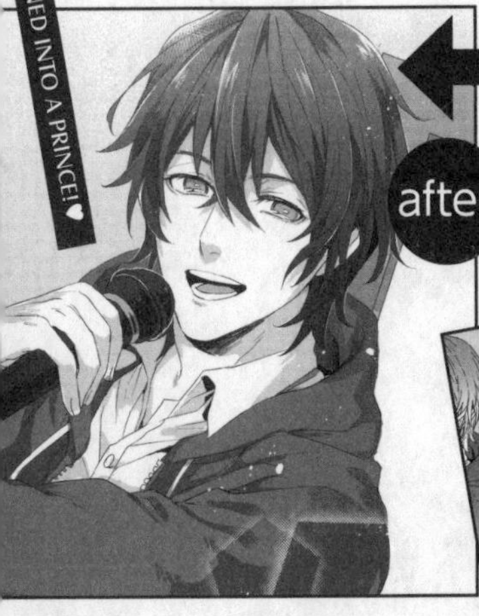

UNEMPLOYED.SHUT-IN.VIRGIN
INTERNET ADDICT.WEIGHS 270 LBS. GIVES OFF PHEROMONES UNCONSCIOUSLY

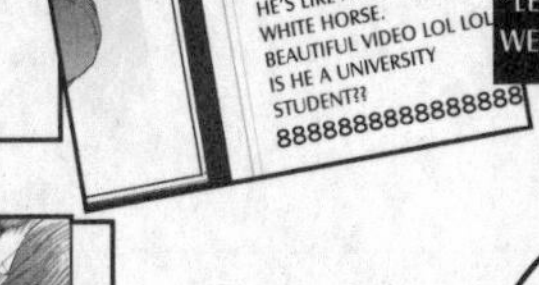
TOP
TRENDING!
FAVORITES: 3,420 / VIEWS: 58
COMMENTS: 1,368
WHO'S THAT?
I HAVE NO IDEA...
HE'S LIKE A PRINCE ON A WHITE HORSE.
BEAUTIFUL VIDEO LOL LOL
IS HE A UNIVERSITY STUDENT??
8888888888888888

HE PRESSED "UPLOAD" BY MISTAKE AND HIS "LET'S DANCE" VIDEO WENT VIRAL!

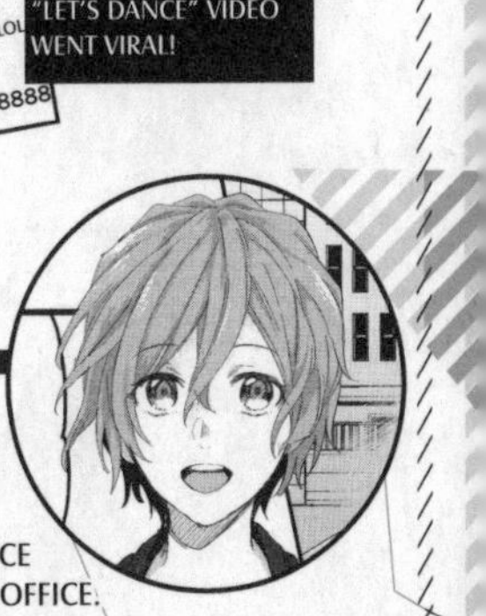

FUMI

FUMI KISARAGI

YOICHI'S BUBBLY NIECE WHO WORKS AT HIS OFFICE. SHE ALWAYS PUTS HER ALL INTO HER WORK.

MI'S HERO, MAN O SAVED R FROM A UBLESOME STOMER, S ACTUALLY OKU BACK EN HE WAS UBBY!

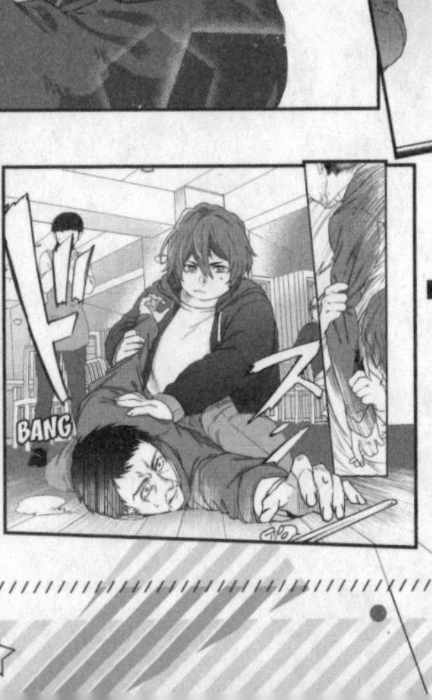
BANG

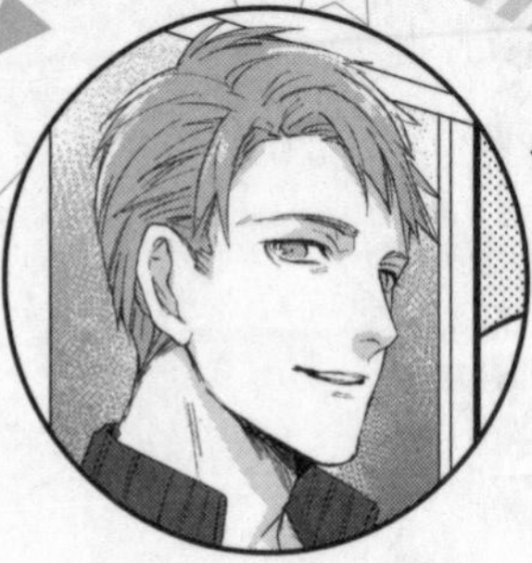

YOICHI (41)

YOICHI KISARAGI

HE WAS OVER 300 LBS, BUT NOW YOICHI IS THE CEO OF A SMALL ENTERTAINMENT COMPANY. HE AND MIROKU MET AT THE GYM. USED TO BE AN IDOL FOR THE SHINEEZ TALENT AGENCY.

SHIJU (40)

SHIJU ONOHARA

A FORMER DANCER AND HOST, NOW UNEMPLOYED AND LEADING A LIFE ON THE EDGE. HE WAS THE ONE WHO SUGGESTED THAT MIROKU TAKE PART IN THE DANCE COMPETITION.

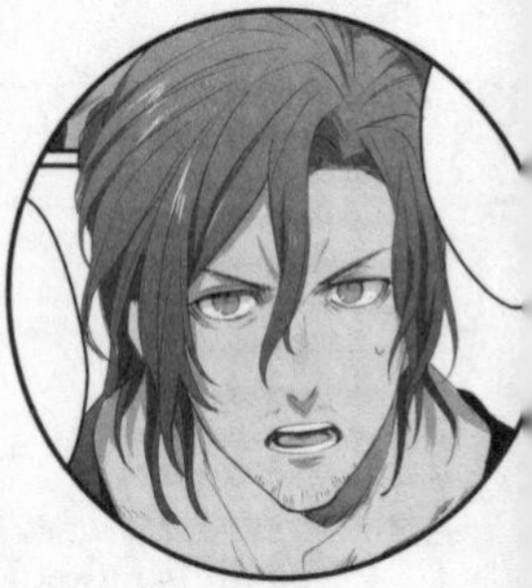

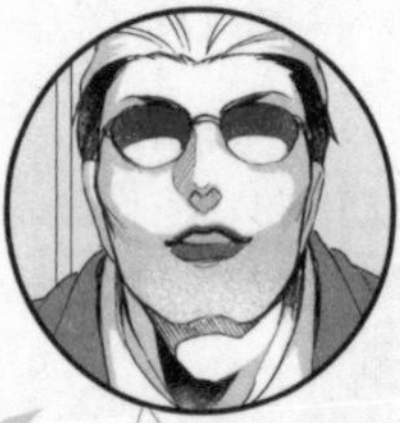

KAMO LAVENDER

PRODUCER EXTRAORDINAIRE OF NATIONALLY TREASURED IDOL GROUPS SUCH AS UGUISUDANI SEVEN.

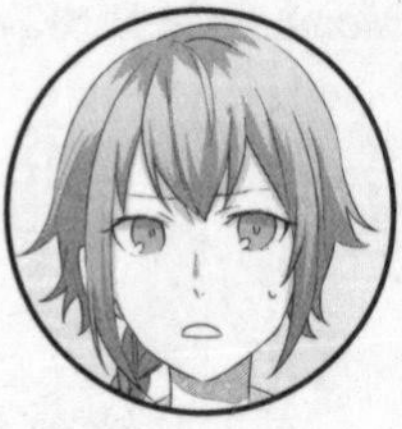

NINA OSAKI

MIROKU'S LITTLE SISTER AND AN ASSISTANT HAIRSTYLIST. SHE HAS MUSICAL TALENT AND HAS EVEN GIVEN SHIJU VOICE LESSONS.

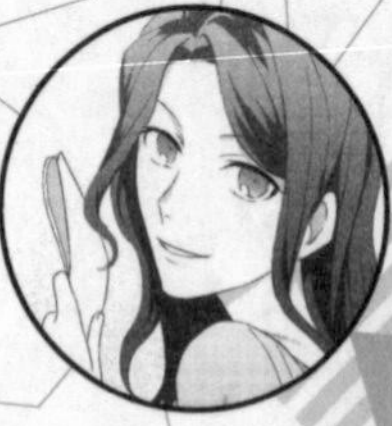

MIHACHI OSAKI

MIROKU'S OLDER SISTER WHO WAS YOICHI'S BIGGEST FAN IN HIS IDOL DAYS AND LOVES HIM EVEN NOW.

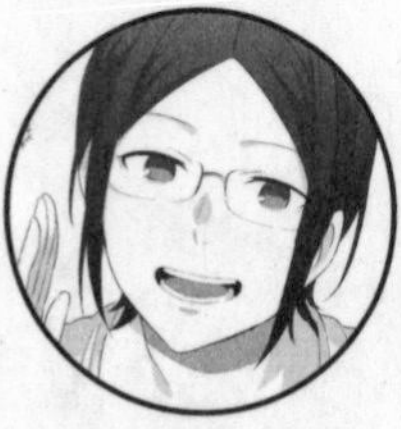

MAKI

FUMI'S BEST FRIEND AND AN OTAKU. SHE SEEMS TO BE OVERLY CAUTIOUS OF MIROKU...?

OSSAN IDOL

CONTENTS

Chapter 18

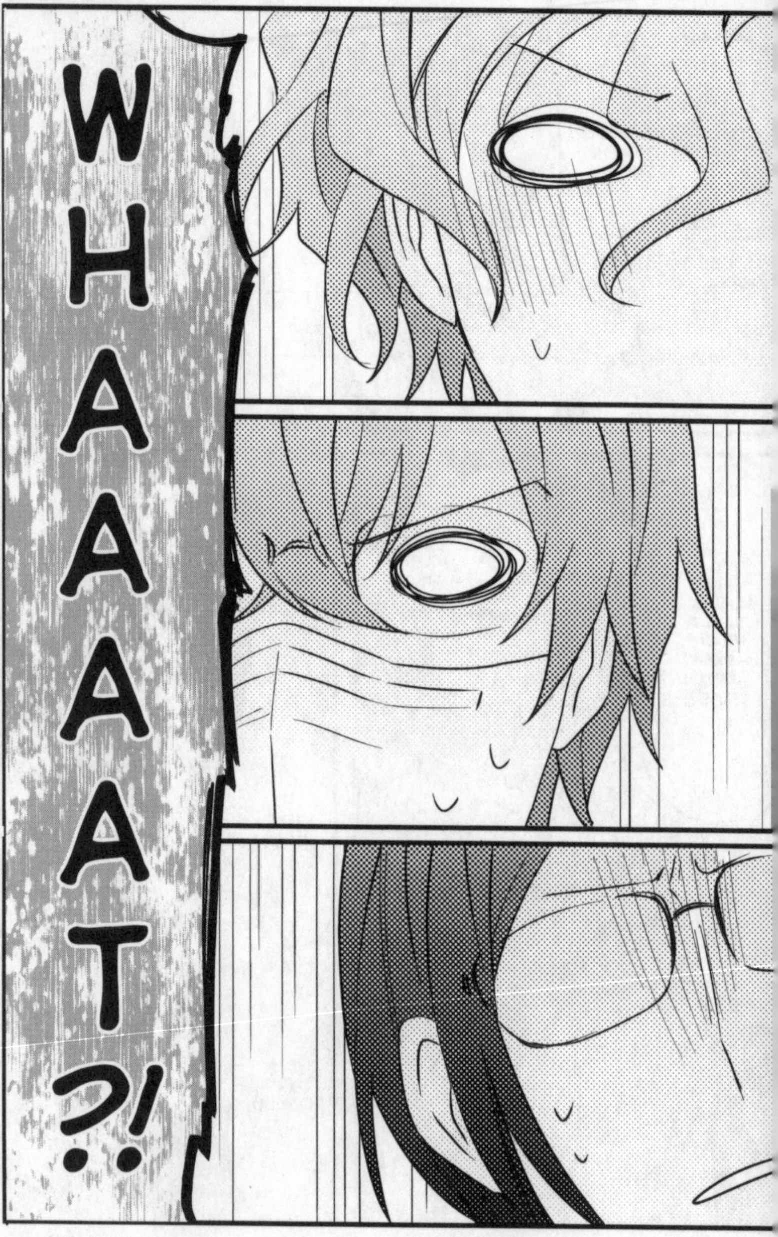
WHAAAAAT?!

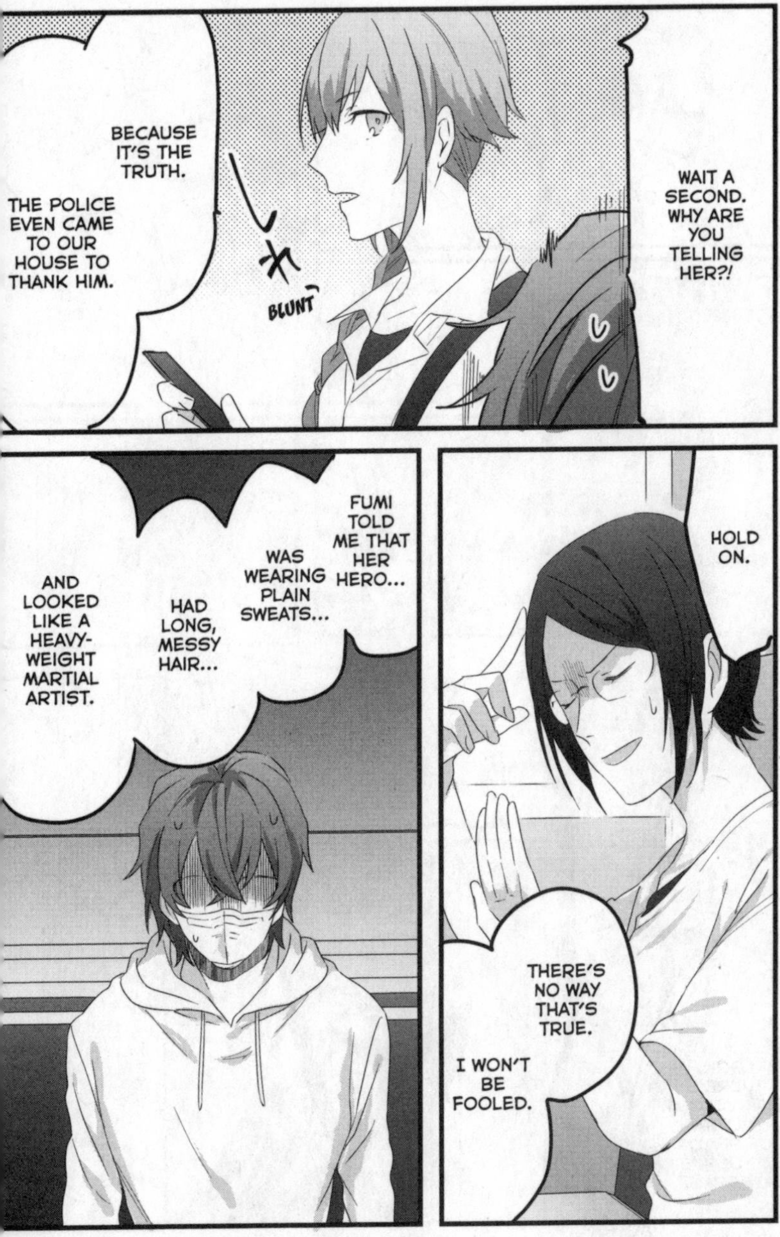
WAIT A SECOND. WHY ARE YOU TELLING HER?!
BECAUSE IT'S THE TRUTH.
THE POLICE EVEN CAME TO OUR HOUSE TO THANK HIM.
BLUNT
HOLD ON.
THERE'S NO WAY THAT'S TRUE.
I WON'T BE FOOLED.
FUMI TOLD ME THAT HER HERO...
WAS WEARING PLAIN SWEATS...
HAD LONG, MESSY HAIR...
AND LOOKED LIKE A HEAVY-WEIGHT MARTIAL ARTIST.

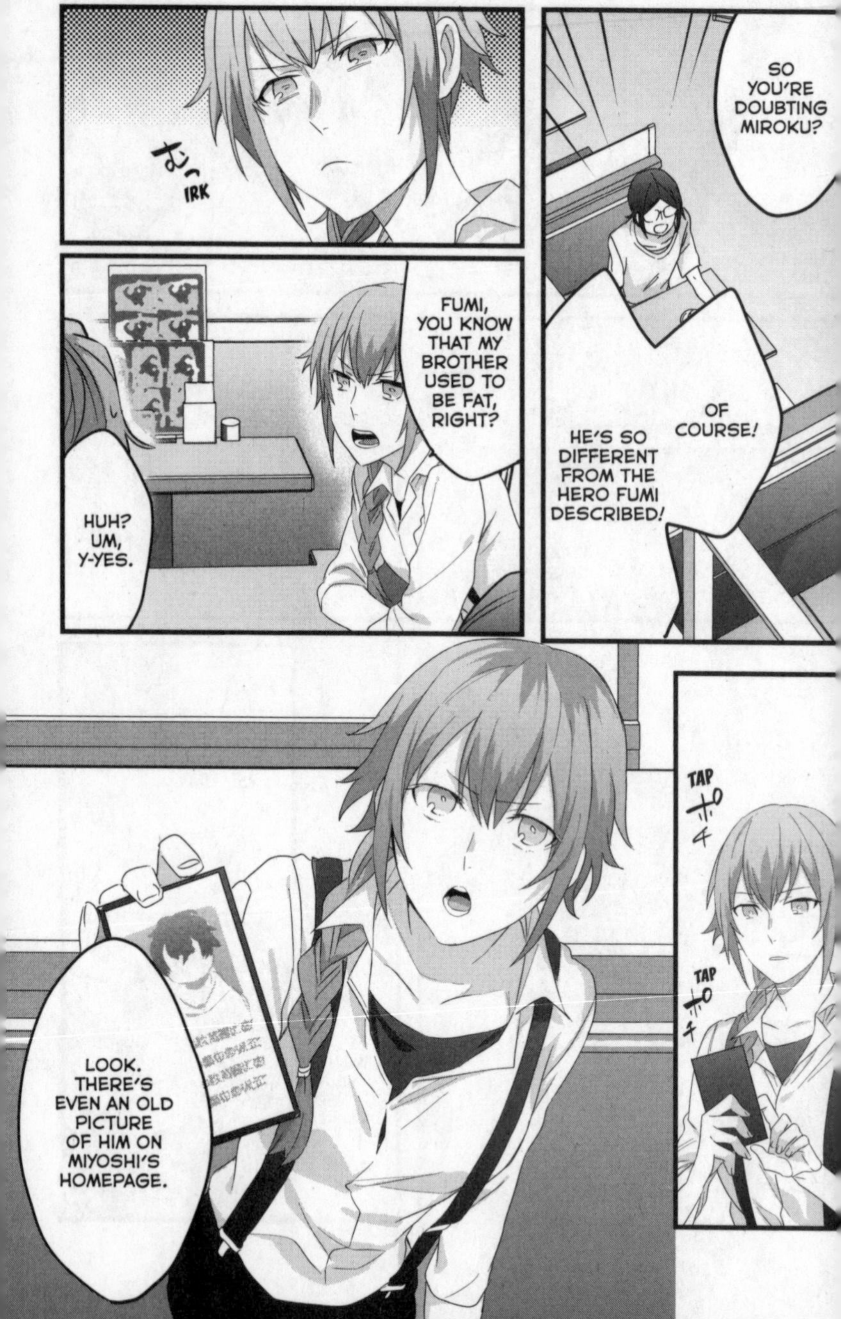
SO YOU'RE DOUBTING MIROKU?
OF COURSE!
HE'S SO DIFFERENT FROM THE HERO FUMI DESCRIBED!
むっ
IRK
FUMI, YOU KNOW THAT MY BROTHER USED TO BE FAT, RIGHT?
HUH? UM, Y-YES.
TAP
ポチ
TAP
ポチ
LOOK. THERE'S EVEN AN OLD PICTURE OF HIM ON MIYOSHI'S HOMEPAGE.

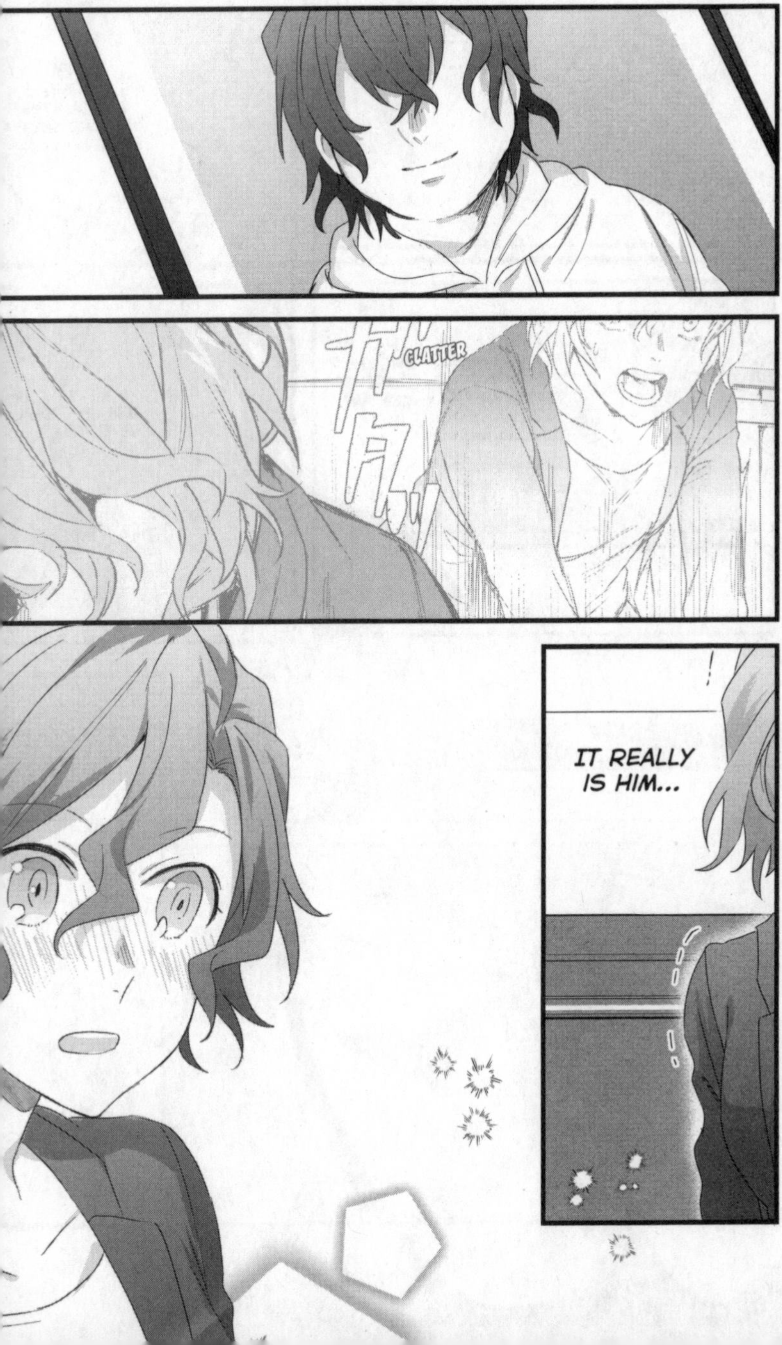
ガタッ
CLATTER
!
IT REALLY IS HIM...

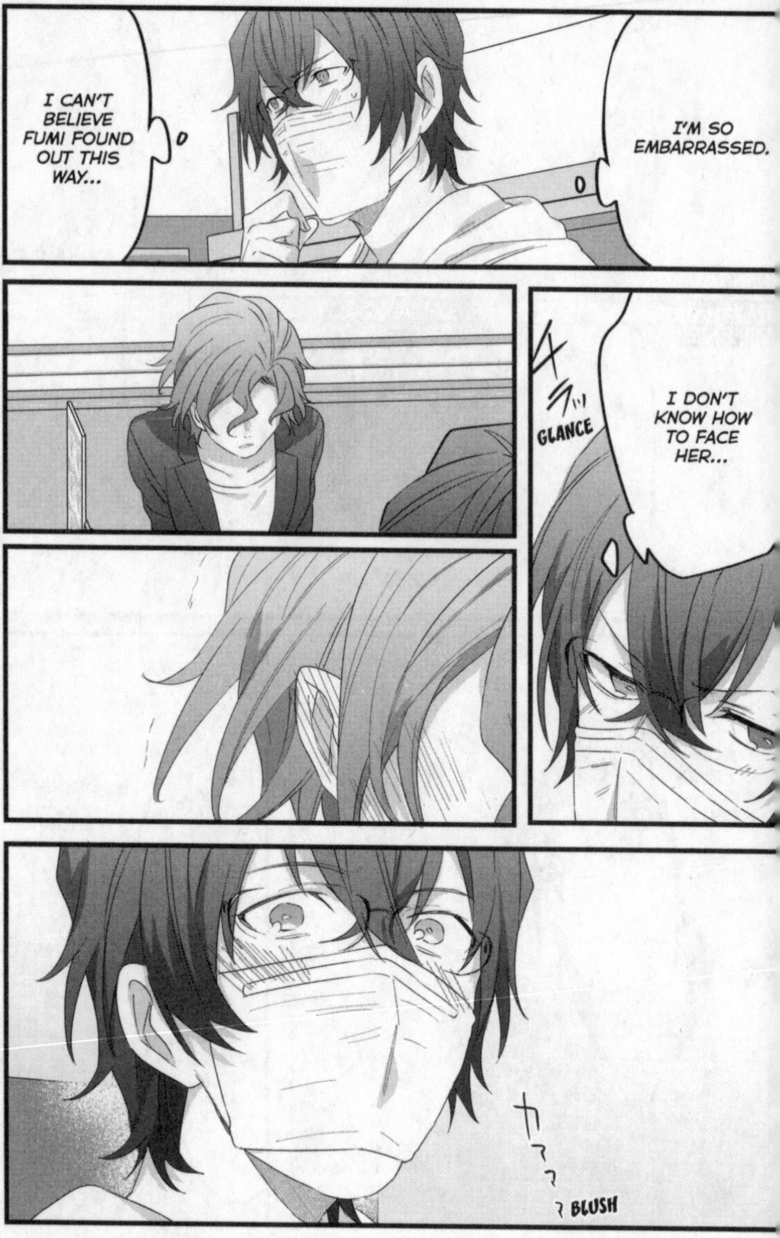
I'M SO EMBARRASSED.
I CAN'T BELIEVE FUMI FOUND OUT THIS WAY...
I DON'T KNOW HOW TO FACE HER...
GLANCE
BLUSH

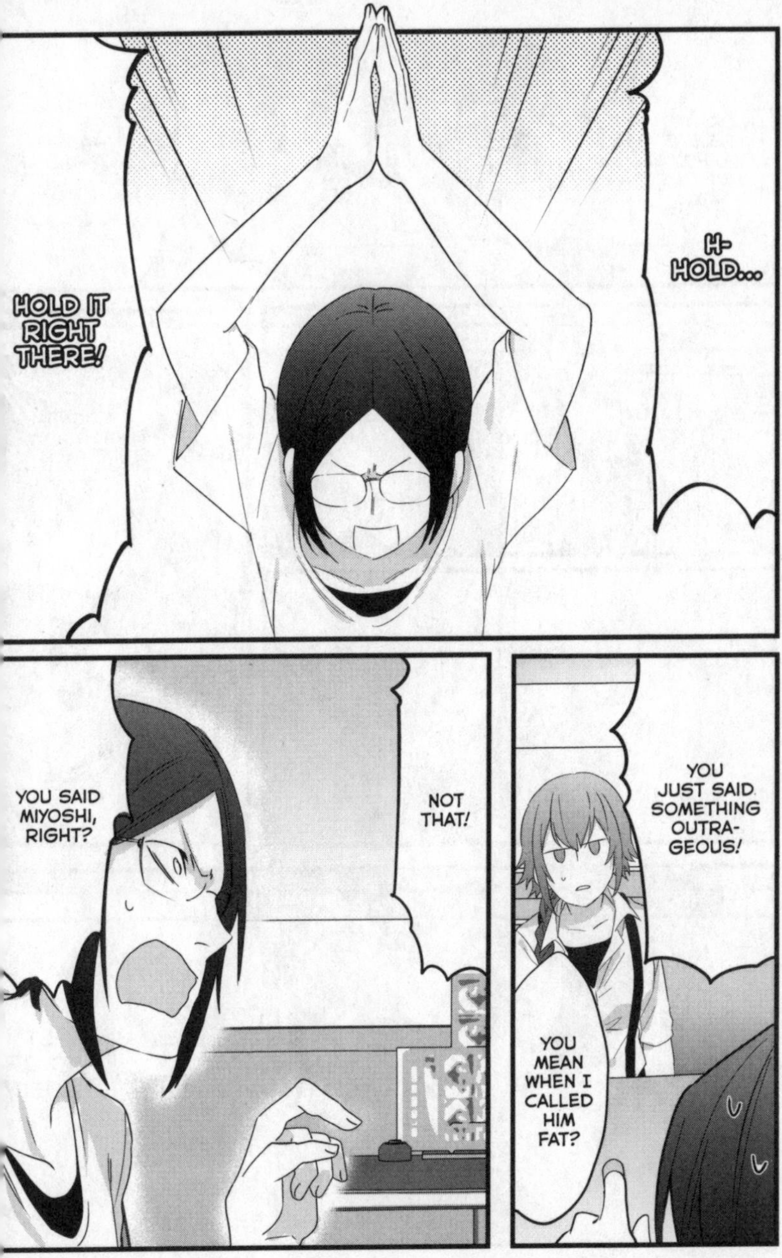
H-HOLD...
HOLD IT RIGHT THERE!
YOU JUST SAID SOMETHING OUTRA-GEOUS!
YOU MEAN WHEN I CALLED HIM FAT?
NOT THAT!
YOU SAID MIYOSHI, RIGHT?

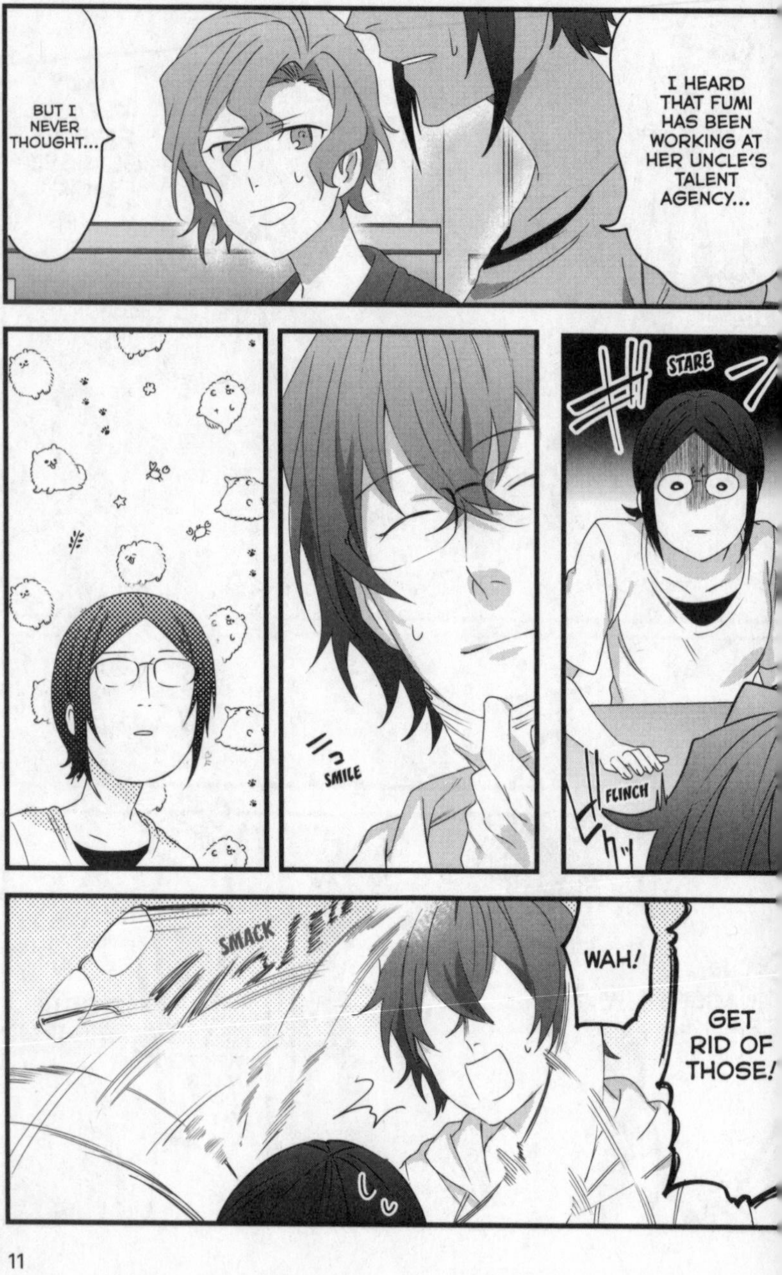

I HEARD THAT FUMI HAS BEEN WORKING AT HER UNCLE'S TALENT AGENCY...
BUT I NEVER THOUGHT...
STARE
FLINCH
SMILE
WAH!
GET RID OF THOSE!
SMACK

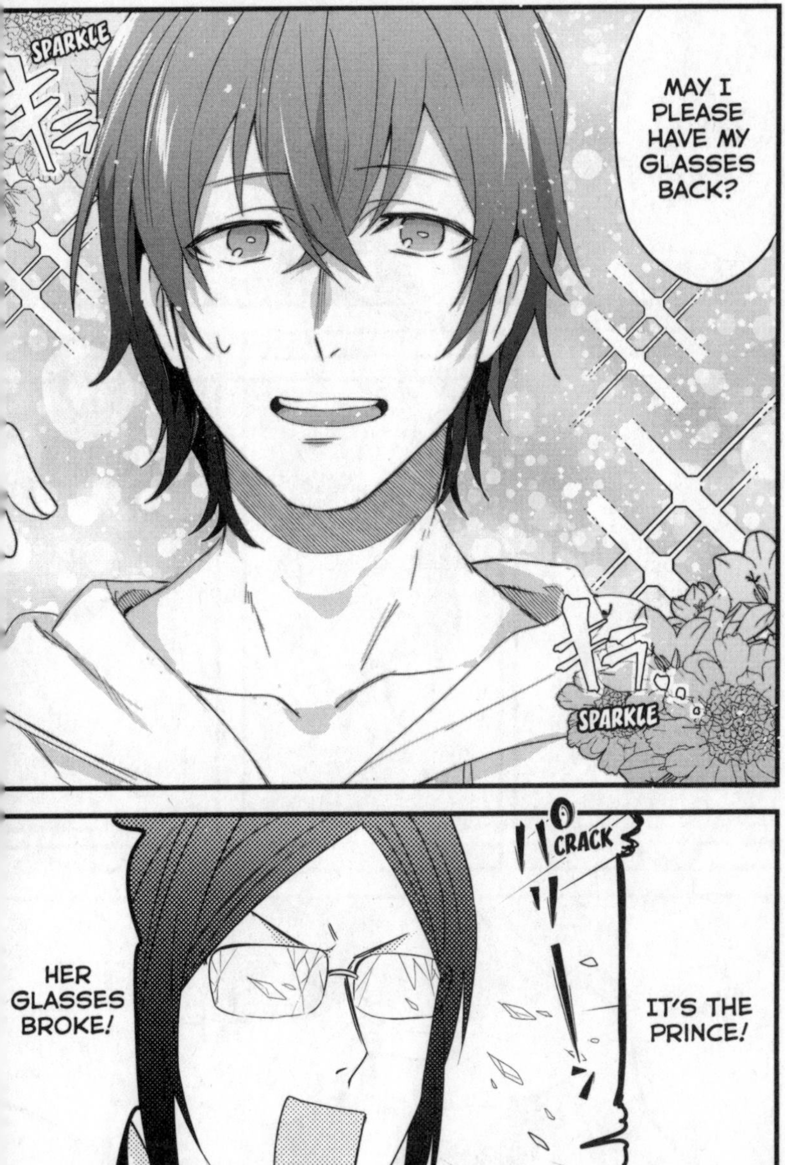
MAY I PLEASE HAVE MY GLASSES BACK?
SPARKLE
SPARKLE
CRACK
IT'S THE PRINCE!
HER GLASSES BROKE!

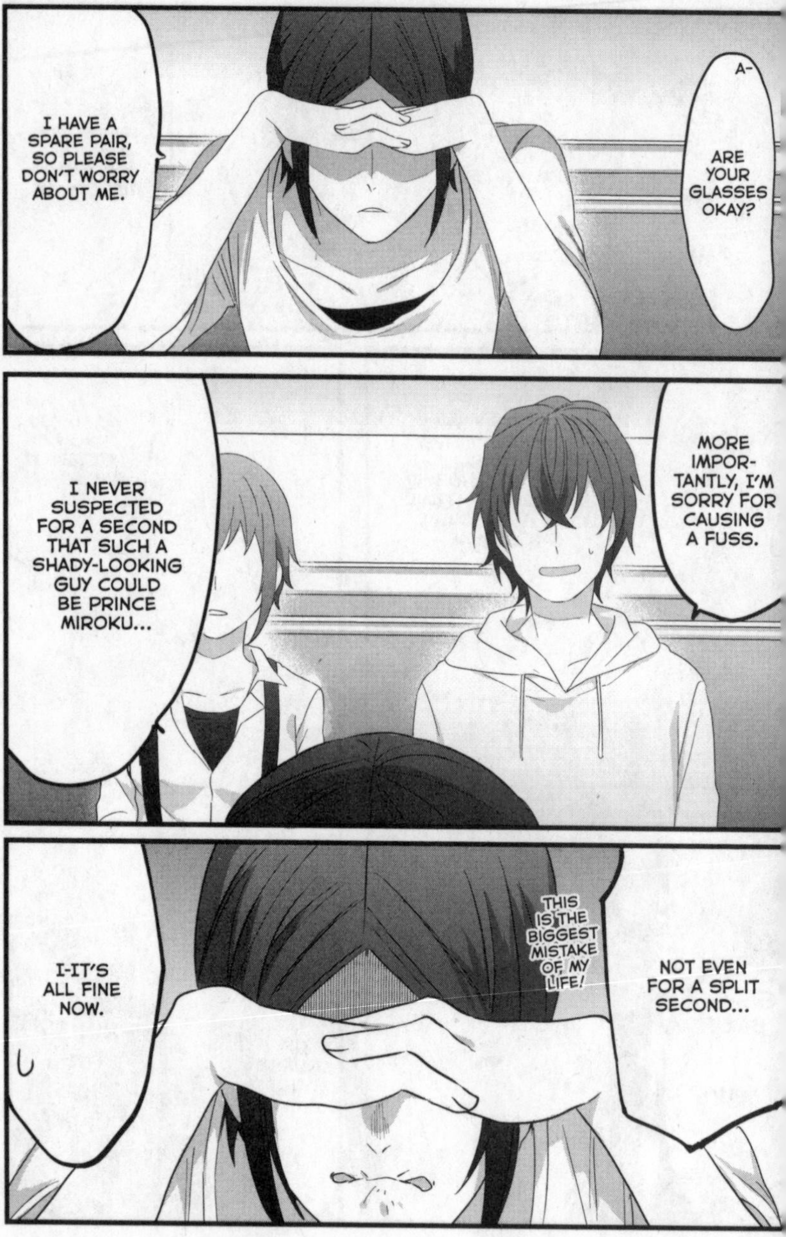
A-
ARE YOUR GLASSES OKAY?
I HAVE A SPARE PAIR, SO PLEASE DON'T WORRY ABOUT ME.
MORE IMPOR-TANTLY, I'M SORRY FOR CAUSING A FUSS.
I NEVER SUSPECTED FOR A SECOND THAT SUCH A SHADY-LOOKING GUY COULD BE PRINCE MIROKU...
NOT EVEN FOR A SPLIT SECOND...
THIS IS THE BIGGEST MISTAKE OF MY LIFE!
I-IT'S ALL FINE NOW.

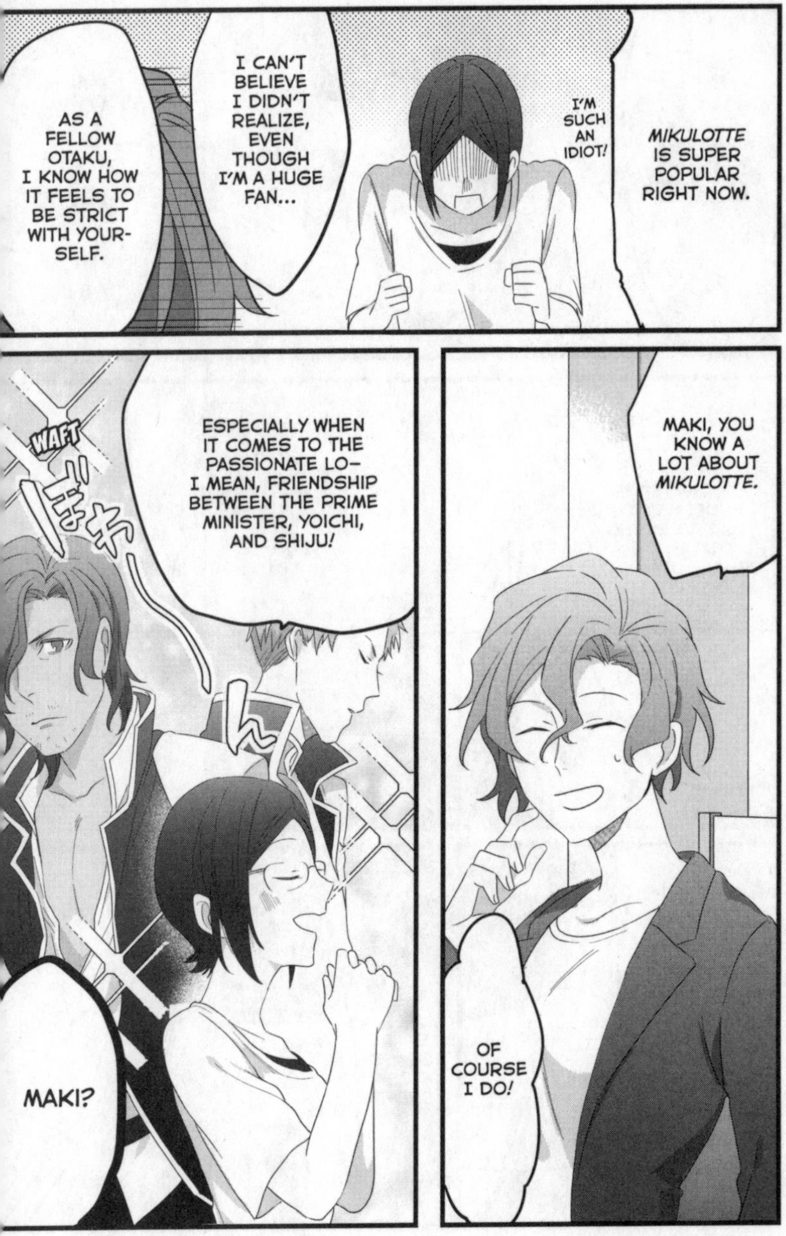
MIKULOTTE IS SUPER POPULAR RIGHT NOW.
I'M SUCH AN IDIOT!
I CAN'T BELIEVE I DIDN'T REALIZE, EVEN THOUGH I'M A HUGE FAN...
AS A FELLOW OTAKU, I KNOW HOW IT FEELS TO BE STRICT WITH YOURSELF.
MAKI, YOU KNOW A LOT ABOUT *MIKULOTTE.*
OF COURSE I DO!
ESPECIALLY WHEN IT COMES TO THE PASSIONATE LO— I MEAN, FRIENDSHIP BETWEEN THE PRIME MINISTER, YOICHI, AND SHIJU!
WAFT
MAKI?

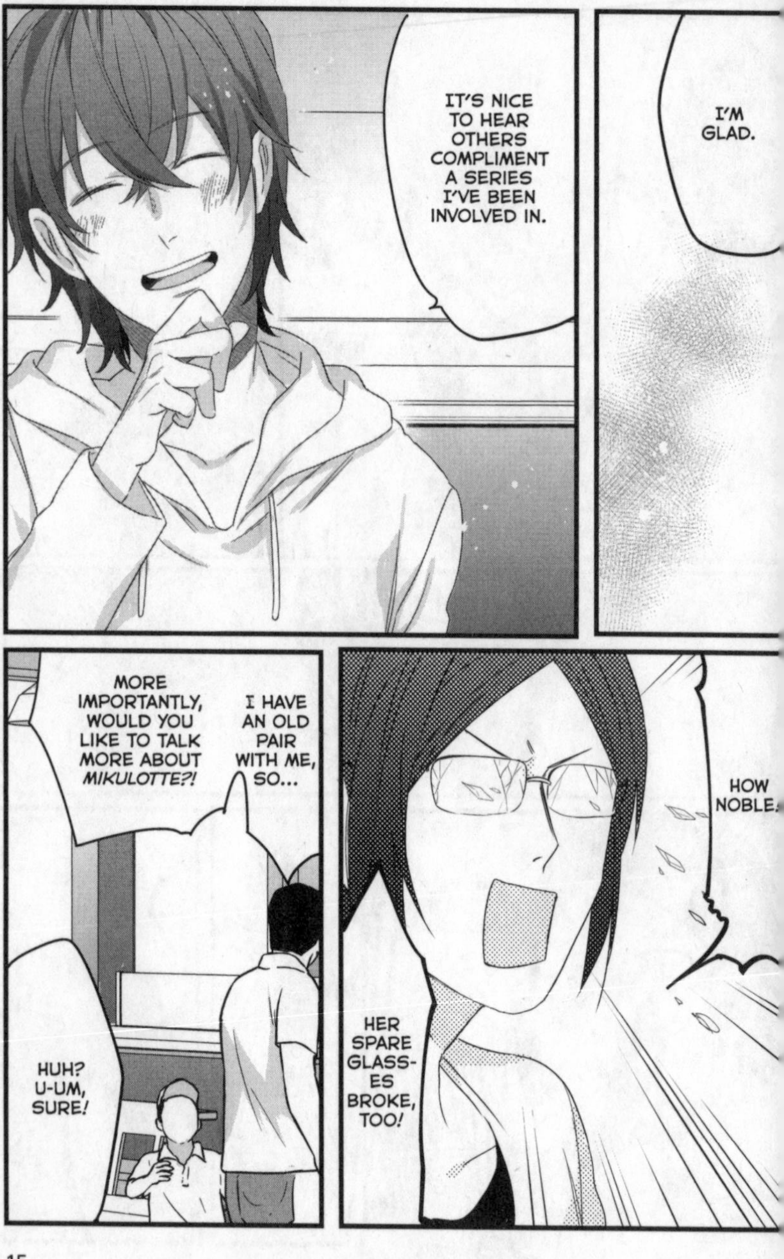
I'M GLAD.
IT'S NICE TO HEAR OTHERS COMPLIMENT A SERIES I'VE BEEN INVOLVED IN.
HOW NOBLE.
HER SPARE GLASS-ES BROKE, TOO!
I HAVE AN OLD PAIR WITH ME, SO...
MORE IMPORTANTLY, WOULD YOU LIKE TO TALK MORE ABOUT *MIKULOTTE?!*
HUH? U-UM, SURE!

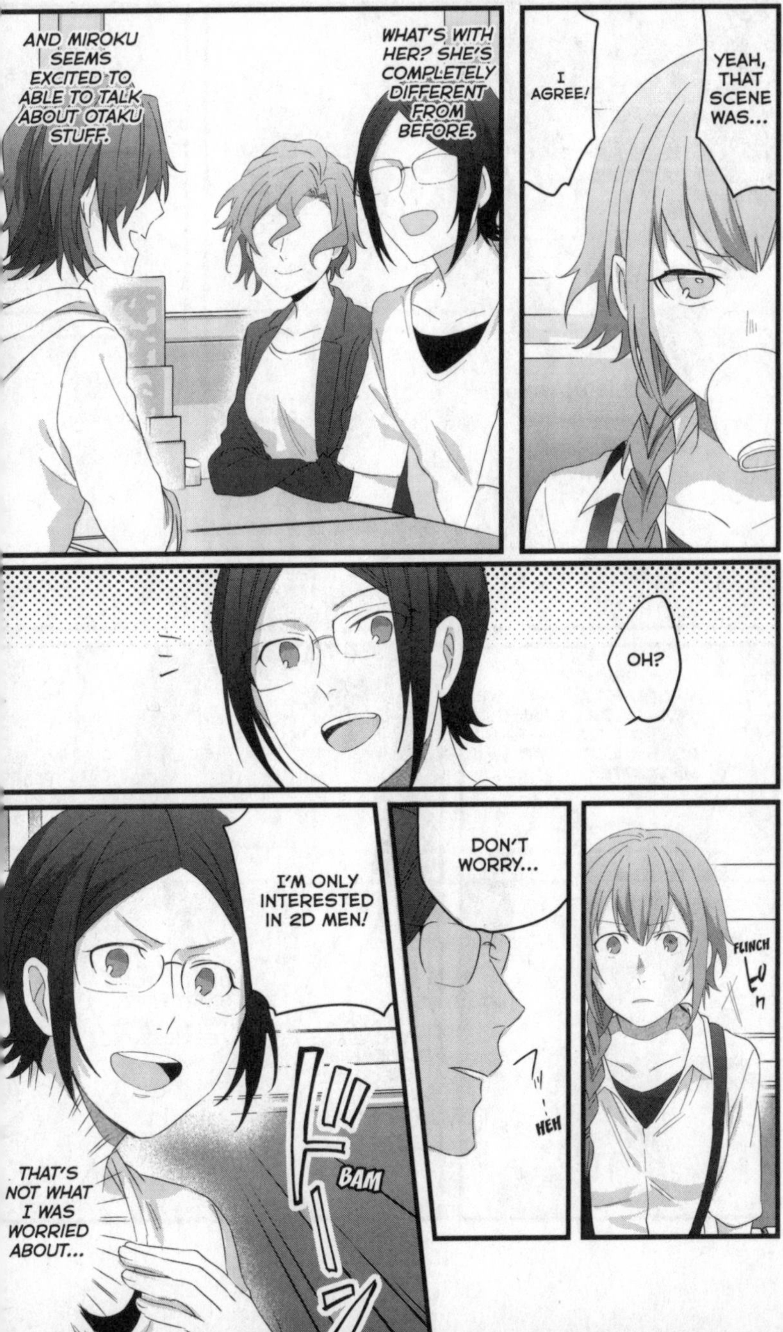
YEAH, THAT SCENE WAS...
I AGREE!
WHAT'S WITH HER? SHE'S COMPLETELY DIFFERENT FROM BEFORE.
AND MIROKU SEEMS EXCITED TO ABLE TO TALK ABOUT OTAKU STUFF.
OH?
FLINCH
DON'T WORRY...
HEH
I'M ONLY INTERESTED IN 2D MEN!
BAM
THAT'S NOT WHAT I WAS WORRIED ABOUT...

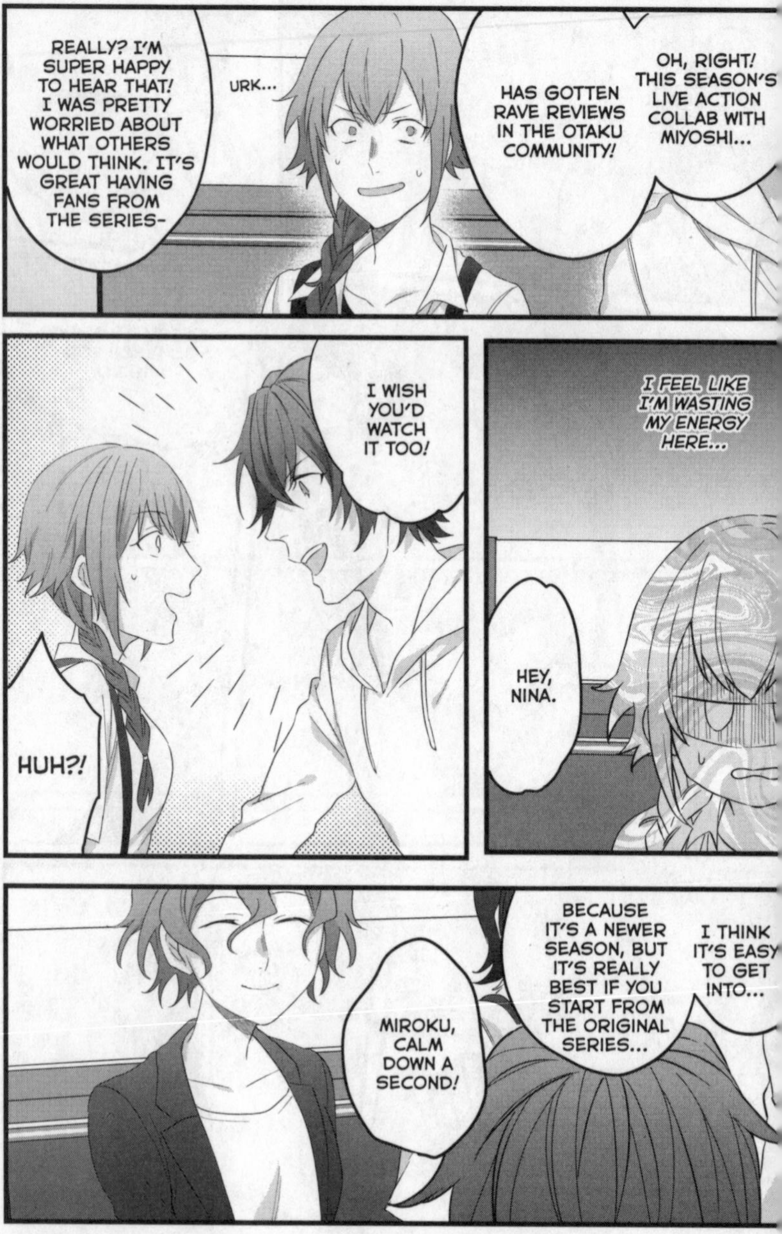
OH, RIGHT! THIS SEASON'S LIVE ACTION COLLAB WITH MIYOSHI...
HAS GOTTEN RAVE REVIEWS IN THE OTAKU COMMUNITY!
URK...
REALLY? I'M SUPER HAPPY TO HEAR THAT! I WAS PRETTY WORRIED ABOUT WHAT OTHERS WOULD THINK. IT'S GREAT HAVING FANS FROM THE SERIES-
I FEEL LIKE I'M WASTING MY ENERGY HERE...
HEY, NINA.
I WISH YOU'D WATCH IT TOO!
HUH?!
I THINK IT'S EASY TO GET INTO...
BECAUSE IT'S A NEWER SEASON, BUT IT'S REALLY BEST IF YOU START FROM THE ORIGINAL SERIES...
MIROKU, CALM DOWN A SECOND!

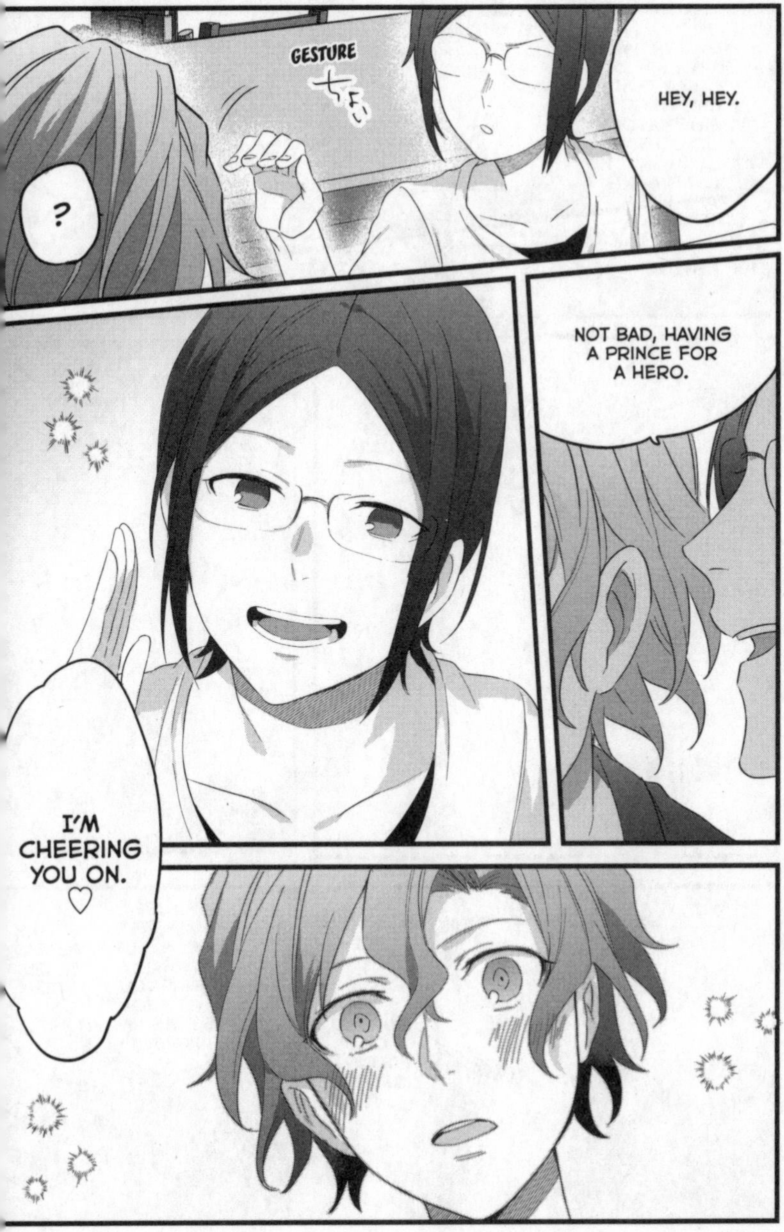
HEY, HEY.
GESTURE
ちょい
?
NOT BAD, HAVING A PRINCE FOR A HERO.
I'M CHEERING YOU ON. ♡

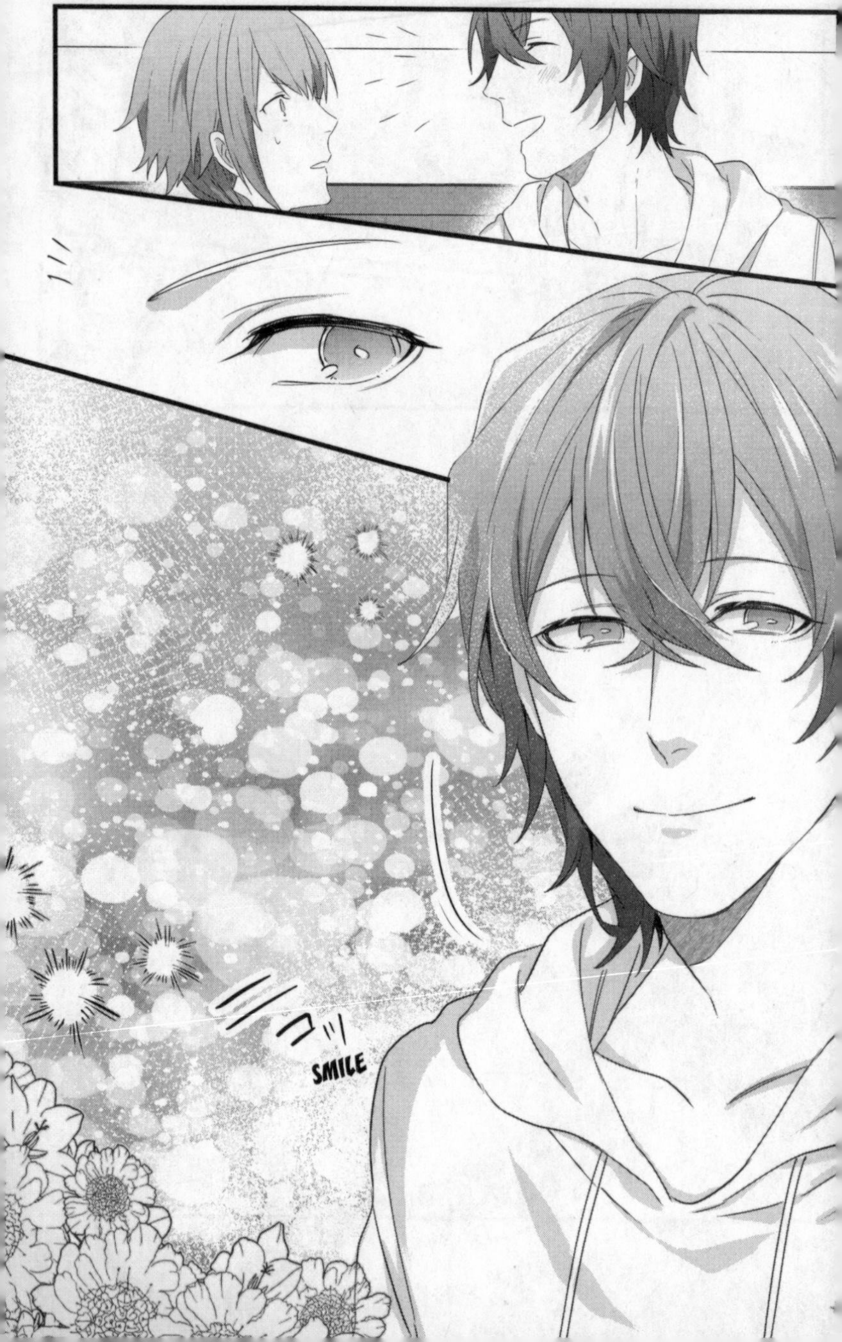
ニコッ
SMILE

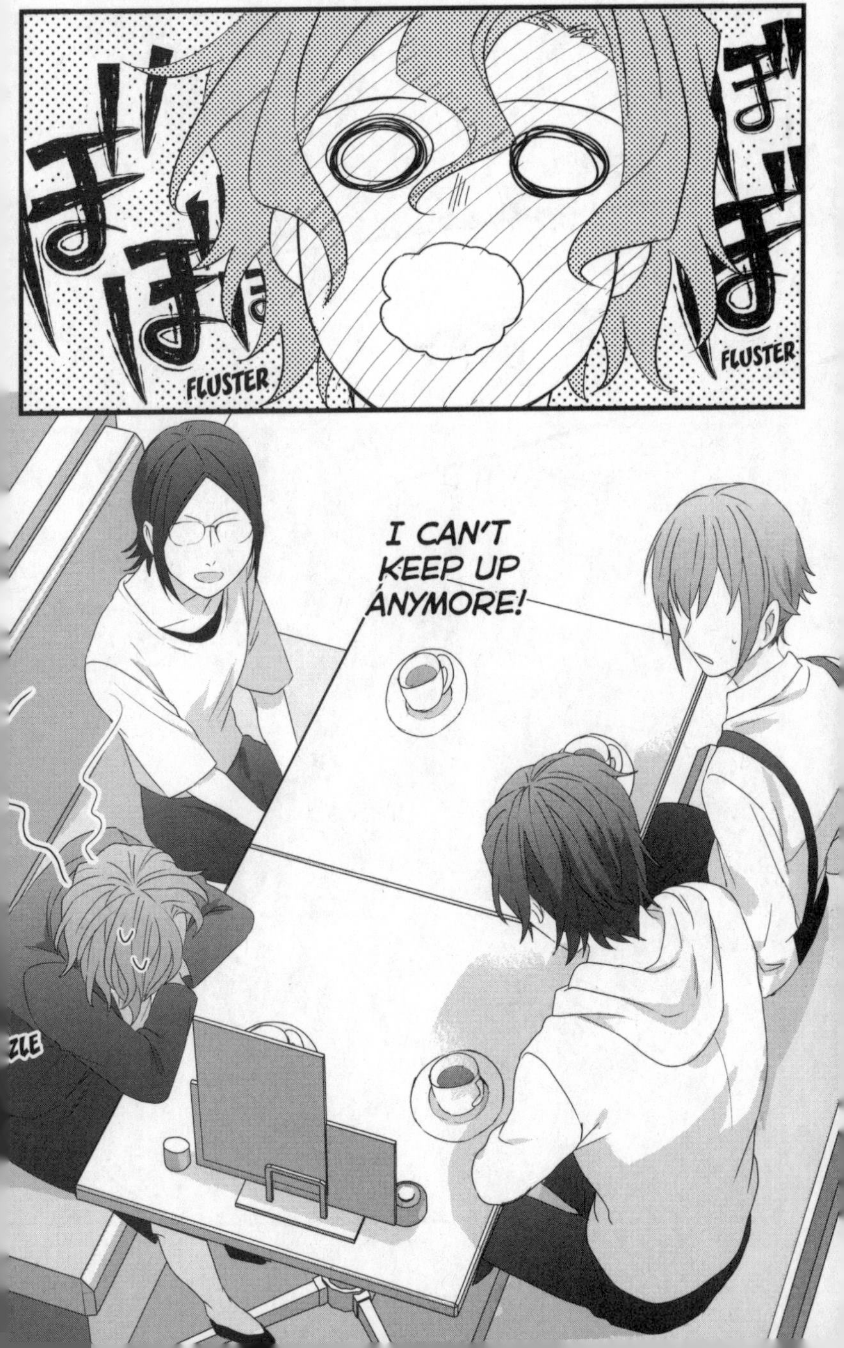
FLUSTER
FLUSTER
I CAN'T KEEP UP ANYMORE!
ZLE

Chapter 19

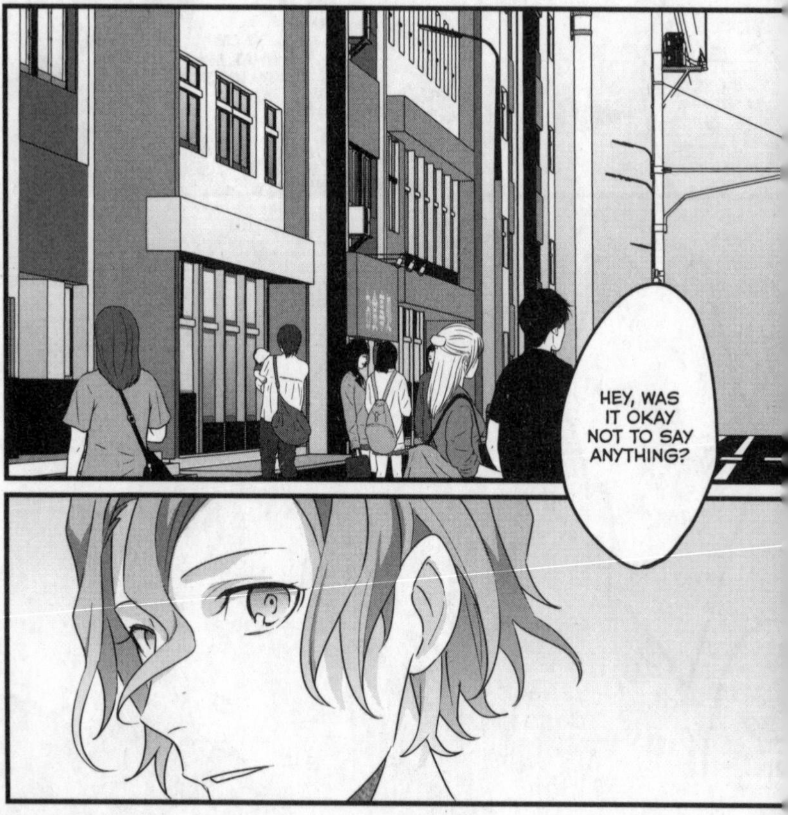
HEY, WAS IT OKAY NOT TO SAY ANYTHING?

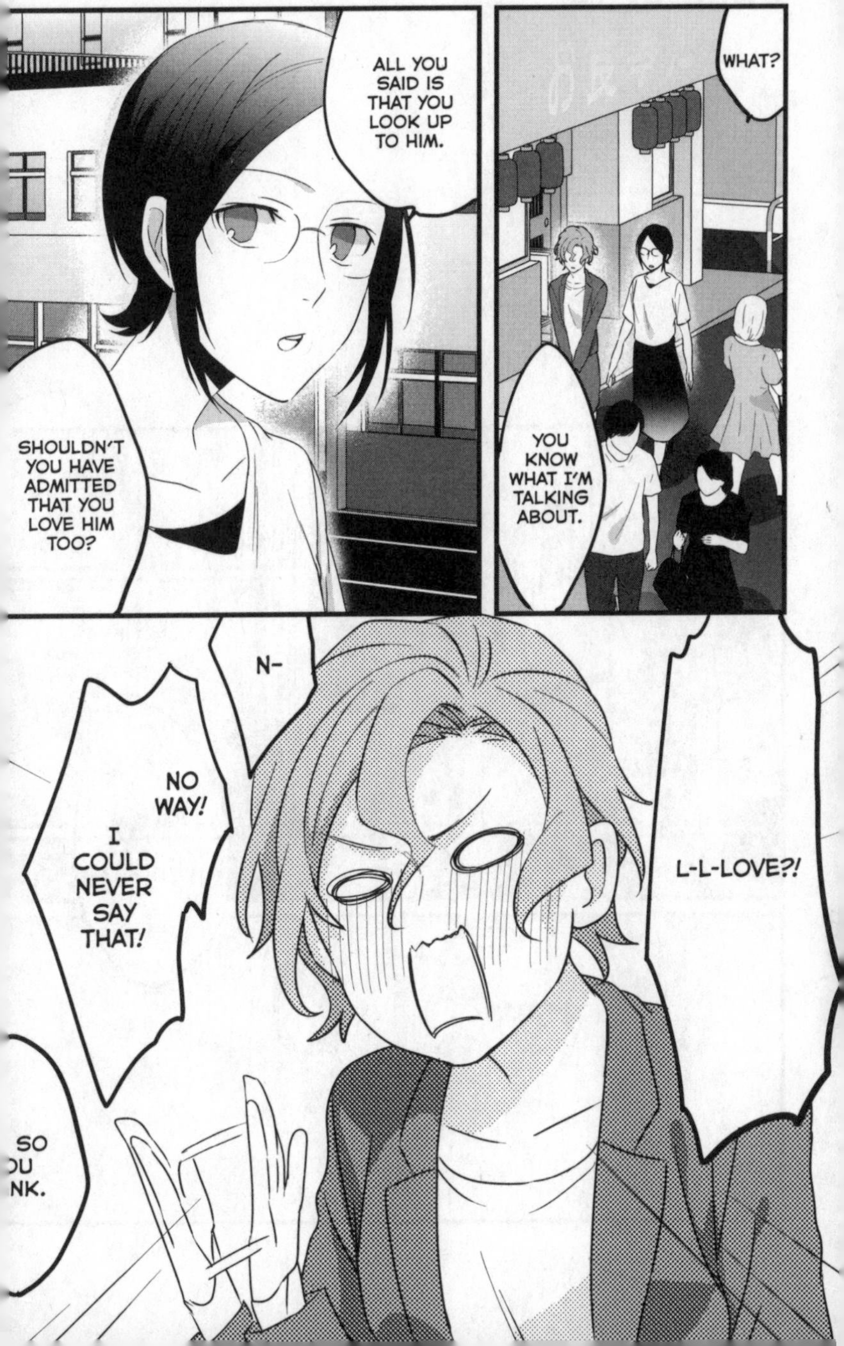
WHAT?
YOU KNOW WHAT I'M TALKING ABOUT.
ALL YOU SAID IS THAT YOU LOOK UP TO HIM.
SHOULDN'T YOU HAVE ADMITTED THAT YOU LOVE HIM TOO?
L-L-LOVE?!
N-
NO WAY! I COULD NEVER SAY THAT!
SO

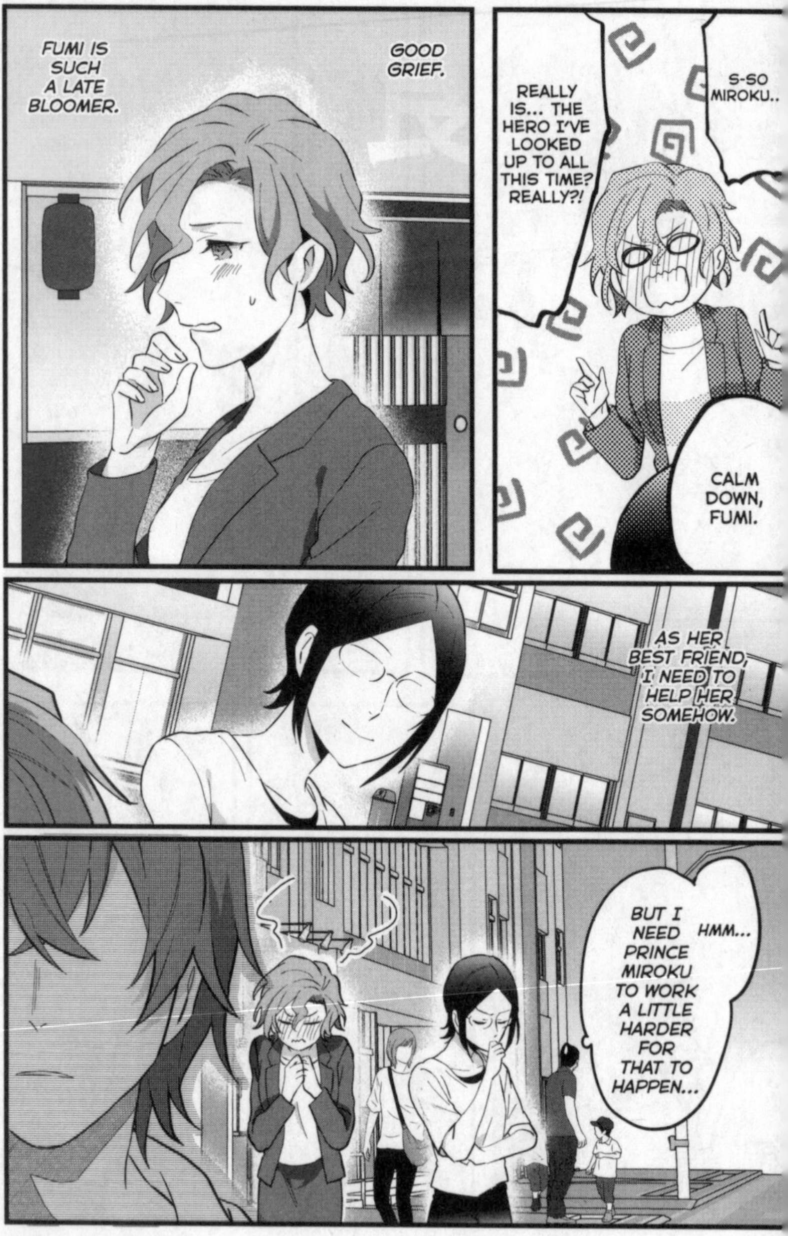
S-SO MIROKU..
REALLY IS... THE HERO I'VE LOOKED UP TO ALL THIS TIME? REALLY?!
CALM DOWN, FUMI.
GOOD GRIEF.
FUMI IS SUCH A LATE BLOOMER.
AS HER BEST FRIEND, I NEED TO HELP HER SOMEHOW.
HMM...
BUT I NEED PRINCE MIROKU TO WORK A LITTLE HARDER FOR THAT TO HAPPEN...

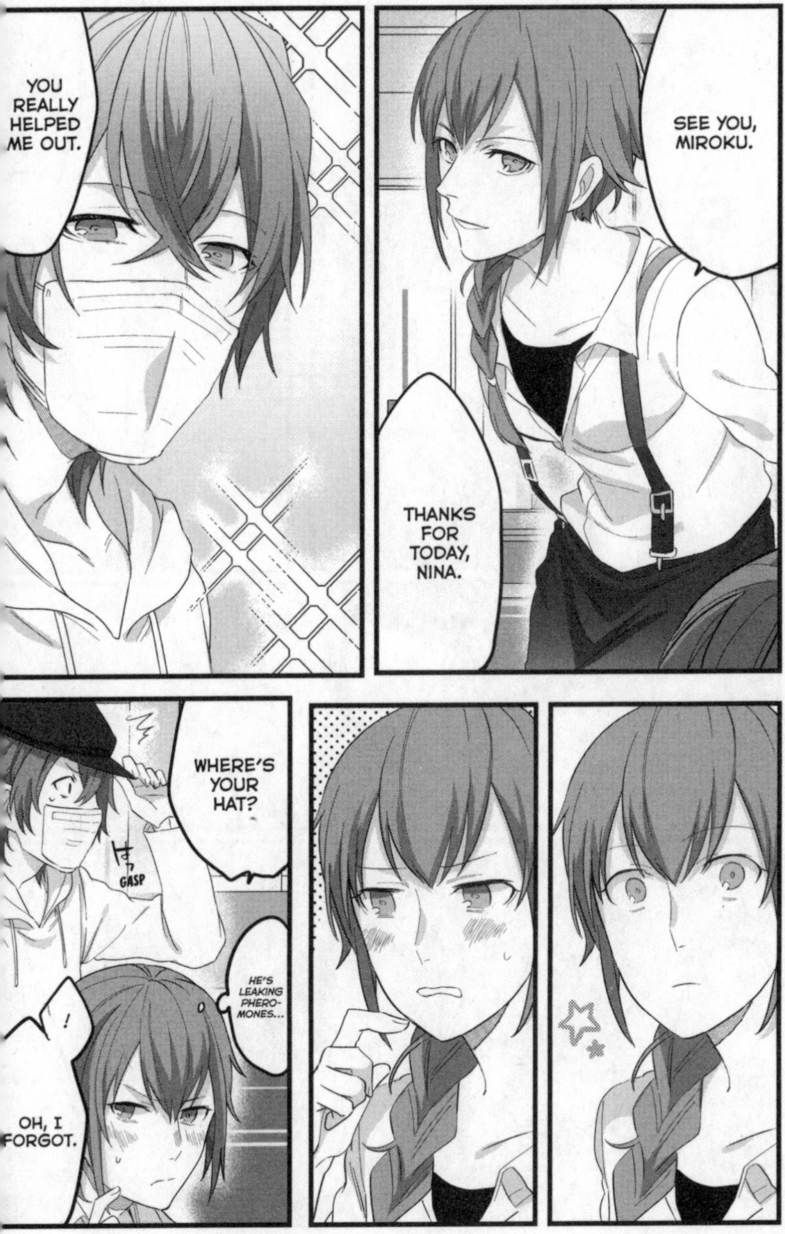
SEE YOU, MIROKU.
THANKS FOR TODAY, NINA.
YOU REALLY HELPED ME OUT.
WHERE'S YOUR HAT?
GASP
!
HE'S LEAKING PHEROMONES...
OH, I FORGOT.

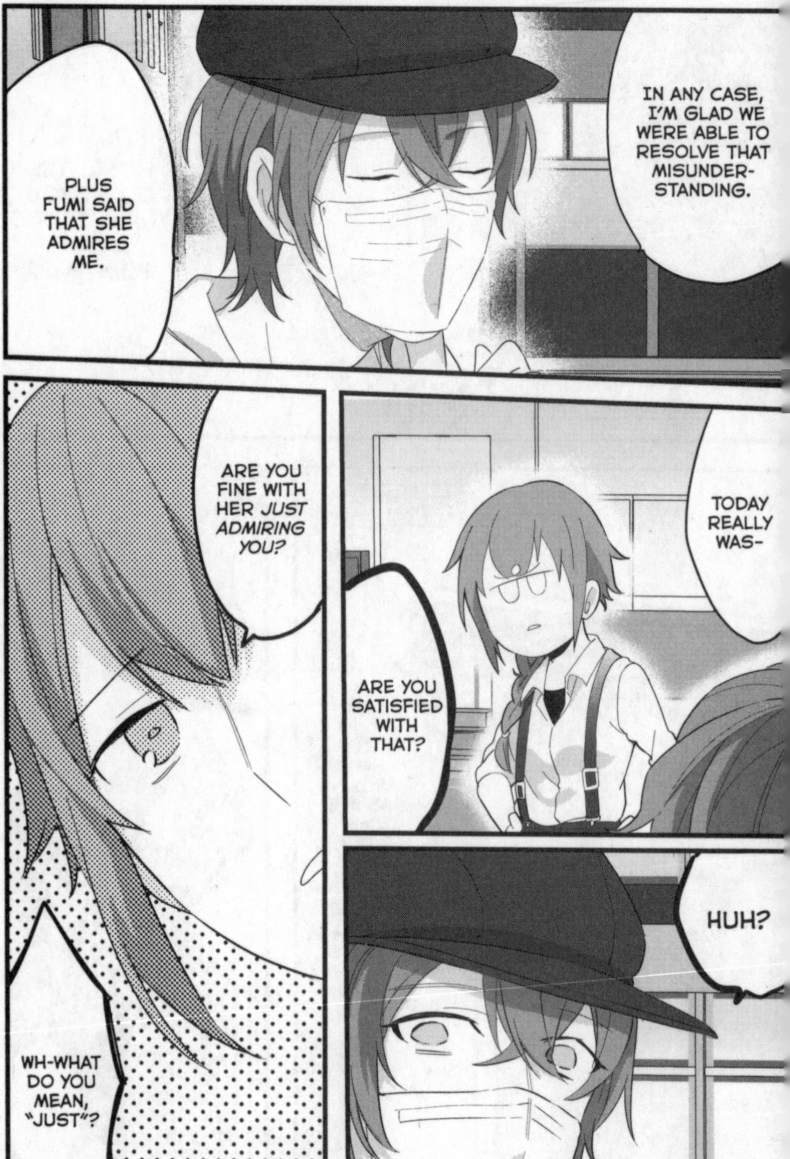
IN ANY CASE, I'M GLAD WE WERE ABLE TO RESOLVE THAT MISUNDERSTANDING.
PLUS FUMI SAID THAT SHE ADMIRES ME.
TODAY REALLY WAS-
ARE YOU SATISFIED WITH THAT?
HUH?
ARE YOU FINE WITH HER *JUST ADMIRING* YOU?
WH-WHAT DO YOU MEAN, "JUST"?

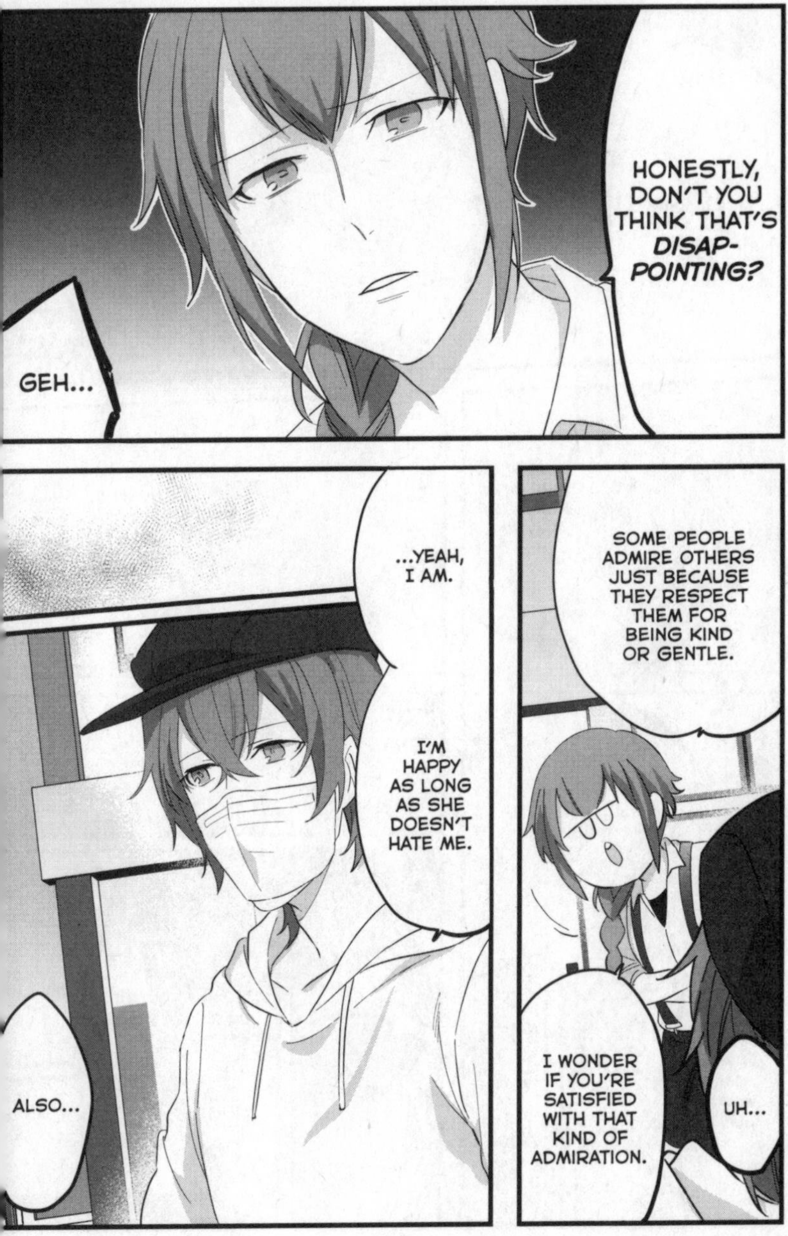
HONESTLY, DON'T YOU THINK THAT'S *DISAP-POINTING?*
GEH...
SOME PEOPLE ADMIRE OTHERS JUST BECAUSE THEY RESPECT THEM FOR BEING KIND OR GENTLE.
I WONDER IF YOU'RE SATISFIED WITH THAT KIND OF ADMIRATION.
UH...
...YEAH, I AM.
I'M HAPPY AS LONG AS SHE DOESN'T HATE ME.
ALSO...

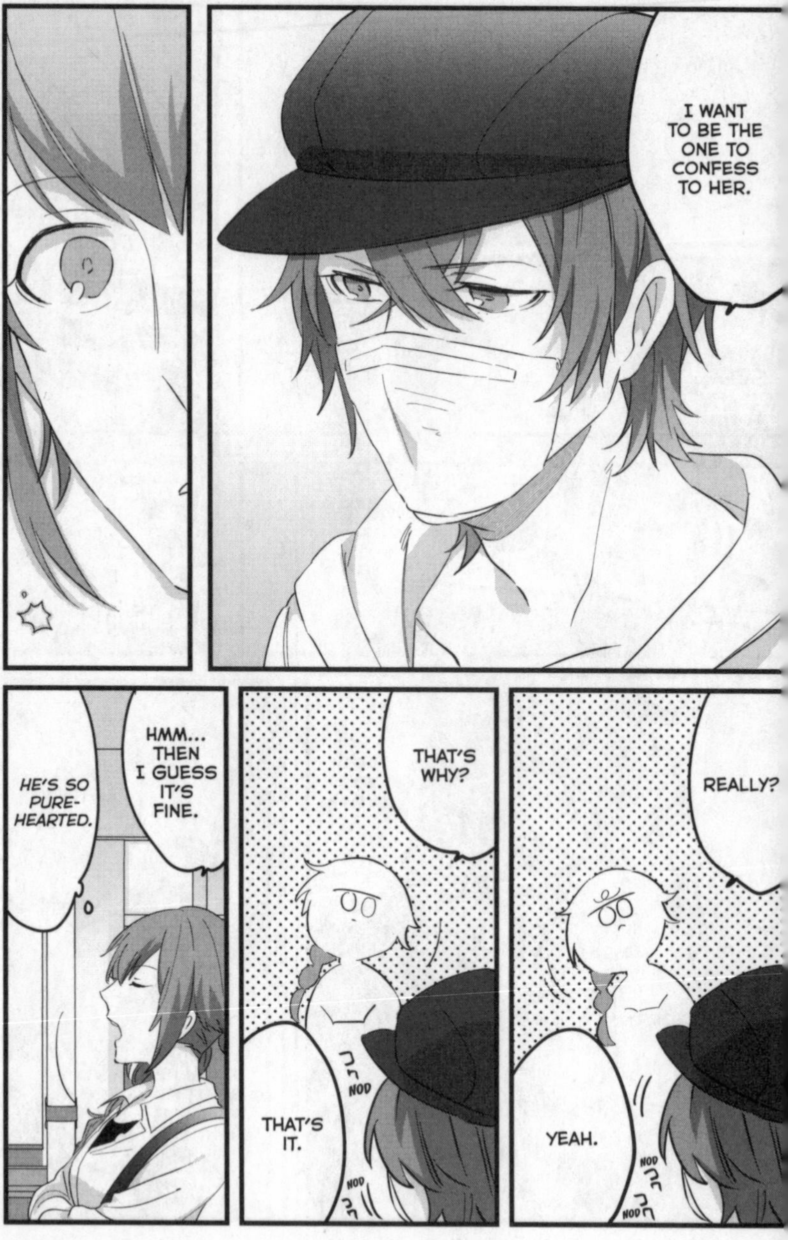
I WANT TO BE THE ONE TO CONFESS TO HER.
REALLY?
YEAH.
NOD
NOD
THAT'S WHY?
THAT'S IT.
NOD
NOD
HMM... THEN I GUESS IT'S FINE.
HE'S SO PURE-HEARTED.

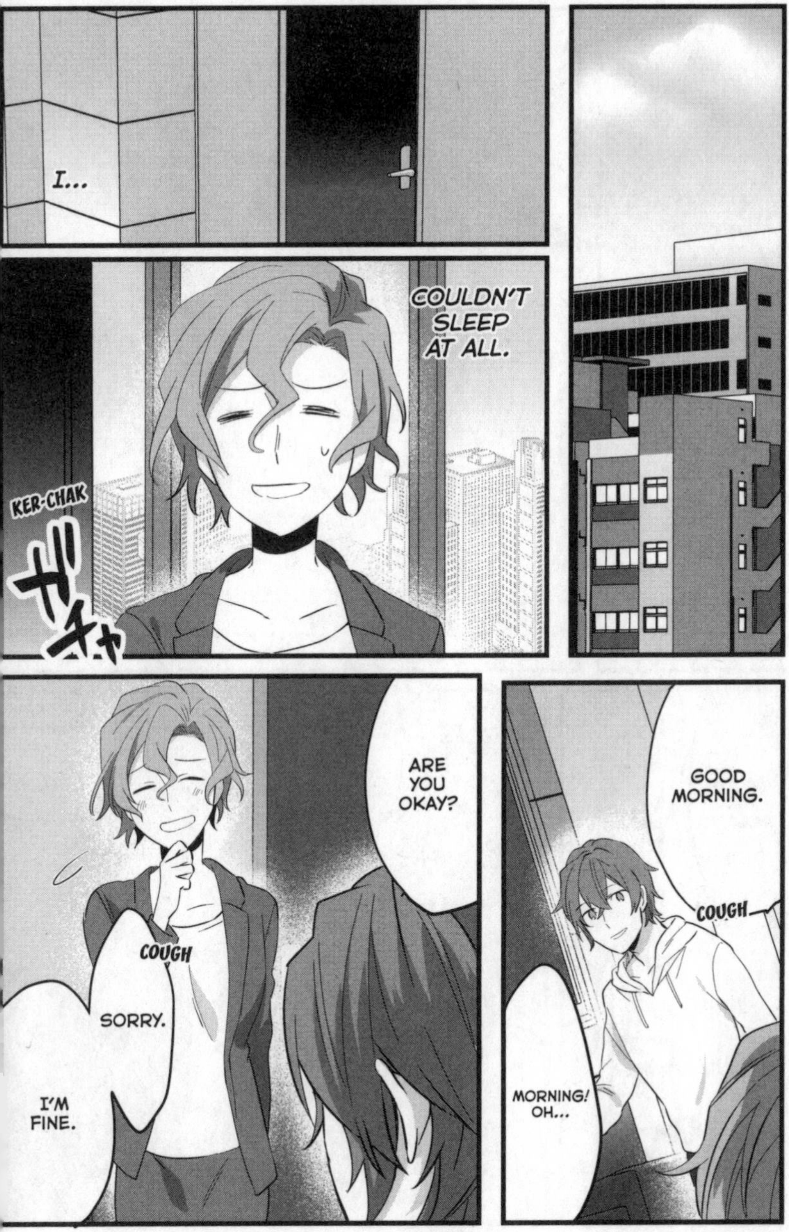
I...
COULDN'T SLEEP AT ALL.
KER-CHAK
ガチャ
GOOD MORNING.
COUGH
MORNING! OH...
ARE YOU OKAY?
COUGH
SORRY.
I'M FINE.

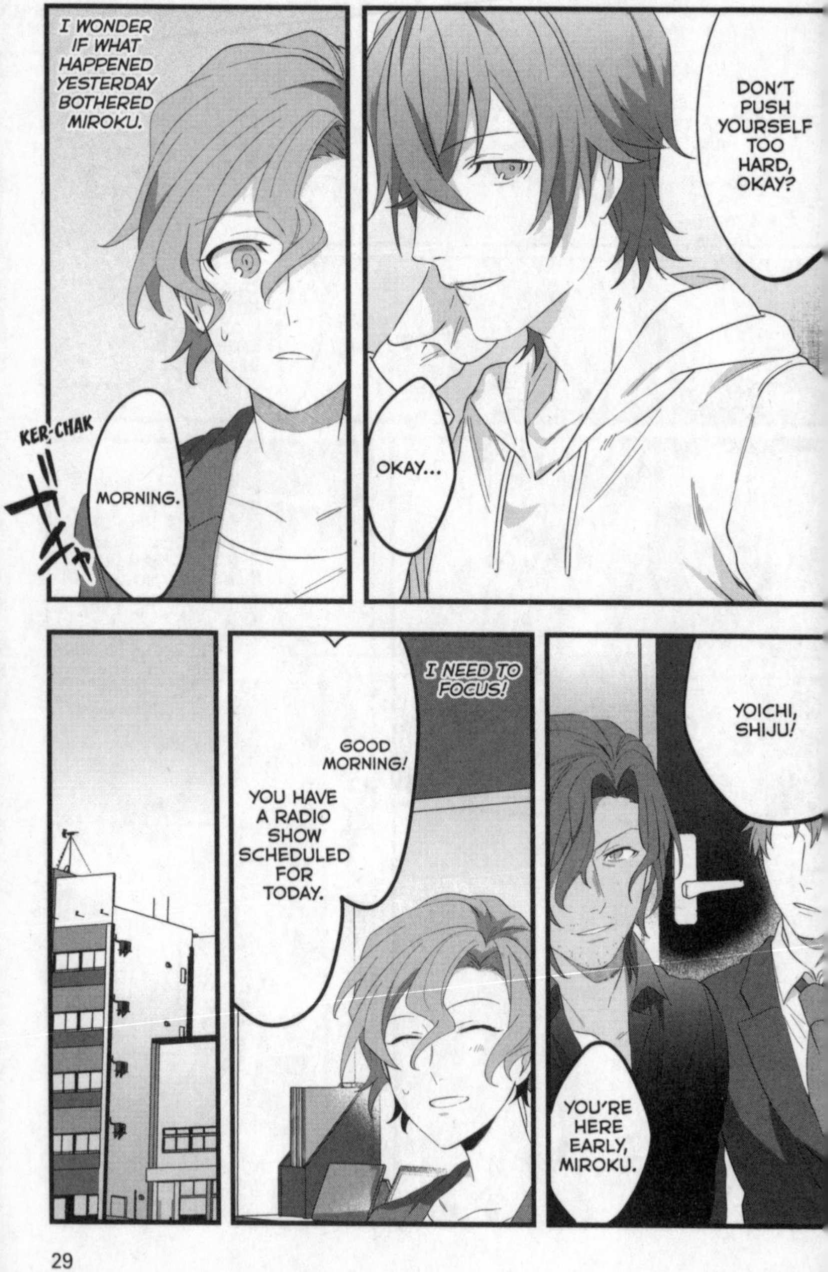
DON'T PUSH YOURSELF TOO HARD, OKAY?
OKAY...
I WONDER IF WHAT HAPPENED YESTERDAY BOTHERED MIROKU.
KER-CHAK
MORNING.
YOICHI, SHIJU!
YOU'RE HERE EARLY, MIROKU.
I NEED TO FOCUS!
GOOD MORNING!
YOU HAVE A RADIO SHOW SCHEDULED FOR TODAY.

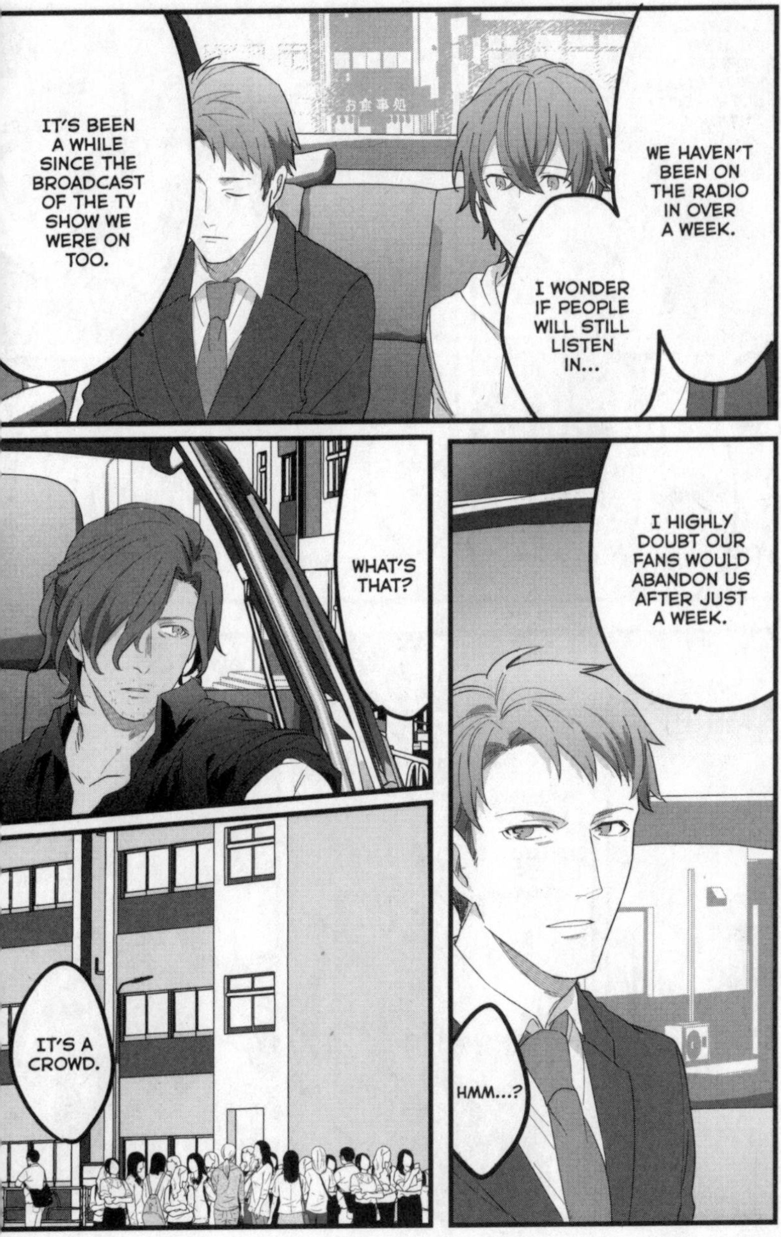
お食事処
WE HAVEN'T BEEN ON THE RADIO IN OVER A WEEK.
I WONDER IF PEOPLE WILL STILL LISTEN IN...
IT'S BEEN A WHILE SINCE THE BROADCAST OF THE TV SHOW WE WERE ON TOO.
I HIGHLY DOUBT OUR FANS WOULD ABANDON US AFTER JUST A WEEK.
HMM...?
WHAT'S THAT?
IT'S A CROWD.

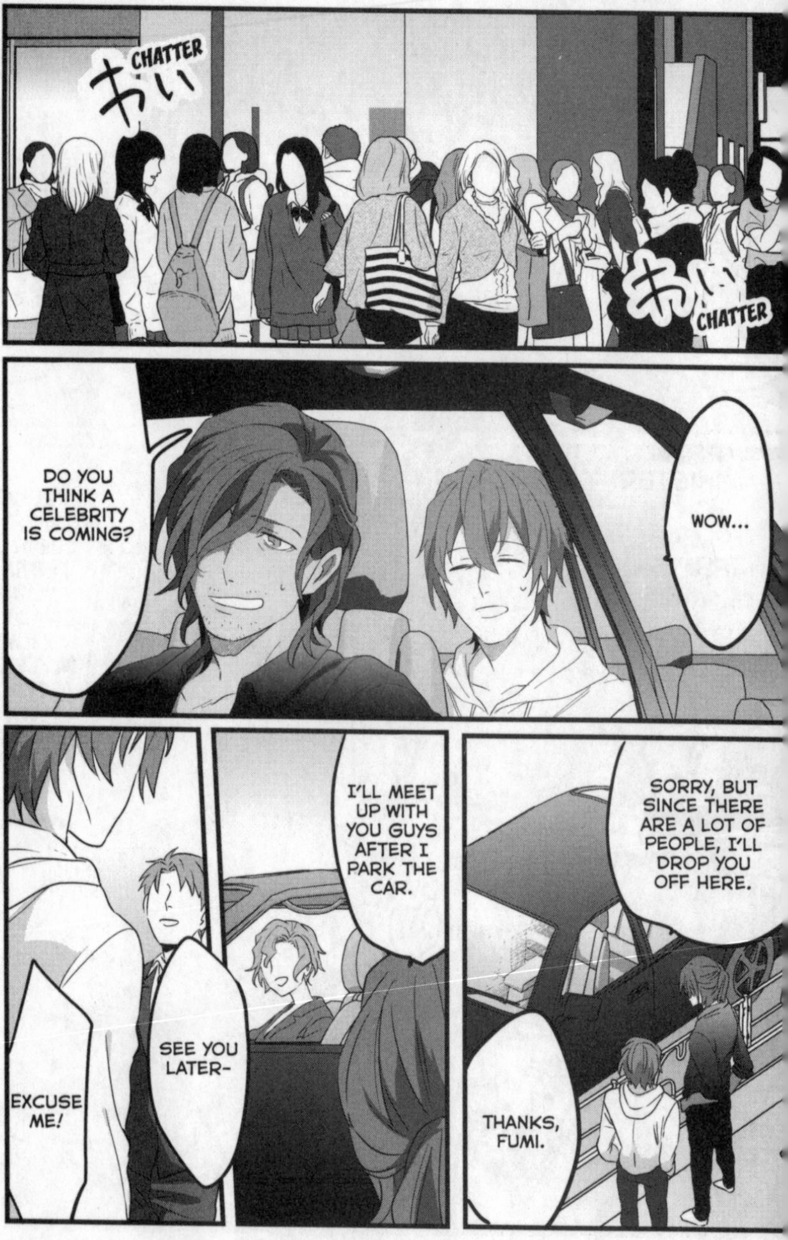
わい
CHATTER
わい
CHATTER
WOW...
DO YOU THINK A CELEBRITY IS COMING?
SORRY, BUT SINCE THERE ARE A LOT OF PEOPLE, I'LL DROP YOU OFF HERE.
THANKS, FUMI.
I'LL MEET UP WITH YOU GUYS AFTER I PARK THE CAR.
SEE YOU LATER-
EXCUSE ME!

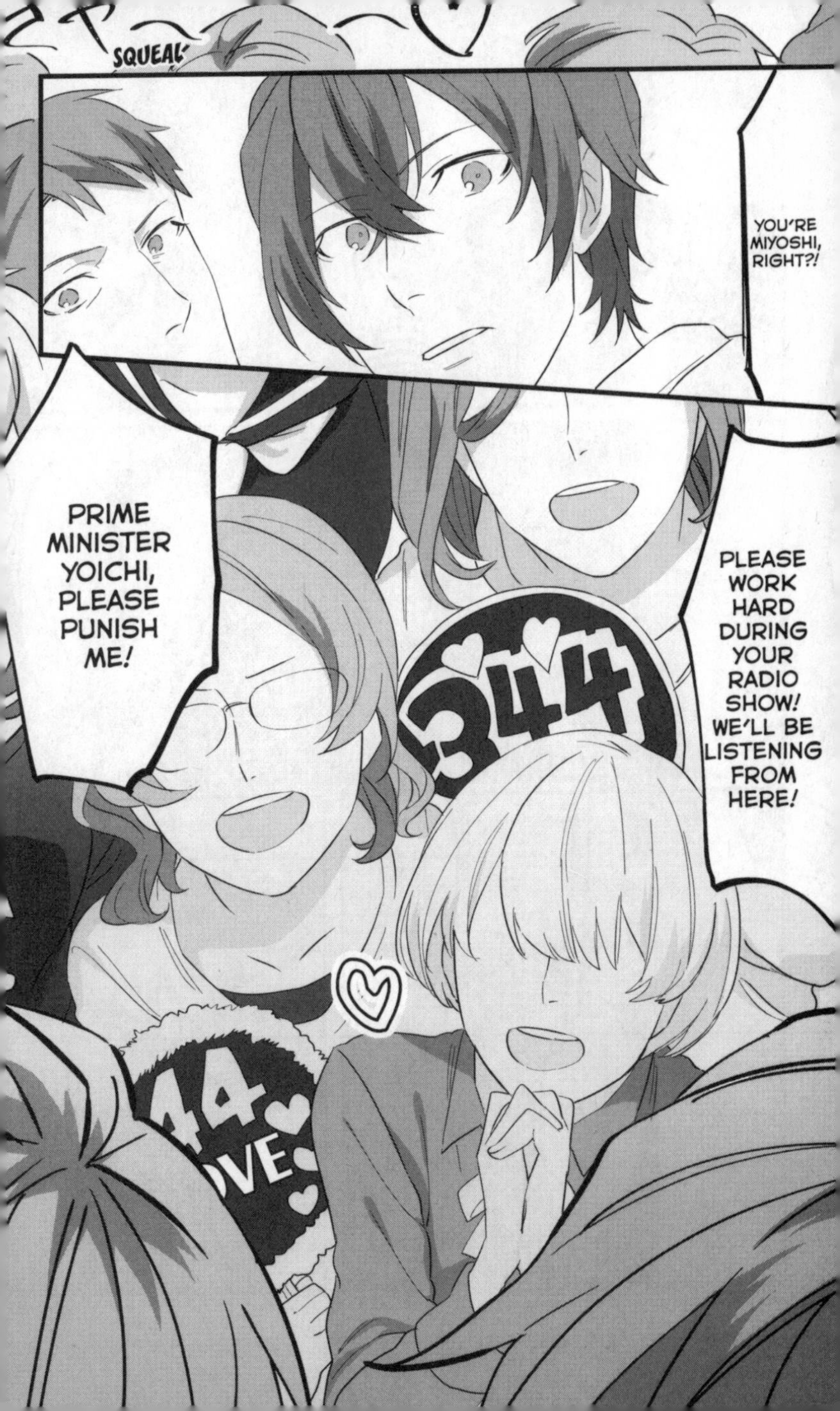
SQUEAL
YOU'RE MIYOSHI, RIGHT?!
PLEASE WORK HARD DURING YOUR RADIO SHOW! WE'LL BE LISTENING FROM HERE!
344
PRIME MINISTER YOICHI, PLEASE PUNISH ME!

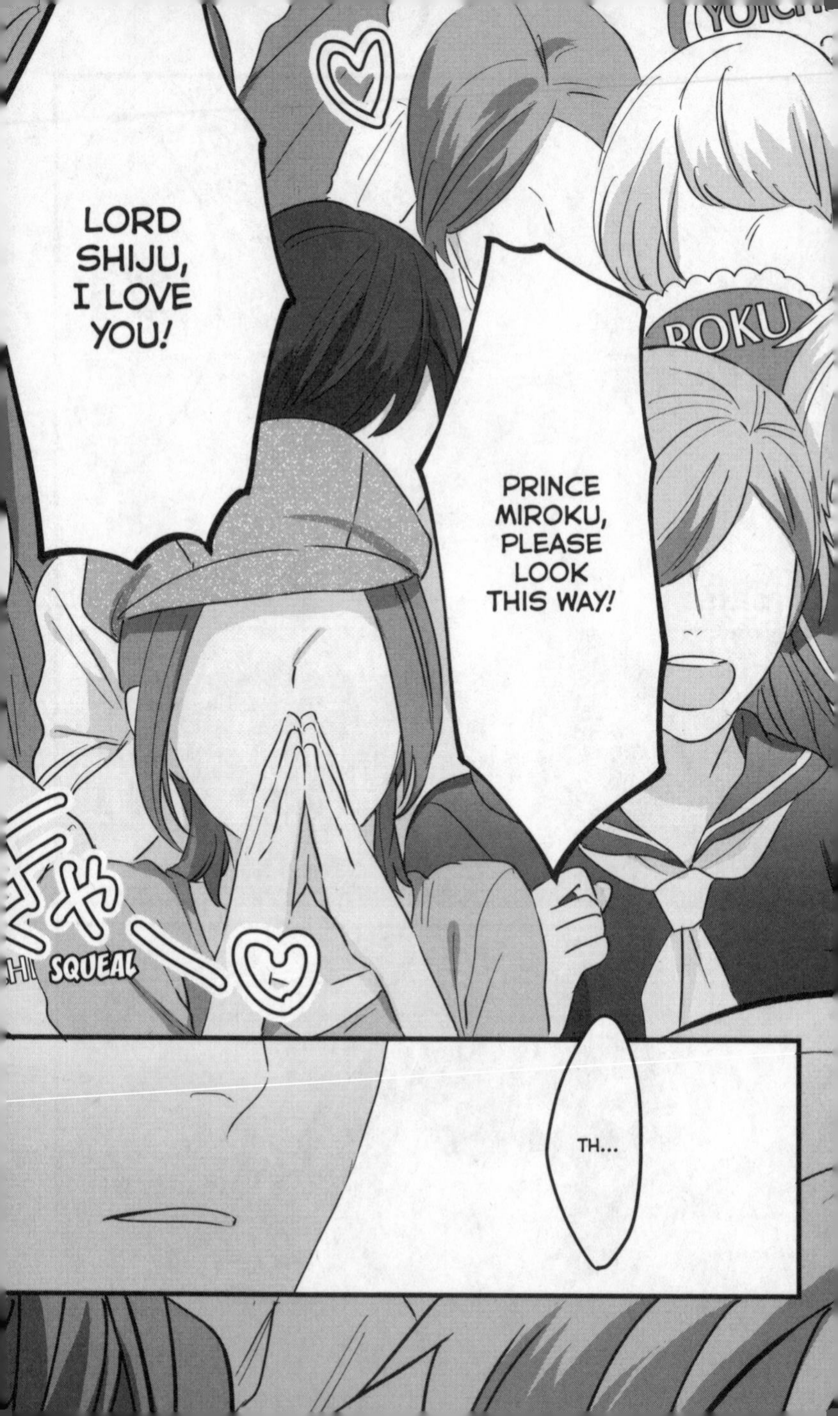
ROKU
PRINCE MIROKU, PLEASE LOOK THIS WAY!
LORD SHIJU, I LOVE YOU!
SQUEAL
TH...

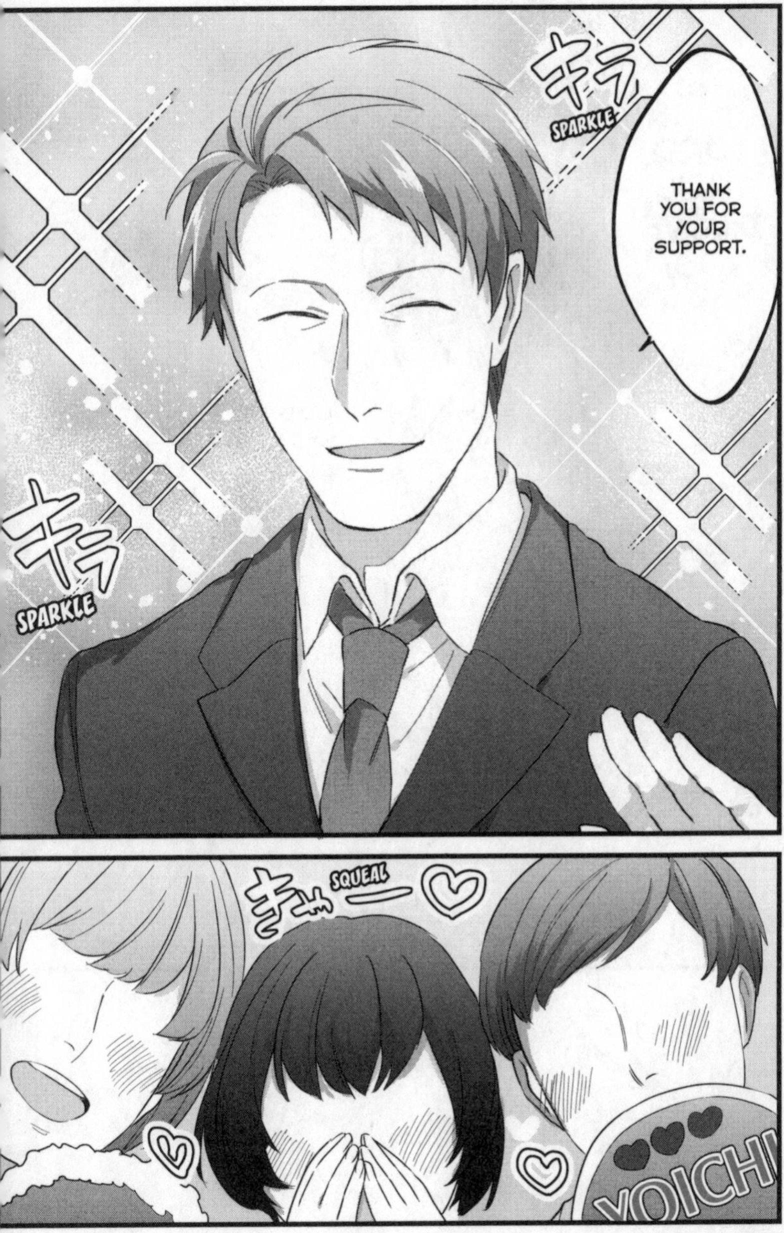
キラ
SPARKLE
THANK YOU FOR YOUR SUPPORT.
キラ
SPARKLE
きゃー
SQUEAL
YOICHI

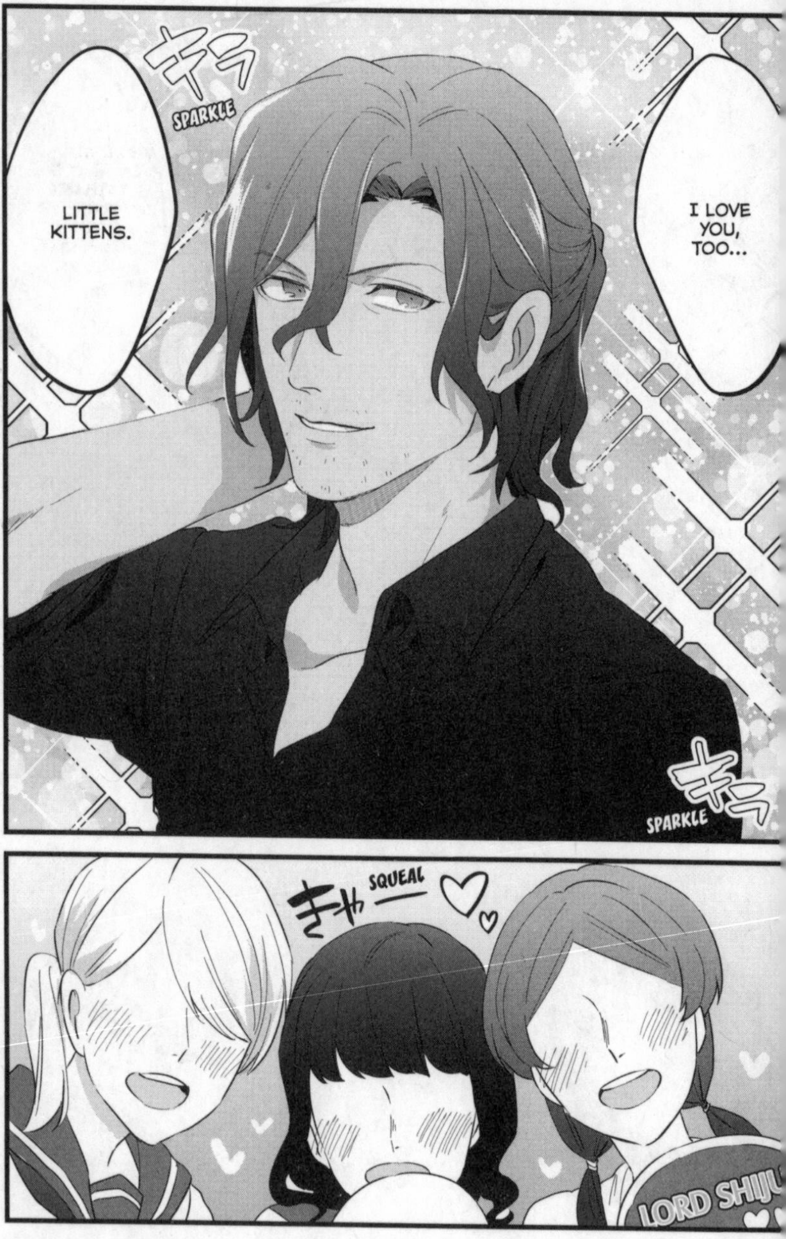
I LOVE YOU, TOO...
キラ
SPARKLE
LITTLE KITTENS.
キラ
SPARKLE
きゃー
SQUEAL
LORD SHIJU

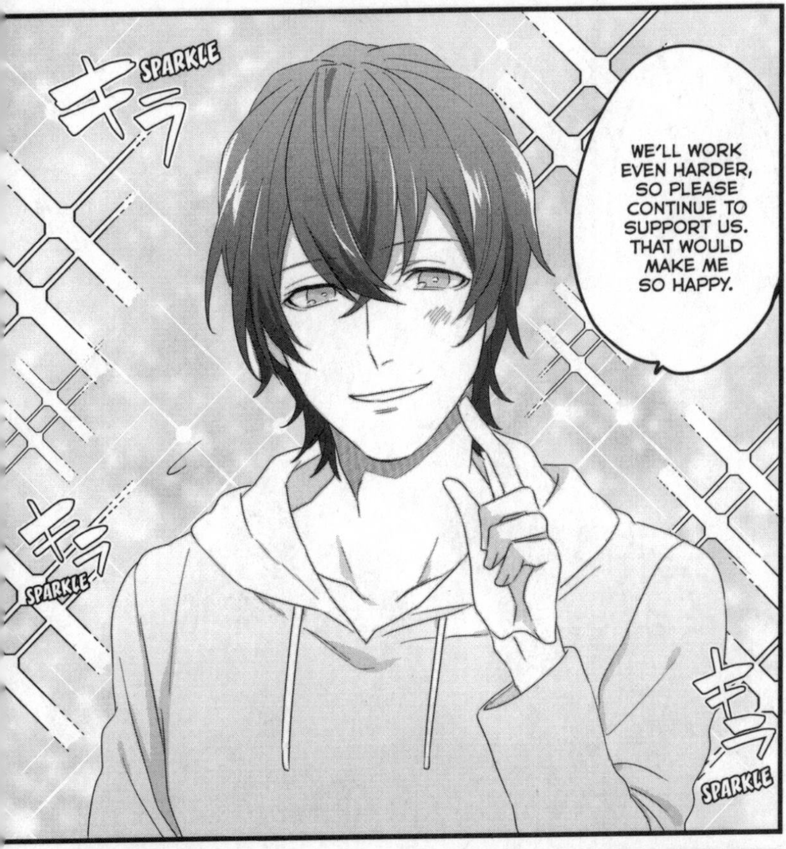
WE'LL WORK EVEN HARDER, SO PLEASE CONTINUE TO SUPPORT US. THAT WOULD MAKE ME SO HAPPY.
キラ
SPARKLE
キラ
SPARKLE
キラ
SPARKLE

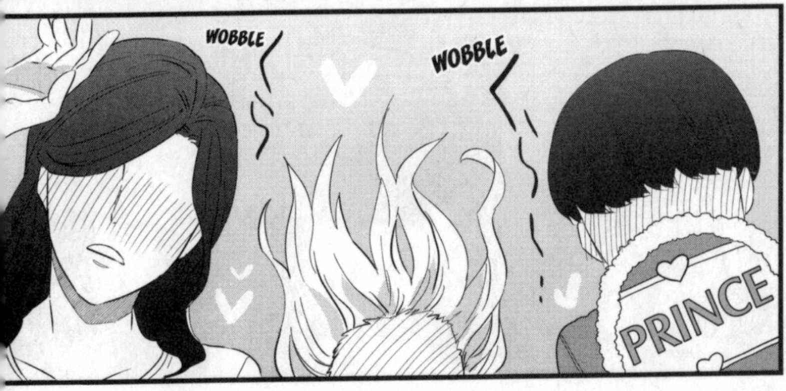
WOBBLE
WOBBLE
PRINCE

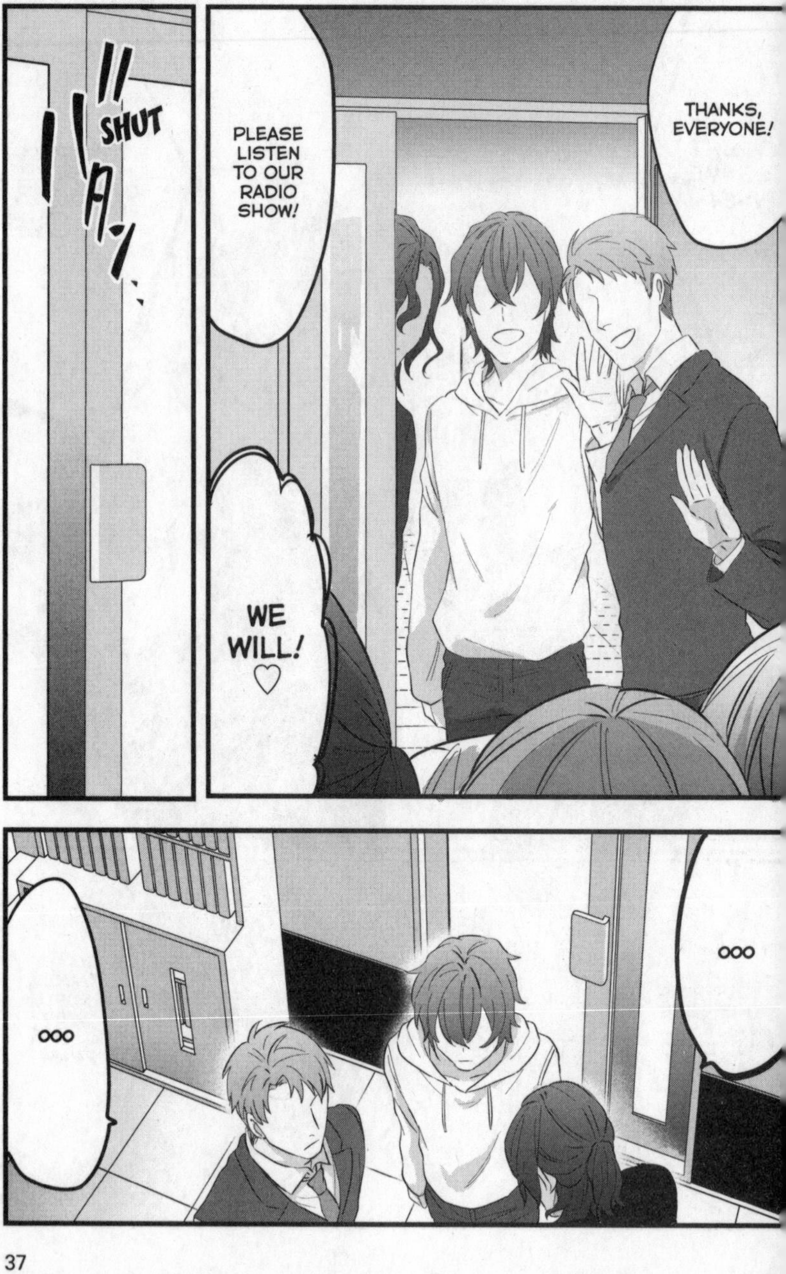
THANKS, EVERYONE!
PLEASE LISTEN TO OUR RADIO SHOW!
WE WILL! ♡
SHUT
…
…

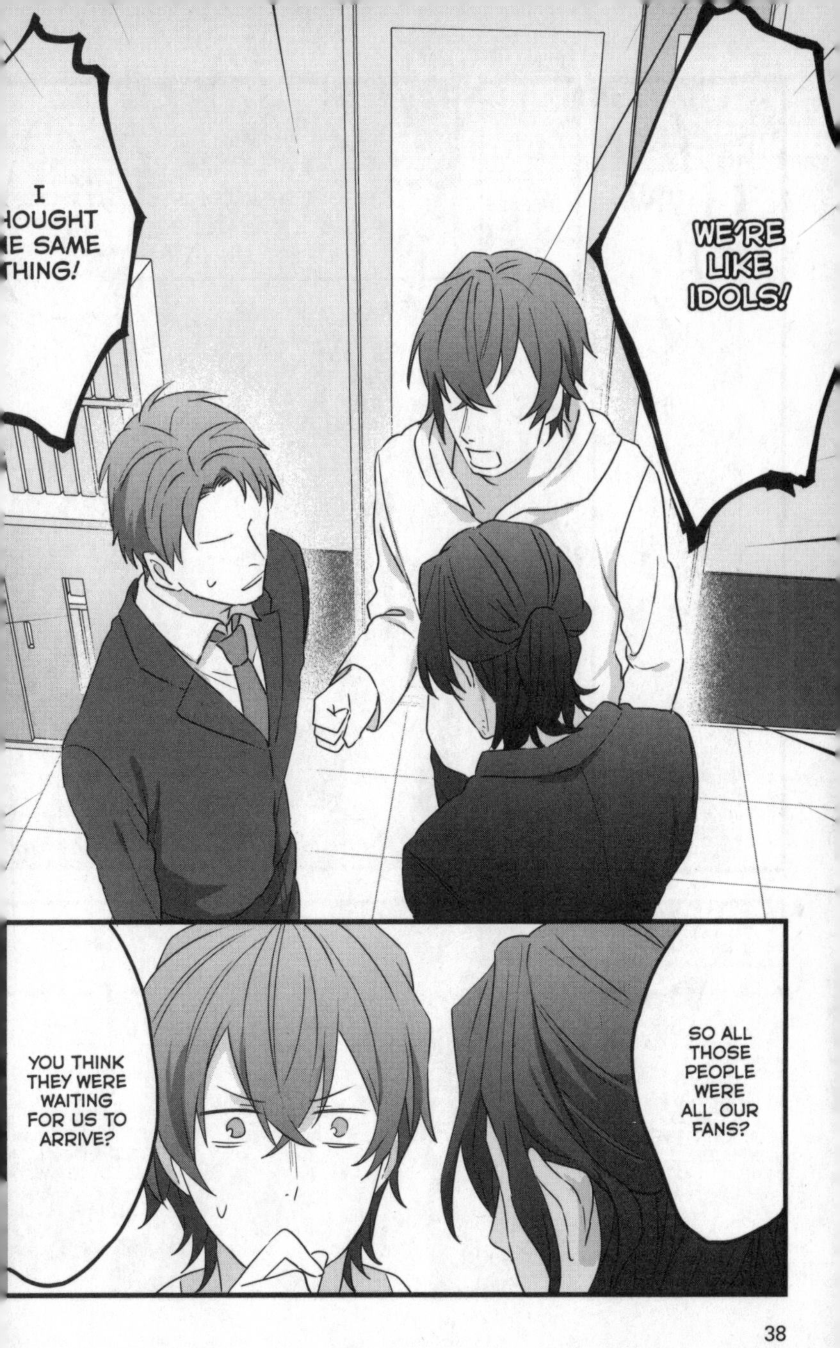
WE'RE LIKE IDOLS!
I HOUGHT IE SAME THING!
SO ALL THOSE PEOPLE WERE ALL OUR FANS?
YOU THINK THEY WERE WAITING FOR US TO ARRIVE?

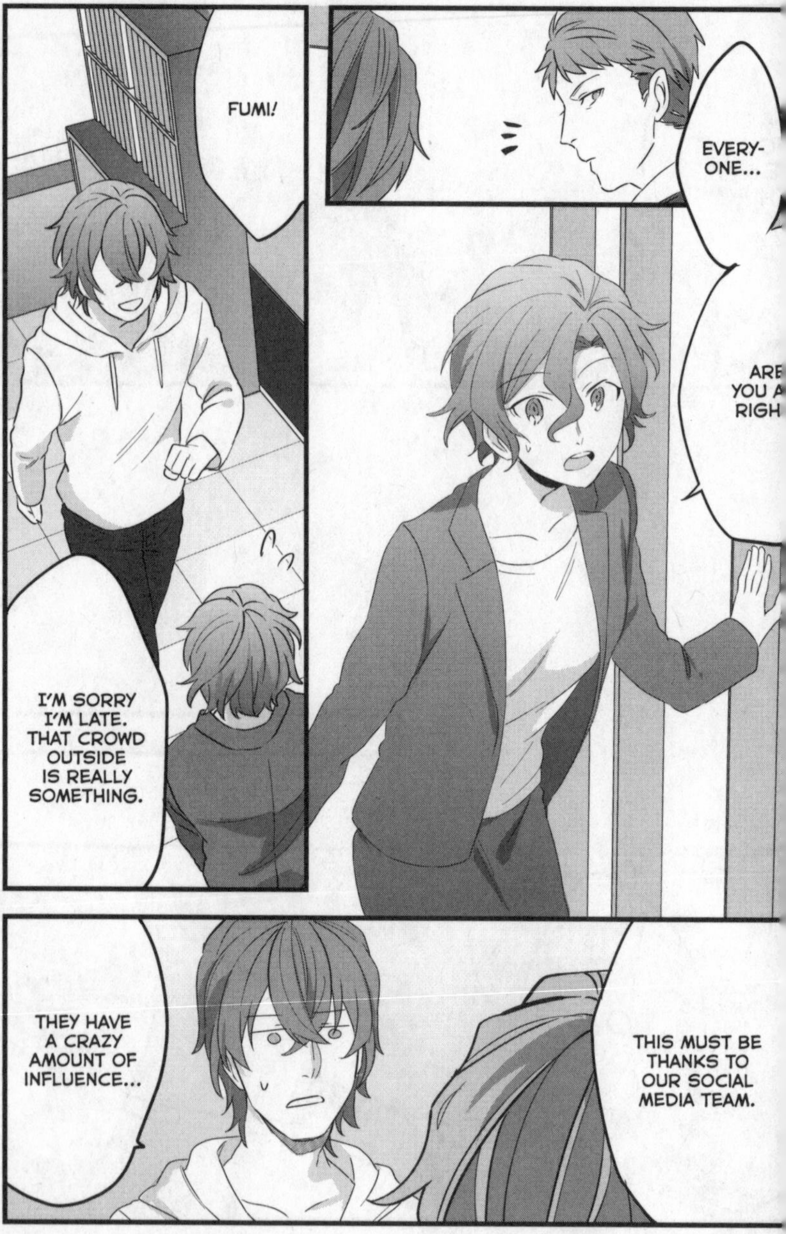
EVERY-ONE...
ARE YOU A RIGH
FUMI!
I'M SORRY I'M LATE. THAT CROWD OUTSIDE IS REALLY SOMETHING.
THIS MUST BE THANKS TO OUR SOCIAL MEDIA TEAM.
THEY HAVE A CRAZY AMOUNT OF INFLUENCE...

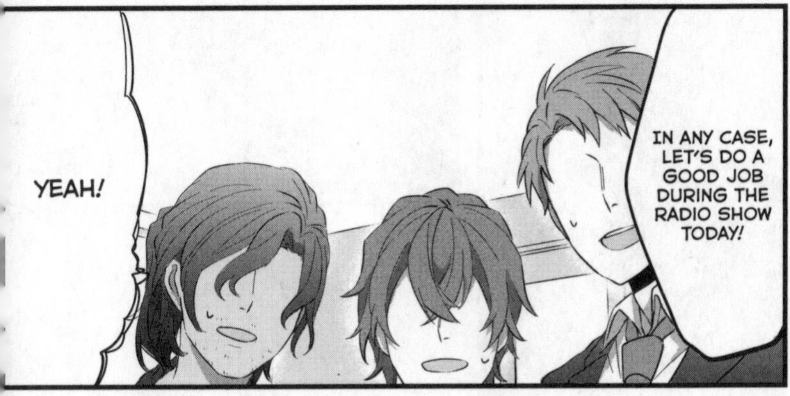
IN ANY CASE, LET'S DO A GOOD JOB DURING THE RADIO SHOW TODAY!
YEAH!

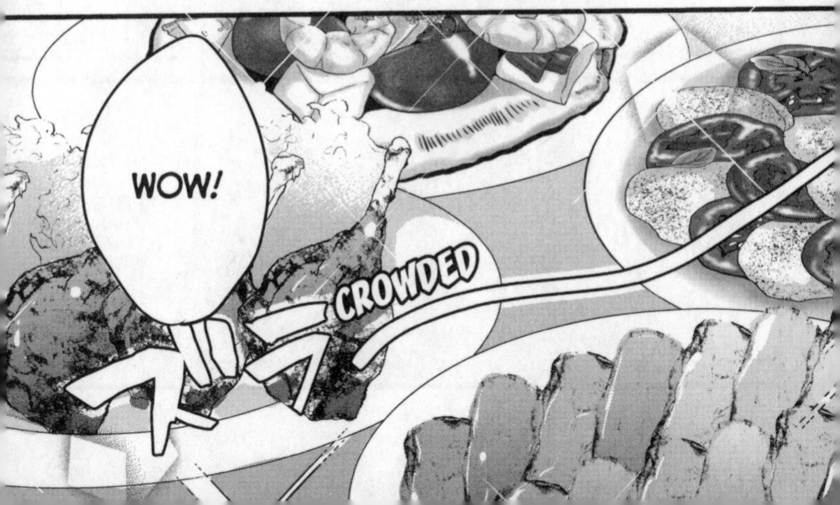
WOW!
CROWDED

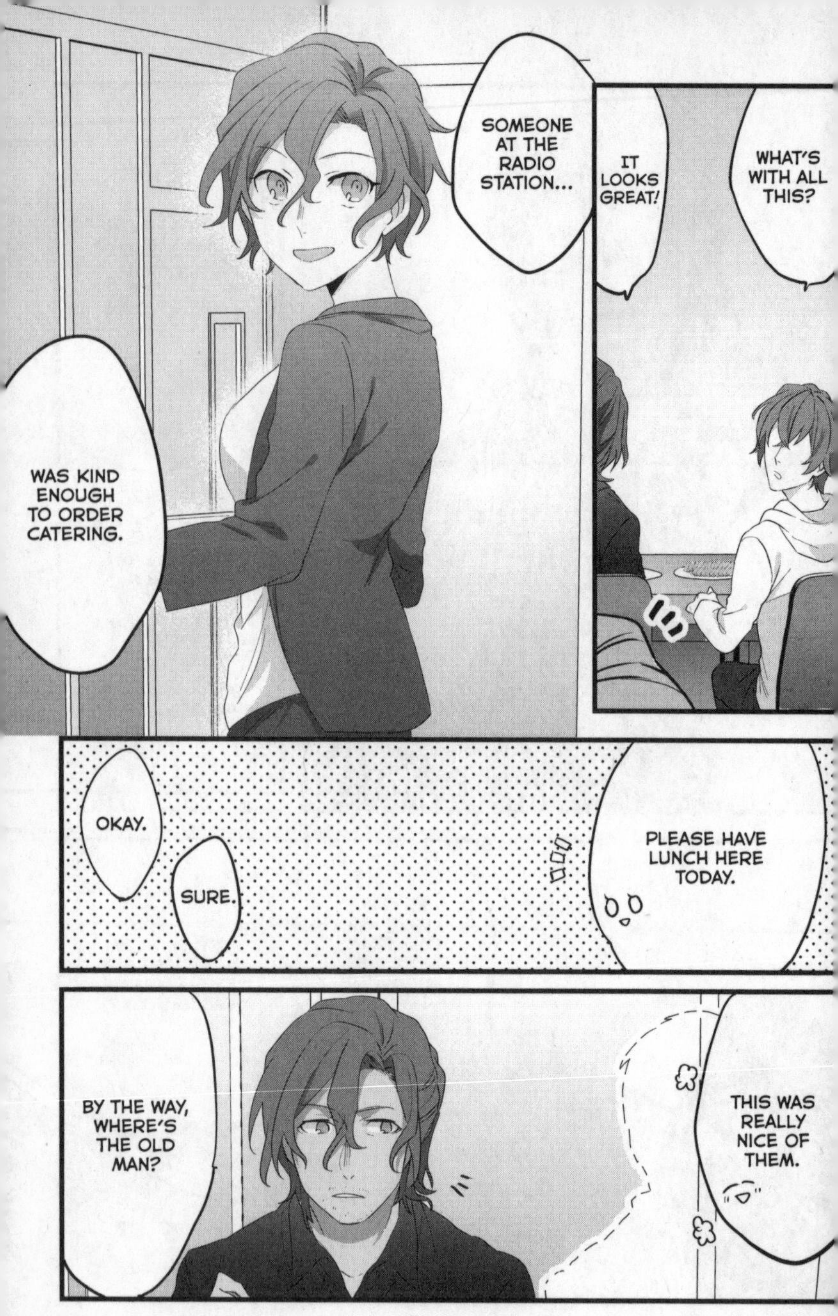
WHAT'S WITH ALL THIS?
IT LOOKS GREAT!
SOMEONE AT THE RADIO STATION...
WAS KIND ENOUGH TO ORDER CATERING.
PLEASE HAVE LUNCH HERE TODAY.
SURE.
OKAY.
THIS WAS REALLY NICE OF THEM.
BY THE WAY, WHERE'S THE OLD MAN?

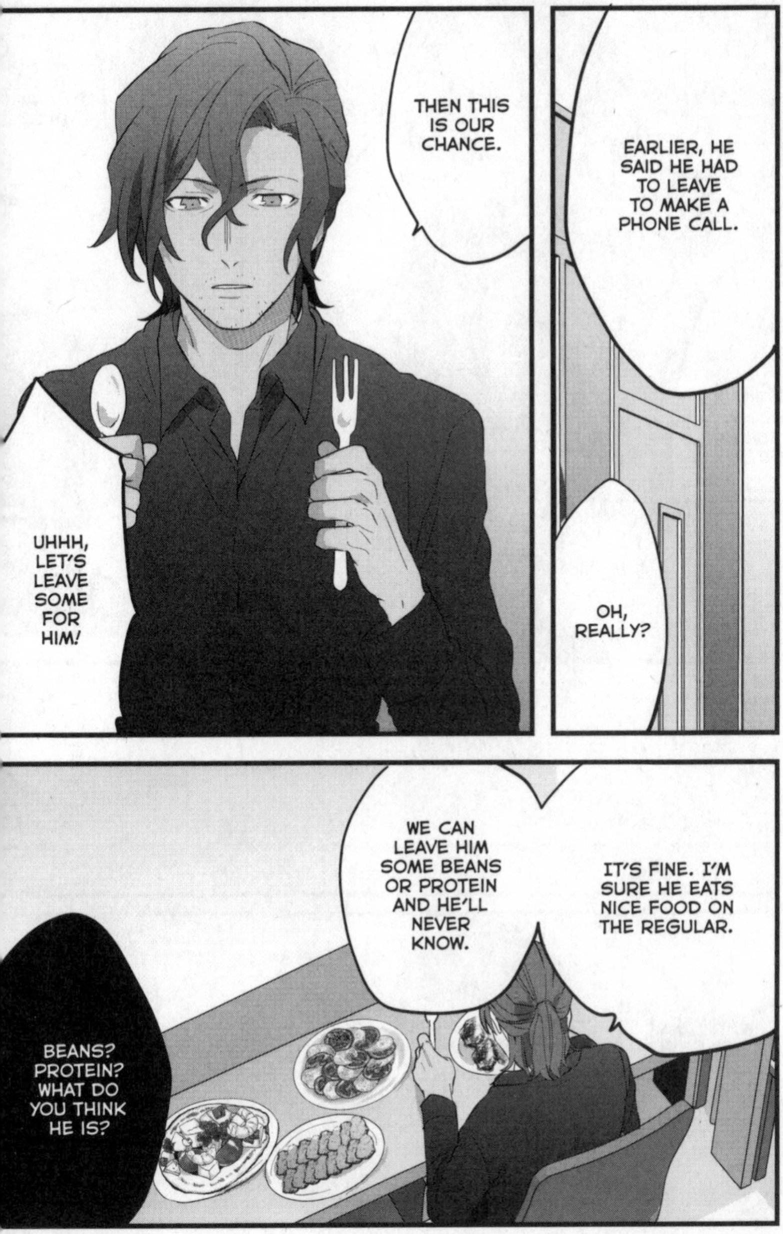
EARLIER, HE SAID HE HAD TO LEAVE TO MAKE A PHONE CALL.
OH, REALLY?
THEN THIS IS OUR CHANCE.
UHHH, LET'S LEAVE SOME FOR HIM!
IT'S FINE. I'M SURE HE EATS NICE FOOD ON THE REGULAR.
WE CAN LEAVE HIM SOME BEANS OR PROTEIN AND HE'LL NEVER KNOW.
BEANS? PROTEIN? WHAT DO YOU THINK HE IS?

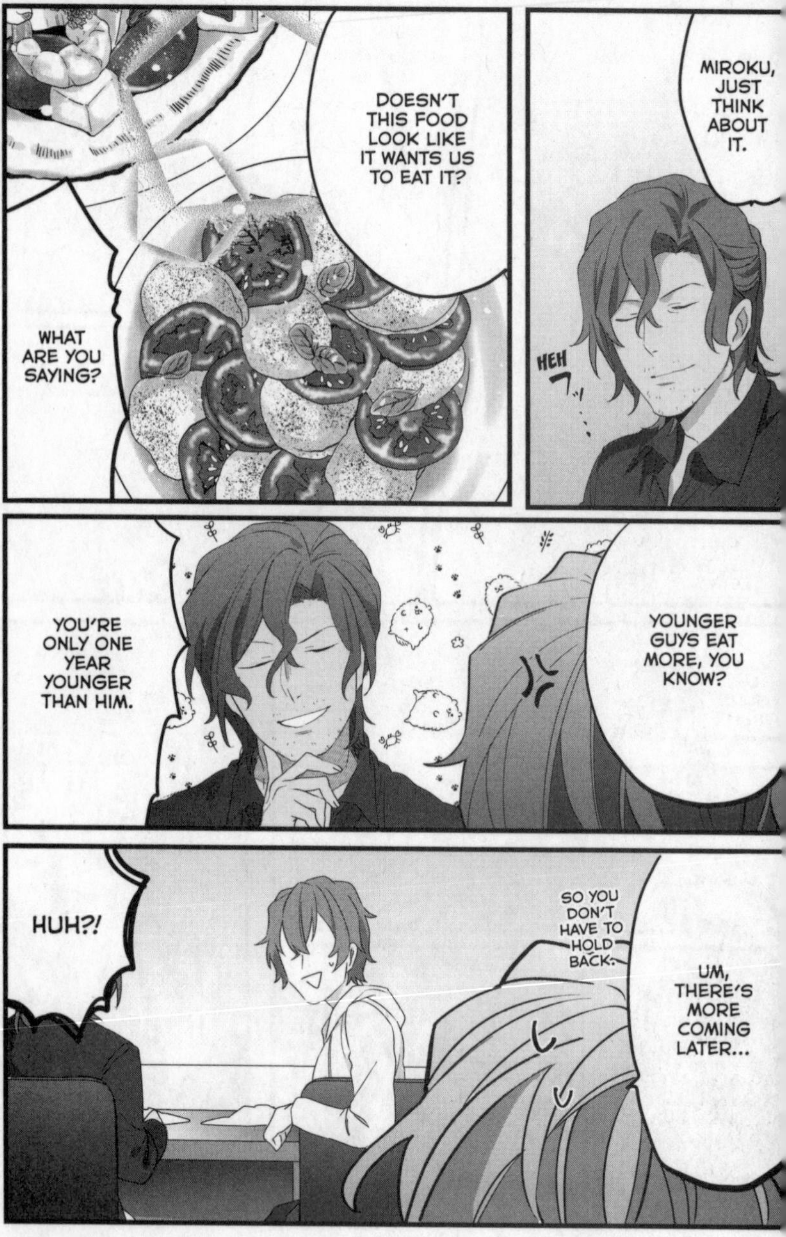
MIROKU, JUST THINK ABOUT IT.
HEH
DOESN'T THIS FOOD LOOK LIKE IT WANTS US TO EAT IT?
WHAT ARE YOU SAYING?
YOUNGER GUYS EAT MORE, YOU KNOW?
YOU'RE ONLY ONE YEAR YOUNGER THAN HIM.
UM, THERE'S MORE COMING LATER...
SO YOU DON'T HAVE TO HOLD BACK.
HUH?!

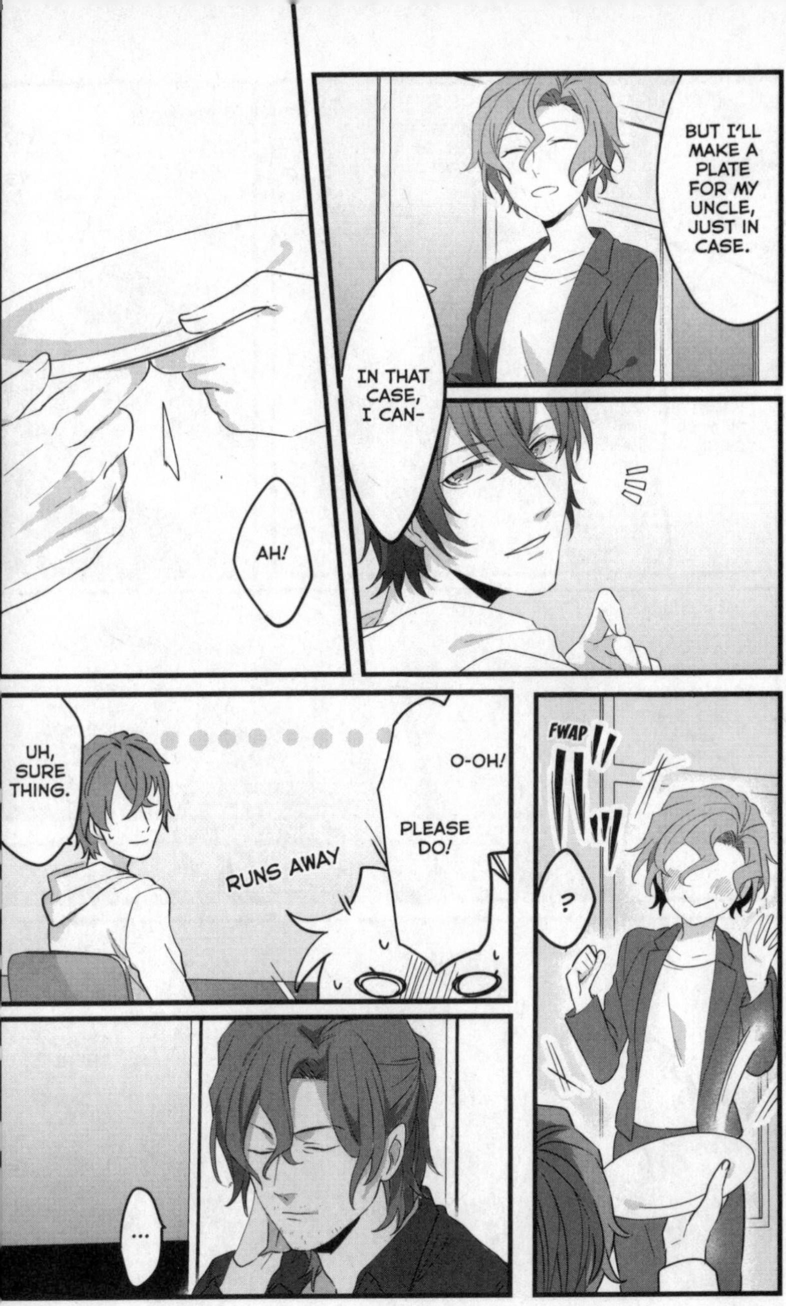
BUT I'LL MAKE A PLATE FOR MY UNCLE, JUST IN CASE.
IN THAT CASE, I CAN-
AH!
FWAP
?
O-OH!
PLEASE DO!
RUNS AWAY
UH, SURE THING.
...

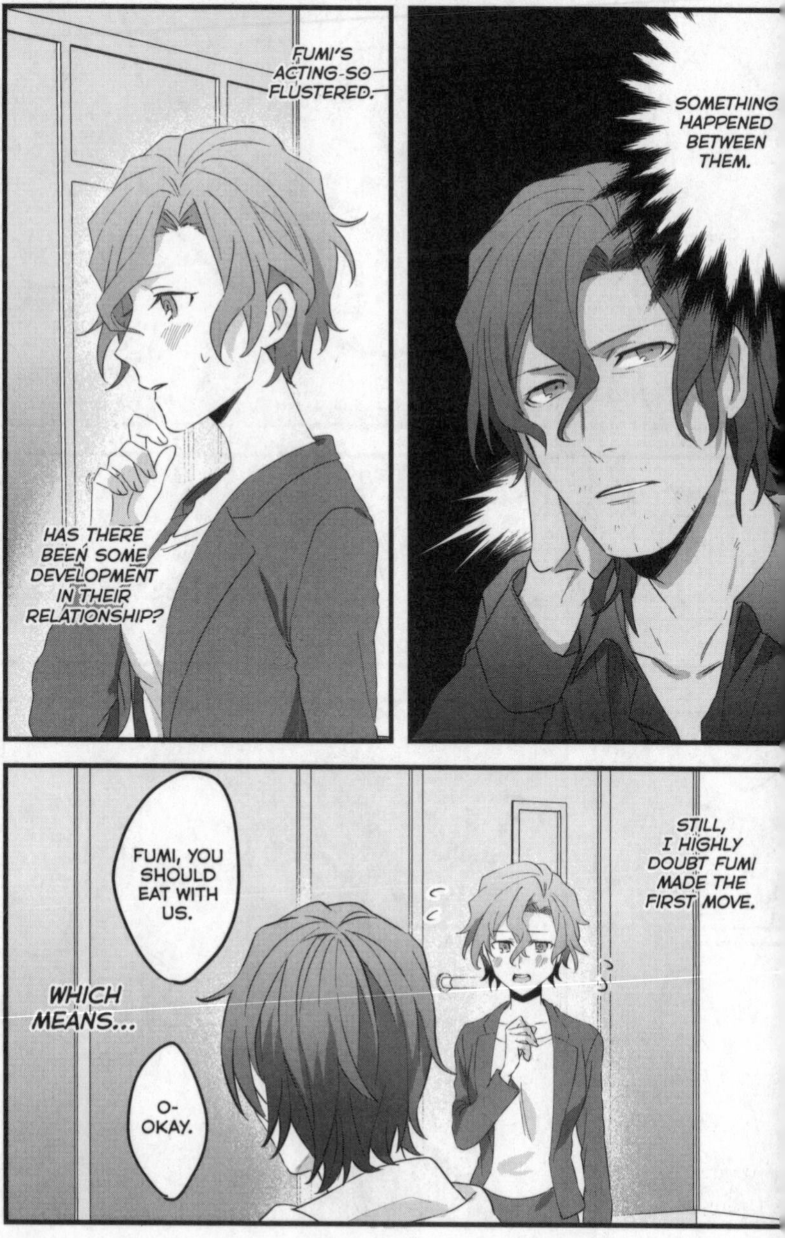
SOMETHING HAPPENED BETWEEN THEM.
FUMI'S ACTING SO FLUSTERED.
HAS THERE BEEN SOME DEVELOPMENT IN THEIR RELATIONSHIP?
STILL, I HIGHLY DOUBT FUMI MADE THE FIRST MOVE.
FUMI, YOU SHOULD EAT WITH US.
WHICH MEANS...
O-OKAY.

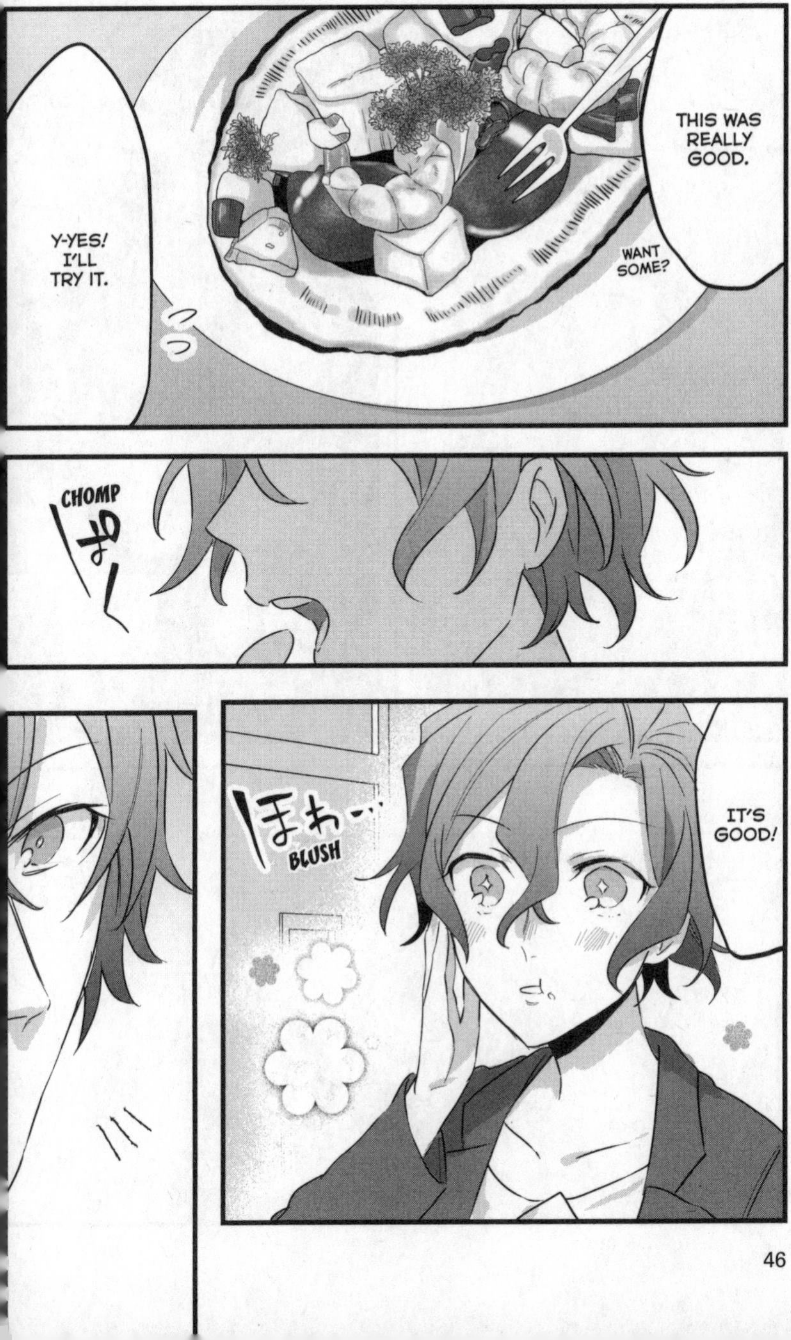
THIS WAS REALLY GOOD.
WANT SOME?
Y-YES! I'LL TRY IT.
CHOMP
IT'S GOOD!
BLUSH

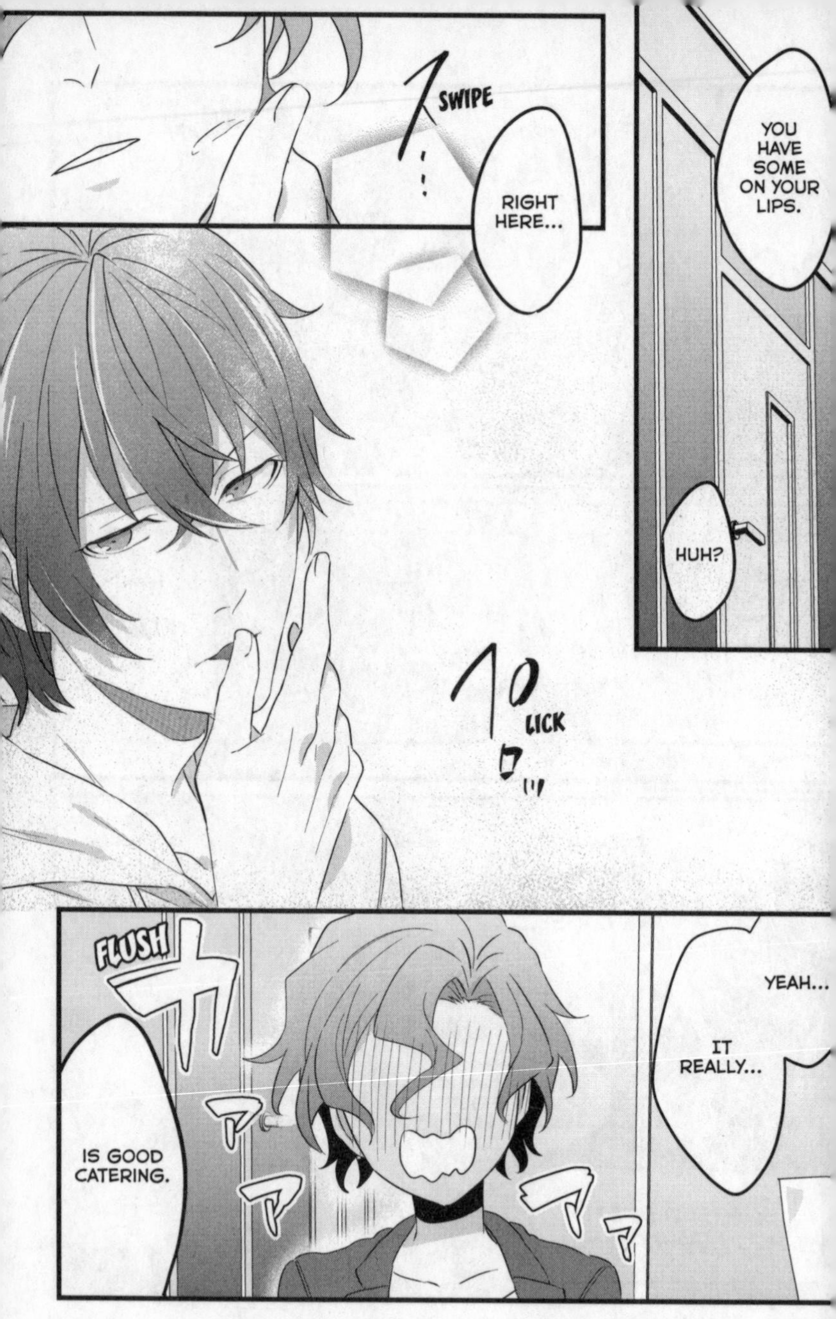
YOU HAVE SOME ON YOUR LIPS.
HUH?
SWIPE
RIGHT HERE...
LICK
YEAH...
IT REALLY...
FLUSH
IS GOOD CATERING.

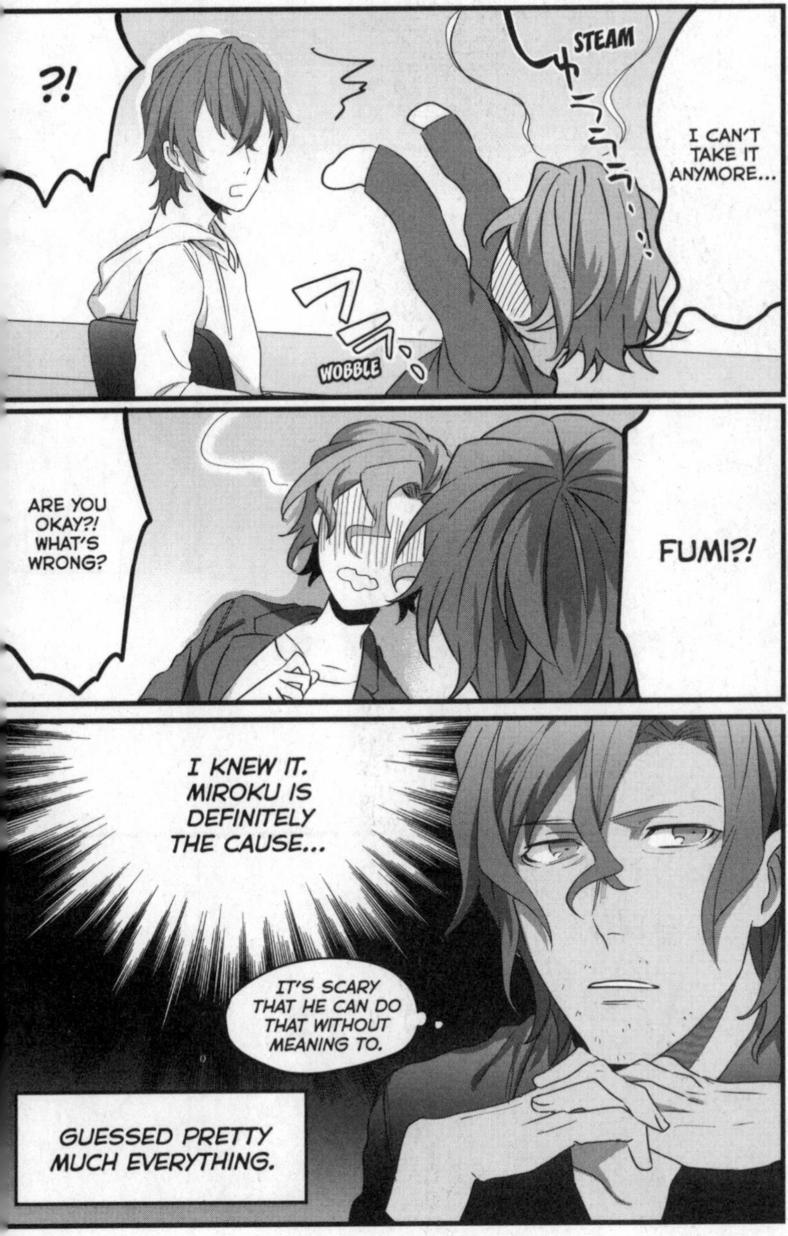
I CAN'T TAKE IT ANYMORE...
STEAM
WOBBLE
?!
FUMI?!
ARE YOU OKAY?! WHAT'S WRONG?
I KNEW IT. MIROKU IS DEFINITELY THE CAUSE...
IT'S SCARY THAT HE CAN DO THAT WITHOUT MEANING TO.
GUESSED PRETTY MUCH EVERYTHING.

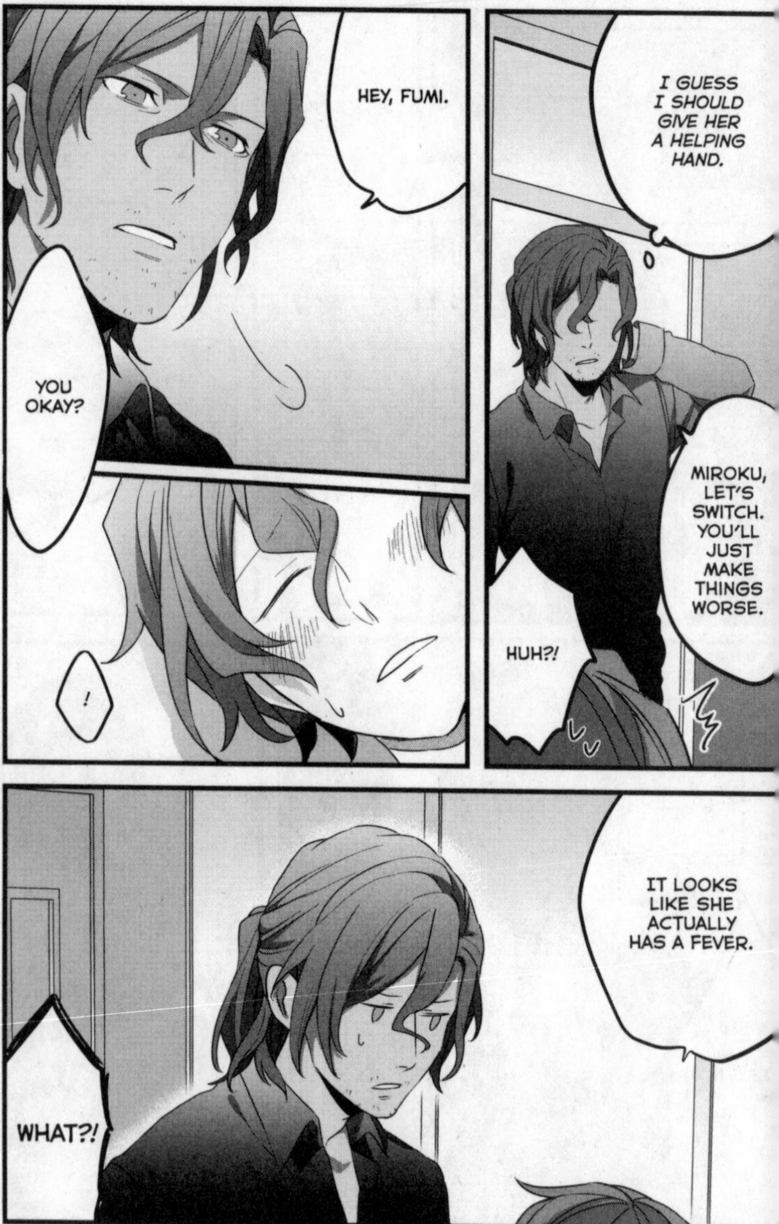
I GUESS I SHOULD GIVE HER A HELPING HAND.
MIROKU, LET'S SWITCH. YOU'LL JUST MAKE THINGS WORSE.
HUH?!
HEY, FUMI.
YOU OKAY?
!
IT LOOKS LIKE SHE ACTUALLY HAS A FEVER.
WHAT?!

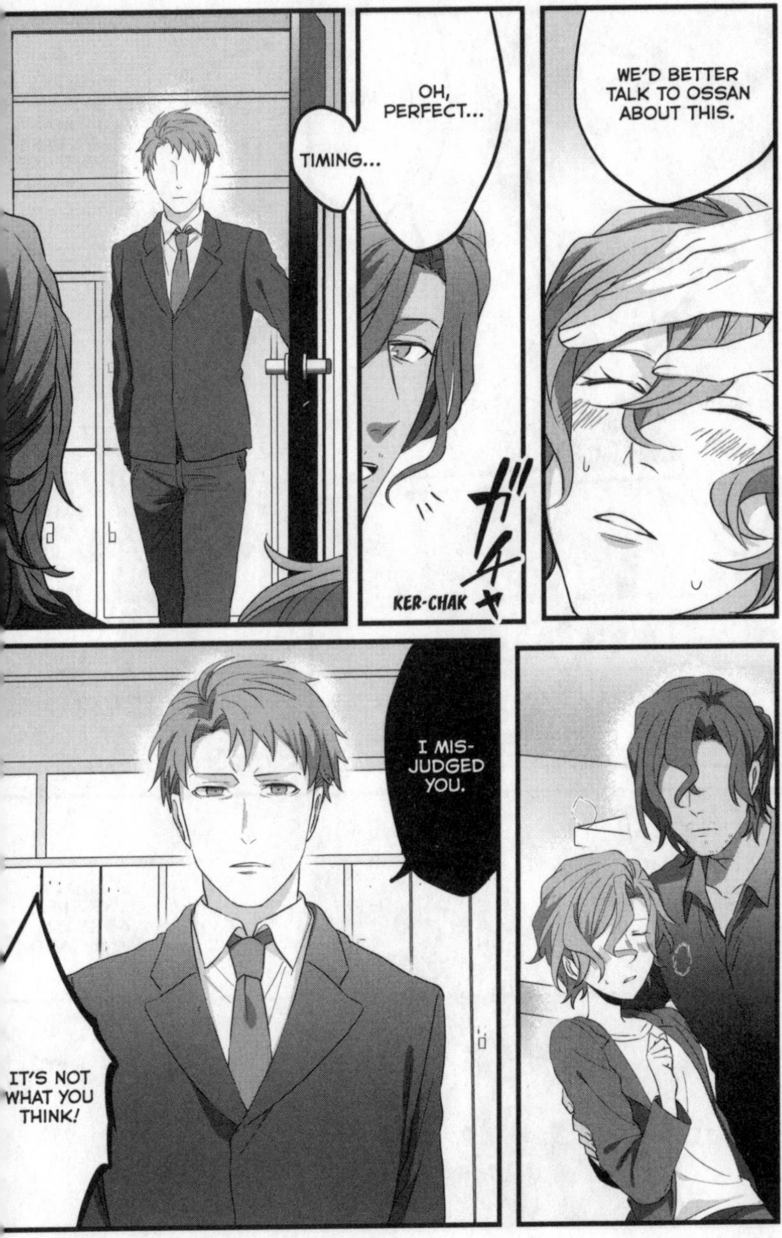
WE'D BETTER TALK TO OSSAN ABOUT THIS.
OH, PERFECT...
TIMING...
ガチャ
KER-CHAK
I MIS-JUDGED YOU.
IT'S NOT WHAT YOU THINK!

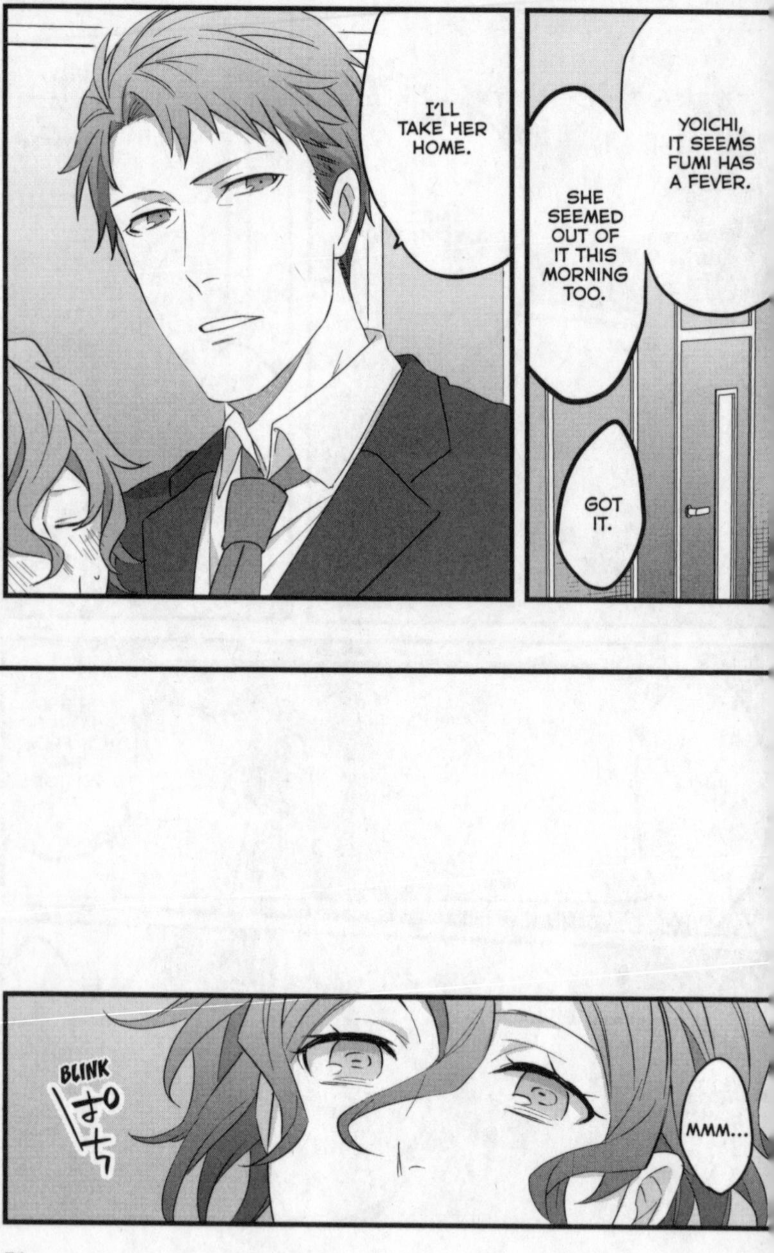
YOICHI, IT SEEMS FUMI HAS A FEVER.
SHE SEEMED OUT OF IT THIS MORNING TOO.
GOT IT.
I'LL TAKE HER HOME.
MMM...
BLINK

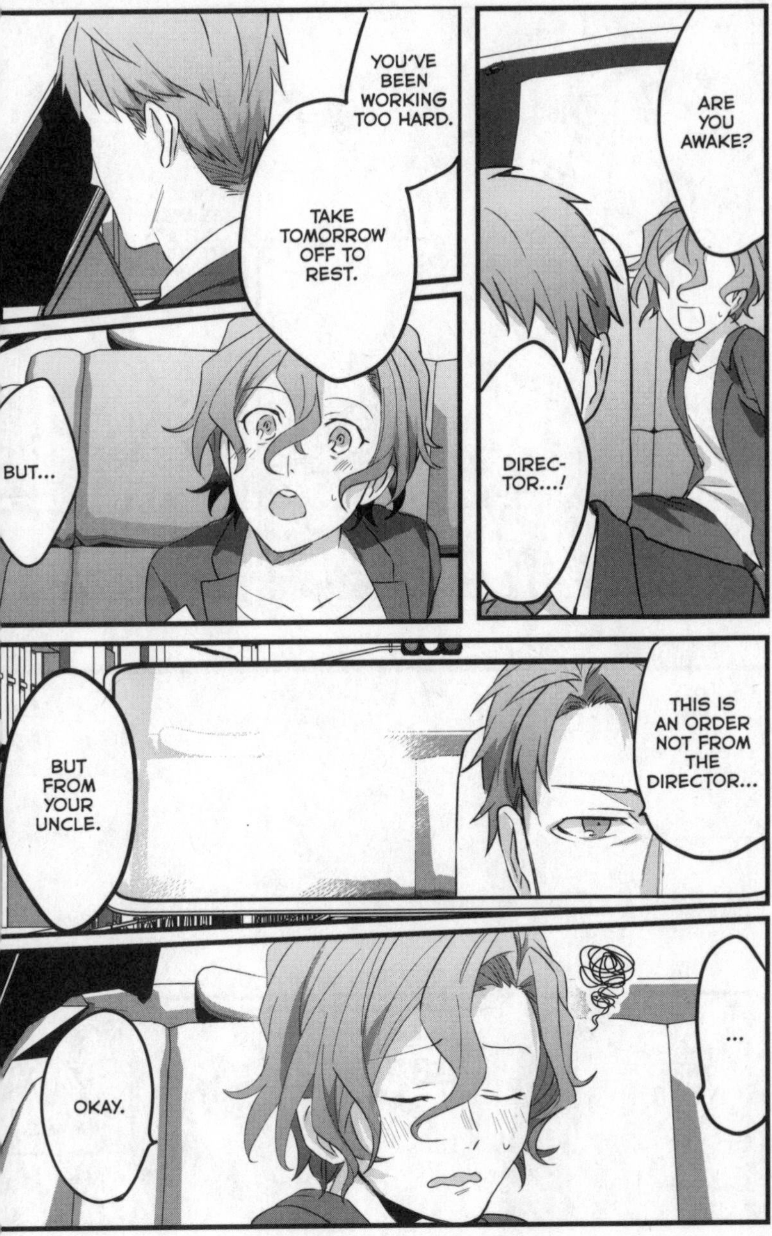
ARE YOU AWAKE?
DIREC- TOR...!
YOU'VE BEEN WORKING TOO HARD.
TAKE TOMORROW OFF TO REST.
BUT...
THIS IS AN ORDER NOT FROM THE DIRECTOR...
BUT FROM YOUR UNCLE.
...
OKAY.

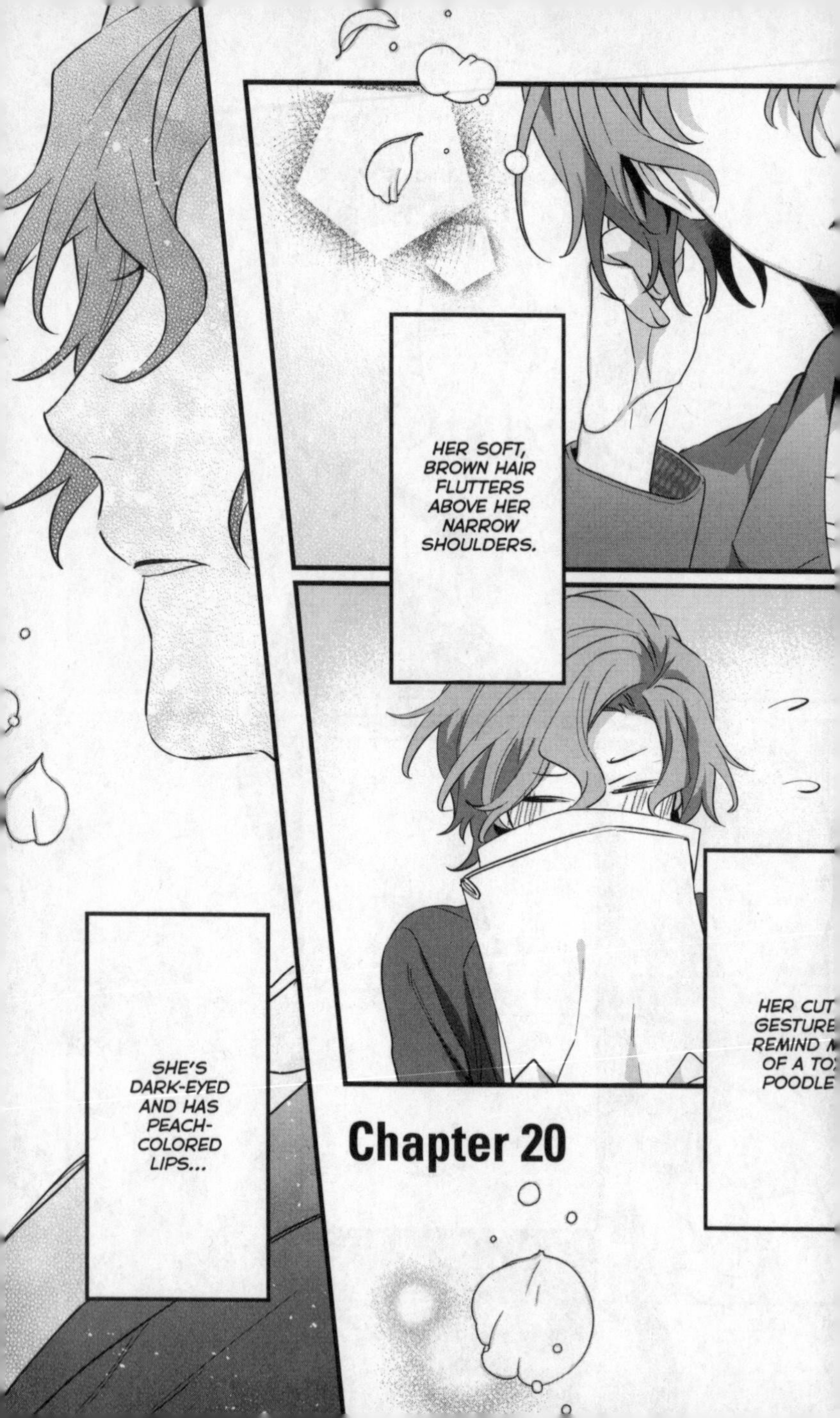
HER SOFT, BROWN HAIR FLUTTERS ABOVE HER NARROW SHOULDERS.
HER CUT GESTURE REMIND OF A TO POODLE
Chapter 20
SHE'S DARK-EYED AND HAS PEACH-COLORED LIPS...

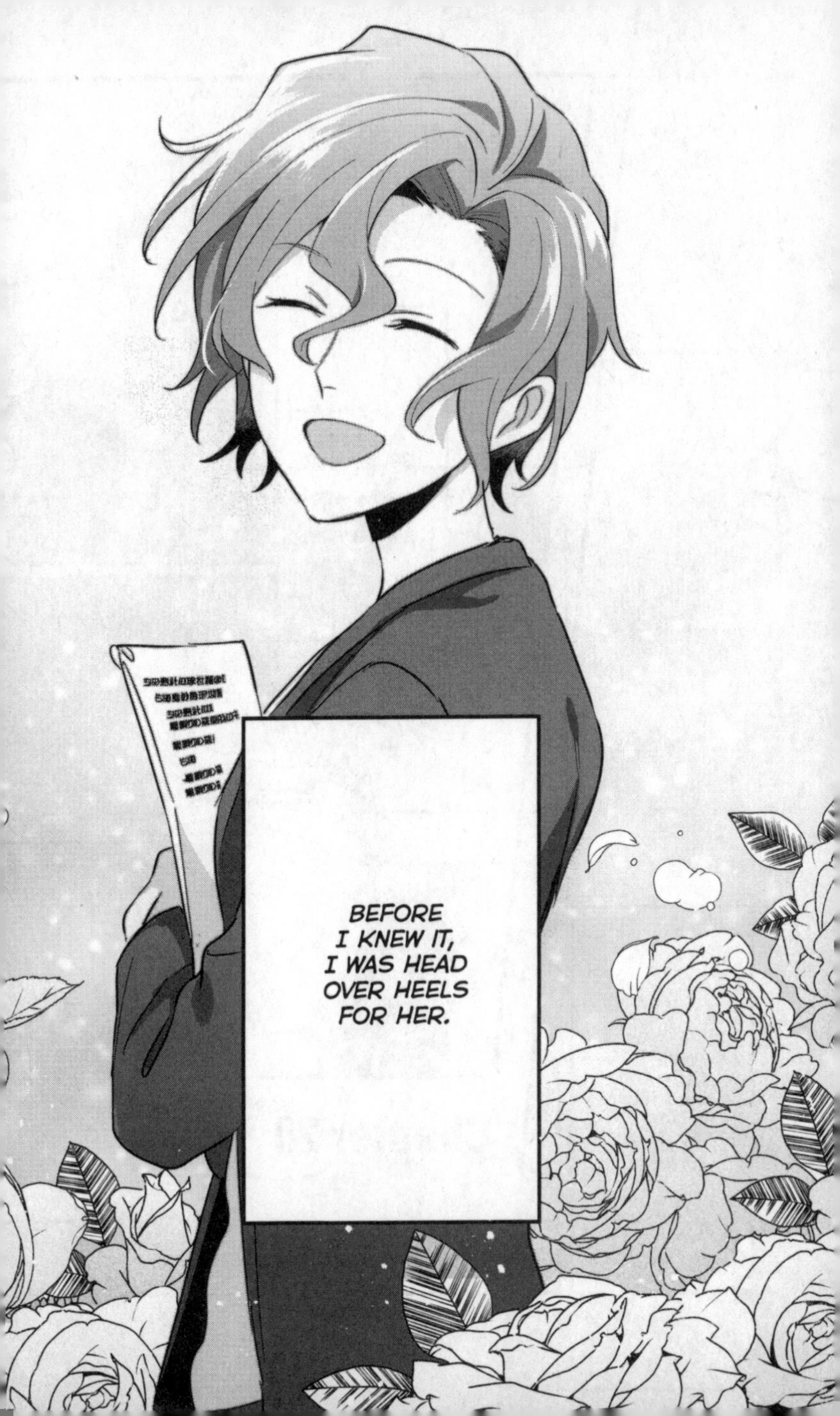
BEFORE I KNEW IT, I WAS HEAD OVER HEELS FOR HER.

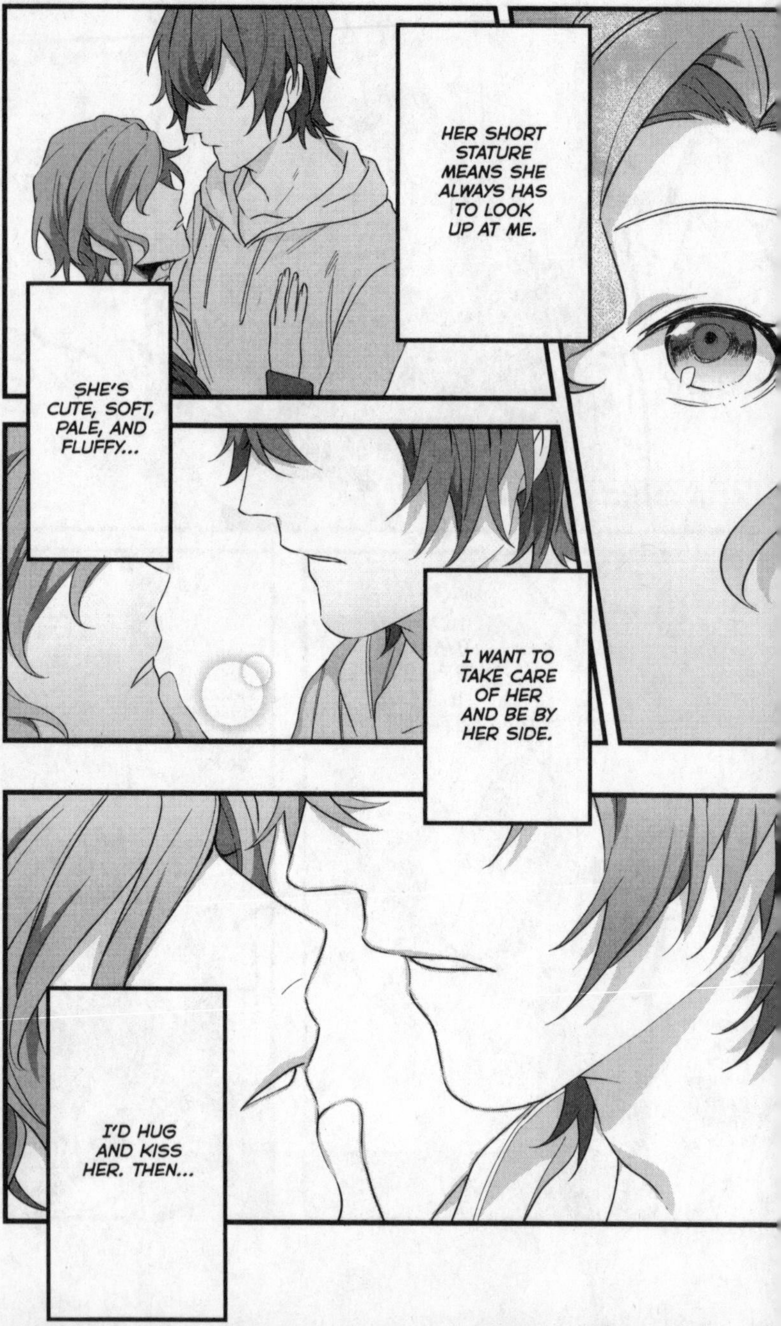
HER SHORT STATURE MEANS SHE ALWAYS HAS TO LOOK UP AT ME.
SHE'S CUTE, SOFT, PALE, AND FLUFFY...
I WANT TO TAKE CARE OF HER AND BE BY HER SIDE.
I'D HUG AND KISS HER. THEN...

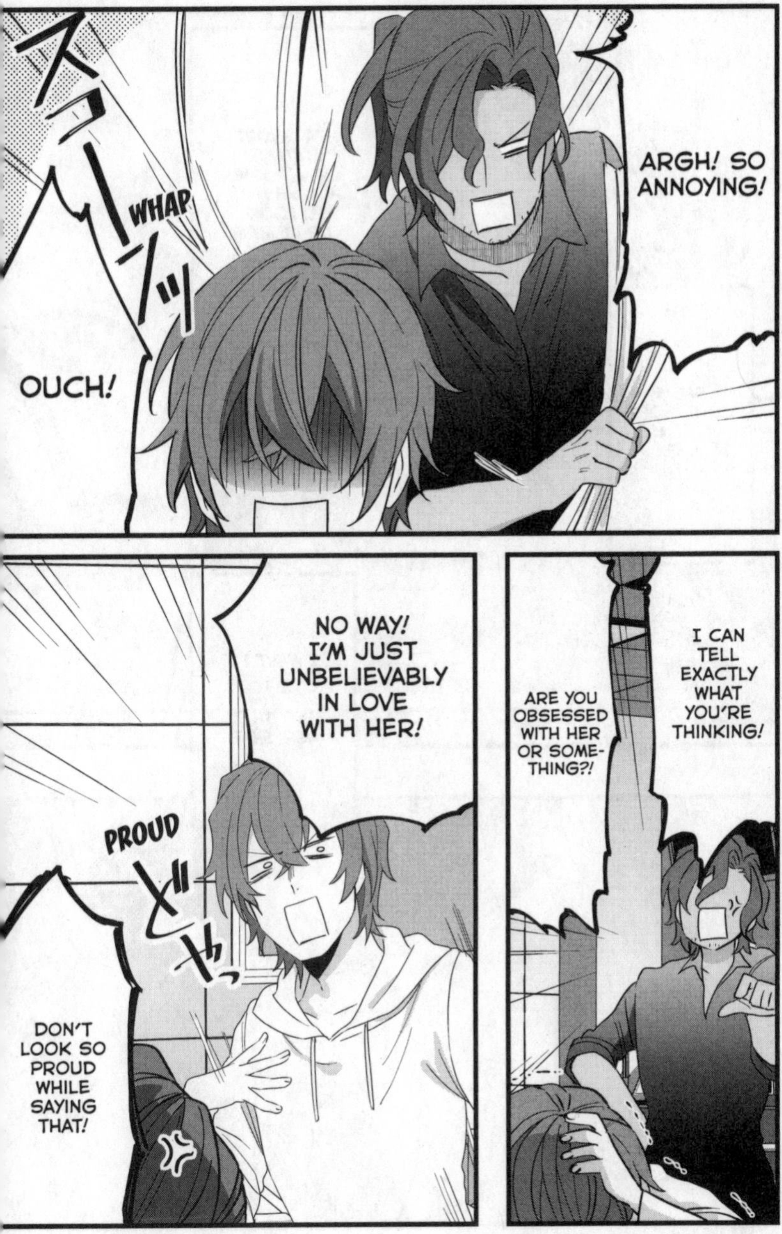
ARGH! SO ANNOYING!
スコーンッ
WHAP
OUCH!
I CAN TELL EXACTLY WHAT YOU'RE THINKING!
ARE YOU OBSESSED WITH HER OR SOMETHING?!
NO WAY! I'M JUST UNBELIEVABLY IN LOVE WITH HER!
どやっ
PROUD
DON'T LOOK SO PROUD WHILE SAYING THAT!

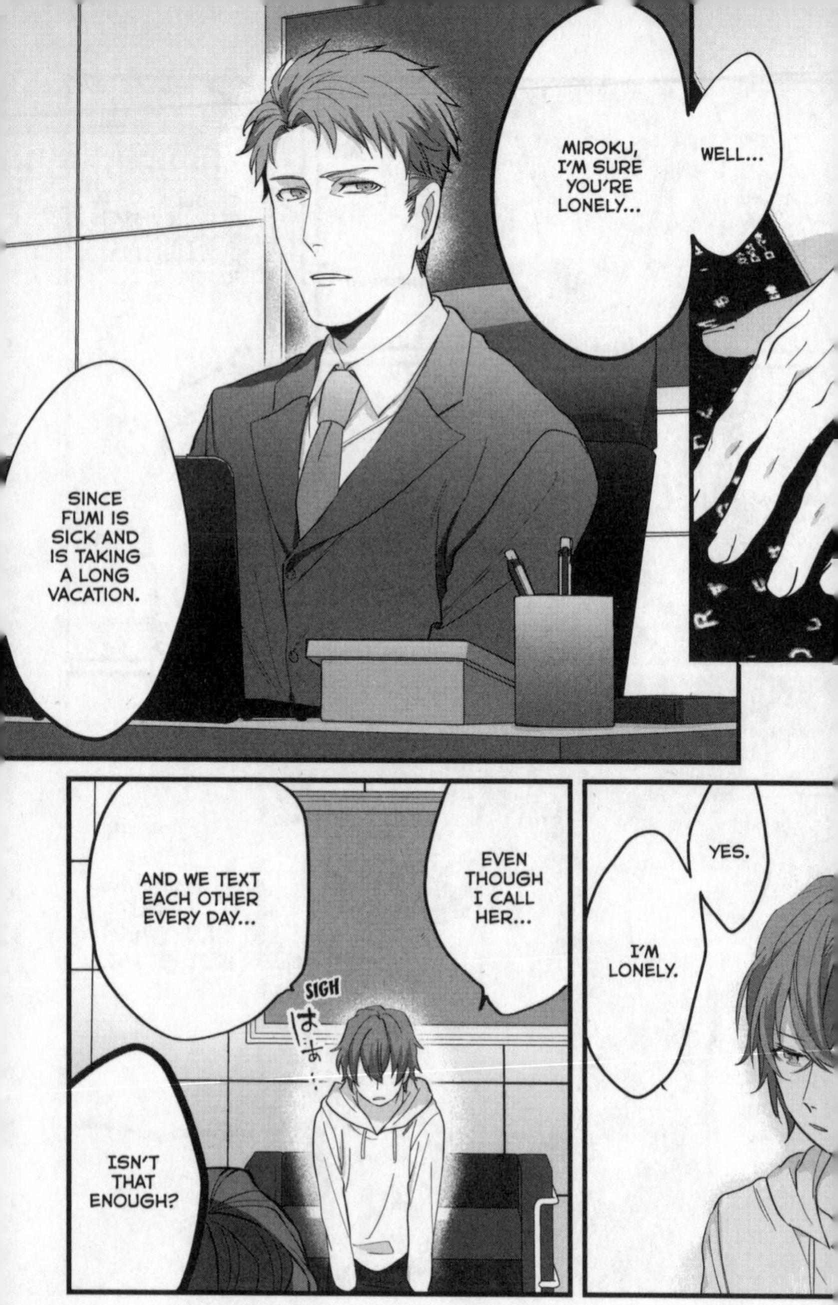
WELL...
MIROKU, I'M SURE YOU'RE LONELY...
SINCE FUMI IS SICK AND IS TAKING A LONG VACATION.
YES.
I'M LONELY.
EVEN THOUGH I CALL HER...
AND WE TEXT EACH OTHER EVERY DAY...
SIGH
ISN'T THAT ENOUGH?

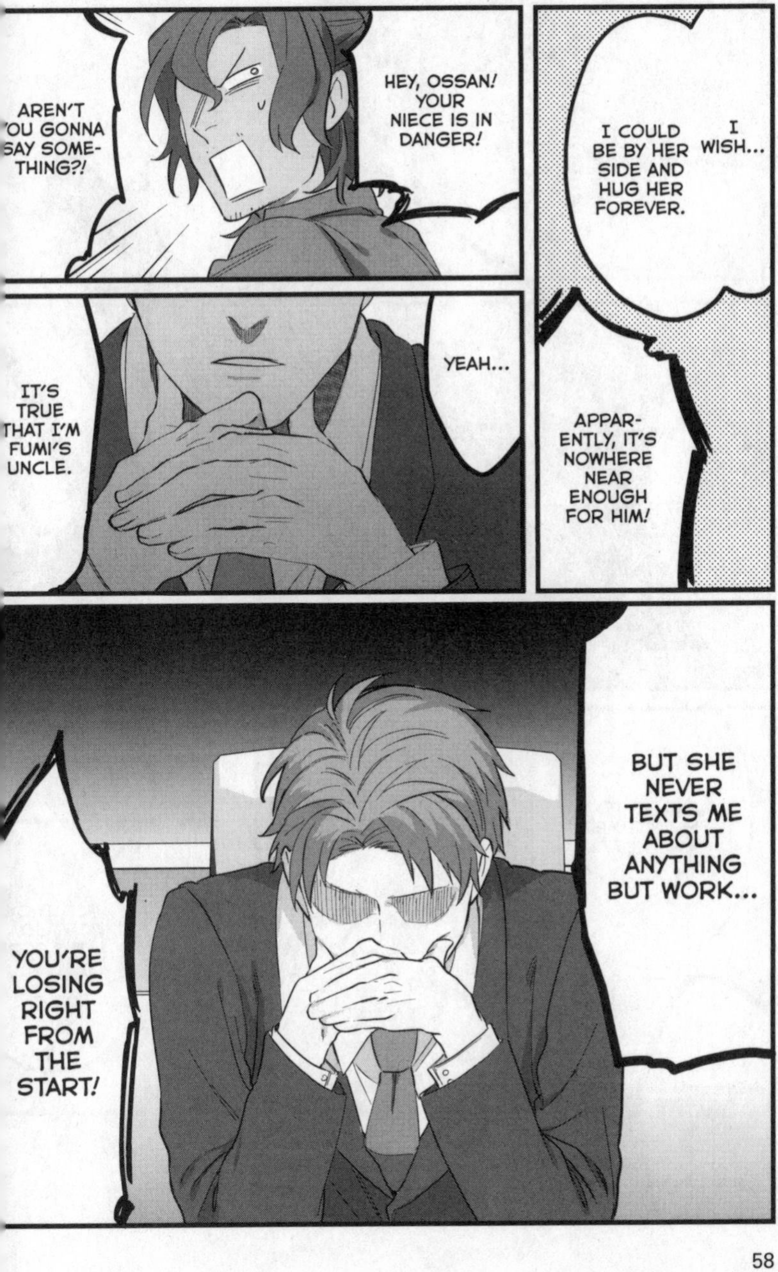
I WISH... I COULD BE BY HER SIDE AND HUG HER FOREVER.
APPARENTLY, IT'S NOWHERE NEAR ENOUGH FOR HIM!
HEY, OSSAN! YOUR NIECE IS IN DANGER!
AREN'T YOU GONNA SAY SOMETHING?!
YEAH...
IT'S TRUE THAT I'M FUMI'S UNCLE.
BUT SHE NEVER TEXTS ME ABOUT ANYTHING BUT WORK...
YOU'RE LOSING RIGHT FROM THE START!

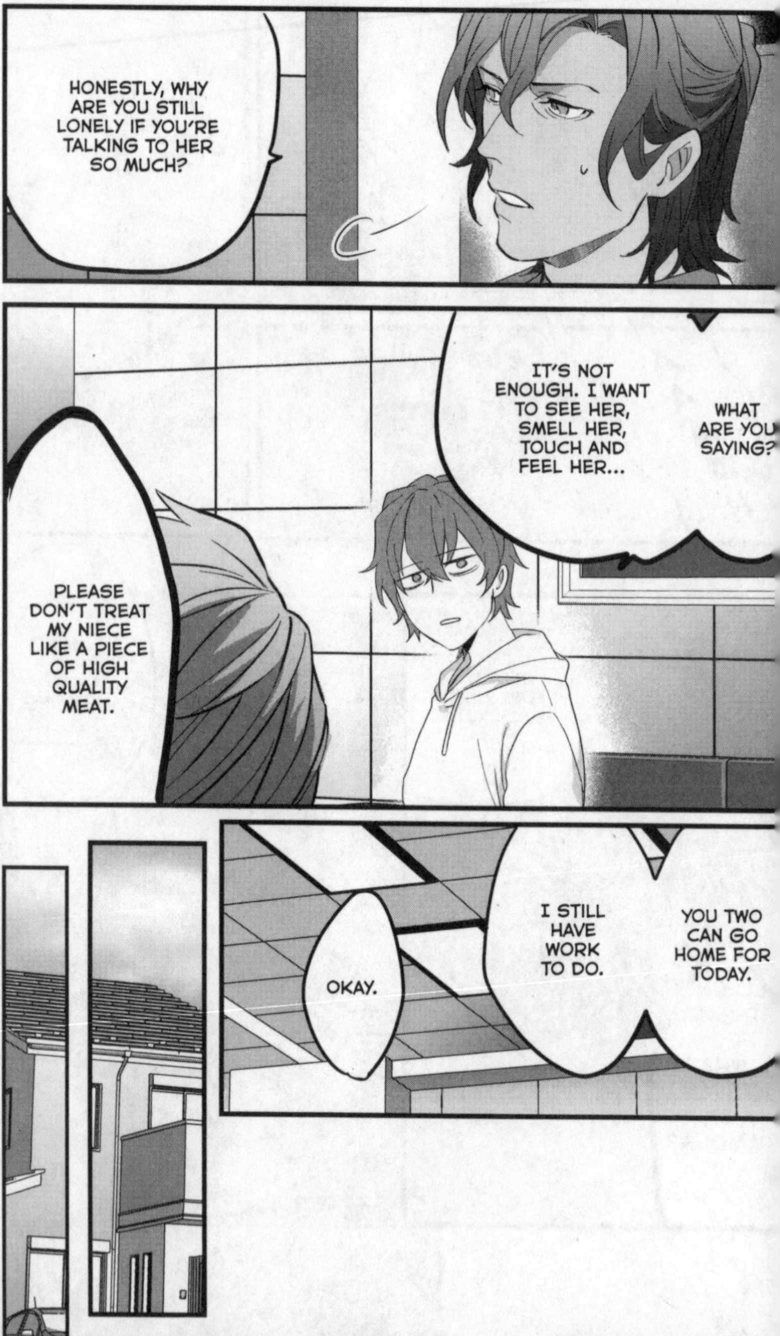
HONESTLY, WHY ARE YOU STILL LONELY IF YOU'RE TALKING TO HER SO MUCH?
WHAT ARE YOU SAYING?
IT'S NOT ENOUGH. I WANT TO SEE HER, SMELL HER, TOUCH AND FEEL HER...
PLEASE DON'T TREAT MY NIECE LIKE A PIECE OF HIGH QUALITY MEAT.
YOU TWO CAN GO HOME FOR TODAY.
I STILL HAVE WORK TO DO.
OKAY.

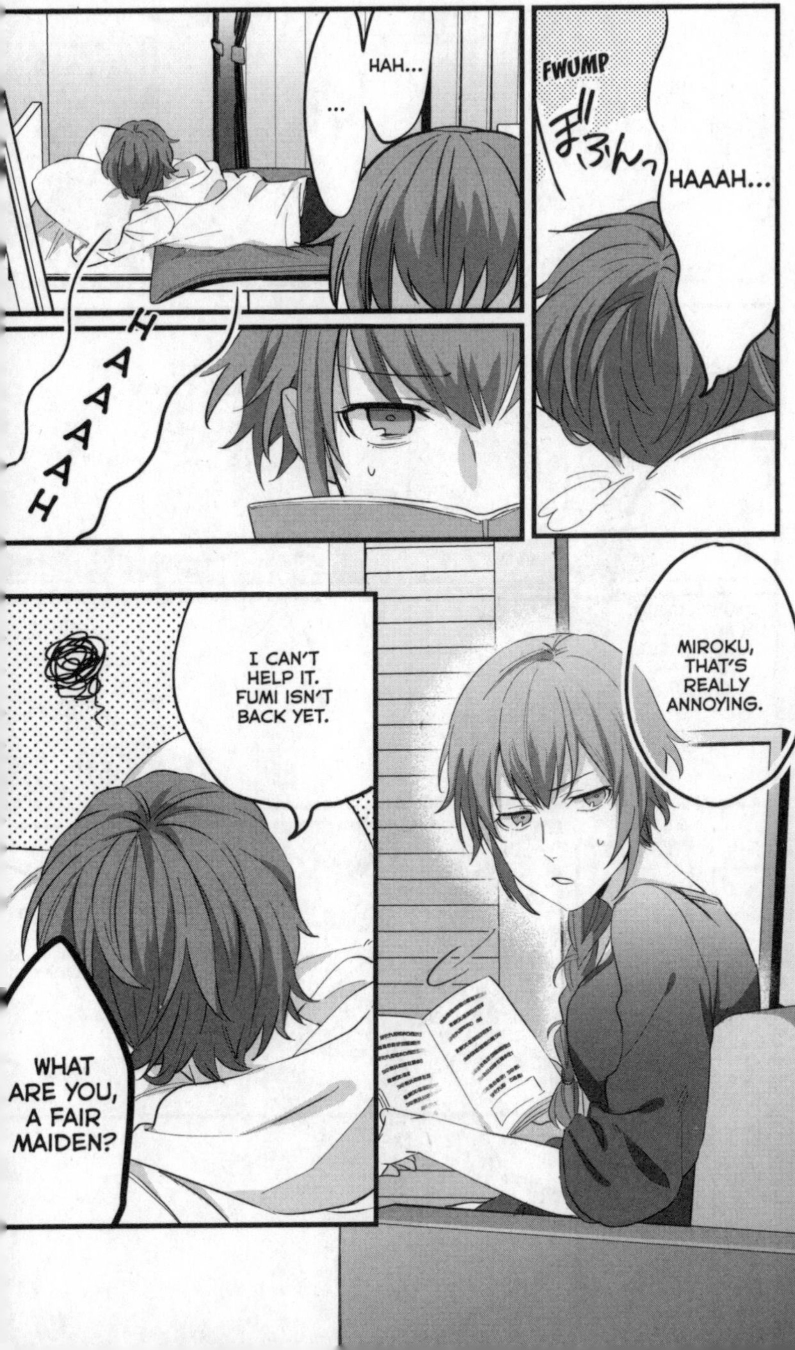
FWUMP
ぼふんっ
HAAAH...
HAH...
...
HAAAAAH
MIROKU, THAT'S REALLY ANNOYING.
I CAN'T HELP IT. FUMI ISN'T BACK YET.
WHAT ARE YOU, A FAIR MAIDEN?

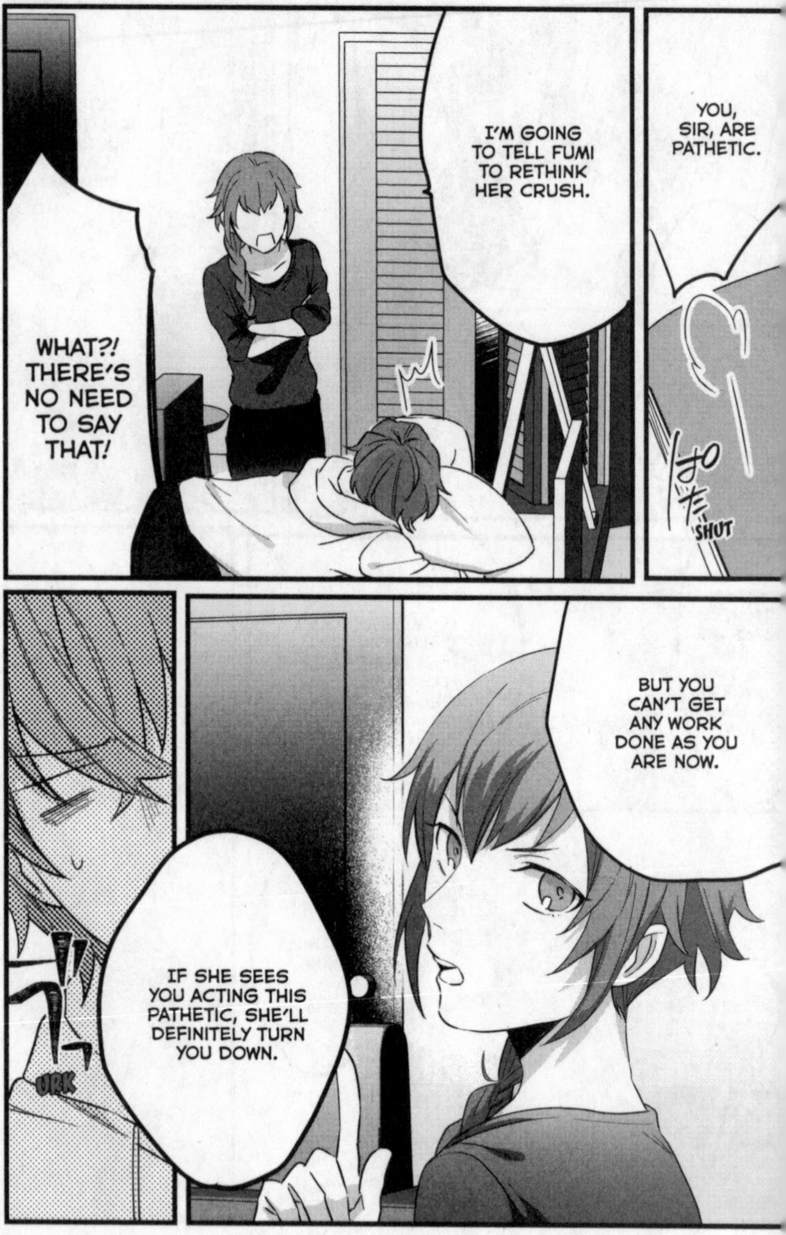
YOU, SIR, ARE PATHETIC.
SHUT
I'M GOING TO TELL FUMI TO RETHINK HER CRUSH.
WHAT?! THERE'S NO NEED TO SAY THAT!
BUT YOU CAN'T GET ANY WORK DONE AS YOU ARE NOW.
IF SHE SEES YOU ACTING THIS PATHETIC, SHE'LL DEFINITELY TURN YOU DOWN.
URK

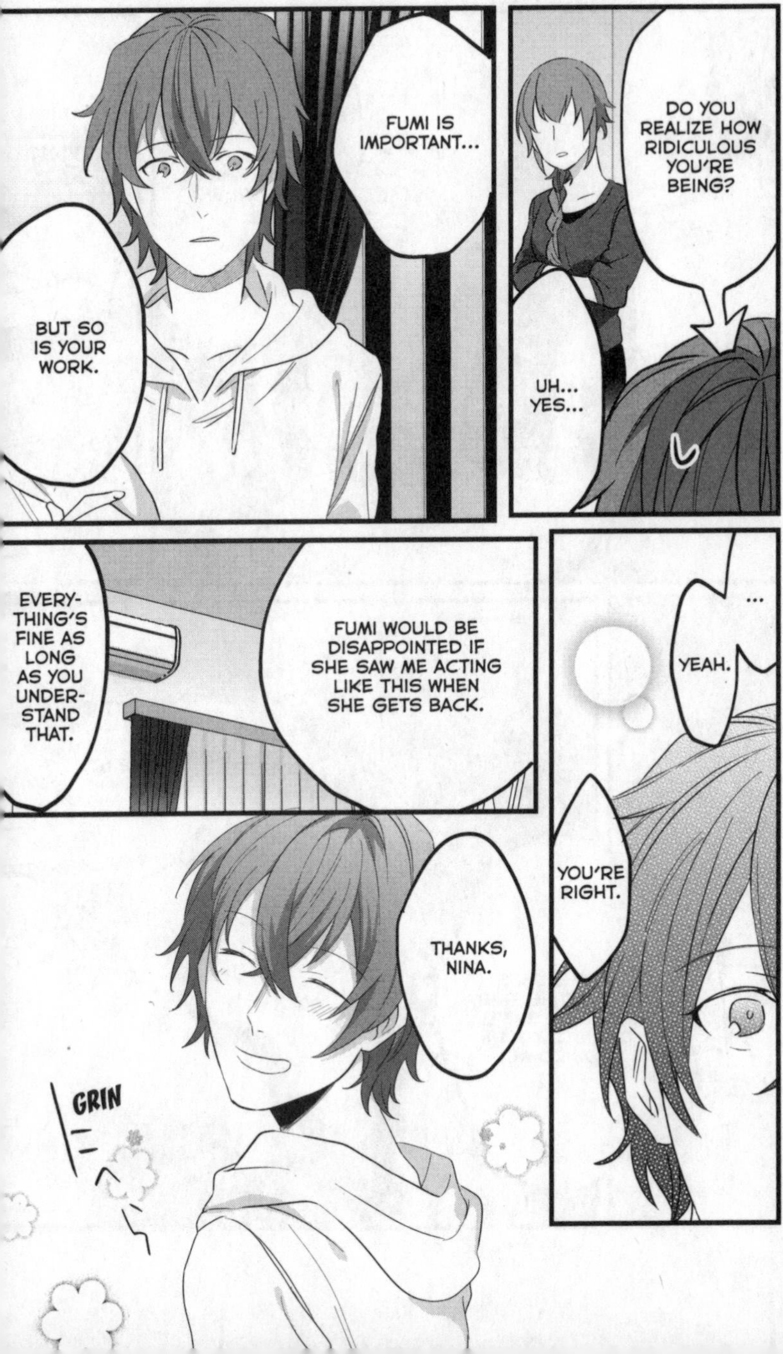
DO YOU REALIZE HOW RIDICULOUS YOU'RE BEING?
UH... YES...
FUMI IS IMPORTANT...
BUT SO IS YOUR WORK.
...
YEAH.
YOU'RE RIGHT.
FUMI WOULD BE DISAPPOINTED IF SHE SAW ME ACTING LIKE THIS WHEN SHE GETS BACK.
EVERY-THING'S FINE AS LONG AS YOU UNDER-STAND THAT.
THANKS, NINA.
GRIN

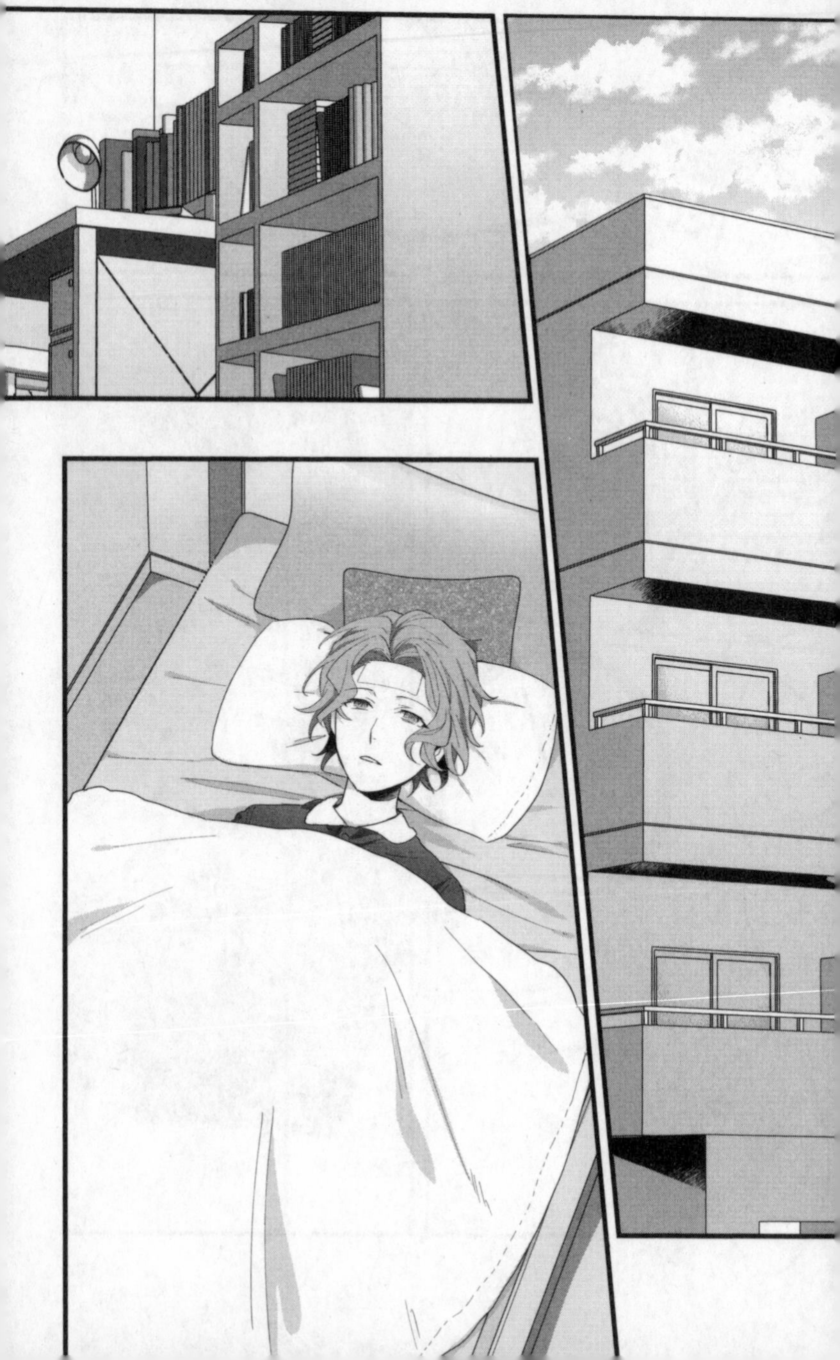

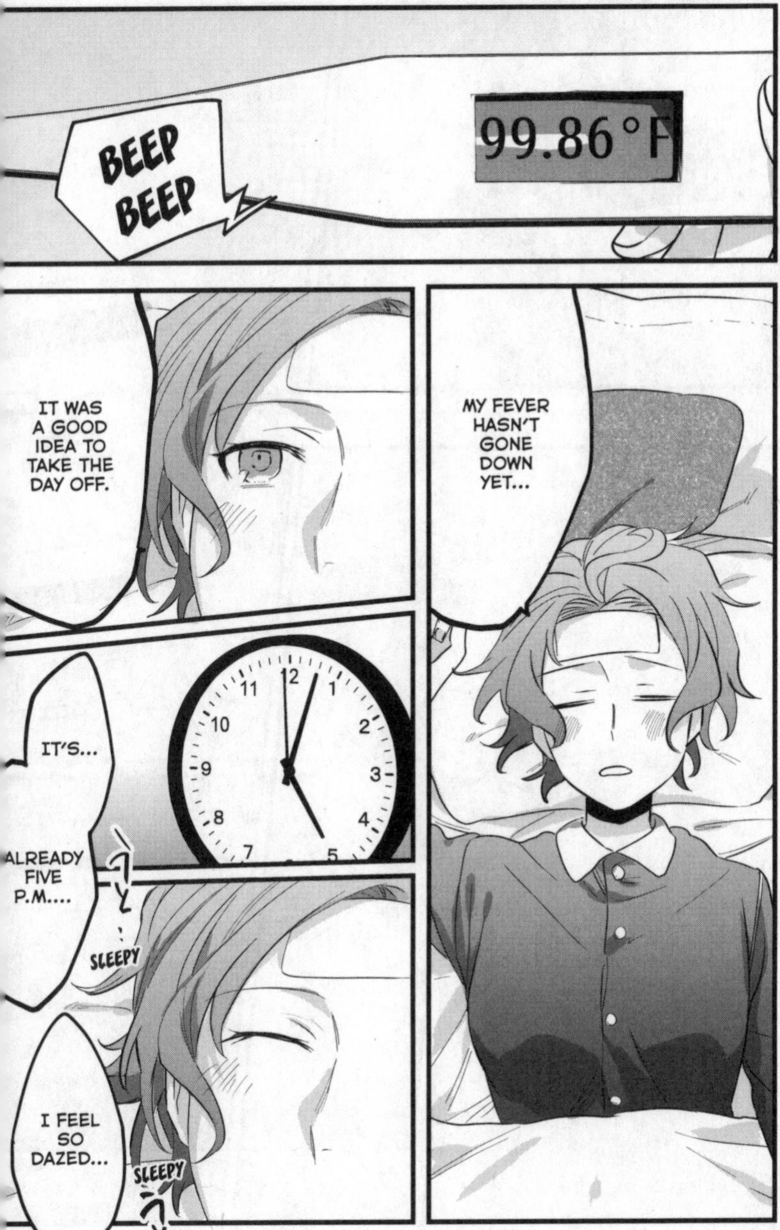
99.86°F
BEEP BEEP
MY FEVER HASN'T GONE DOWN YET...
IT WAS A GOOD IDEA TO TAKE THE DAY OFF.
IT'S...
ALREADY FIVE P.M....
SLEEPY
I FEEL SO DAZED...
SLEEPY

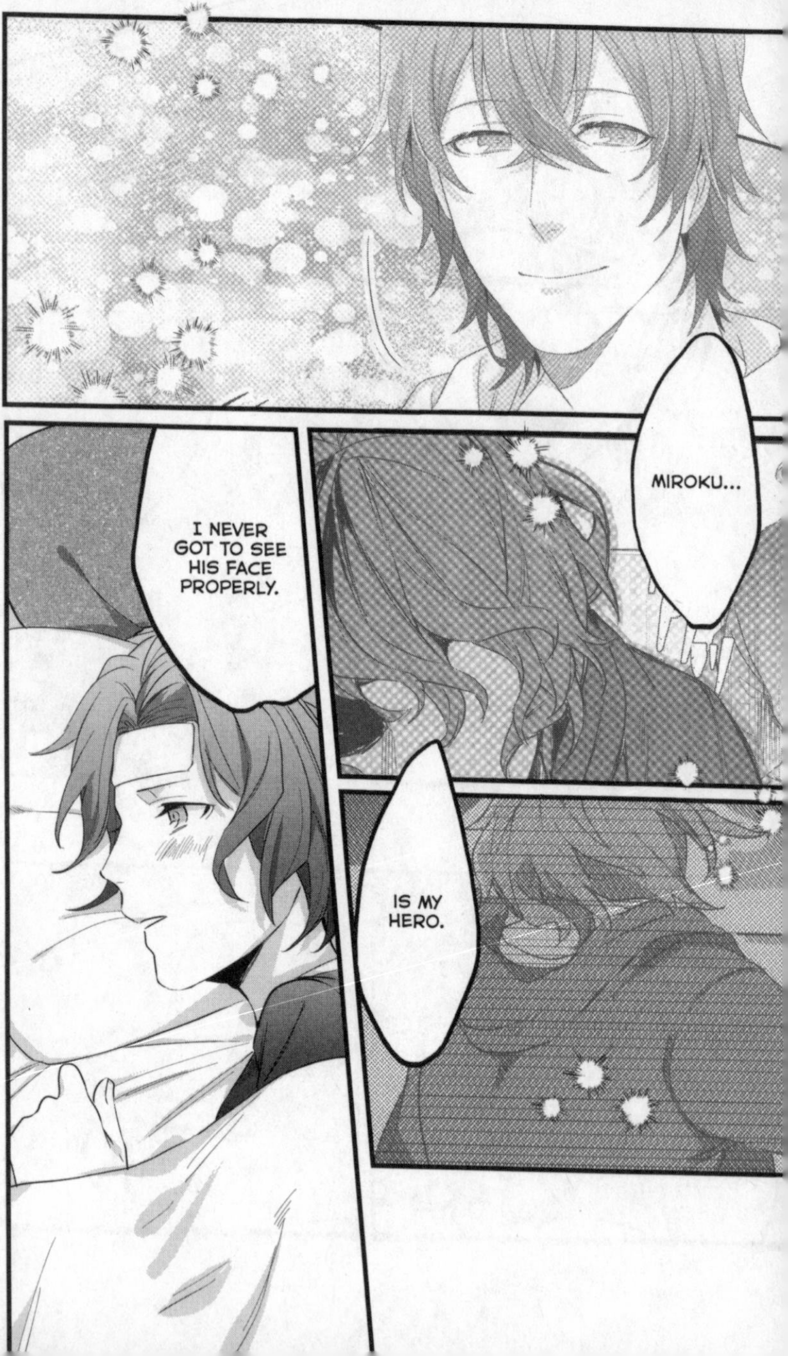
MIROKU...
IS MY HERO.
I NEVER GOT TO SEE HIS FACE PROPERLY.

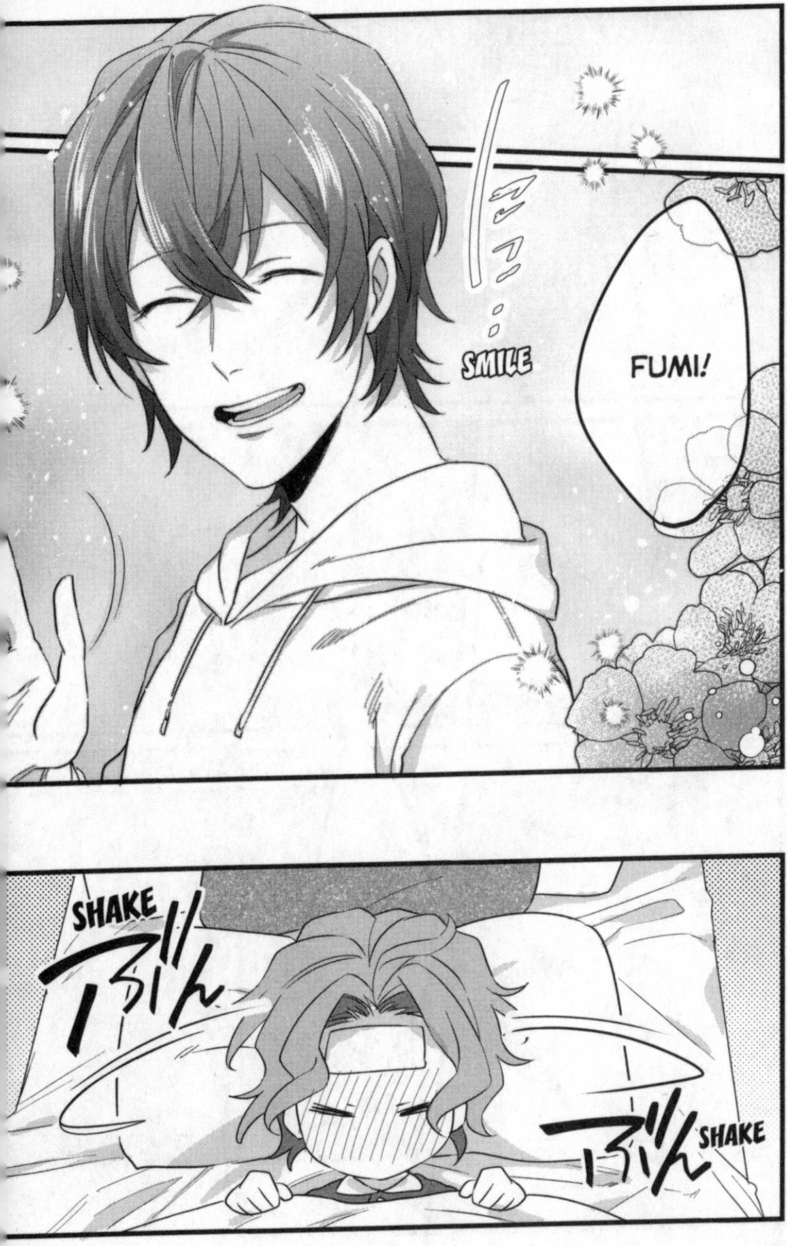
FUMI!
SMILE
SHAKE
SHAKE

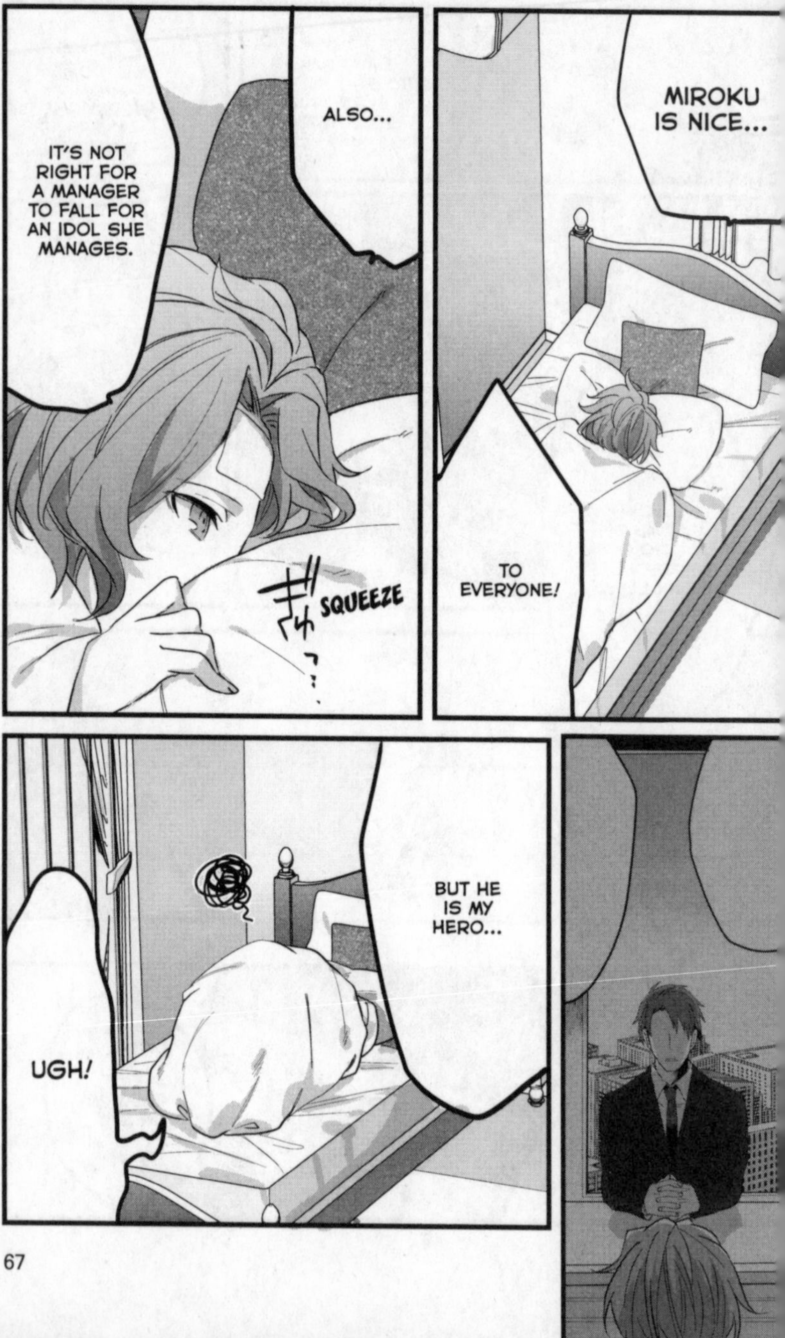
MIROKU IS NICE...
TO EVERYONE!
ALSO...
IT'S NOT RIGHT FOR A MANAGER TO FALL FOR AN IDOL SHE MANAGES.
SQUEEZE
BUT HE IS MY HERO...
UGH!

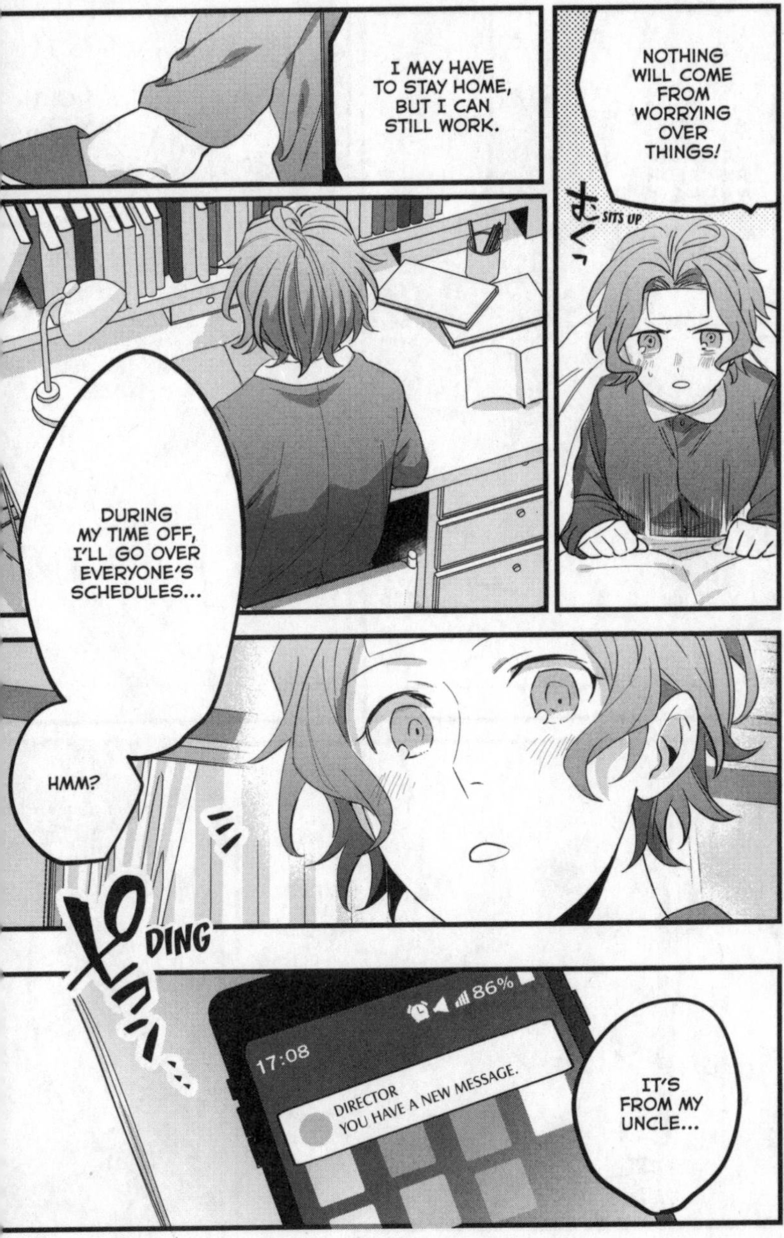
NOTHING WILL COME FROM WORRYING OVER THINGS!
SITS UP
I MAY HAVE TO STAY HOME, BUT I CAN STILL WORK.
DURING MY TIME OFF, I'LL GO OVER EVERYONE'S SCHEDULES...
HMM?
DING
86%
17:08
DIRECTOR
YOU HAVE A NEW MESSAGE.
IT'S FROM MY UNCLE...

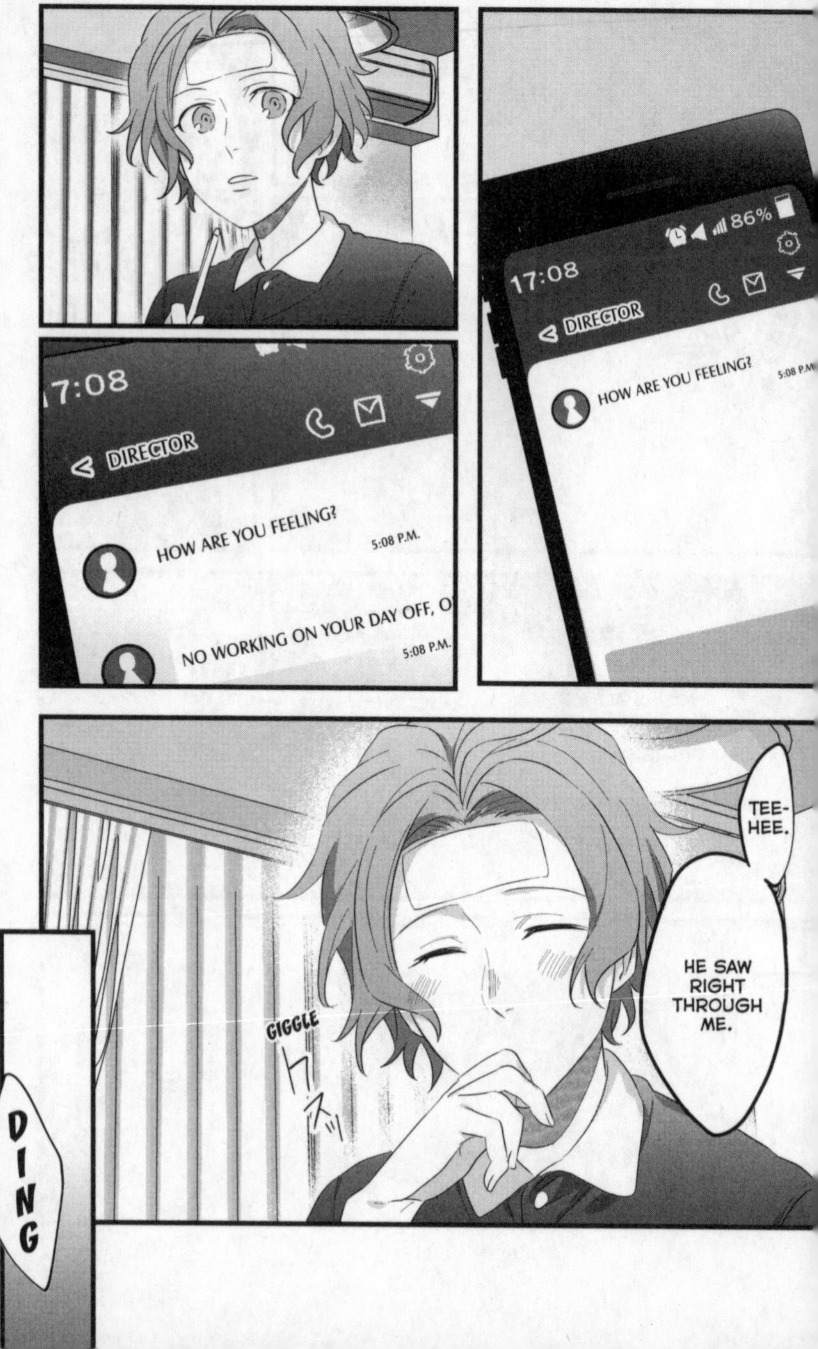
86%
17:08
DIRECTOR
HOW ARE YOU FEELING?
5:08 P.M
7:08
DIRECTOR
HOW ARE YOU FEELING?
5:08 P.M.
NO WORKING ON YOUR DAY OFF, O
5:08 P.M.
TEE-HEE.
HE SAW RIGHT THROUGH ME.
GIGGLE
クスッ
DING

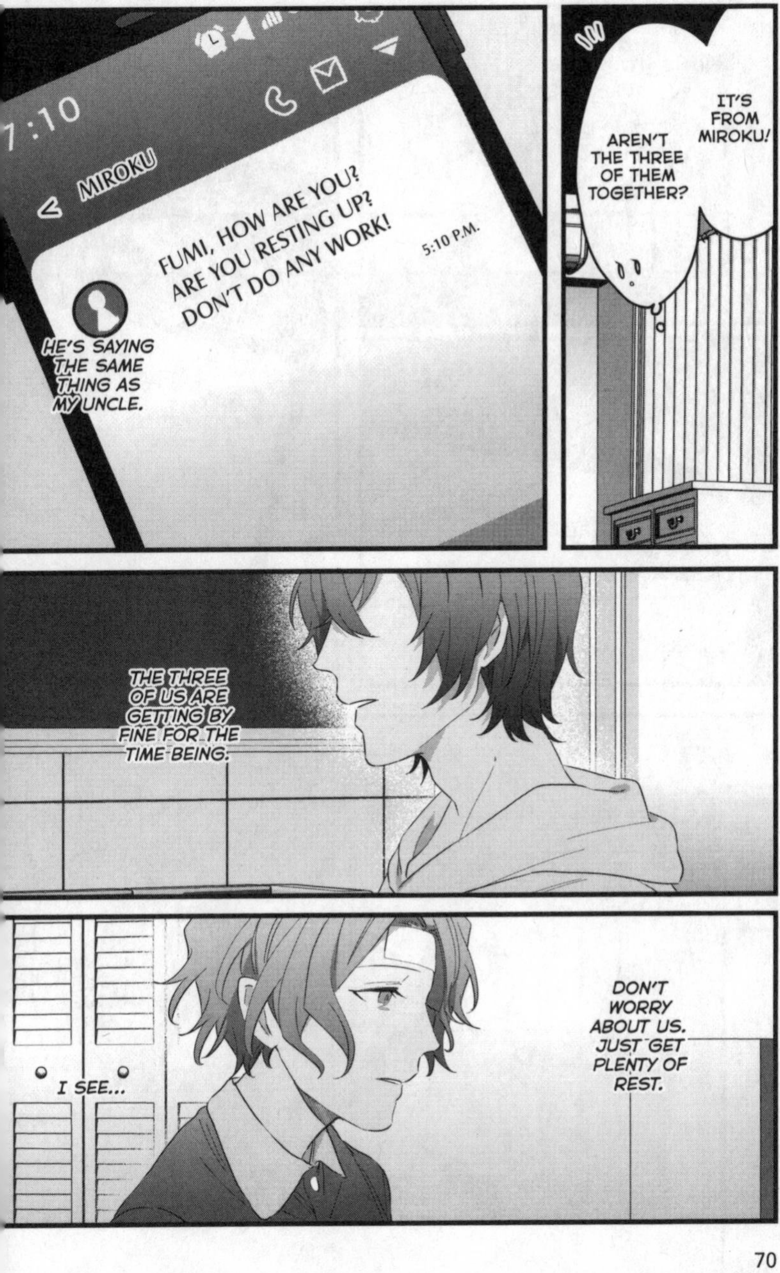
IT'S FROM MIROKU!
AREN'T THE THREE OF THEM TOGETHER?
7:10
MIROKU
FUMI, HOW ARE YOU? ARE YOU RESTING UP? DON'T DO ANY WORK!
5:10 P.M.
HE'S SAYING THE SAME THING AS MY UNCLE.
THE THREE OF US ARE GETTING BY FINE FOR THE TIME BEING.
DON'T WORRY ABOUT US. JUST GET PLENTY OF REST.
I SEE...

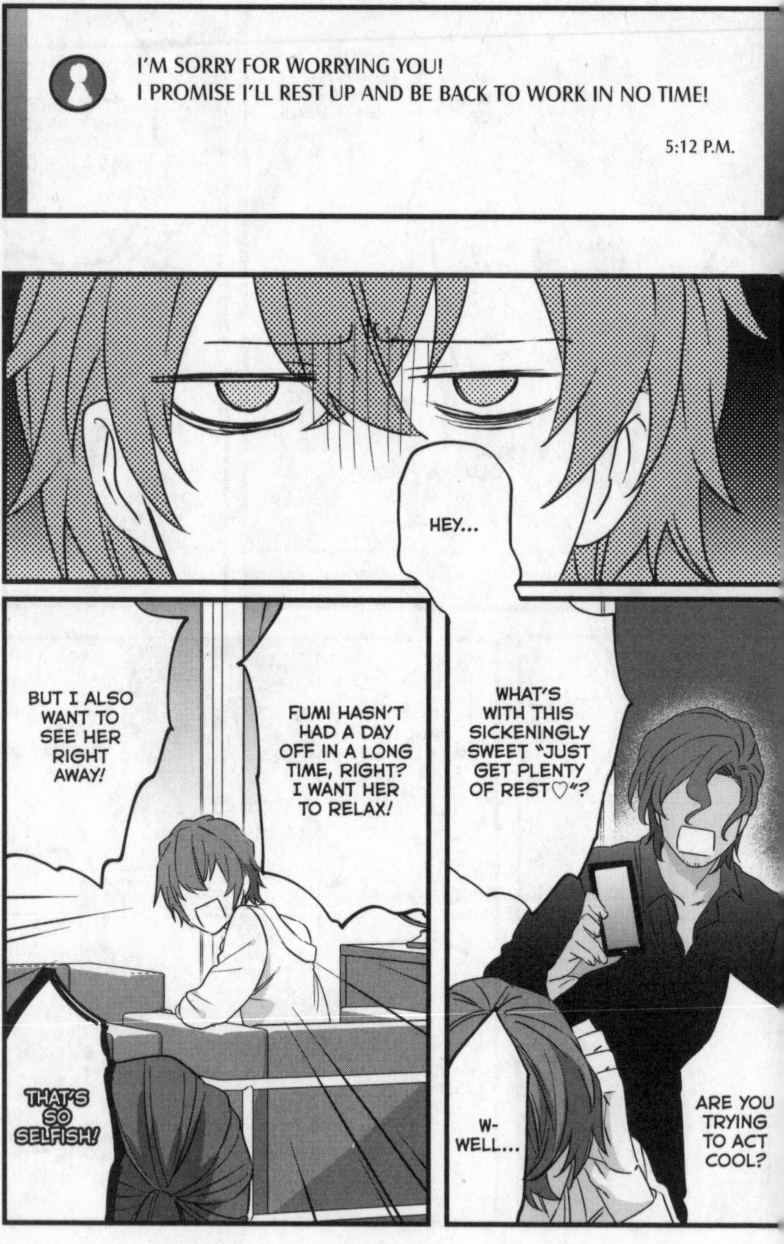
I'M SORRY FOR WORRYING YOU!
I PROMISE I'LL REST UP AND BE BACK TO WORK IN NO TIME!
5:12 P.M.
HEY...
WHAT'S WITH THIS SICKENINGLY SWEET "JUST GET PLENTY OF REST♡"?
ARE YOU TRYING TO ACT COOL?
W- WELL...
FUMI HASN'T HAD A DAY OFF IN A LONG TIME, RIGHT? I WANT HER TO RELAX!
BUT I ALSO WANT TO SEE HER RIGHT AWAY!
THAT'S SO SELFISH!

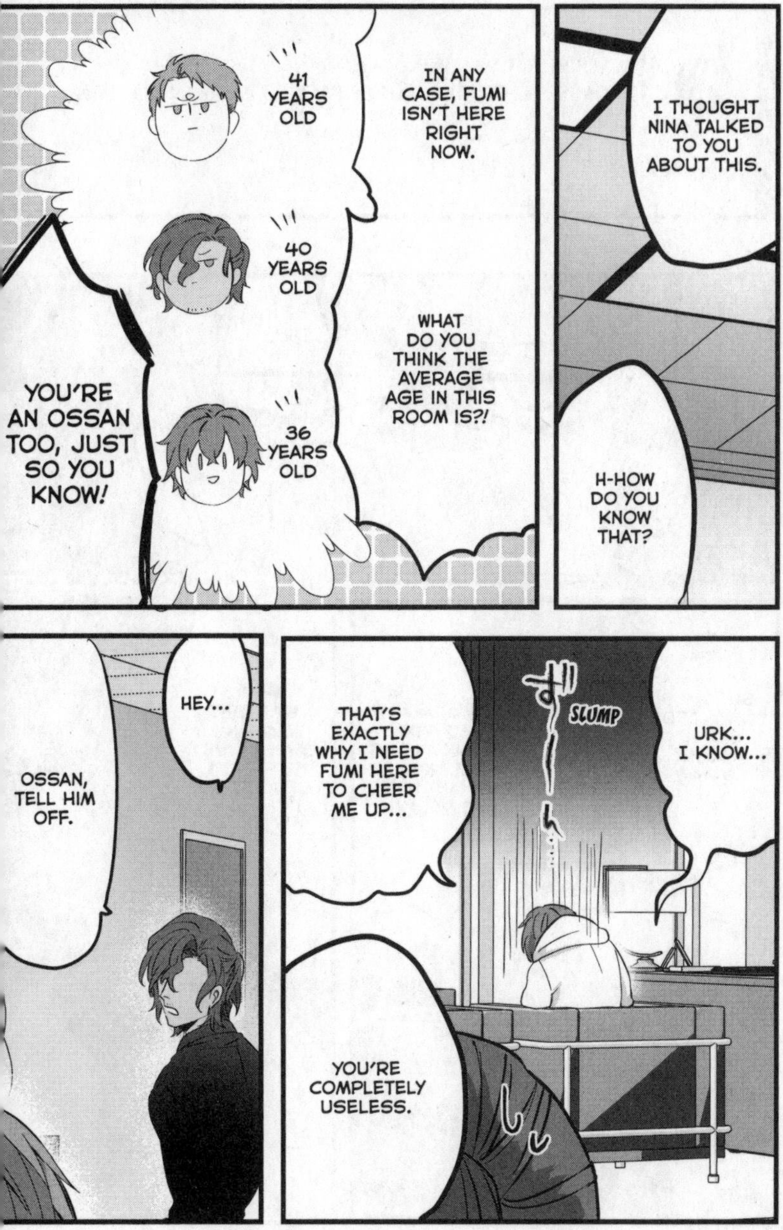
I THOUGHT NINA TALKED TO YOU ABOUT THIS.
H-HOW DO YOU KNOW THAT?
IN ANY CASE, FUMI ISN'T HERE RIGHT NOW.
WHAT DO YOU THINK THE AVERAGE AGE IN THIS ROOM IS?!
41 YEARS OLD
40 YEARS OLD
36 YEARS OLD
YOU'RE AN OSSAN TOO, JUST SO YOU KNOW!
URK... I KNOW...
SLUMP
THAT'S EXACTLY WHY I NEED FUMI HERE TO CHEER ME UP...
YOU'RE COMPLETELY USELESS.
HEY...
OSSAN, TELL HIM OFF.

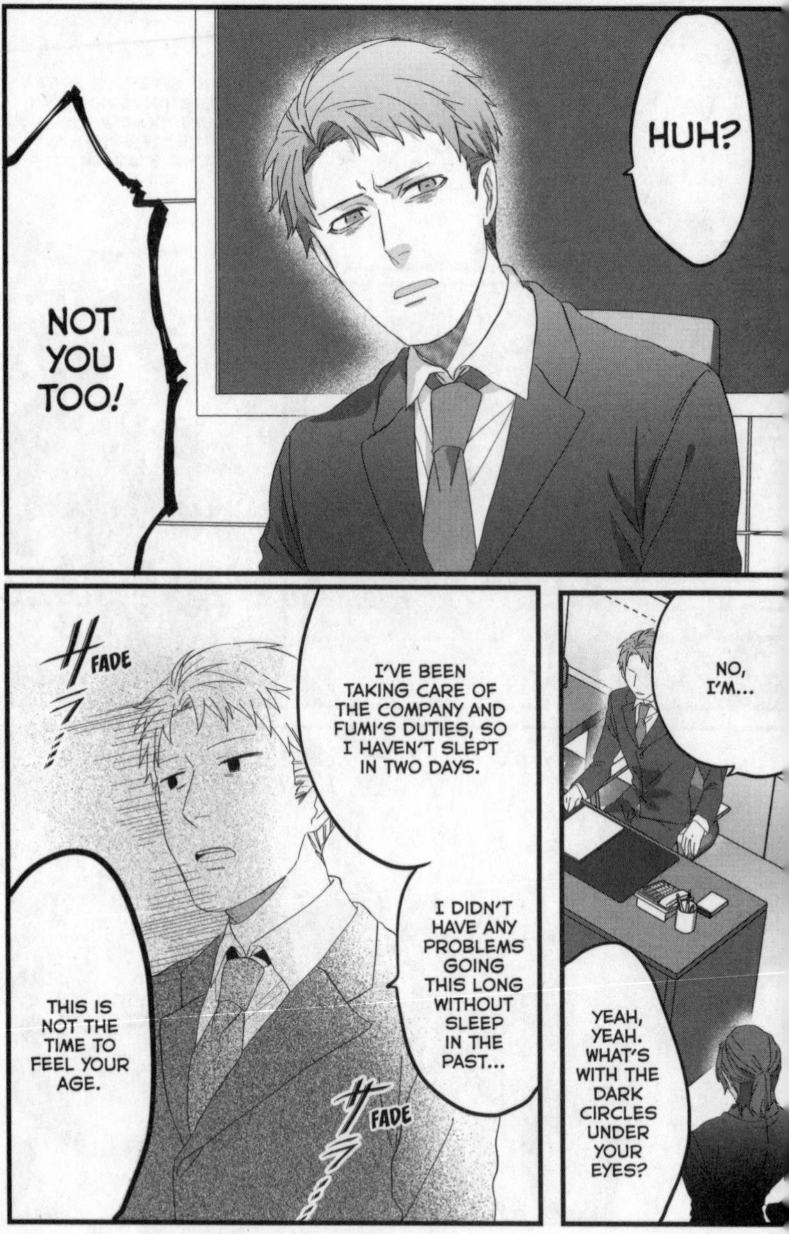
HUH?
NOT YOU TOO!
NO, I'M...
YEAH, YEAH. WHAT'S WITH THE DARK CIRCLES UNDER YOUR EYES?
I'VE BEEN TAKING CARE OF THE COMPANY AND FUMI'S DUTIES, SO I HAVEN'T SLEPT IN TWO DAYS.
FADE
I DIDN'T HAVE ANY PROBLEMS GOING THIS LONG WITHOUT SLEEP IN THE PAST...
THIS IS NOT THE TIME TO FEEL YOUR AGE.
FADE

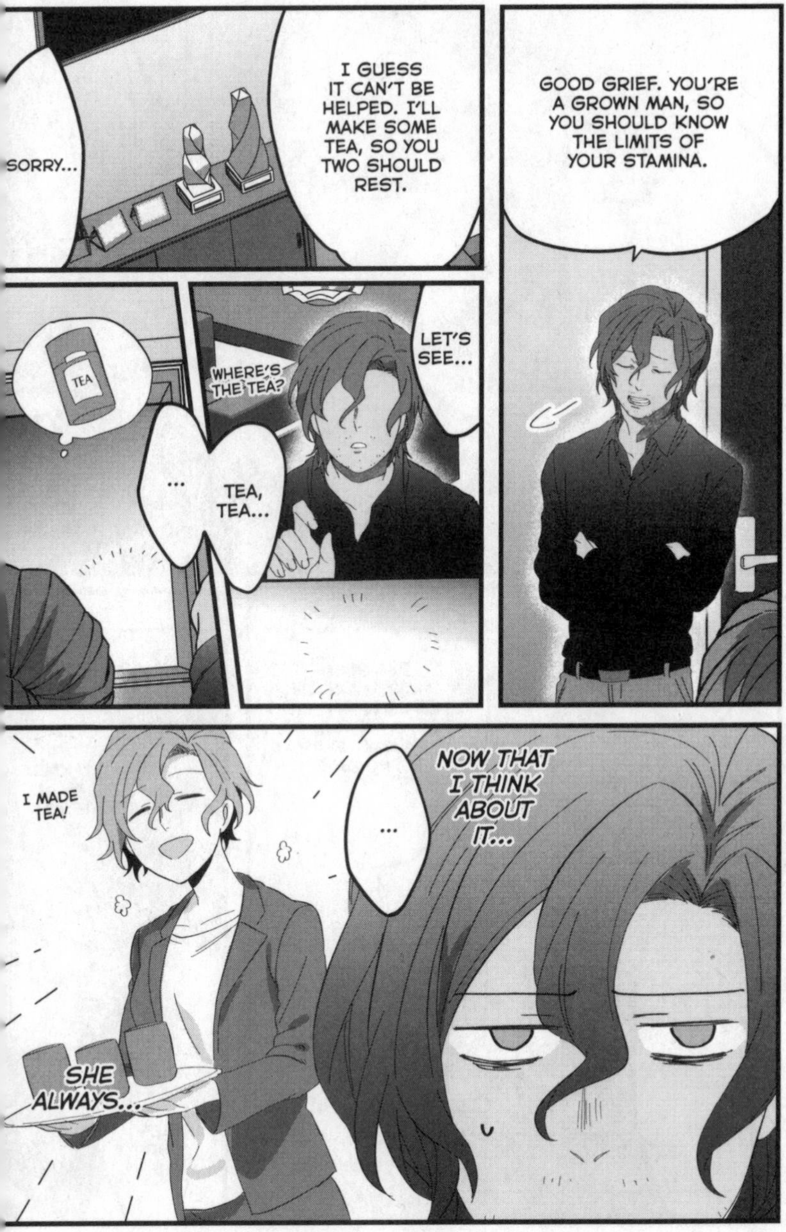
GOOD GRIEF. YOU'RE A GROWN MAN, SO YOU SHOULD KNOW THE LIMITS OF YOUR STAMINA.
SORRY...
I GUESS IT CAN'T BE HELPED. I'LL MAKE SOME TEA, SO YOU TWO SHOULD REST.
LET'S SEE...
WHERE'S THE TEA?
TEA, TEA...
...
TEA
NOW THAT I THINK ABOUT IT...
...
I MADE TEA!
SHE ALWAYS...

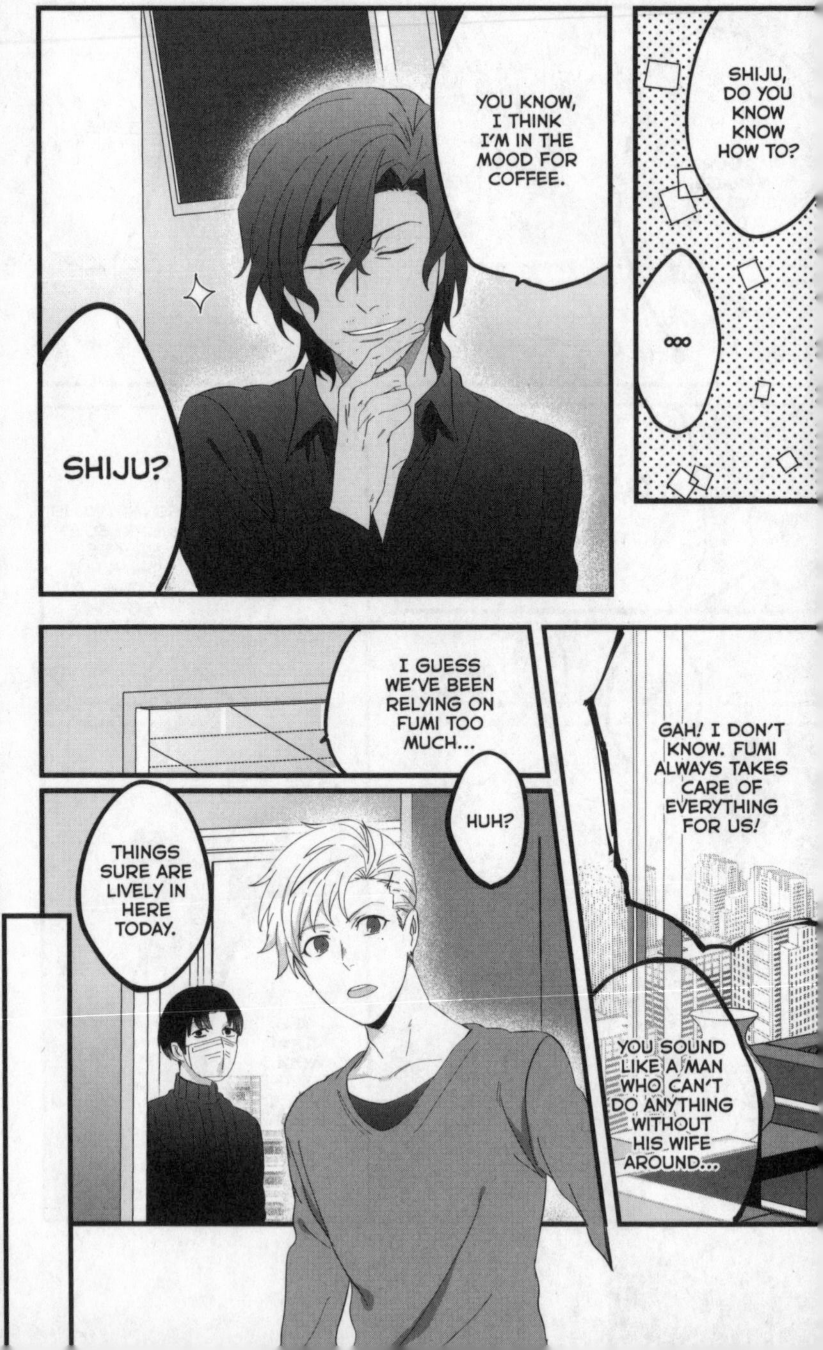
SHIJU, DO YOU KNOW KNOW HOW TO?
...
YOU KNOW, I THINK I'M IN THE MOOD FOR COFFEE.
SHIJU?
GAH! I DON'T KNOW. FUMI ALWAYS TAKES CARE OF EVERYTHING FOR US!
YOU SOUND LIKE A MAN WHO CAN'T DO ANYTHING WITHOUT HIS WIFE AROUND...
I GUESS WE'VE BEEN RELYING ON FUMI TOO MUCH...
HUH?
THINGS SURE ARE LIVELY IN HERE TODAY.

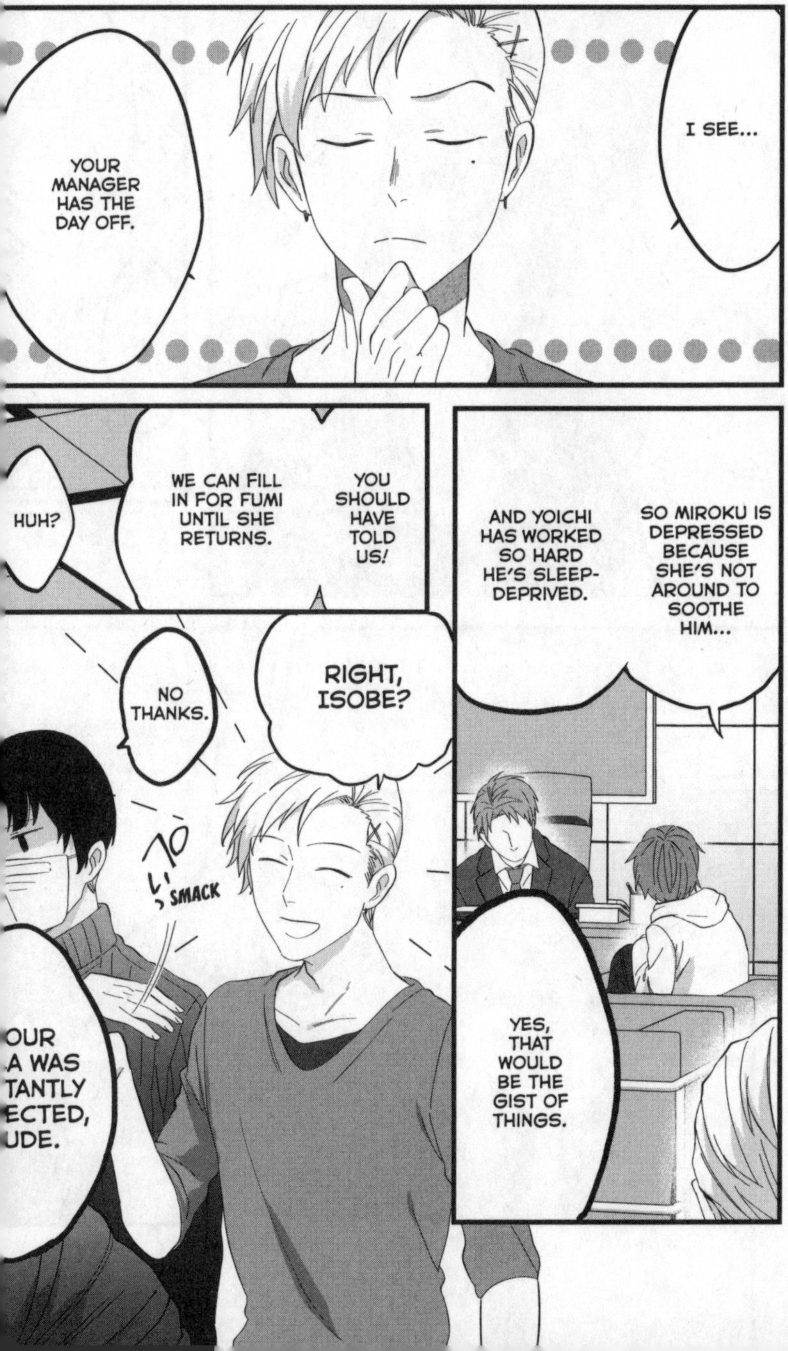
I SEE...
YOUR MANAGER HAS THE DAY OFF.
SO MIROKU IS DEPRESSED BECAUSE SHE'S NOT AROUND TO SOOTHE HIM...
AND YOICHI HAS WORKED SO HARD HE'S SLEEP-DEPRIVED.
YES, THAT WOULD BE THE GIST OF THINGS.
YOU SHOULD HAVE TOLD US!
WE CAN FILL IN FOR FUMI UNTIL SHE RETURNS.
HUH?
RIGHT, ISOBE?
NO THANKS.
SMACK
OUR A WAS TANTLY ECTED, UDE.

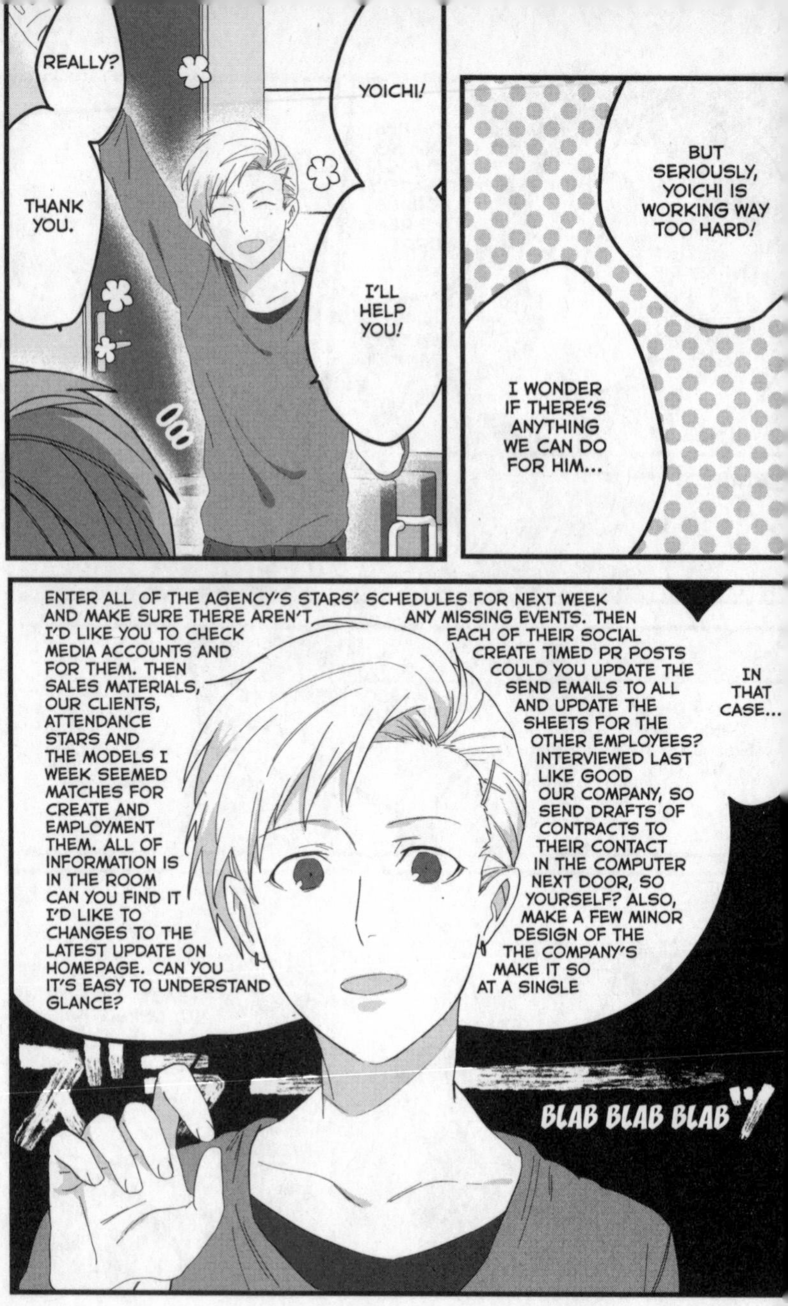
BUT SERIOUSLY, YOICHI IS WORKING WAY TOO HARD!
I WONDER IF THERE'S ANYTHING WE CAN DO FOR HIM...
YOICHI!
I'LL HELP YOU!
REALLY?
THANK YOU.
IN THAT CASE...
ENTER ALL OF THE AGENCY'S STARS' SCHEDULES FOR NEXT WEEK AND MAKE SURE THERE AREN'T ANY MISSING EVENTS. THEN I'D LIKE YOU TO CHECK EACH OF THEIR SOCIAL MEDIA ACCOUNTS AND CREATE TIMED PR POSTS FOR THEM. THEN COULD YOU UPDATE THE SALES MATERIALS, SEND EMAILS TO ALL OUR CLIENTS, AND UPDATE THE ATTENDANCE SHEETS FOR THE STARS AND OTHER EMPLOYEES? THE MODELS I INTERVIEWED LAST WEEK SEEMED LIKE GOOD MATCHES FOR OUR COMPANY, SO CREATE AND SEND DRAFTS OF EMPLOYMENT CONTRACTS TO THEM. ALL OF THEIR CONTACT INFORMATION IS IN THE COMPUTER IN THE ROOM NEXT DOOR, SO CAN YOU FIND IT YOURSELF? ALSO, I'D LIKE TO MAKE A FEW MINOR CHANGES TO THE DESIGN OF THE LATEST UPDATE ON THE COMPANY'S HOMEPAGE. CAN YOU MAKE IT SO IT'S EASY TO UNDERSTAND AT A SINGLE GLANCE?
BLAB BLAB BLAB

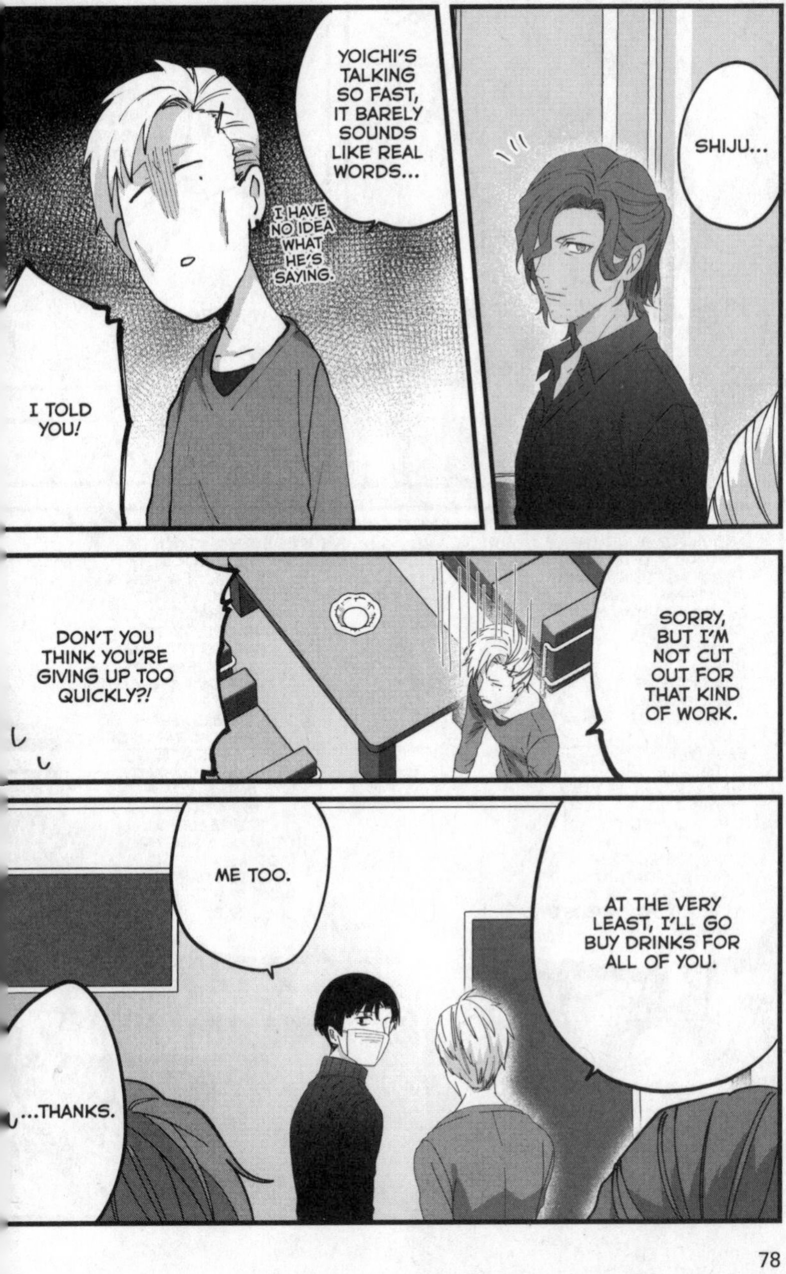
SHIJU...
YOICHI'S TALKING SO FAST, IT BARELY SOUNDS LIKE REAL WORDS...
I HAVE NO IDEA WHAT HE'S SAYING.
I TOLD YOU!
SORRY, BUT I'M NOT CUT OUT FOR THAT KIND OF WORK.
DON'T YOU THINK YOU'RE GIVING UP TOO QUICKLY?!
AT THE VERY LEAST, I'LL GO BUY DRINKS FOR ALL OF YOU.
ME TOO.
...THANKS.

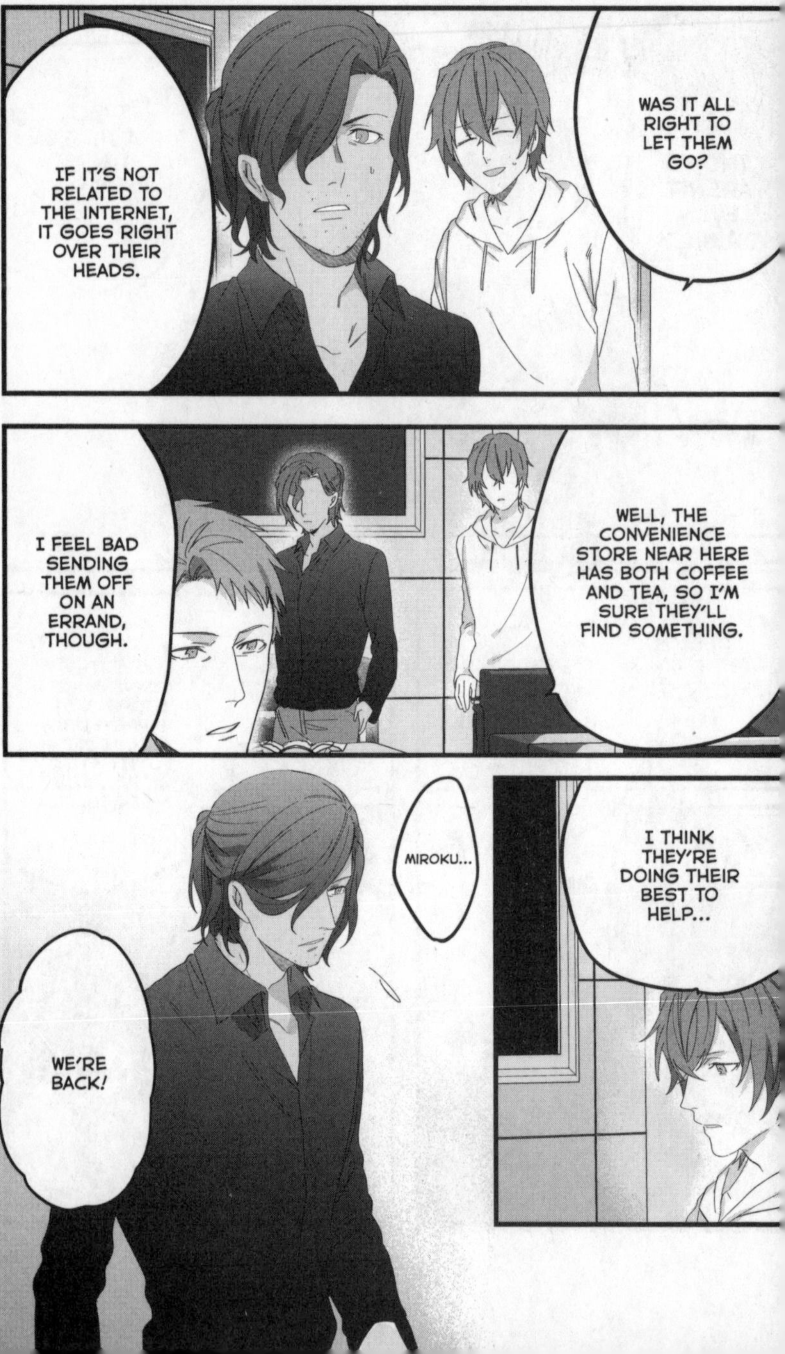
WAS IT ALL RIGHT TO LET THEM GO?
IF IT'S NOT RELATED TO THE INTERNET, IT GOES RIGHT OVER THEIR HEADS.
WELL, THE CONVENIENCE STORE NEAR HERE HAS BOTH COFFEE AND TEA, SO I'M SURE THEY'LL FIND SOMETHING.
I FEEL BAD SENDING THEM OFF ON AN ERRAND, THOUGH.
I THINK THEY'RE DOING THEIR BEST TO HELP...
MIROKU...
WE'RE BACK!

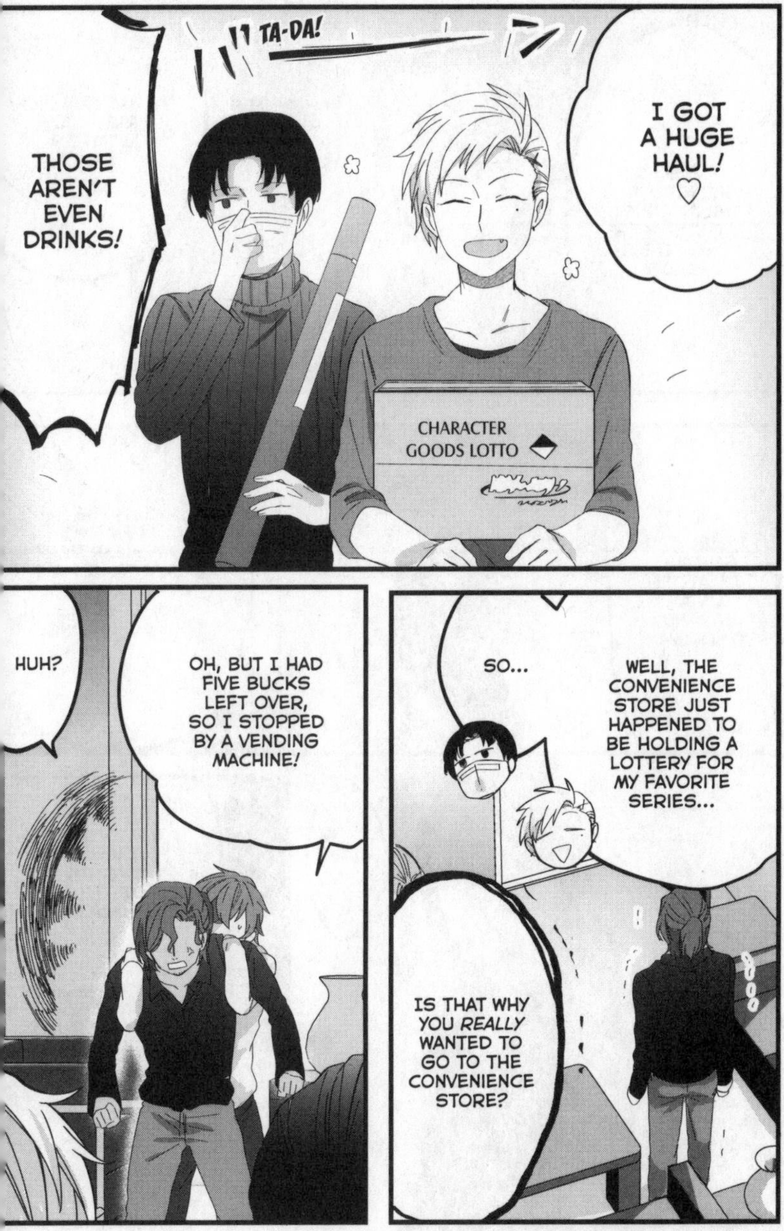
TA-DA!
I GOT A HUGE HAUL! ♡
CHARACTER GOODS LOTTO
THOSE AREN'T EVEN DRINKS!
WELL, THE CONVENIENCE STORE JUST HAPPENED TO BE HOLDING A LOTTERY FOR MY FAVORITE SERIES...
SO...
IS THAT WHY YOU *REALLY* WANTED TO GO TO THE CONVENIENCE STORE?
OH, BUT I HAD FIVE BUCKS LEFT OVER, SO I STOPPED BY A VENDING MACHINE!
HUH?

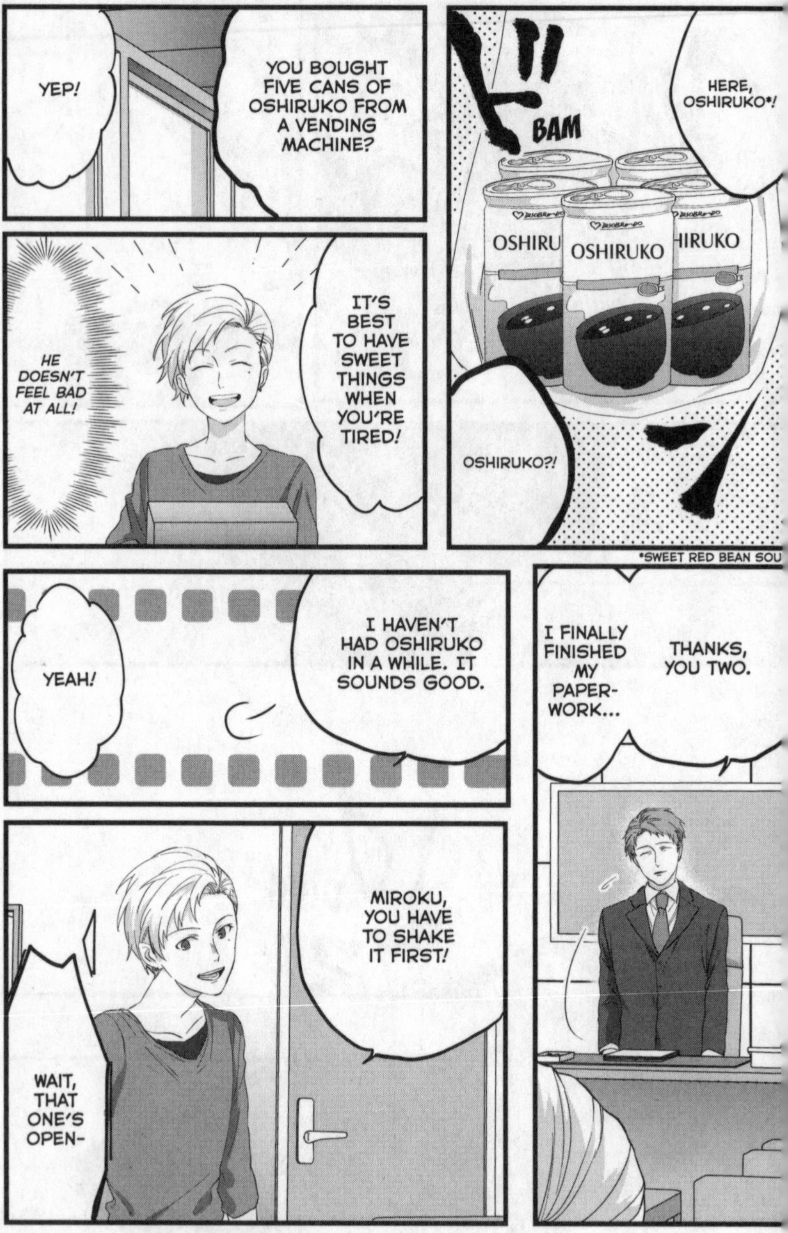
HERE, OSHIRUKO*!
BAM
OSHIRUKO
OSHIRUKO?!
YOU BOUGHT FIVE CANS OF OSHIRUKO FROM A VENDING MACHINE?
YEP!
IT'S BEST TO HAVE SWEET THINGS WHEN YOU'RE TIRED!
HE DOESN'T FEEL BAD AT ALL!
THANKS, YOU TWO.
I FINALLY FINISHED MY PAPER-WORK...
I HAVEN'T HAD OSHIRUKO IN A WHILE. IT SOUNDS GOOD.
YEAH!
MIROKU, YOU HAVE TO SHAKE IT FIRST!
WAIT, THAT ONE'S OPEN-

*SWEET RED BEAN SOU

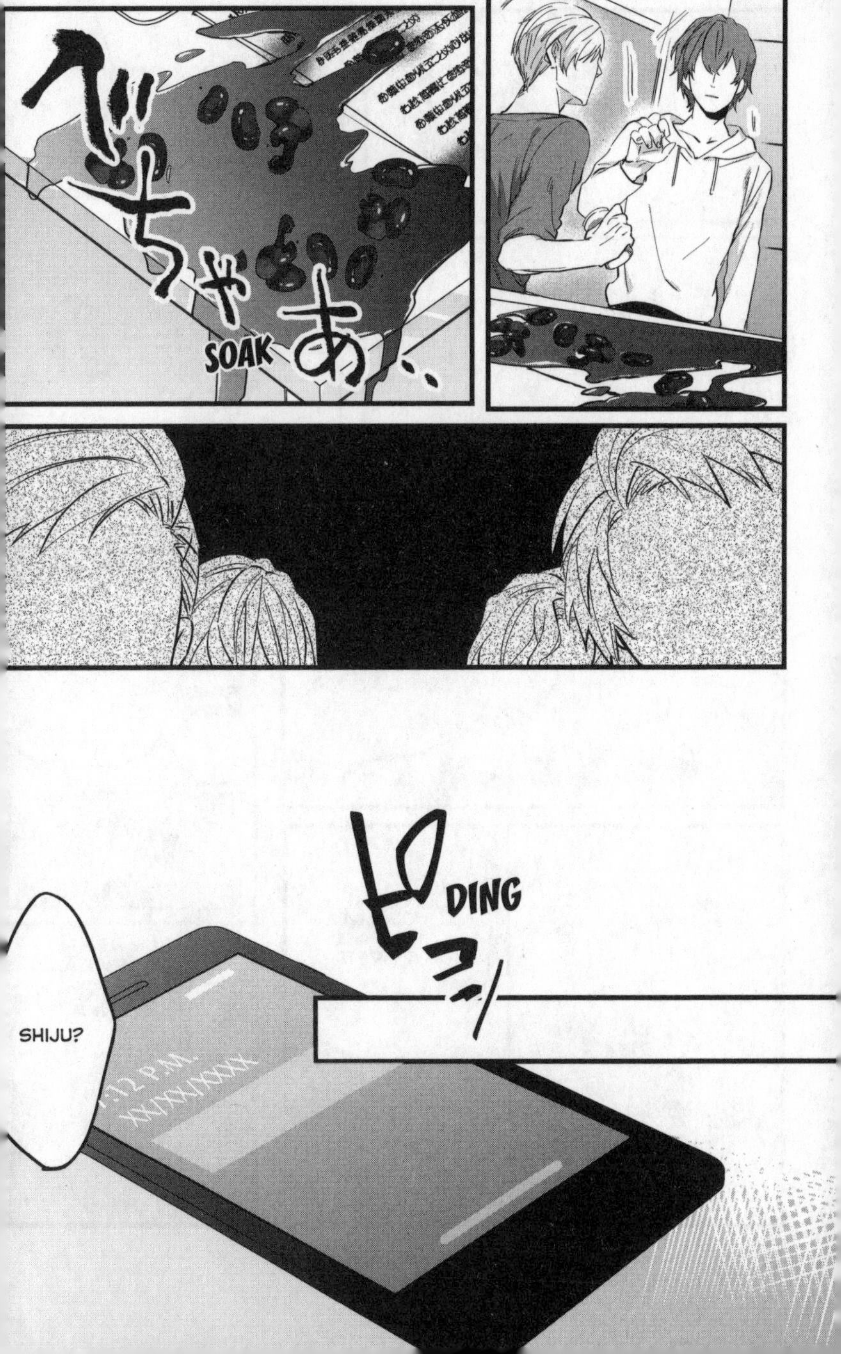

べちゃあ
SOAK
ピコッ
DING
XX/XX/XXXX
SHIJU?

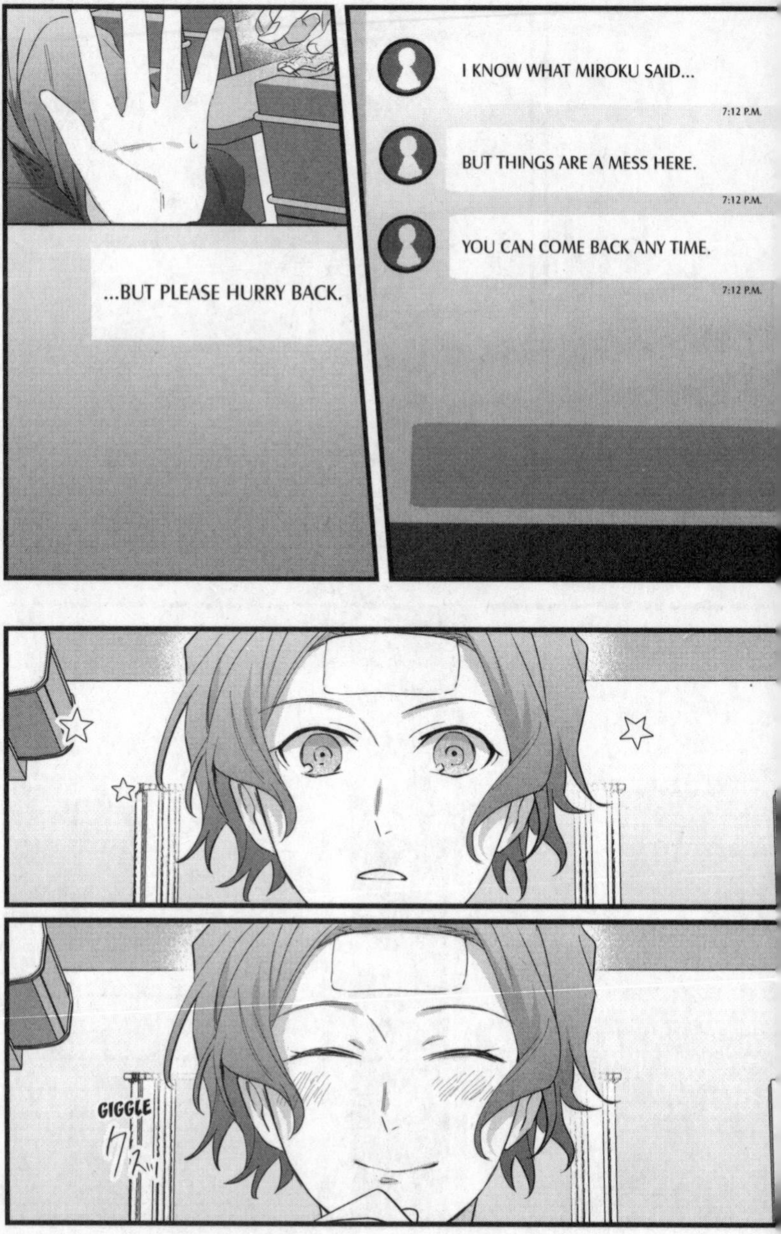
I KNOW WHAT MIROKU SAID...
7:12 P.M.
BUT THINGS ARE A MESS HERE.
7:12 P.M.
YOU CAN COME BACK ANY TIME.
7:12 P.M.
...BUT PLEASE HURRY BACK.
GIGGLE
クスッ

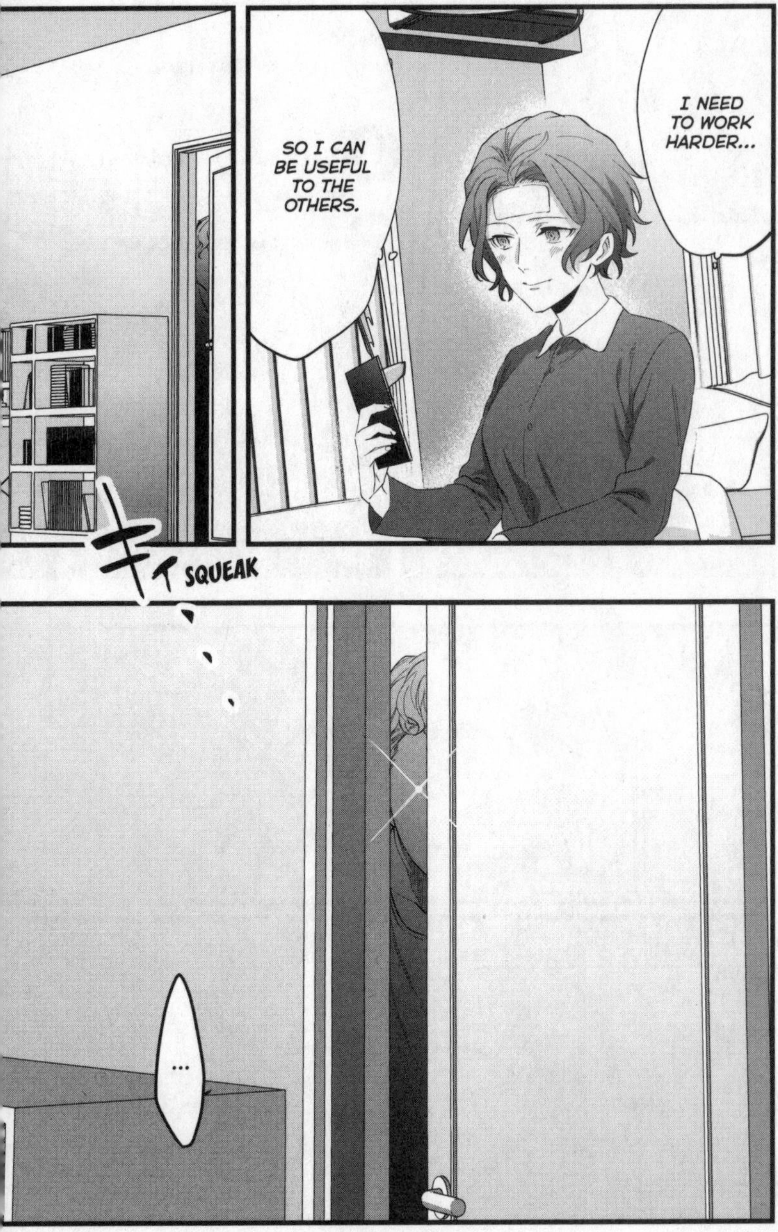
I NEED TO WORK HARDER...
SO I CAN BE USEFUL TO THE OTHERS.
キィ SQUEAK
...

Chapter 21

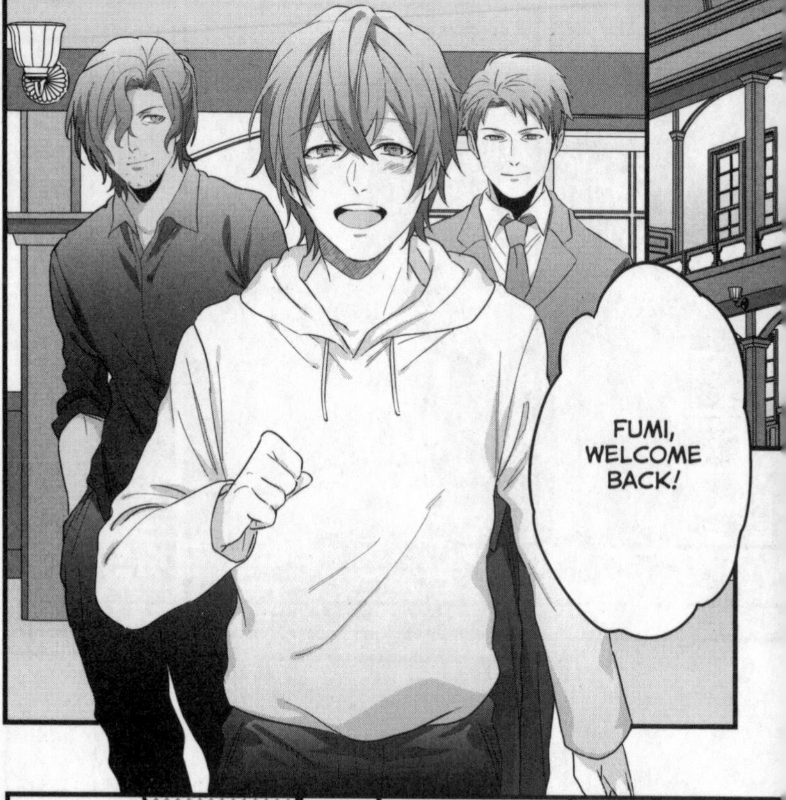
FUMI, WELCOME BACK!

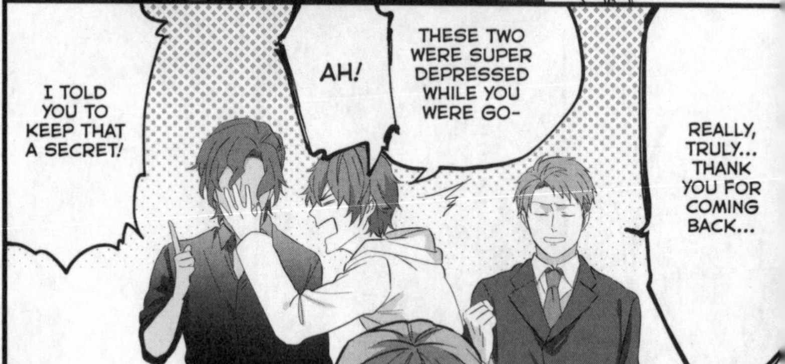
REALLY, TRULY... THANK YOU FOR COMING BACK...
THESE TWO WERE SUPER DEPRESSED WHILE YOU WERE GO-
AH!
I TOLD YOU TO KEEP THAT A SECRET!

FWAP

I'M SORRY FOR ALL THE TROUBLE I CAUSED!

YOU GUYS...

FUMI...

THAT'S RIGHT.

I WASN'T RESPONSIBLE ENOUGH TO TAKE CARE OF MY OWN HEALTH...

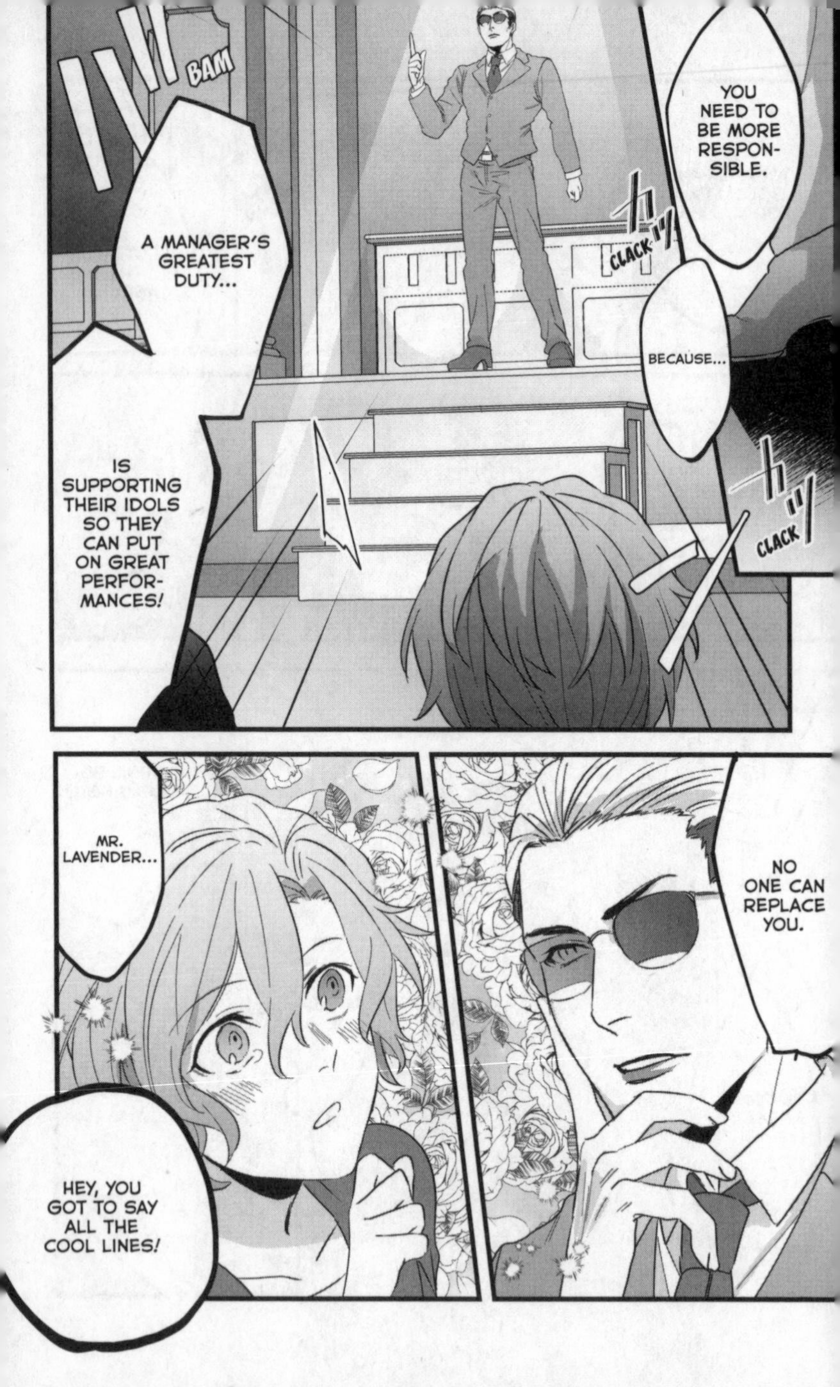
YOU NEED TO BE MORE RESPONSIBLE.
CLACK
BECAUSE...
CLACK
BAM
A MANAGER'S GREATEST DUTY...
IS SUPPORTING THEIR IDOLS SO THEY CAN PUT ON GREAT PERFORMANCES!
NO ONE CAN REPLACE YOU.
MR. LAVENDER...
HEY, YOU GOT TO SAY ALL THE COOL LINES!

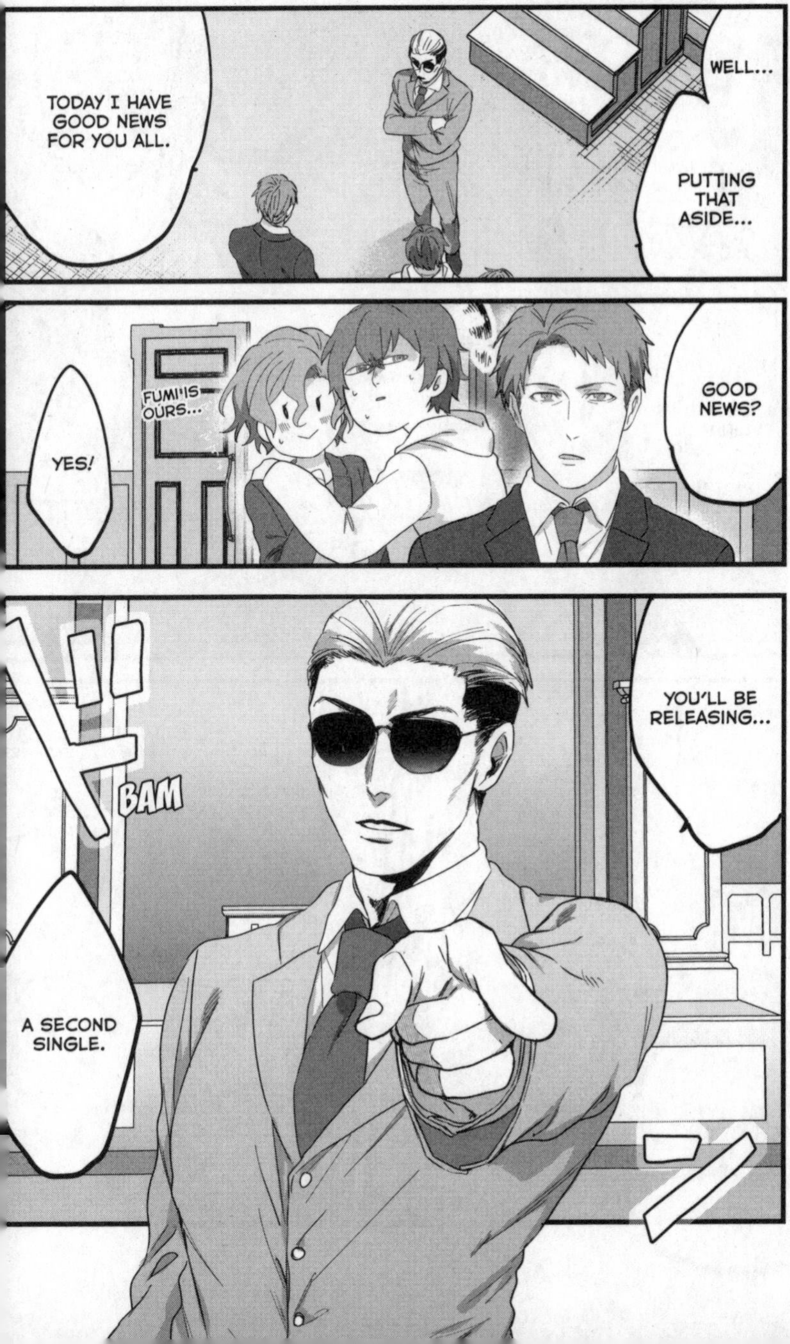
WELL...
PUTTING THAT ASIDE...
TODAY I HAVE GOOD NEWS FOR YOU ALL.
GOOD NEWS?
FUMI IS OURS...
YES!
YOU'LL BE RELEASING...
BAM
A SECOND SINGLE.

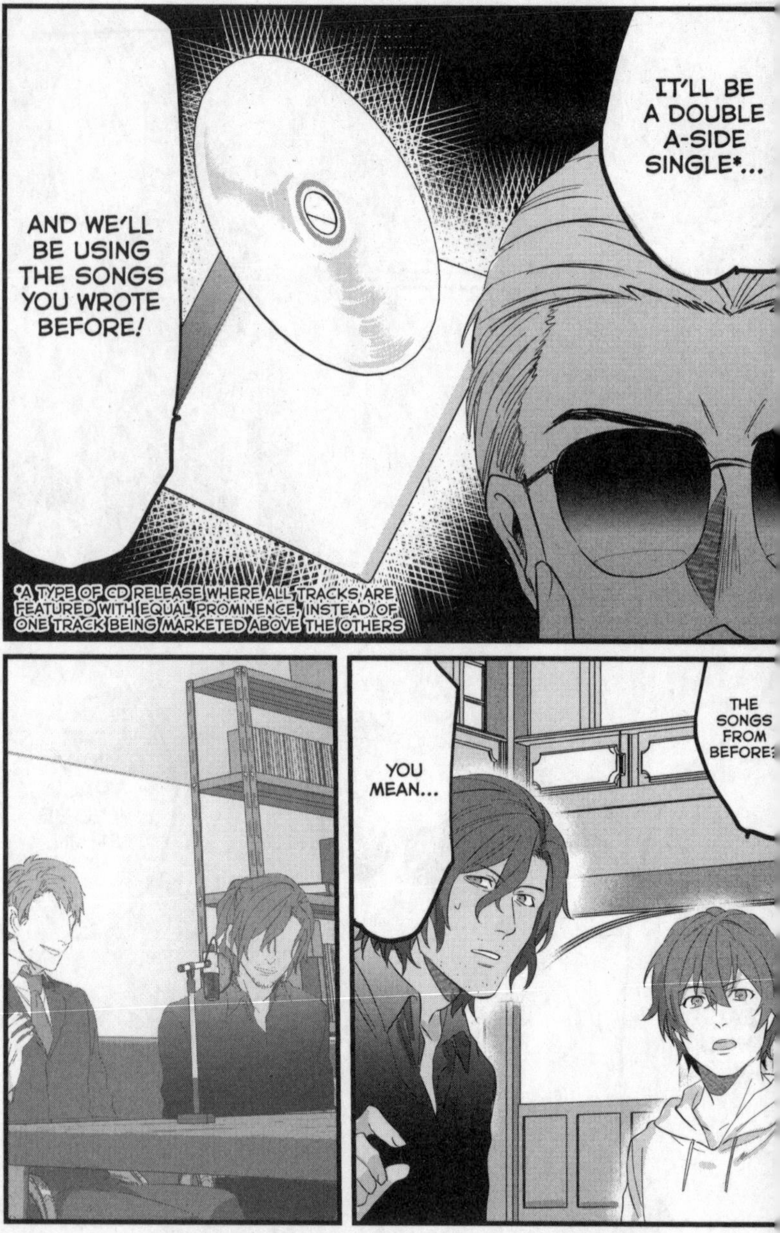
IT'LL BE A DOUBLE A-SIDE SINGLE*...
AND WE'LL BE USING THE SONGS YOU WROTE BEFORE!
*A TYPE OF CD RELEASE WHERE ALL TRACKS ARE FEATURED WITH EQUAL PROMINENCE, INSTEAD OF ONE TRACK BEING MARKETED ABOVE THE OTHERS
THE SONGS FROM BEFORE?
YOU MEAN...

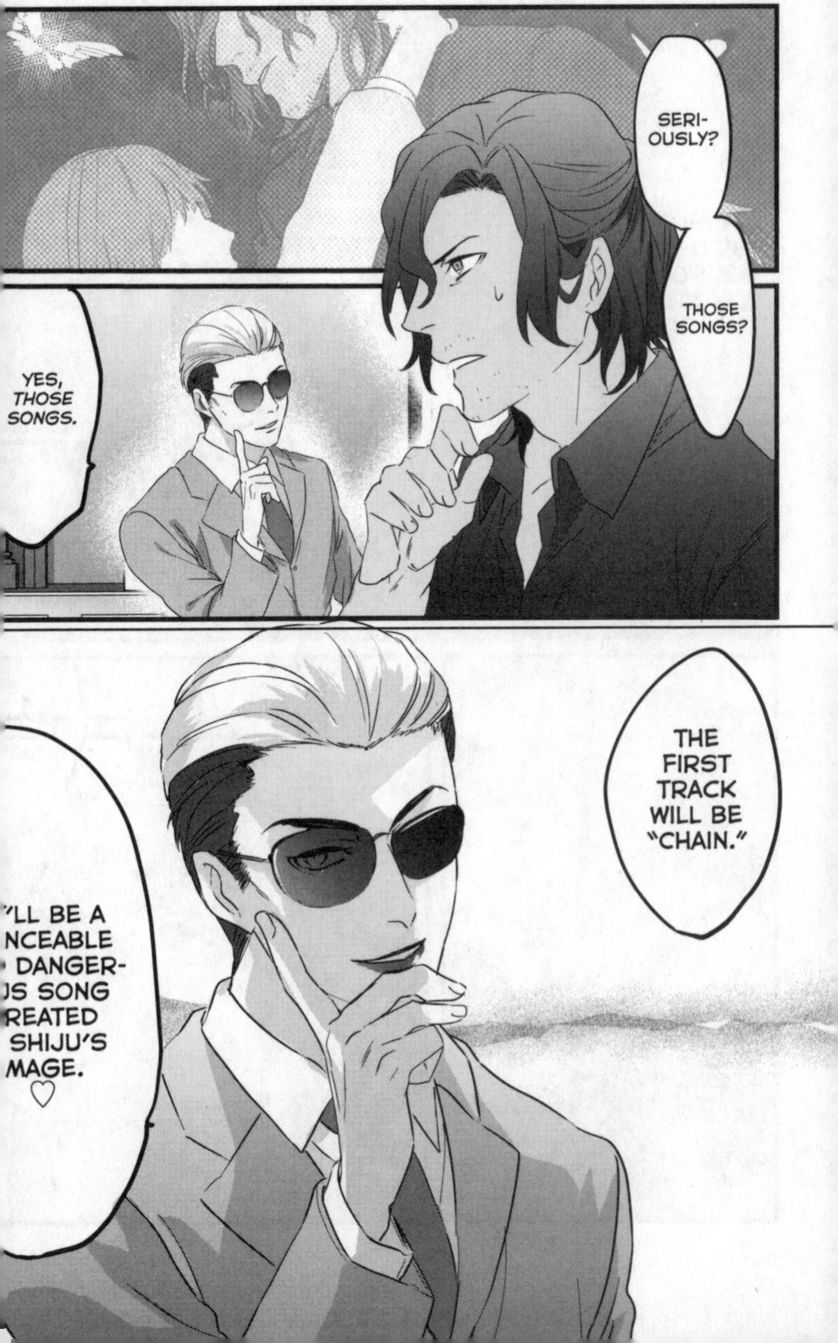
SERI-OUSLY?
THOSE SONGS?
YES, *THOSE* SONGS.
THE FIRST TRACK WILL BE "CHAIN."
'LL BE A NCEABLE DANGER- US SONG REATED SHIJU'S MAGE. ♡

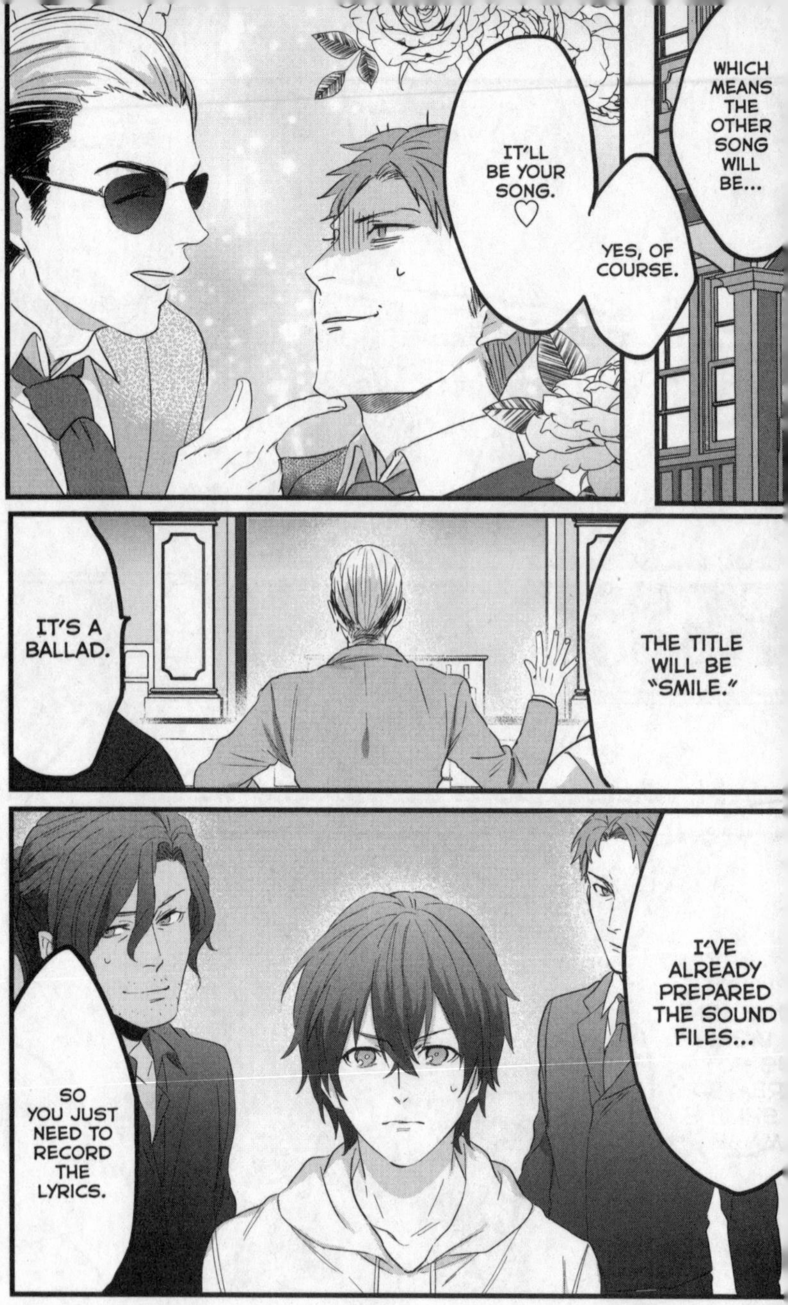
WHICH MEANS THE OTHER SONG WILL BE...
IT'LL BE YOUR SONG. ♡
YES, OF COURSE.
THE TITLE WILL BE "SMILE."
IT'S A BALLAD.
I'VE ALREADY PREPARED THE SOUND FILES...
SO YOU JUST NEED TO RECORD THE LYRICS.

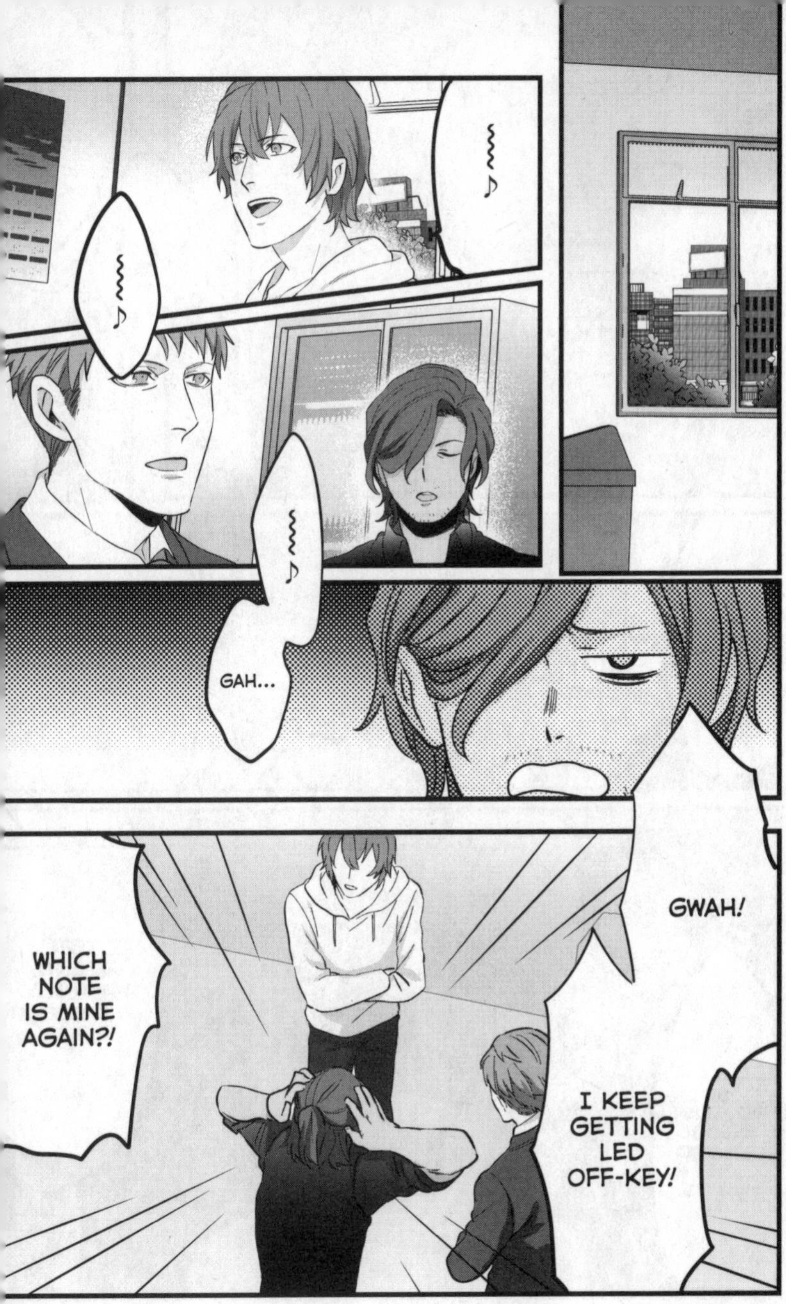
~~♪
~~♪
~~♪
GAH...
GWAH!
I KEEP GETTING LED OFF-KEY!
WHICH NOTE IS MINE AGAIN?!

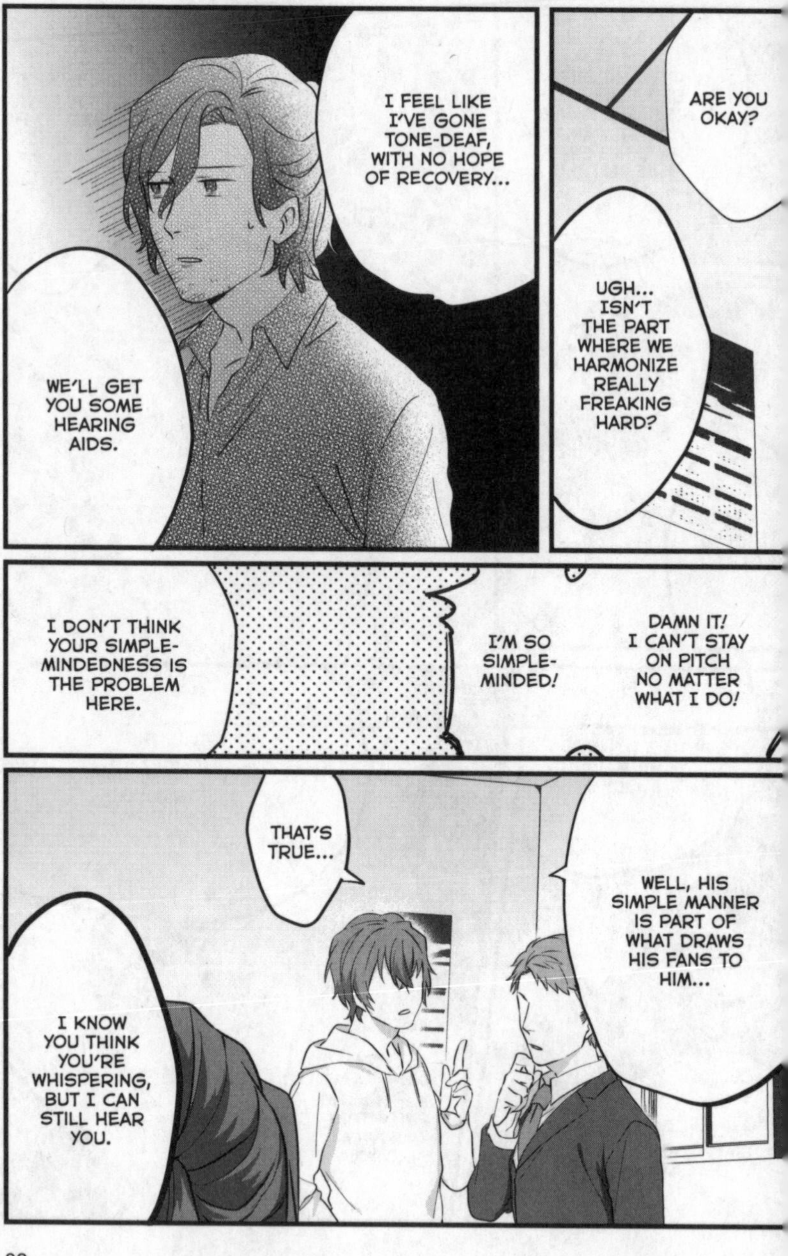
ARE YOU OKAY?
UGH... ISN'T THE PART WHERE WE HARMONIZE REALLY FREAKING HARD?
I FEEL LIKE I'VE GONE TONE-DEAF, WITH NO HOPE OF RECOVERY...
WE'LL GET YOU SOME HEARING AIDS.
DAMN IT! I CAN'T STAY ON PITCH NO MATTER WHAT I DO!
I'M SO SIMPLE-MINDED!
I DON'T THINK YOUR SIMPLE-MINDEDNESS IS THE PROBLEM HERE.
WELL, HIS SIMPLE MANNER IS PART OF WHAT DRAWS HIS FANS TO HIM...
THAT'S TRUE...
I KNOW YOU THINK YOU'RE WHISPERING, BUT I CAN STILL HEAR YOU.

IN ANY CASE, WE NEED TO FIND A WAY TO KEEP YOU ON-PITCH.
UNTIL HE GETS USED TO IT, LET'S SING OUR PARTS QUIETLY AND HAVE HIM SING THE MELODY.
SORRY, GUYS...
STILL, THE ONLY WAY FOR YOU TO MEMORIZE IT IS THROUGH REPETITION.
YOU DIDN'T HAVE A PROBLEM WITH THIS LAST TIME, DID YOU?
WELL, LAST TIME I SANG THE MAIN MELODY...
BUT THIS TIME, OSSAN IS THE LEAD.

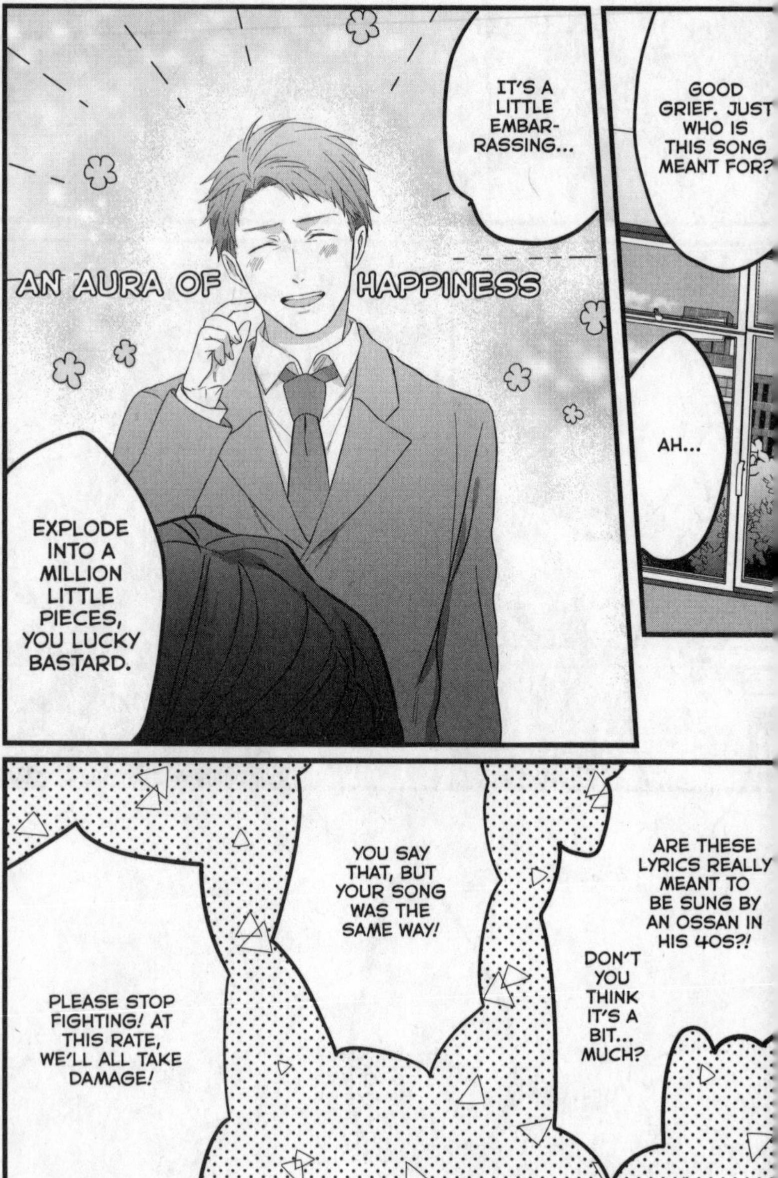
GOOD GRIEF. JUST WHO IS THIS SONG MEANT FOR?
AH...
IT'S A LITTLE EMBAR-RASSING...
AN AURA OF HAPPINESS
EXPLODE INTO A MILLION LITTLE PIECES, YOU LUCKY BASTARD.
ARE THESE LYRICS REALLY MEANT TO BE SUNG BY AN OSSAN IN HIS 40S?!
DON'T YOU THINK IT'S A BIT... MUCH?
YOU SAY THAT, BUT YOUR SONG WAS THE SAME WAY!
PLEASE STOP FIGHTING! AT THIS RATE, WE'LL ALL TAKE DAMAGE!

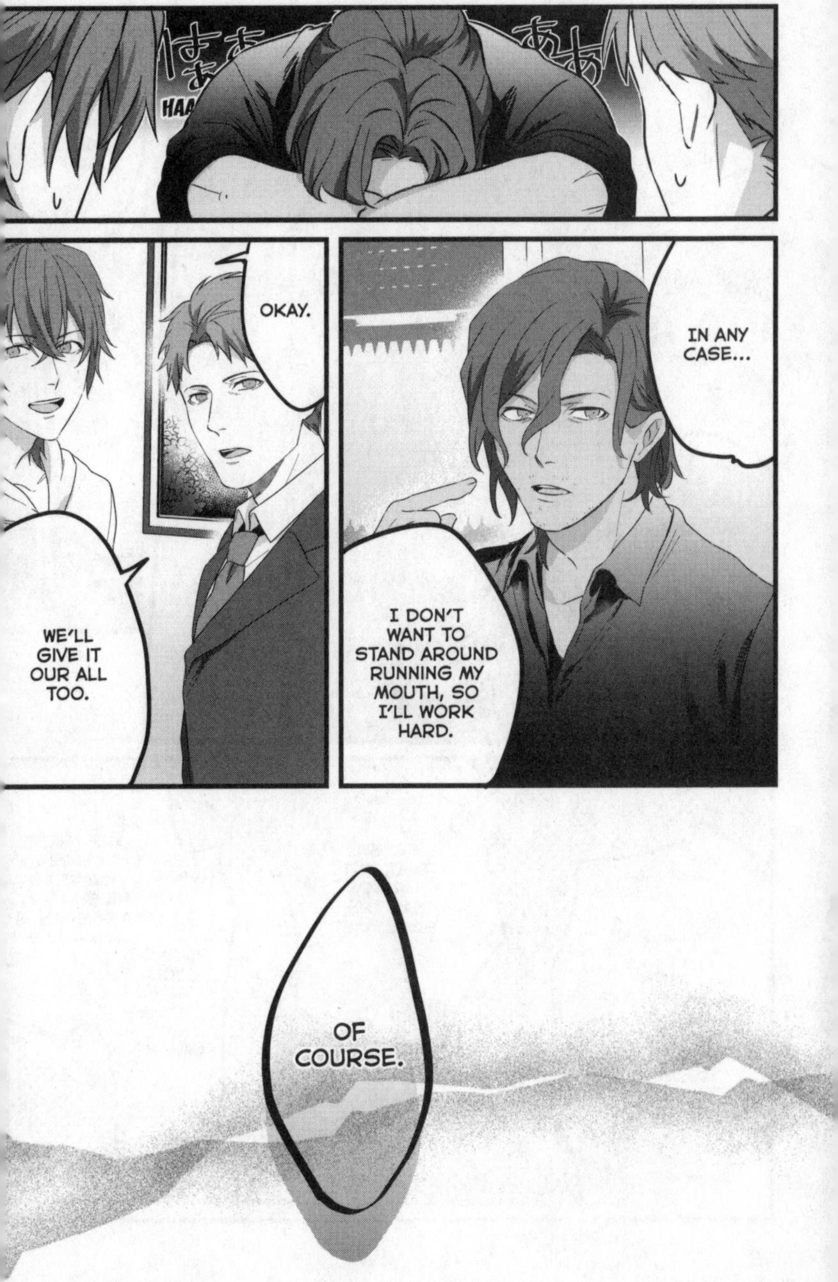
HAA
IN ANY CASE...
I DON'T WANT TO STAND AROUND RUNNING MY MOUTH, SO I'LL WORK HARD.
OKAY.
WE'LL GIVE IT OUR ALL TOO.
OF COURSE.

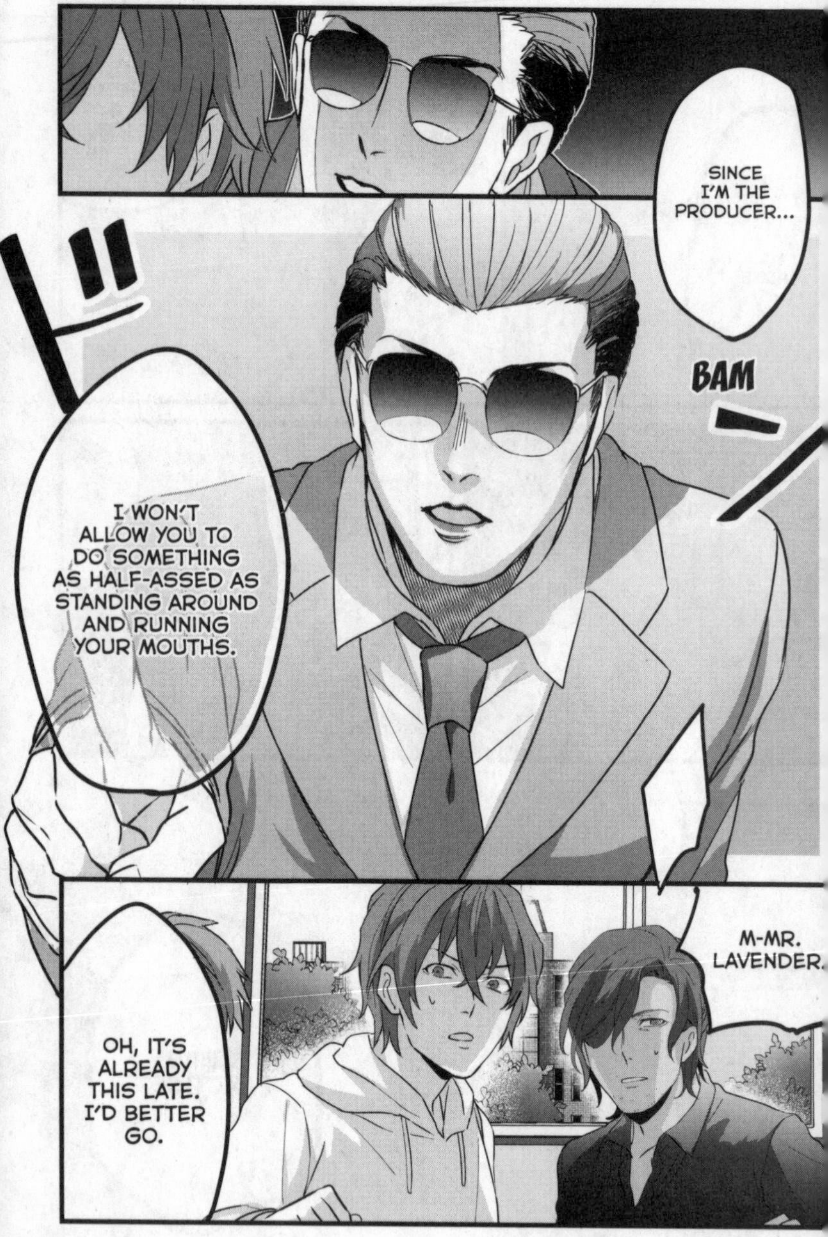
SINCE I'M THE PRODUCER...
BAM
I WON'T ALLOW YOU TO DO SOMETHING AS HALF-ASSED AS STANDING AROUND AND RUNNING YOUR MOUTHS.
M-MR. LAVENDER.
OH, IT'S ALREADY THIS LATE. I'D BETTER GO.

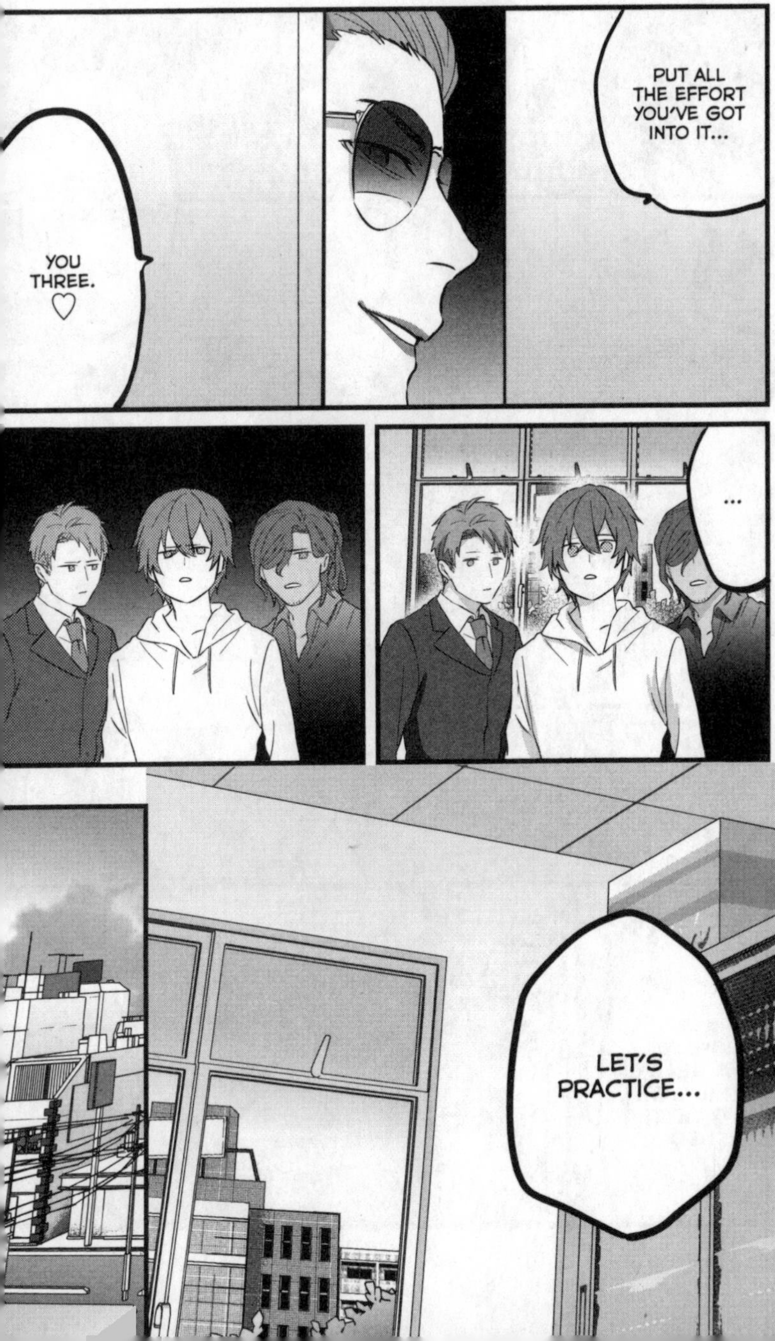
PUT ALL THE EFFORT YOU'VE GOT INTO IT...
YOU THREE. ♡
...
LET'S PRACTICE...

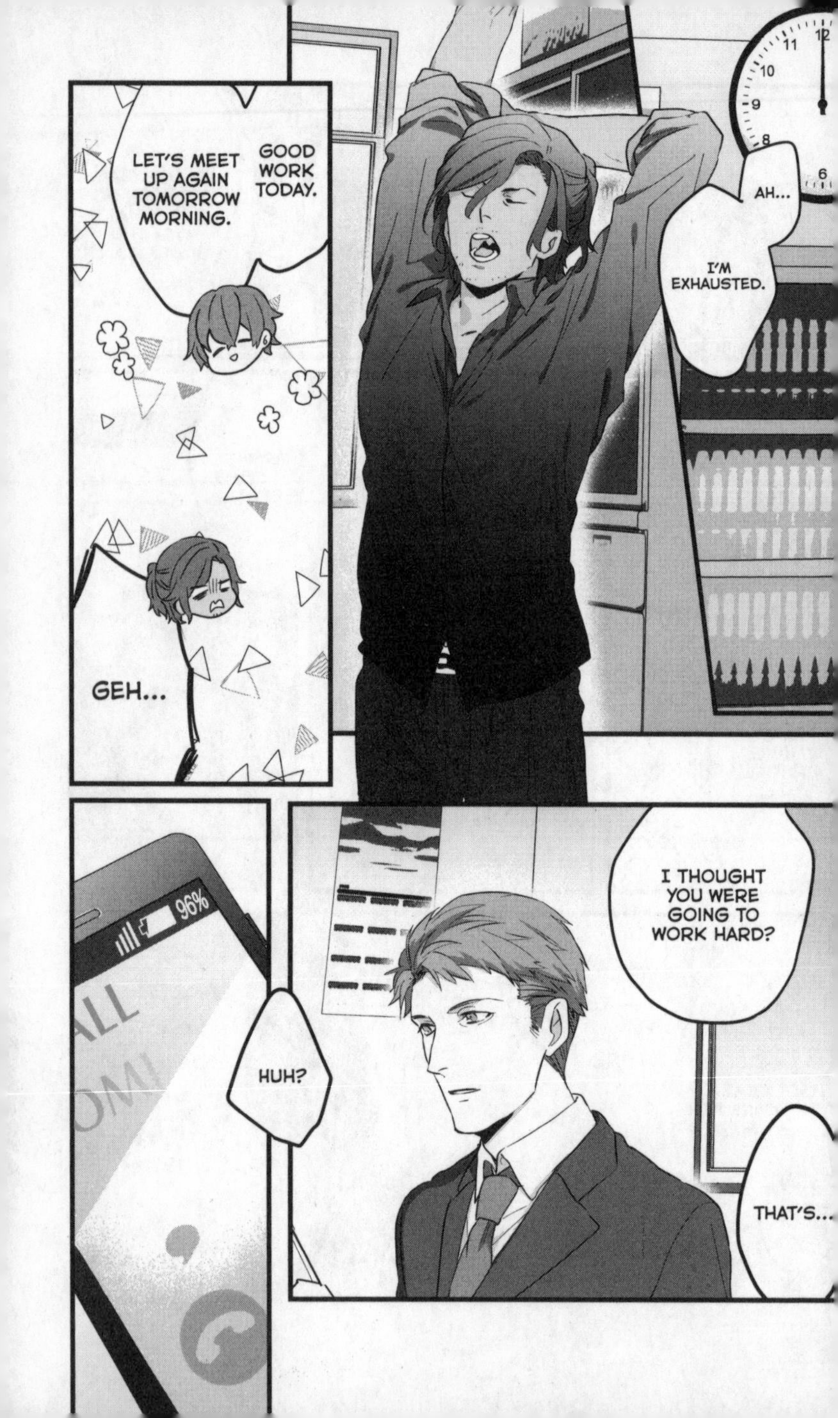
AH...
I'M EXHAUSTED.
GOOD WORK TODAY.
LET'S MEET UP AGAIN TOMORROW MORNING.
GEH...
I THOUGHT YOU WERE GOING TO WORK HARD?
THAT'S...
HUH?
96%

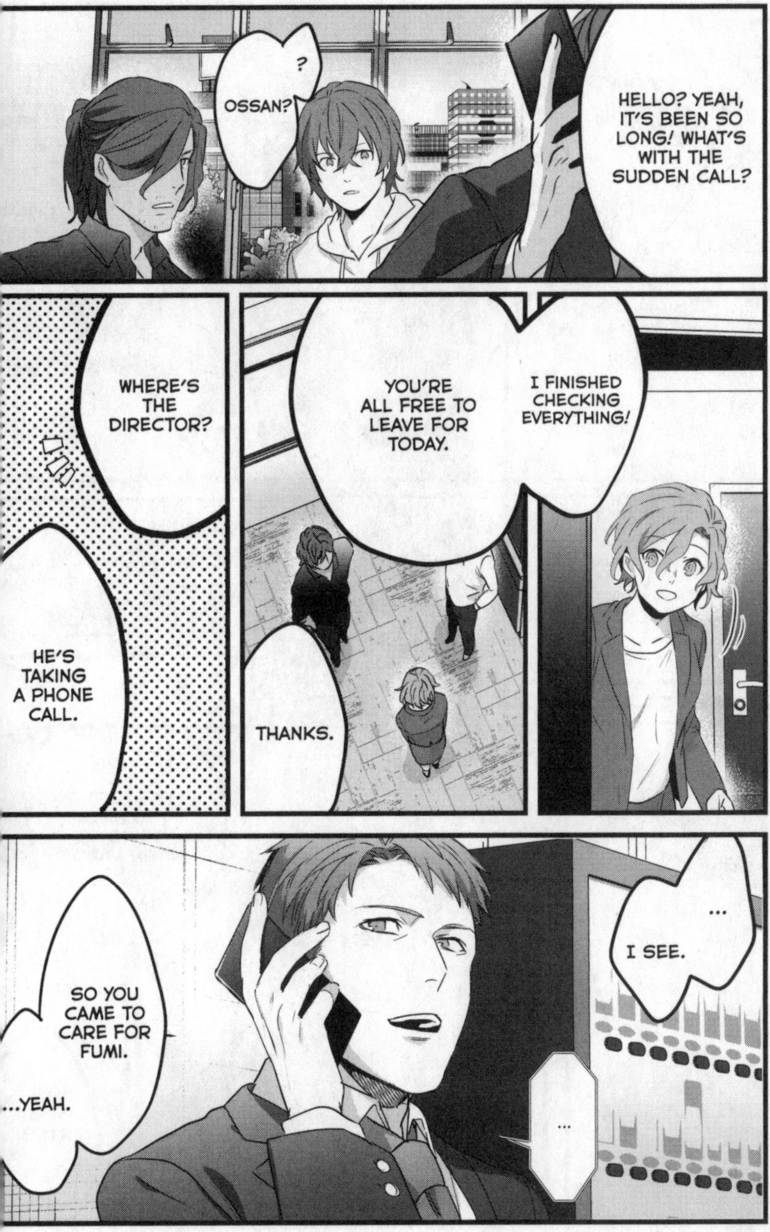
HELLO? YEAH, IT'S BEEN SO LONG! WHAT'S WITH THE SUDDEN CALL?
? OSSAN?
I FINISHED CHECKING EVERYTHING!
YOU'RE ALL FREE TO LEAVE FOR TODAY.
THANKS.
WHERE'S THE DIRECTOR?
HE'S TAKING A PHONE CALL.
... I SEE.
...
SO YOU CAME TO CARE FOR FUMI.
...YEAH.

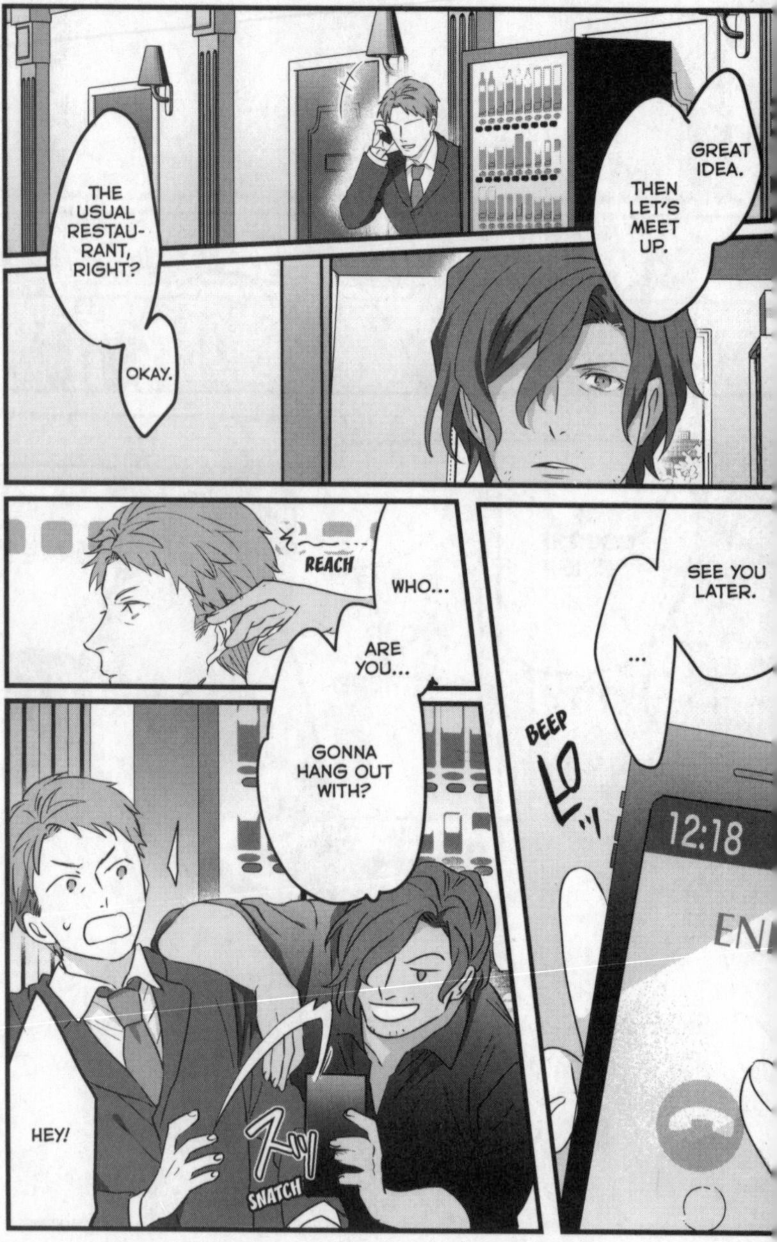
GREAT IDEA.
THEN LET'S MEET UP.
THE USUAL RESTAURANT, RIGHT?
OKAY.
SEE YOU LATER.
...
BEEP
REACH
WHO...
ARE YOU...
GONNA HANG OUT WITH?
HEY!
SNATCH

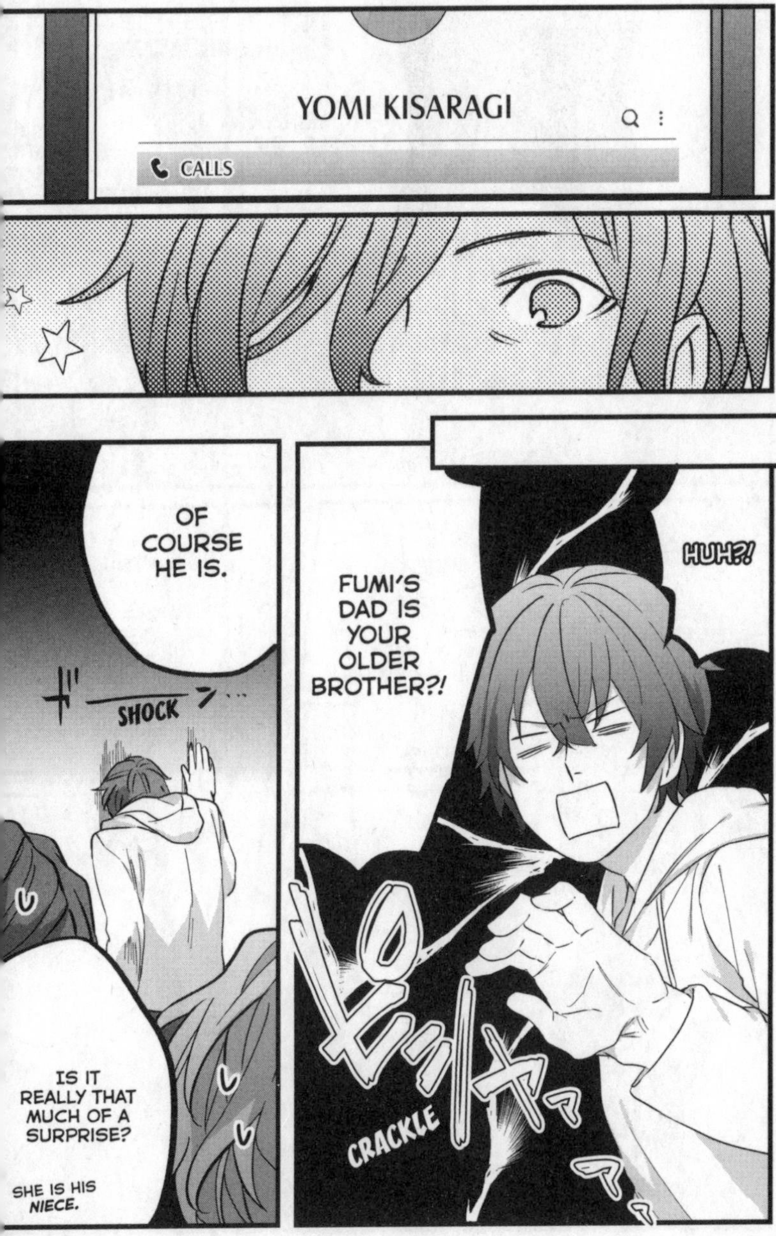
YOMI KISARAGI
CALLS
HUH?!
FUMI'S DAD IS YOUR OLDER BROTHER?!
CRACKLE
OF COURSE HE IS.
SHOCK
IS IT REALLY THAT MUCH OF A SURPRISE?
SHE IS HIS NIECE.

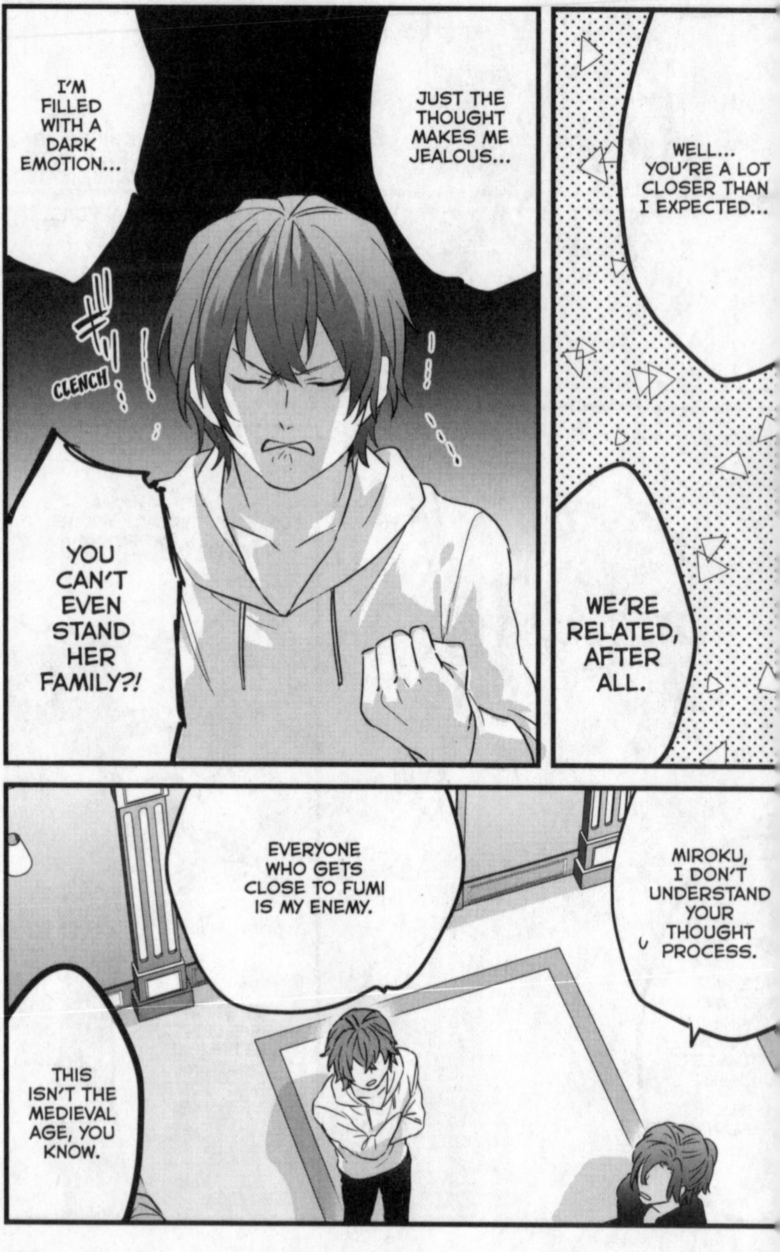
WELL... YOU'RE A LOT CLOSER THAN I EXPECTED...
WE'RE RELATED, AFTER ALL.
JUST THE THOUGHT MAKES ME JEALOUS...
I'M FILLED WITH A DARK EMOTION...
CLENCH
YOU CAN'T EVEN STAND HER FAMILY?!
MIROKU, I DON'T UNDERSTAND YOUR THOUGHT PROCESS.
EVERYONE WHO GETS CLOSE TO FUMI IS MY ENEMY.
THIS ISN'T THE MEDIEVAL AGE, YOU KNOW.

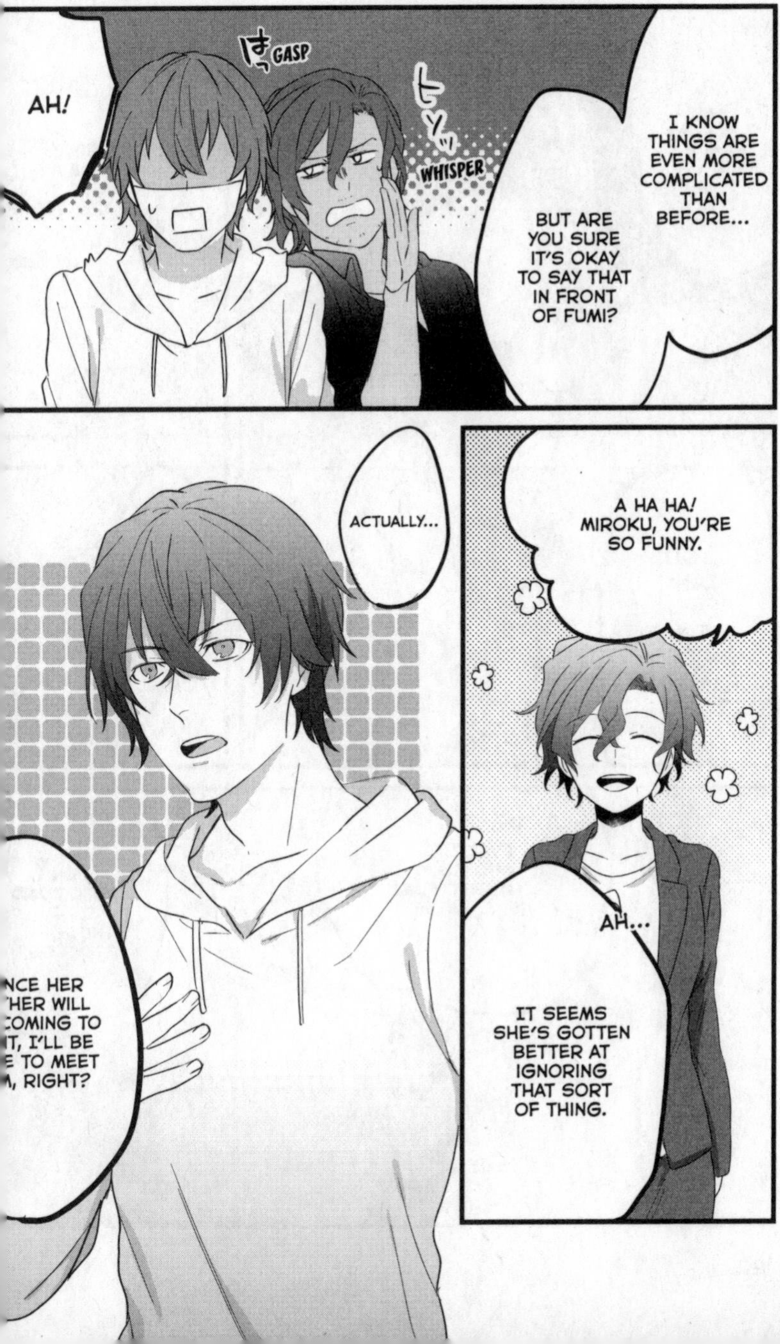
I KNOW THINGS ARE EVEN MORE COMPLICATED THAN BEFORE...
BUT ARE YOU SURE IT'S OKAY TO SAY THAT IN FRONT OF FUMI?
ヒソッ WHISPER
はっ GASP
AH!
A HA HA! MIROKU, YOU'RE SO FUNNY.
AH...
IT SEEMS SHE'S GOTTEN BETTER AT IGNORING THAT SORT OF THING.
ACTUALLY...
NCE HER
HER WILL
COMING TO
IT, I'LL BE
E TO MEET
M, RIGHT?

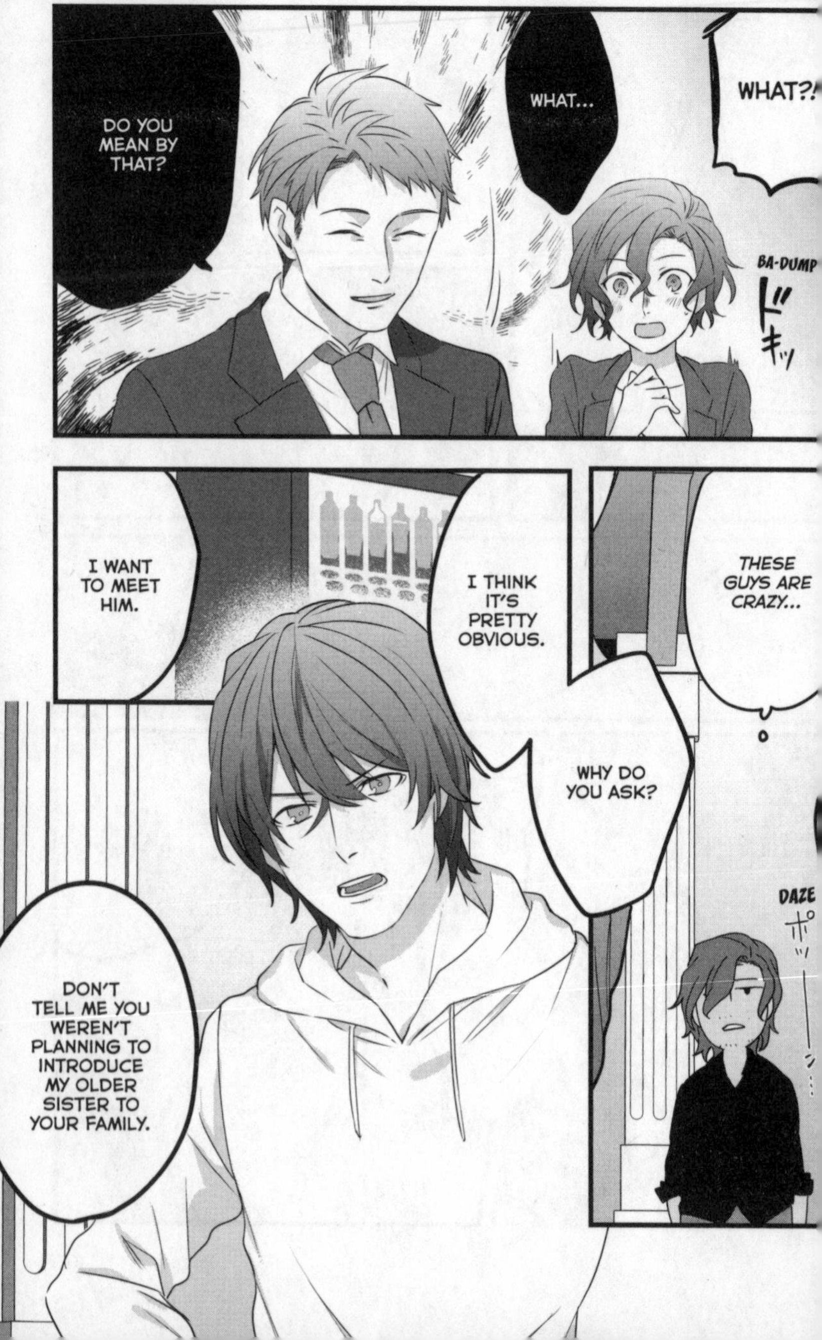
WHAT?!
BA-DUMP
ドキッ
WHAT...
DO YOU MEAN BY THAT?
THESE GUYS ARE CRAZY...
DAZE
ポッー…
I WANT TO MEET HIM.
WHY DO YOU ASK?
I THINK IT'S PRETTY OBVIOUS.
DON'T TELL ME YOU WEREN'T PLANNING TO INTRODUCE MY OLDER SISTER TO YOUR FAMILY.

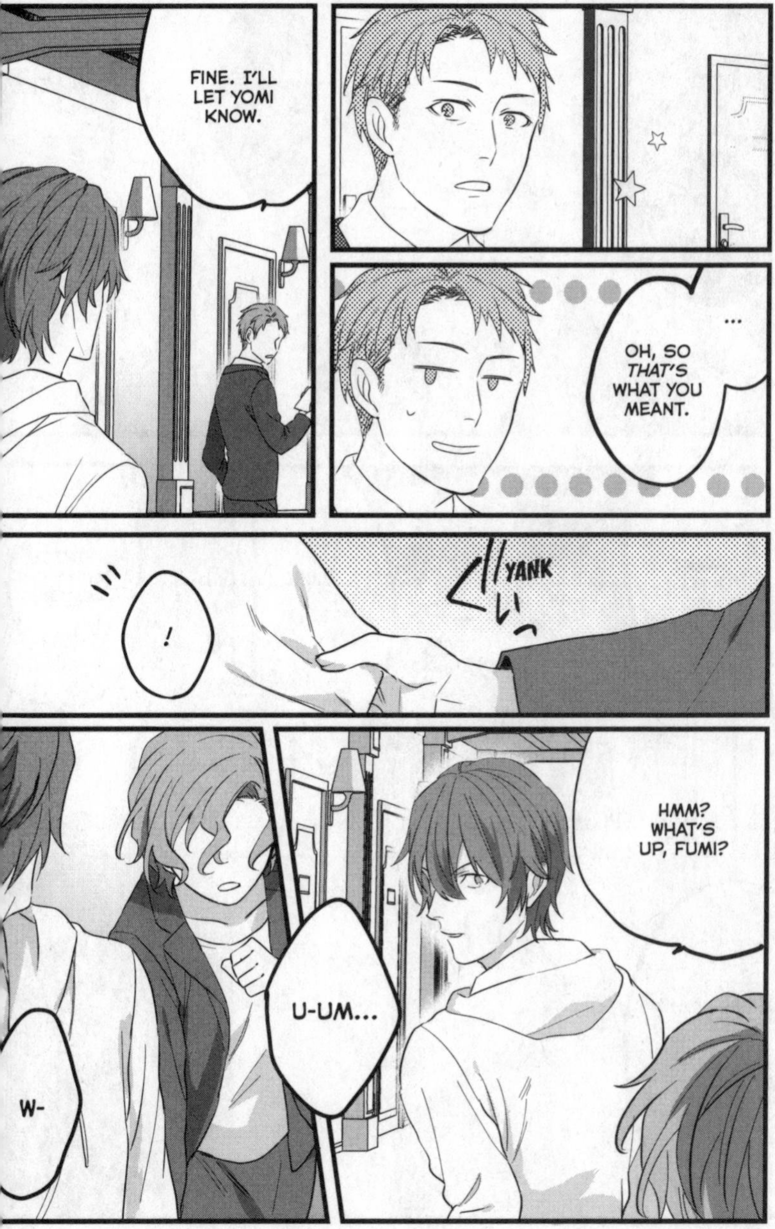
...
OH, SO *THAT'S* WHAT YOU MEANT.
FINE. I'LL LET YOMI KNOW.
YANK
!
HMM? WHAT'S UP, FUMI?
U-UM...
W-

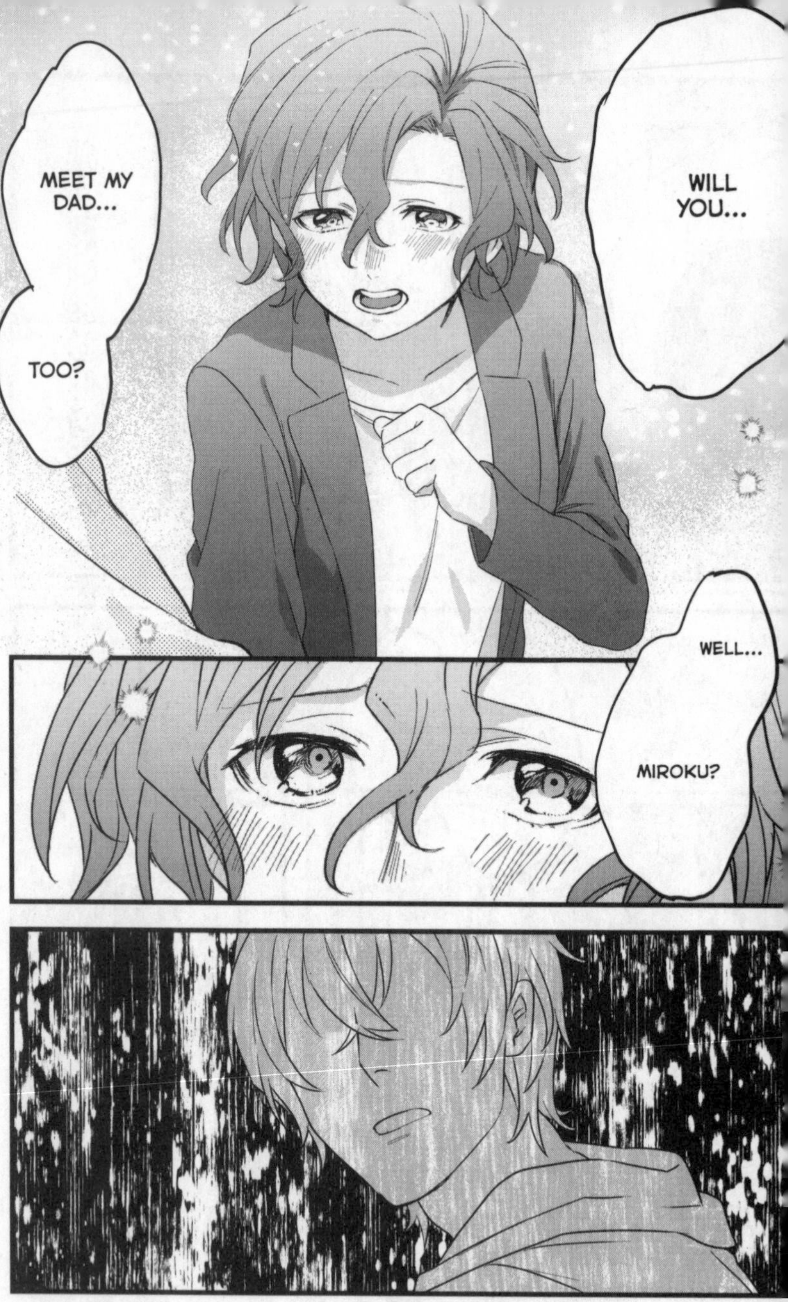
WILL YOU...
MEET MY DAD...
TOO?
WELL...
MIROKU?

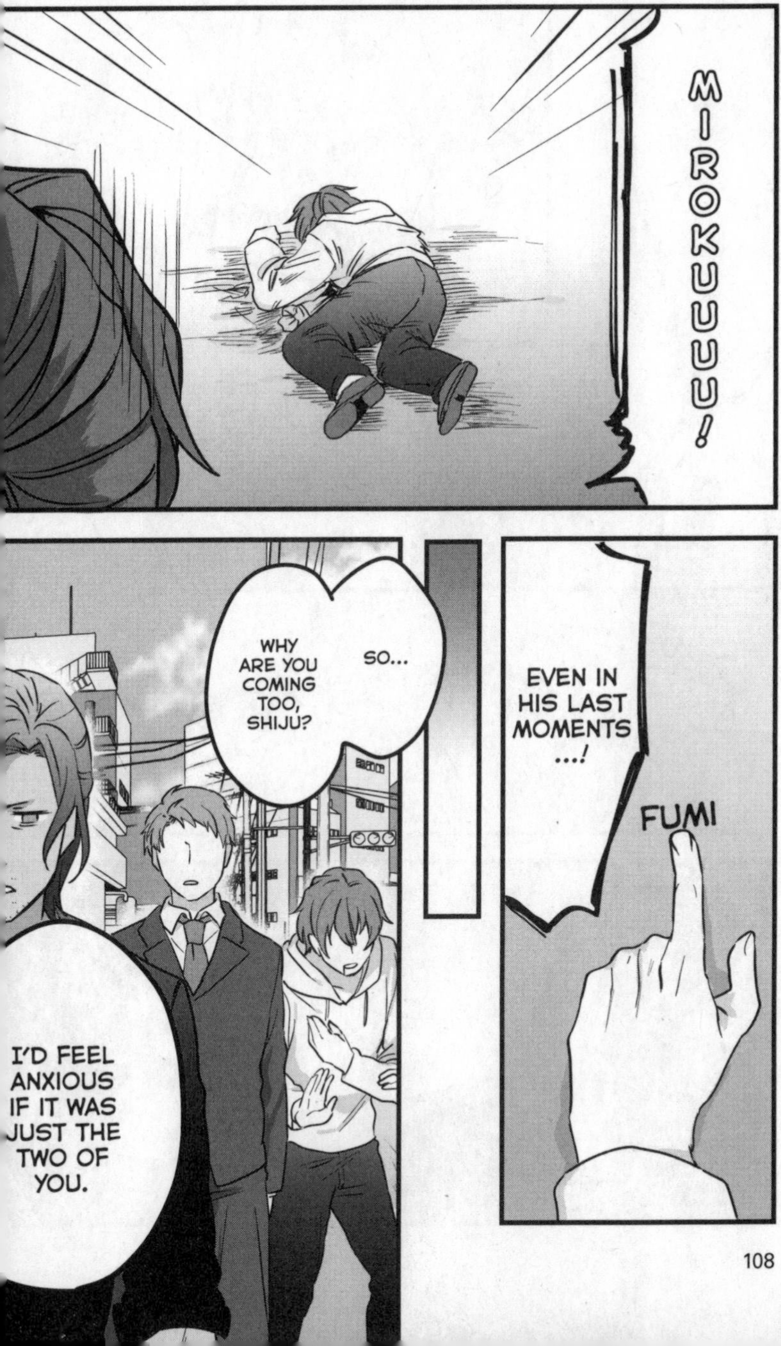
MIROKUUUU!
EVEN IN HIS LAST MOMENTS ...!
FUMI
SO...
WHY ARE YOU COMING TOO, SHIJU?
I'D FEEL ANXIOUS IF IT WAS JUST THE TWO OF YOU.

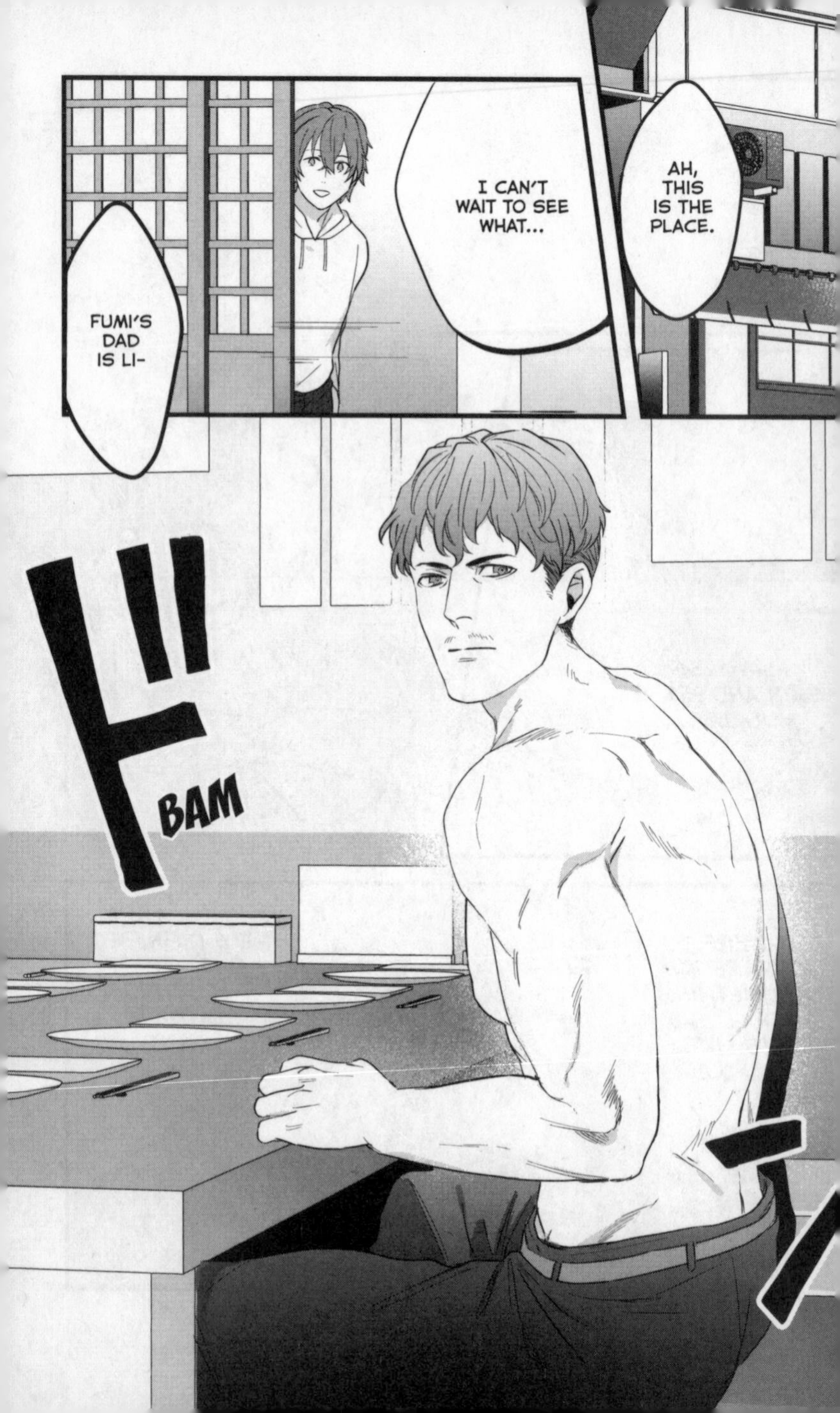
AH, THIS IS THE PLACE.
I CAN'T WAIT TO SEE WHAT...
FUMI'S DAD IS LI-
ド
BAM

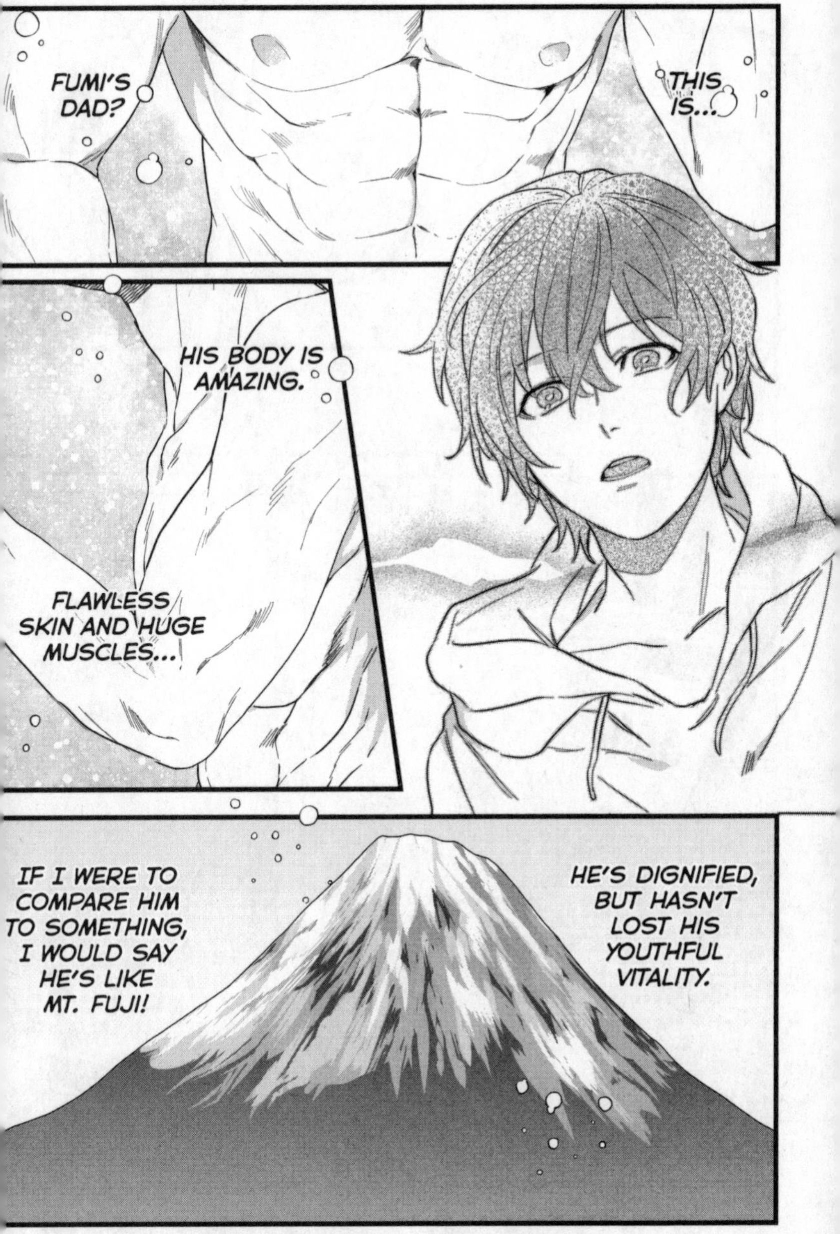
THIS IS...
FUMI'S DAD?
HIS BODY IS AMAZING.
FLAWLESS SKIN AND HUGE MUSCLES...
HE'S DIGNIFIED, BUT HASN'T LOST HIS YOUTHFUL VITALITY.
IF I WERE TO COMPARE HIM TO SOMETHING, I WOULD SAY HE'S LIKE MT. FUJI!

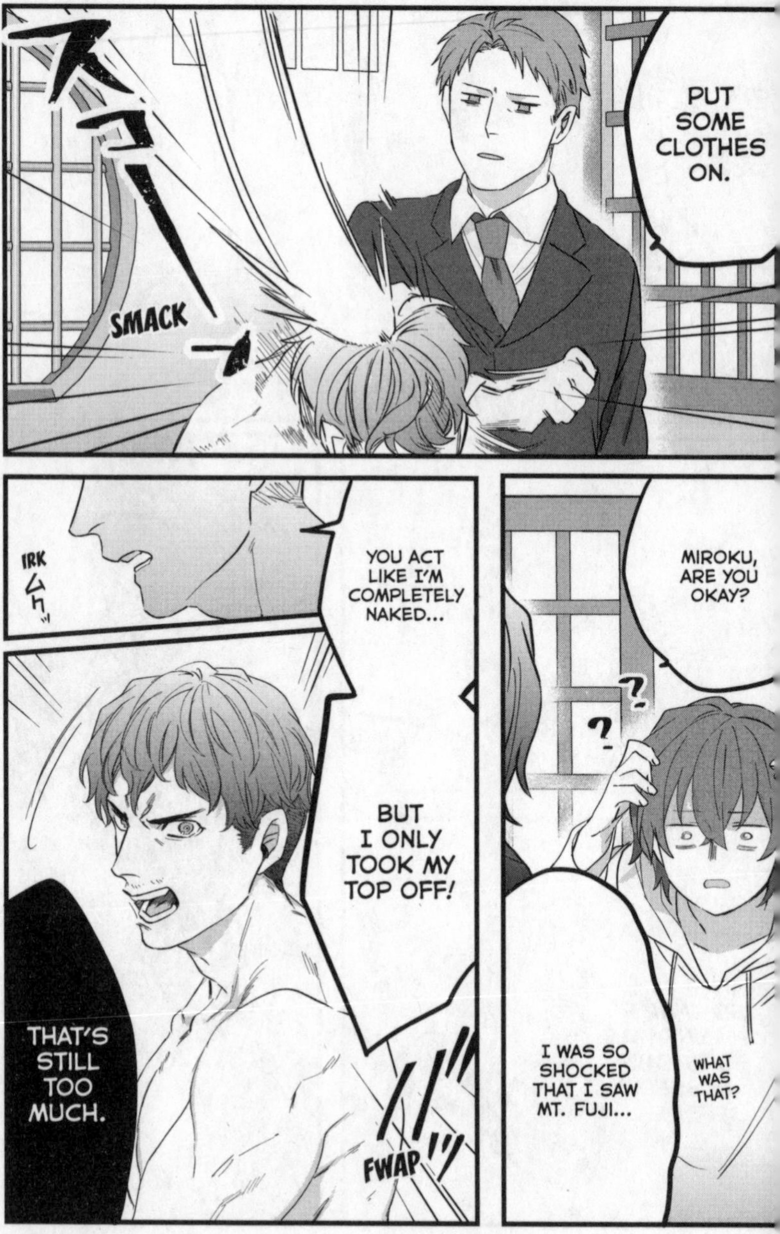
スコー
SMACK
PUT SOME CLOTHES ON.
MIROKU, ARE YOU OKAY?
??
WHAT WAS THAT?
I WAS SO SHOCKED THAT I SAW MT. FUJI...
YOU ACT LIKE I'M COMPLETELY NAKED...
IRK
ムカッ
BUT I ONLY TOOK MY TOP OFF!
THAT'S STILL TOO MUCH.
FWAP

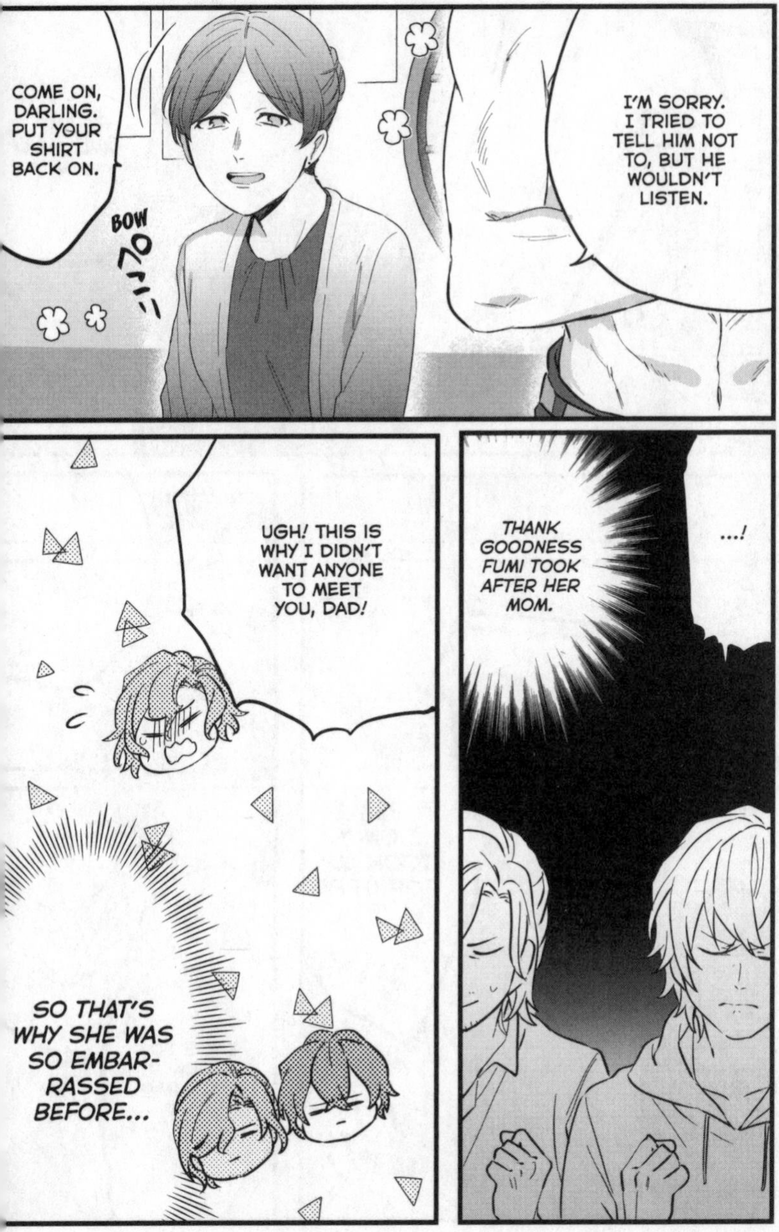
I'M SORRY. I TRIED TO TELL HIM NOT TO, BUT HE WOULDN'T LISTEN.
COME ON, DARLING. PUT YOUR SHIRT BACK ON.
BOW
...!
THANK GOODNESS FUMI TOOK AFTER HER MOM.
UGH! THIS IS WHY I DIDN'T WANT ANYONE TO MEET YOU, DAD!
SO THAT'S WHY SHE WAS SO EMBAR-RASSED BEFORE...

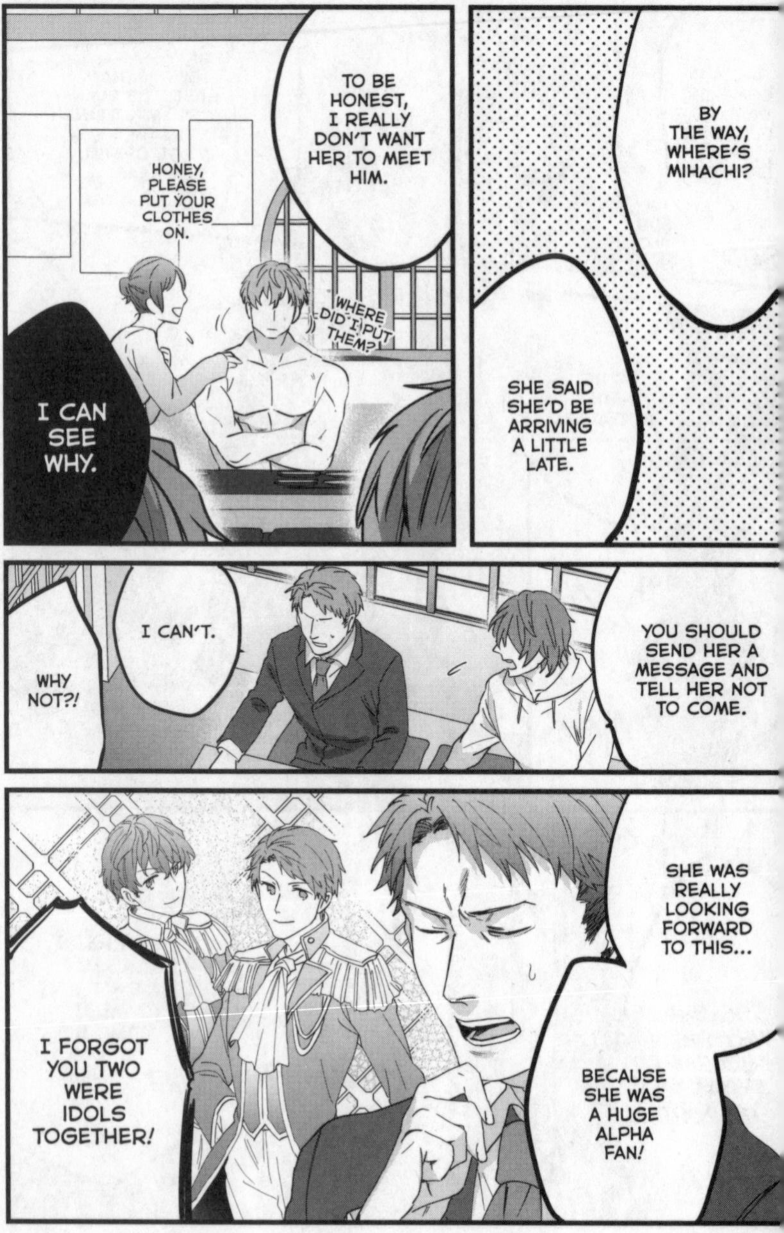
BY THE WAY, WHERE'S MIHACHI?
SHE SAID SHE'D BE ARRIVING A LITTLE LATE.
TO BE HONEST, I REALLY DON'T WANT HER TO MEET HIM.
HONEY, PLEASE PUT YOUR CLOTHES ON.
WHERE DID I PUT THEM?
I CAN SEE WHY.
YOU SHOULD SEND HER A MESSAGE AND TELL HER NOT TO COME.
I CAN'T.
WHY NOT?!
SHE WAS REALLY LOOKING FORWARD TO THIS...
BECAUSE SHE WAS A HUGE ALPHA FAN!
I FORGOT YOU TWO WERE IDOLS TOGETHER!

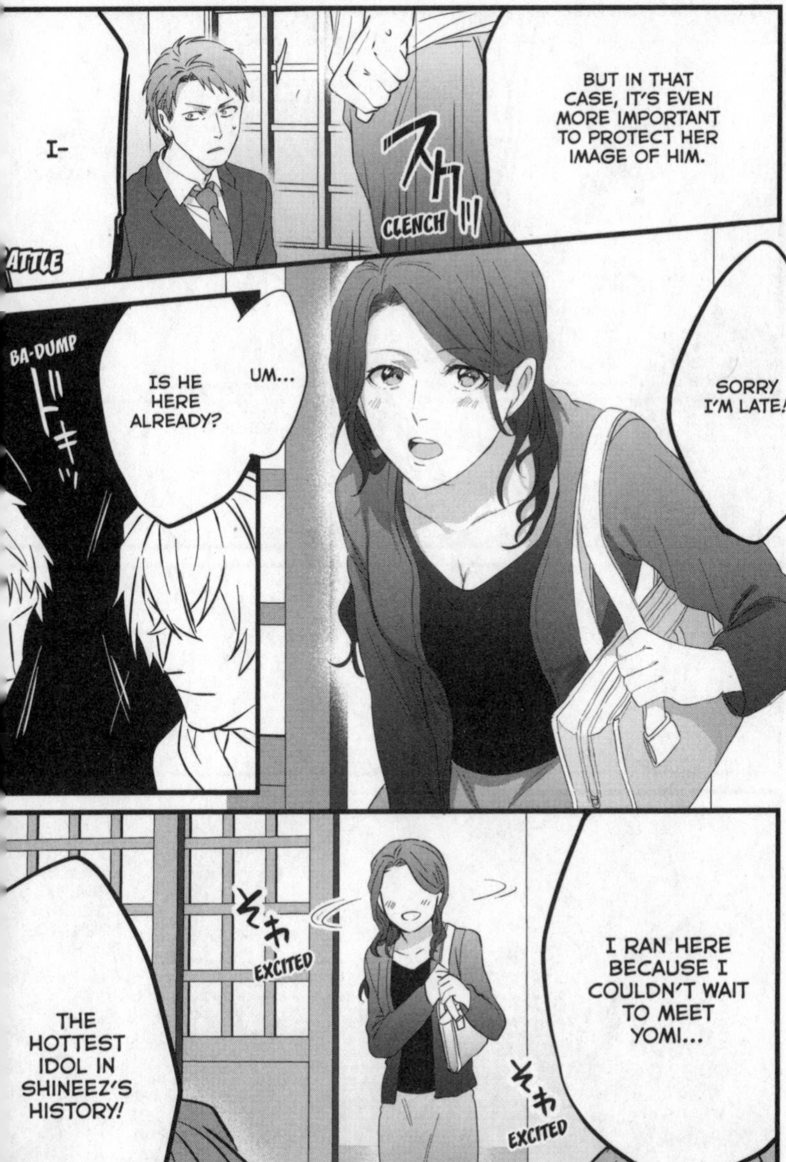
BUT IN THAT CASE, IT'S EVEN MORE IMPORTANT TO PROTECT HER IMAGE OF HIM.
CLENCH
I-
ATTLE
SORRY I'M LATE!
UM...
IS HE HERE ALREADY?
BA-DUMP
I RAN HERE BECAUSE I COULDN'T WAIT TO MEET YOMI...
EXCITED
EXCITED
THE HOTTEST IDOL IN SHINEEZ'S HISTORY!

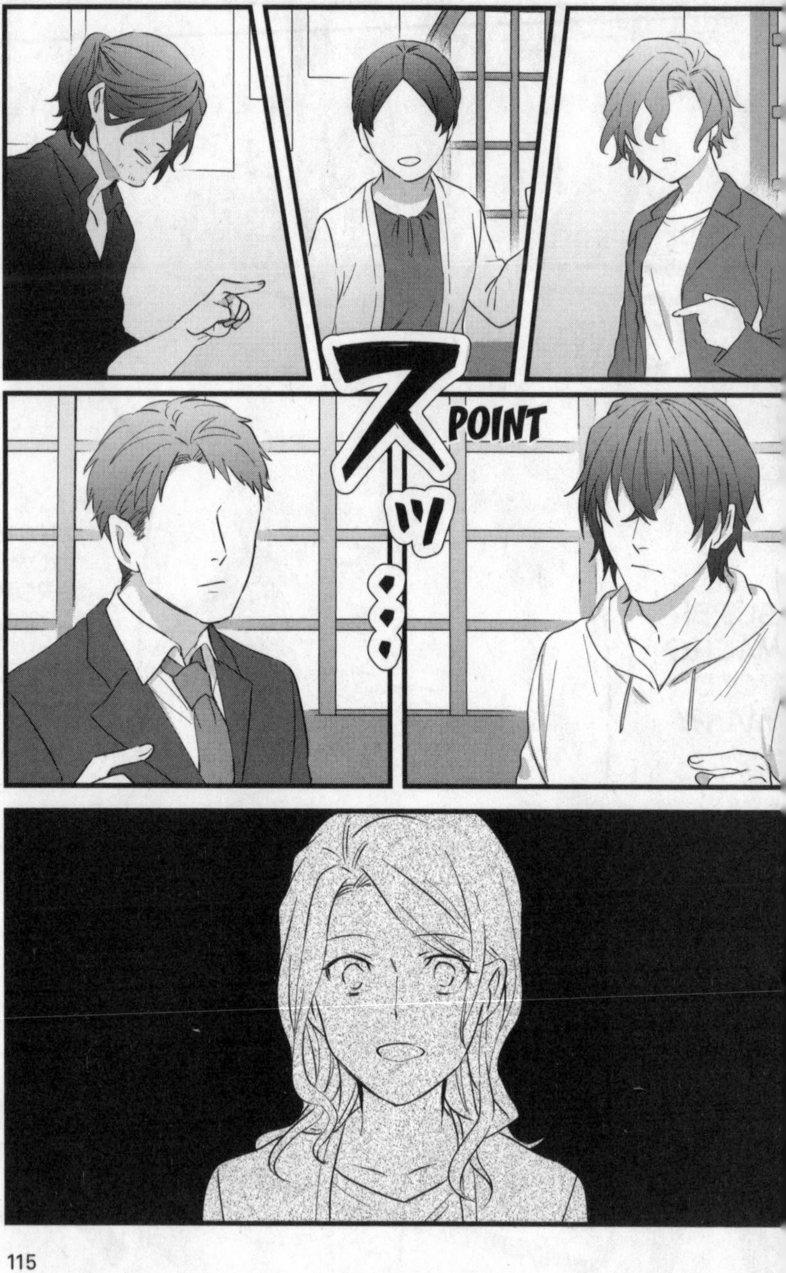
スッ
POINT

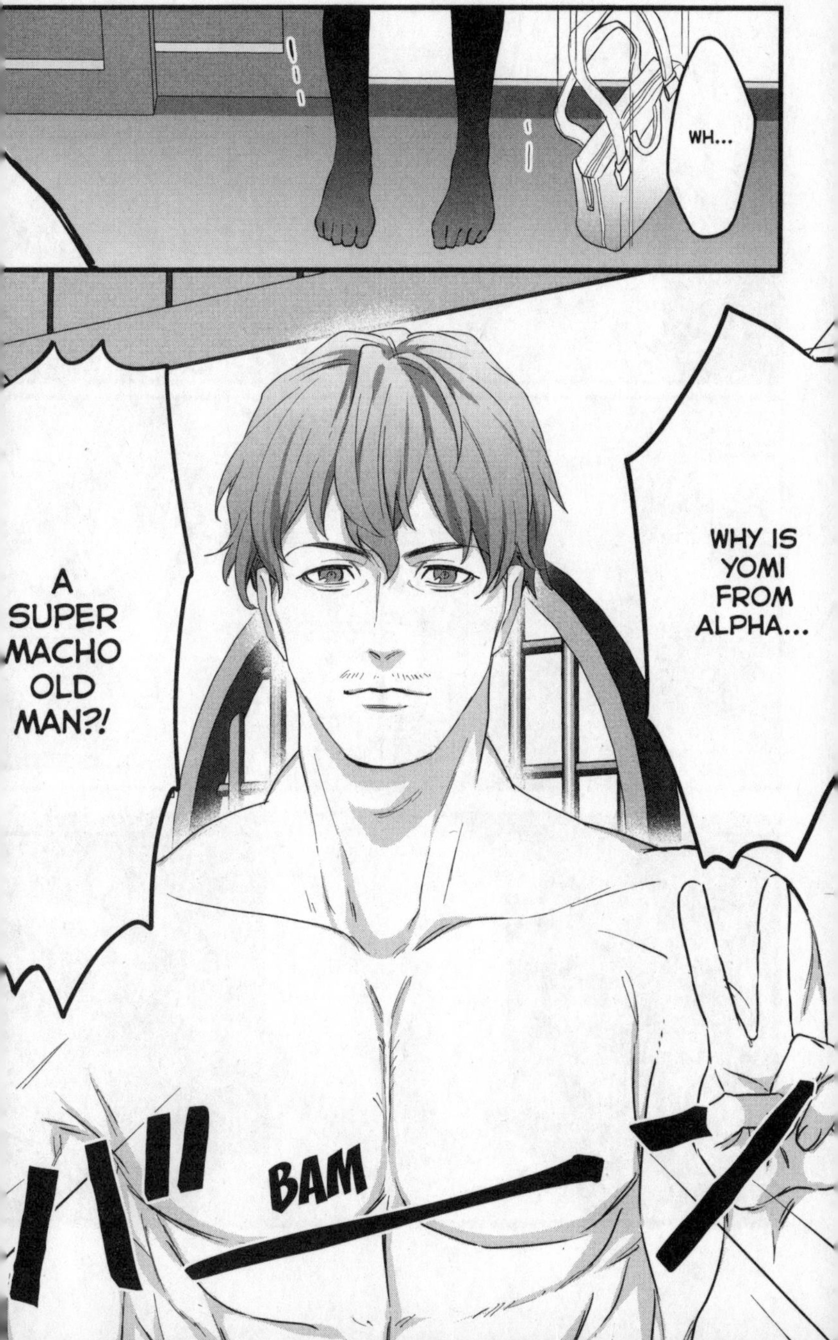
WH...
WHY IS YOMI FROM ALPHA...
A SUPER MACHO OLD MAN?!
BAM

Chapter 22

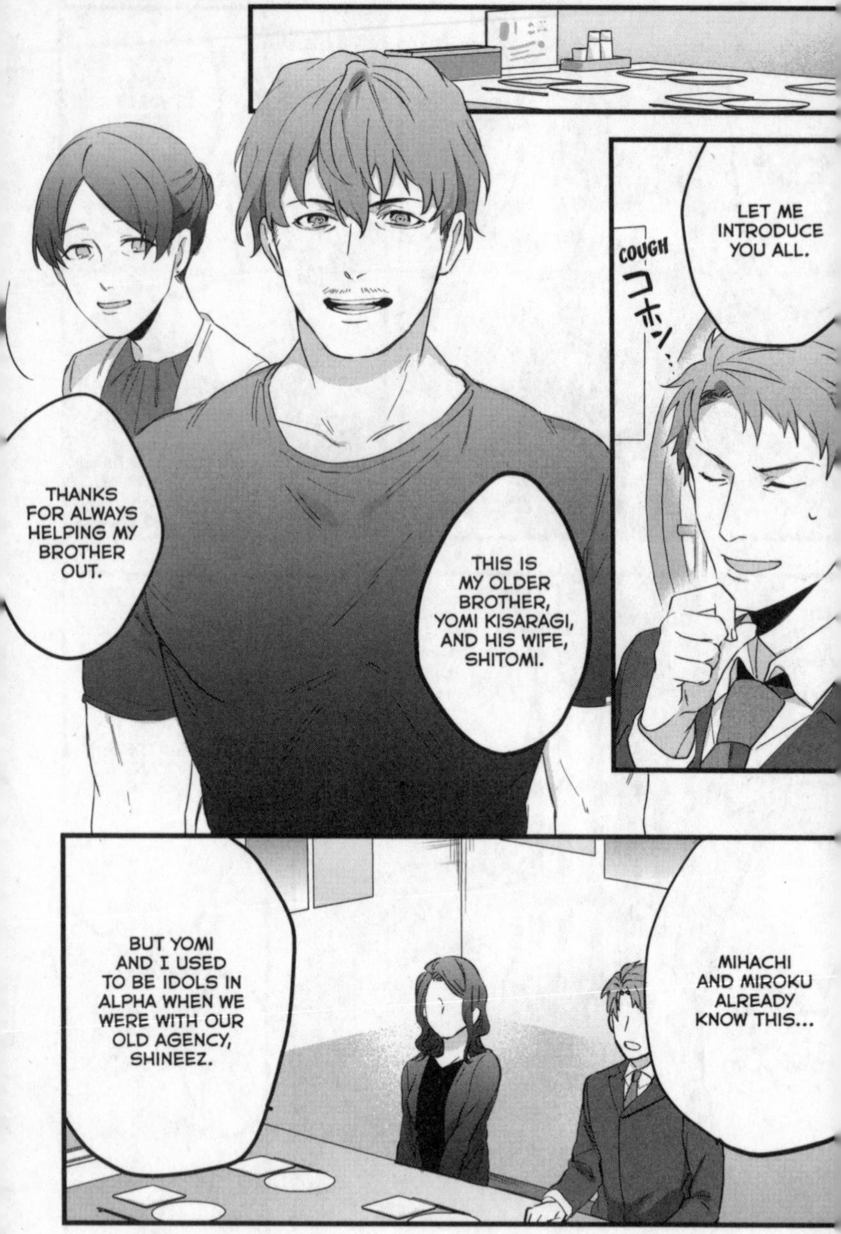

LET ME INTRODUCE YOU ALL.
COUGH
コホン…
THIS IS MY OLDER BROTHER, YOMI KISARAGI, AND HIS WIFE, SHITOMI.
THANKS FOR ALWAYS HELPING MY BROTHER OUT.
MIHACHI AND MIROKU ALREADY KNOW THIS...
BUT YOMI AND I USED TO BE IDOLS IN ALPHA WHEN WE WERE WITH OUR OLD AGENCY, SHINEEZ.

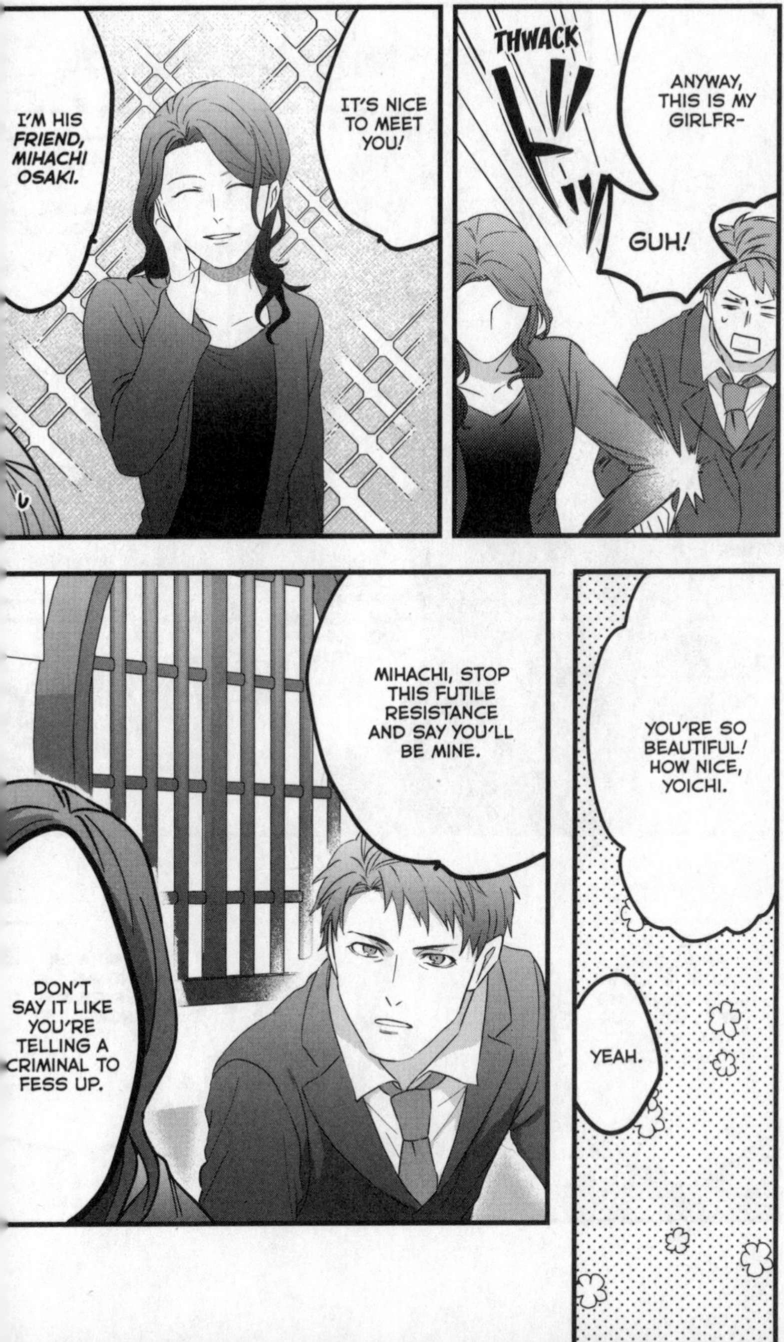
THWACK
ANYWAY, THIS IS MY GIRLFR-
GUH!
IT'S NICE TO MEET YOU!
I'M HIS FRIEND, MIHACHI OSAKI.
YOU'RE SO BEAUTIFUL! HOW NICE, YOICHI.
YEAH.
MIHACHI, STOP THIS FUTILE RESISTANCE AND SAY YOU'LL BE MINE.
DON'T SAY IT LIKE YOU'RE TELLING A CRIMINAL TO FESS UP.

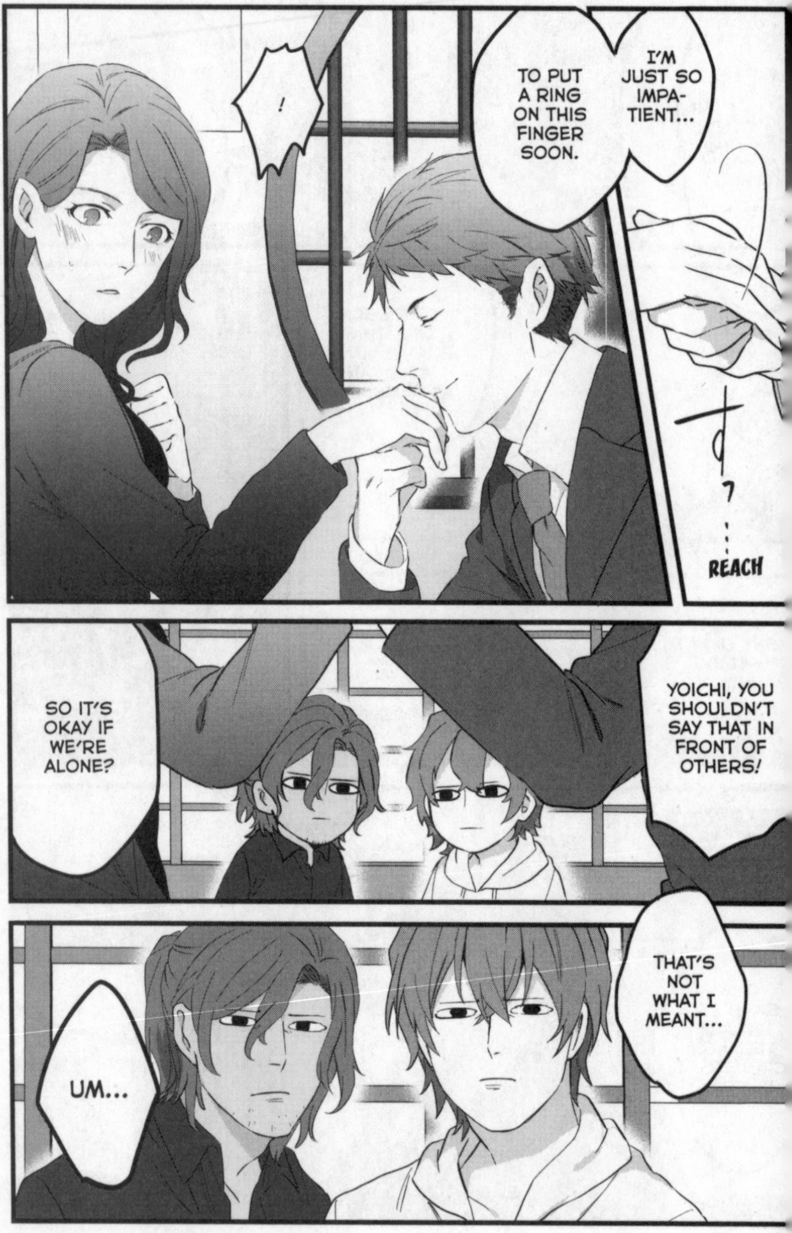
REACH
I'M JUST SO IMPATIENT...
TO PUT A RING ON THIS FINGER SOON.
!
YOICHI, YOU SHOULDN'T SAY THAT IN FRONT OF OTHERS!
SO IT'S OKAY IF WE'RE ALONE?
THAT'S NOT WHAT I MEANT...
UM...

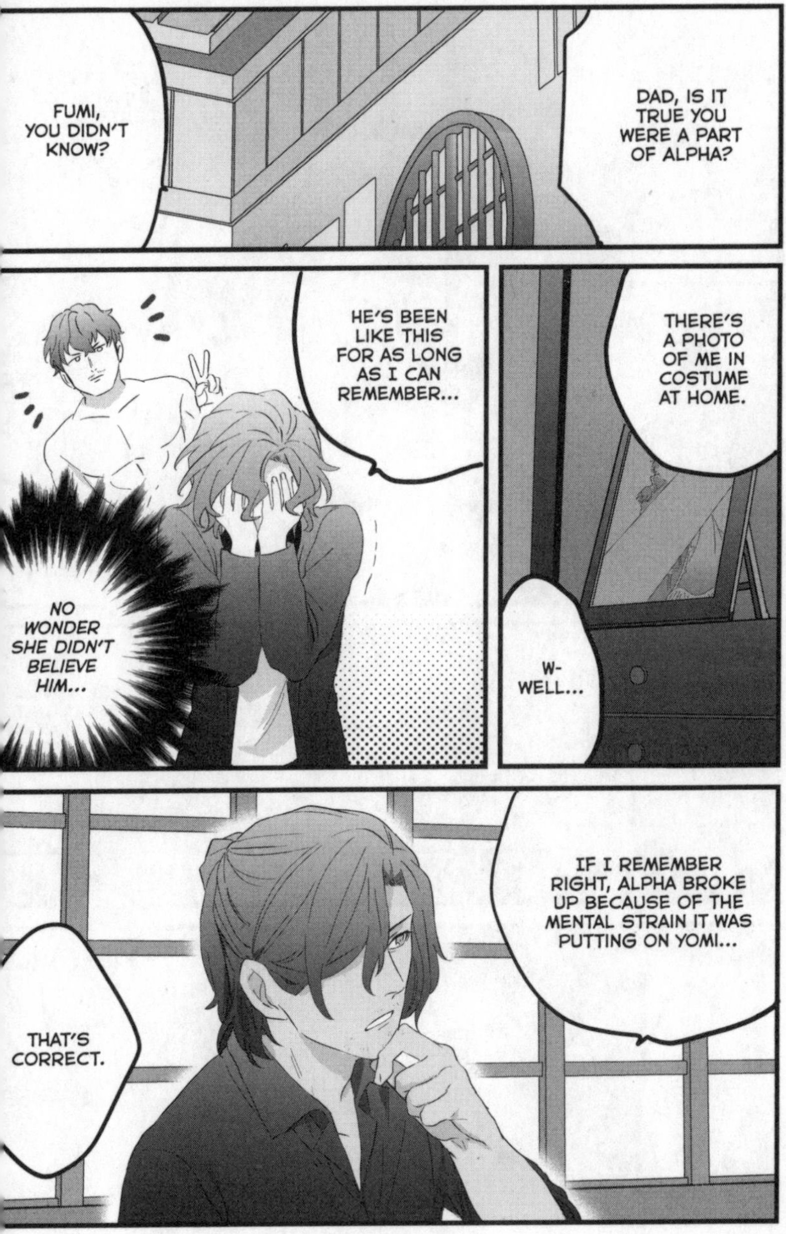
DAD, IS IT TRUE YOU WERE A PART OF ALPHA?
FUMI, YOU DIDN'T KNOW?
THERE'S A PHOTO OF ME IN COSTUME AT HOME.
W-WELL...
HE'S BEEN LIKE THIS FOR AS LONG AS I CAN REMEMBER...
NO WONDER SHE DIDN'T BELIEVE HIM...
IF I REMEMBER RIGHT, ALPHA BROKE UP BECAUSE OF THE MENTAL STRAIN IT WAS PUTTING ON YOMI...
THAT'S CORRECT.

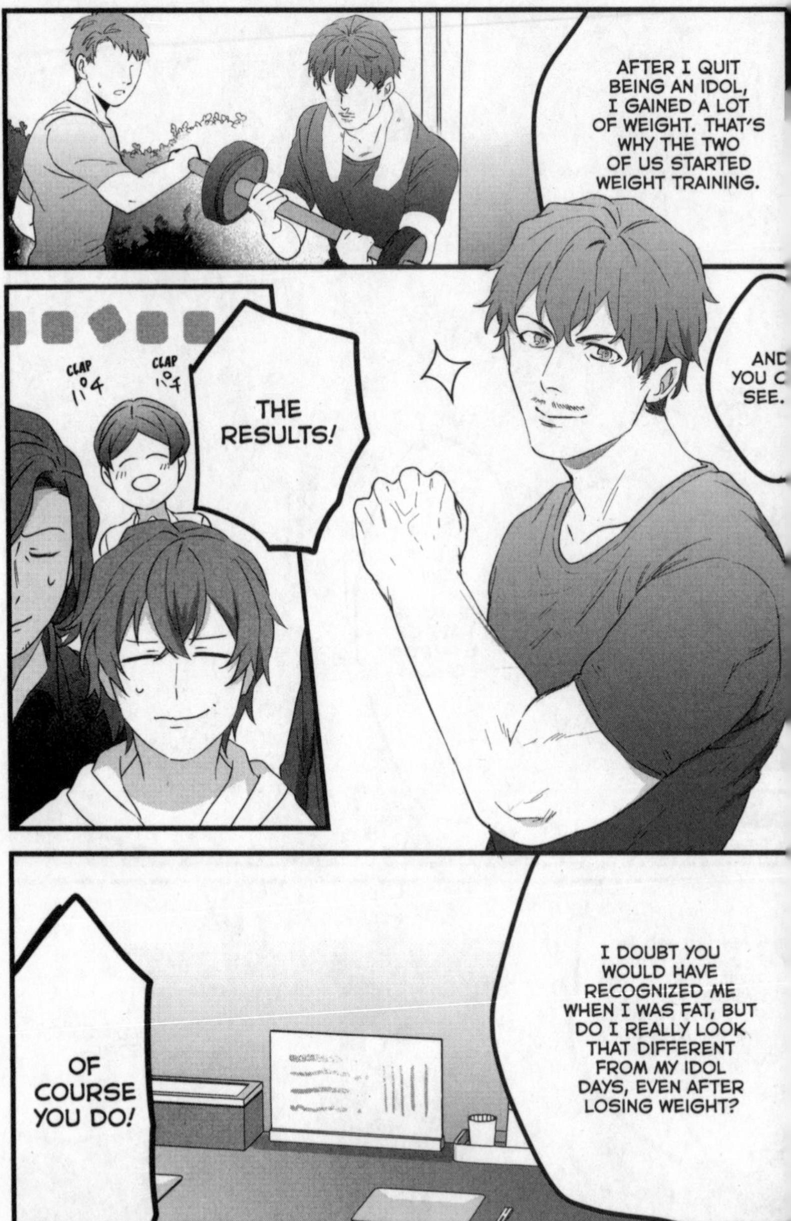
AFTER I QUIT BEING AN IDOL, I GAINED A LOT OF WEIGHT. THAT'S WHY THE TWO OF US STARTED WEIGHT TRAINING.
AND YOU C SEE.
THE RESULTS!
CLAP パチ
CLAP パチ
I DOUBT YOU WOULD HAVE RECOGNIZED ME WHEN I WAS FAT, BUT DO I REALLY LOOK THAT DIFFERENT FROM MY IDOL DAYS, EVEN AFTER LOSING WEIGHT?
OF COURSE YOU DO!

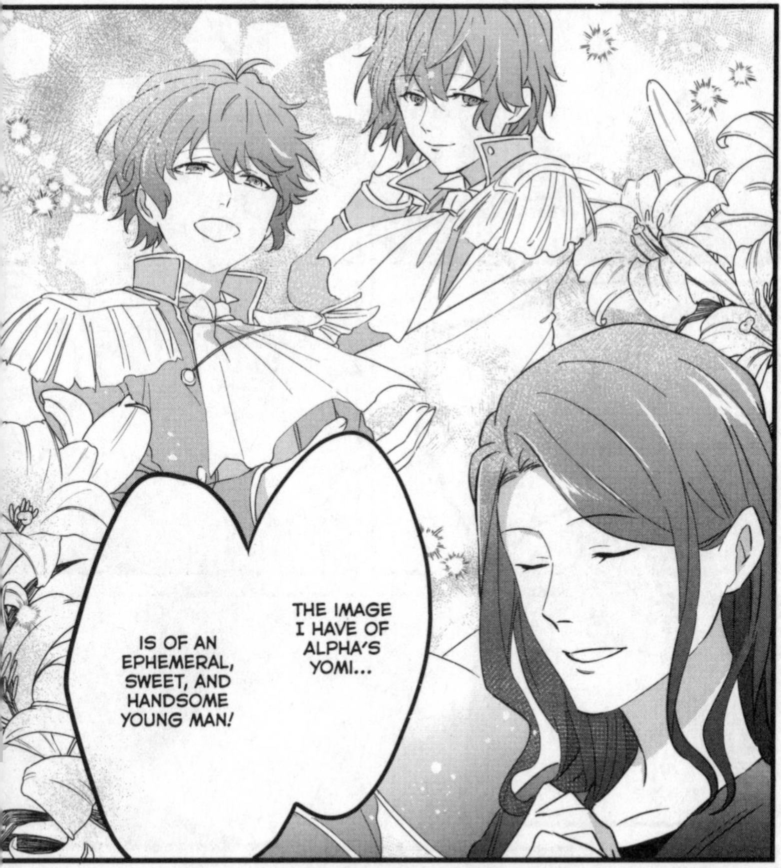
THE IMAGE I HAVE OF ALPHA'S YOMI...
IS OF AN EPHEMERAL, SWEET, AND HANDSOME YOUNG MAN!

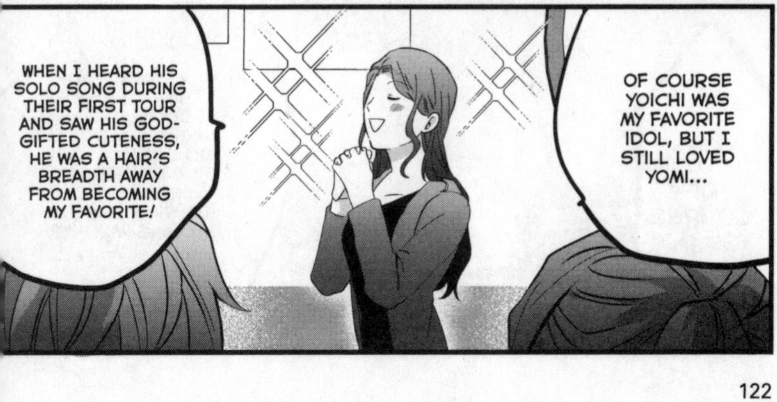
OF COURSE YOICHI WAS MY FAVORITE IDOL, BUT I STILL LOVED YOMI...
WHEN I HEARD HIS SOLO SONG DURING THEIR FIRST TOUR AND SAW HIS GOD-GIFTED CUTENESS, HE WAS A HAIR'S BREADTH AWAY FROM BECOMING MY FAVORITE!

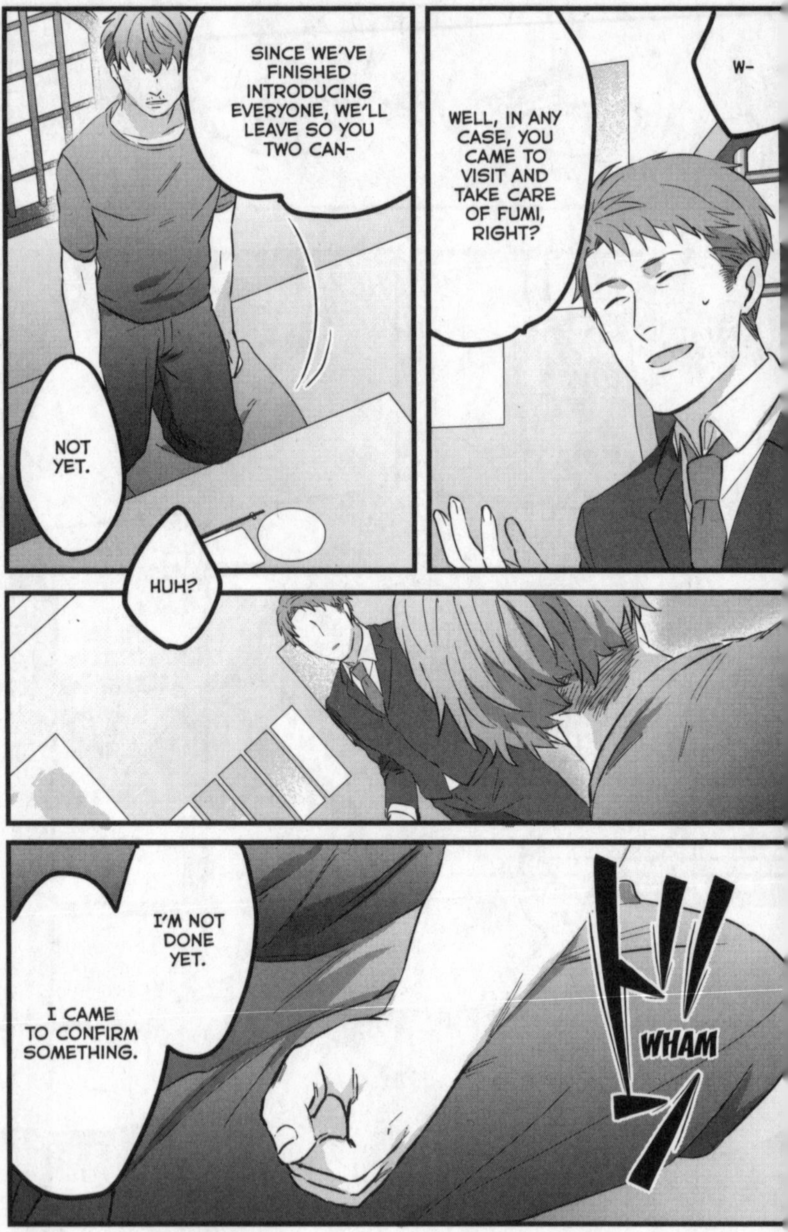
W-
WELL, IN ANY CASE, YOU CAME TO VISIT AND TAKE CARE OF FUMI, RIGHT?
SINCE WE'VE FINISHED INTRODUCING EVERYONE, WE'LL LEAVE SO YOU TWO CAN-
NOT YET.
HUH?
WHAM
I'M NOT DONE YET.
I CAME TO CONFIRM SOMETHING.

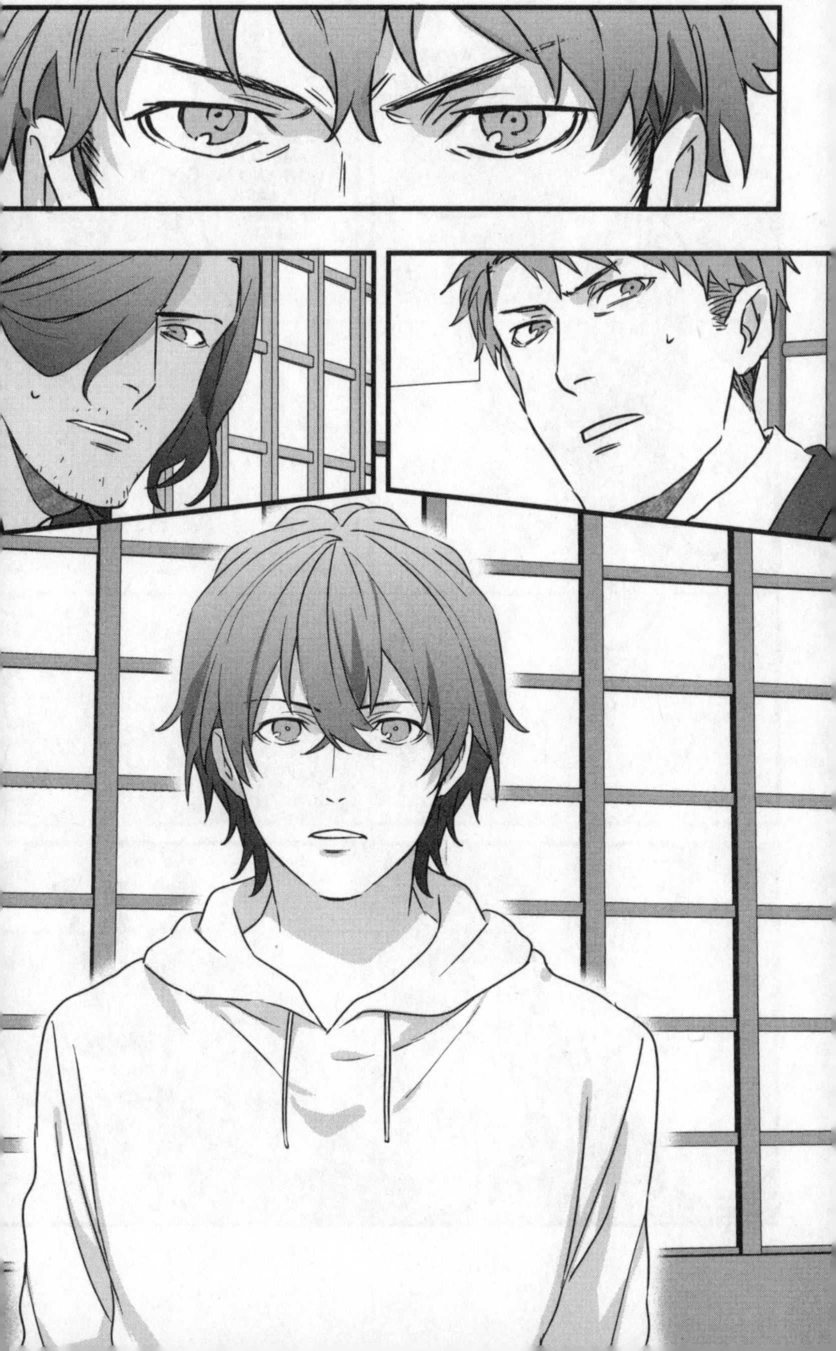

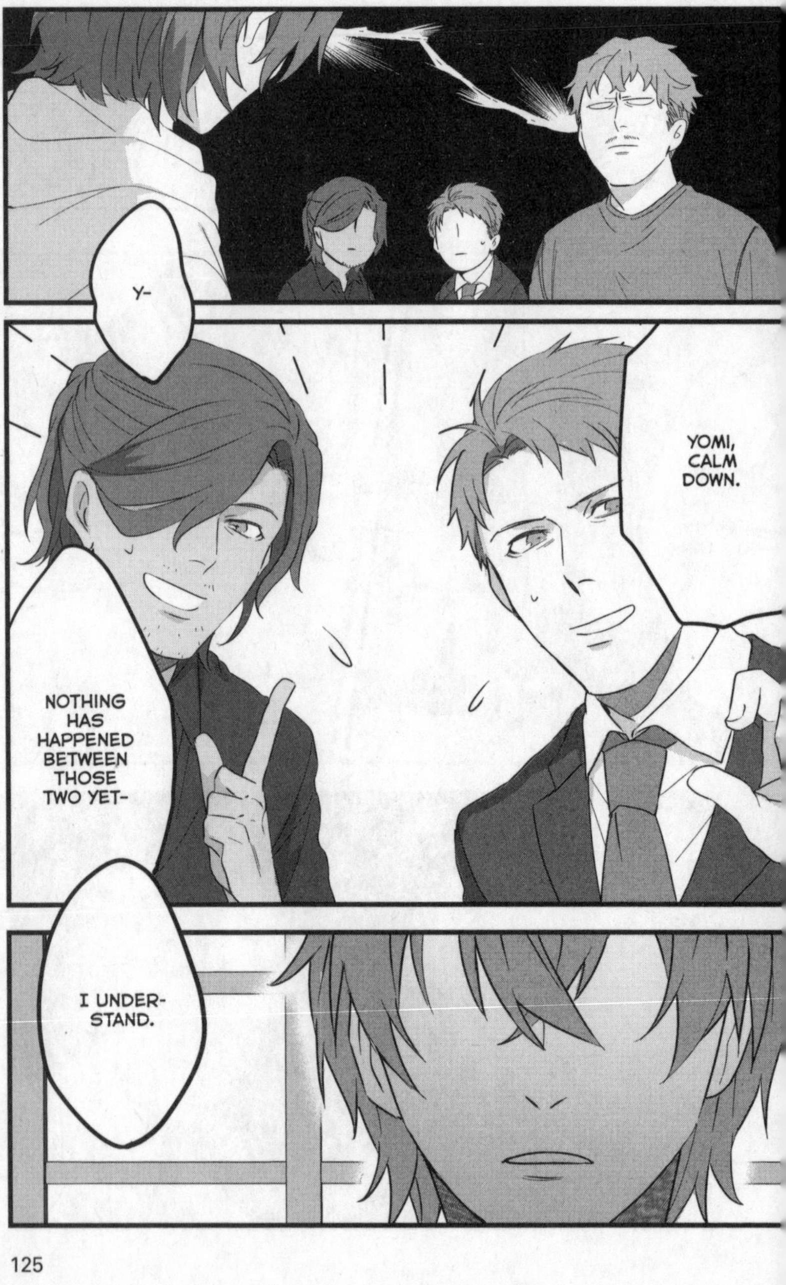
Y-
YOMI, CALM DOWN.
NOTHING HAS HAPPENED BETWEEN THOSE TWO YET-
I UNDER-STAND.

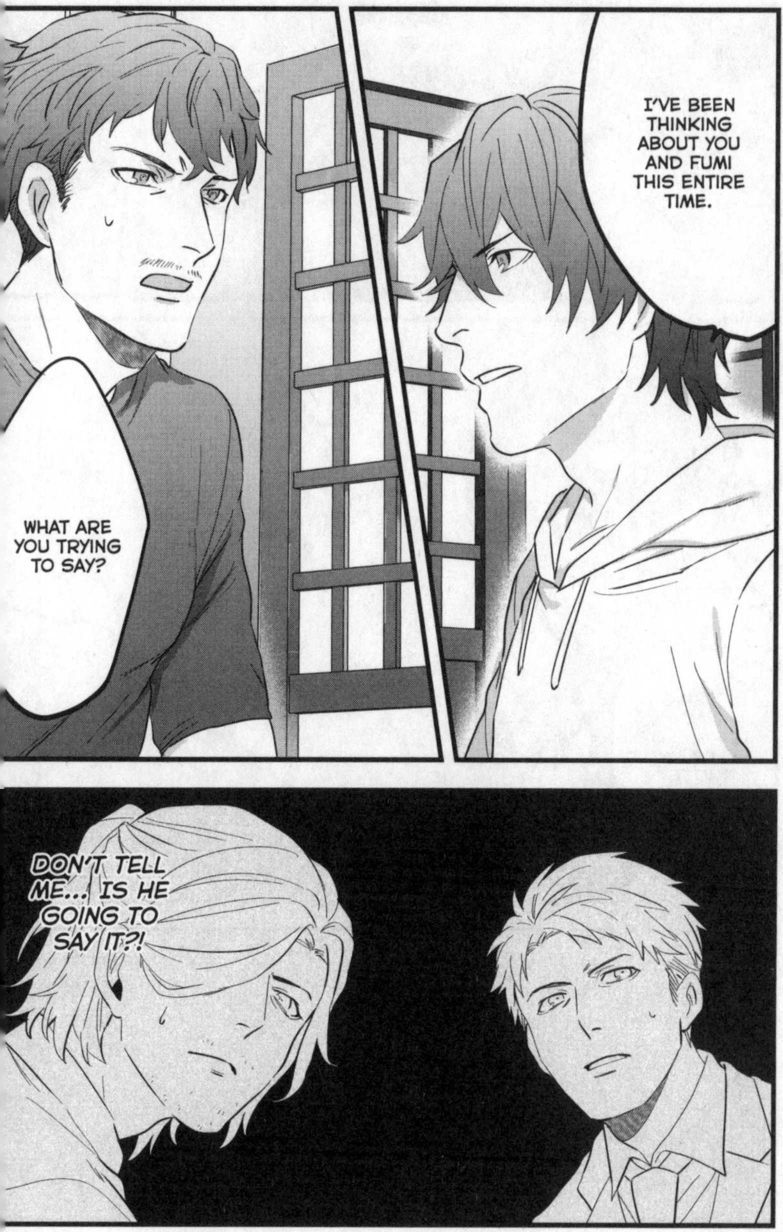
I'VE BEEN THINKING ABOUT YOU AND FUMI THIS ENTIRE TIME.
WHAT ARE YOU TRYING TO SAY?
DON'T TELL ME... IS HE GOING TO SAY IT?!

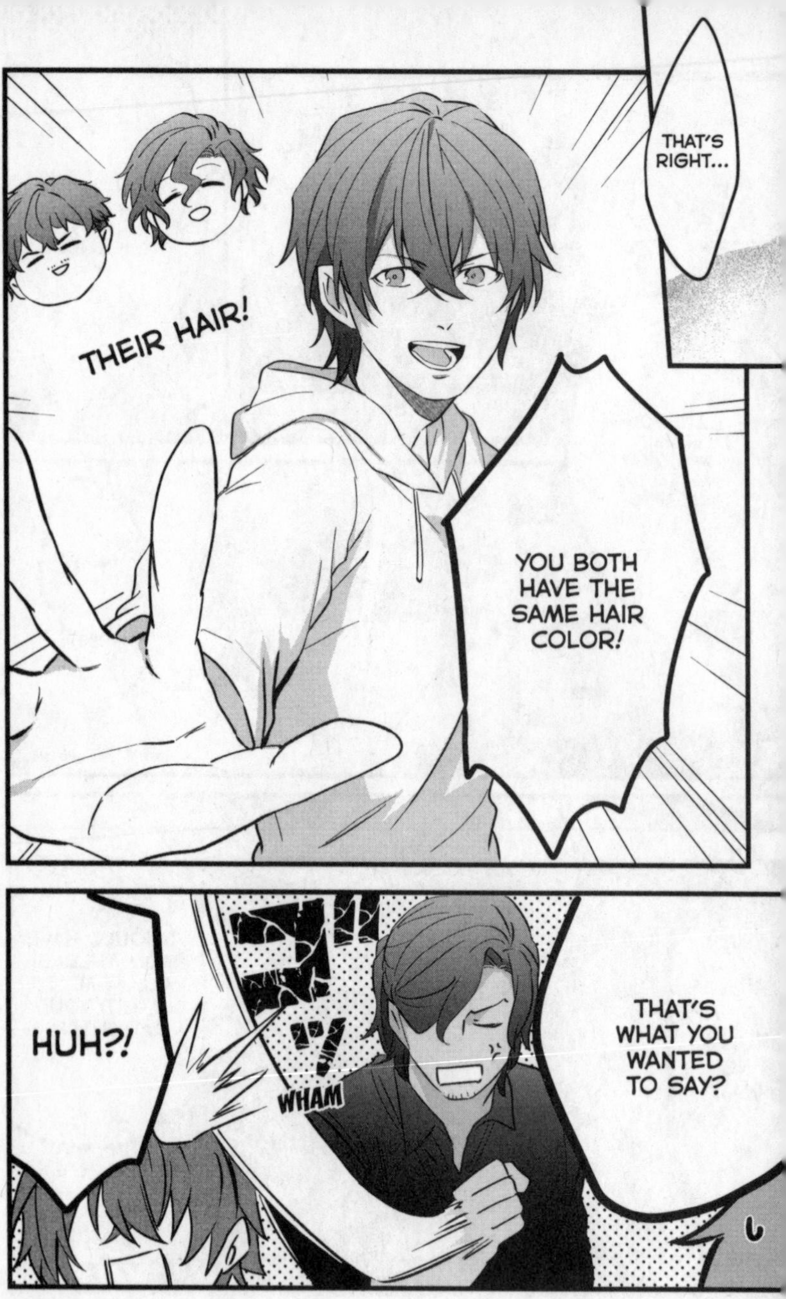
THAT'S RIGHT...
THEIR HAIR!
YOU BOTH HAVE THE SAME HAIR COLOR!
THAT'S WHAT YOU WANTED TO SAY?
WHAM
HUH?!

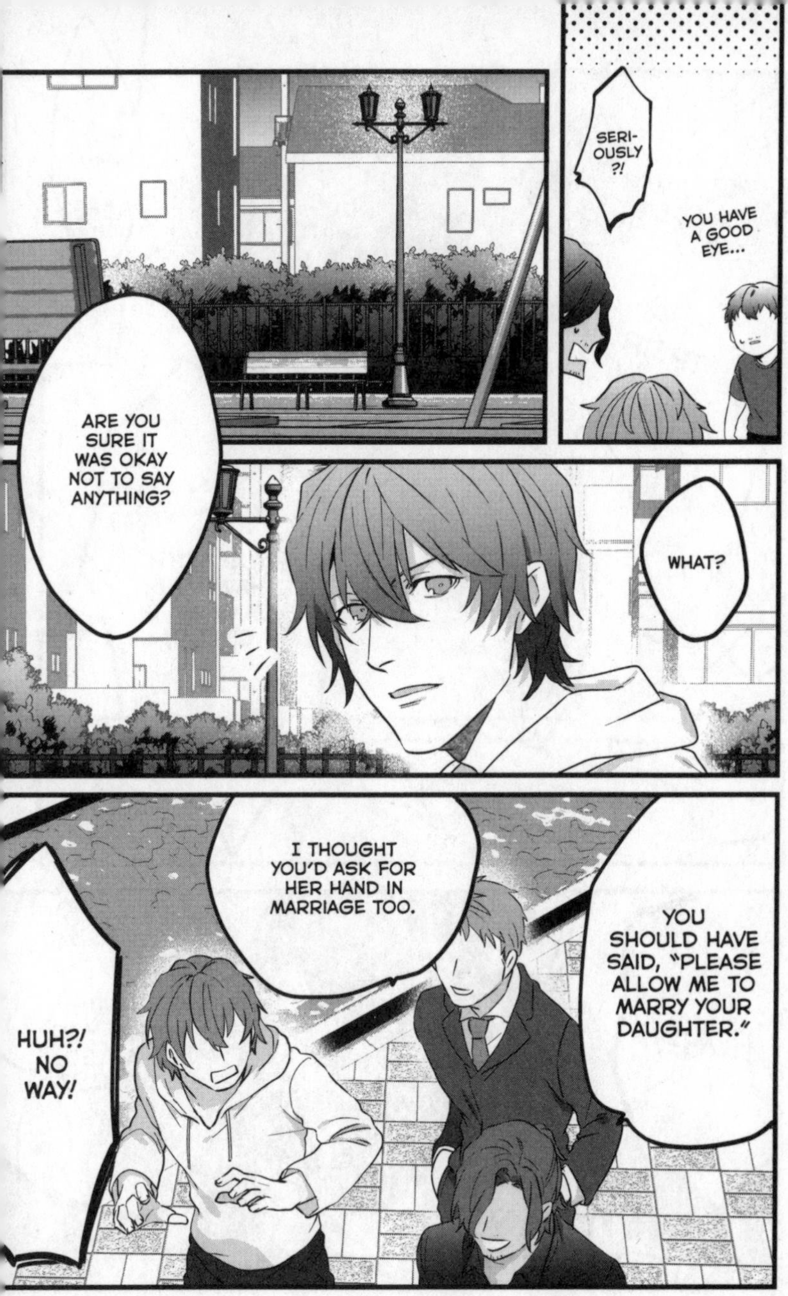
SERI-OUSLY?!
YOU HAVE A GOOD EYE...
ARE YOU SURE IT WAS OKAY NOT TO SAY ANYTHING?
WHAT?
YOU SHOULD HAVE SAID, "PLEASE ALLOW ME TO MARRY YOUR DAUGHTER."
I THOUGHT YOU'D ASK FOR HER HAND IN MARRIAGE TOO.
HUH?! NO WAY!

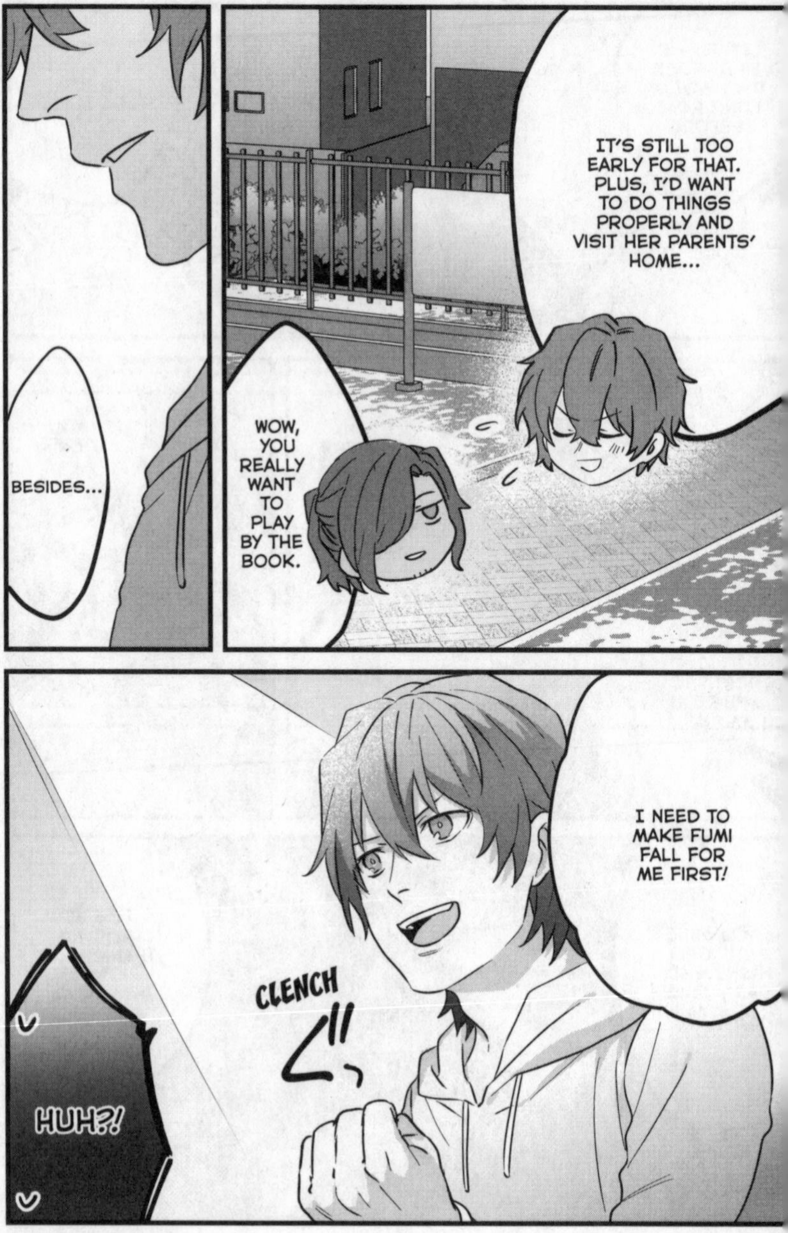
IT'S STILL TOO EARLY FOR THAT. PLUS, I'D WANT TO DO THINGS PROPERLY AND VISIT HER PARENTS' HOME...
WOW, YOU REALLY WANT TO PLAY BY THE BOOK.
BESIDES...
I NEED TO MAKE FUMI FALL FOR ME FIRST!
CLENCH
HUH?!

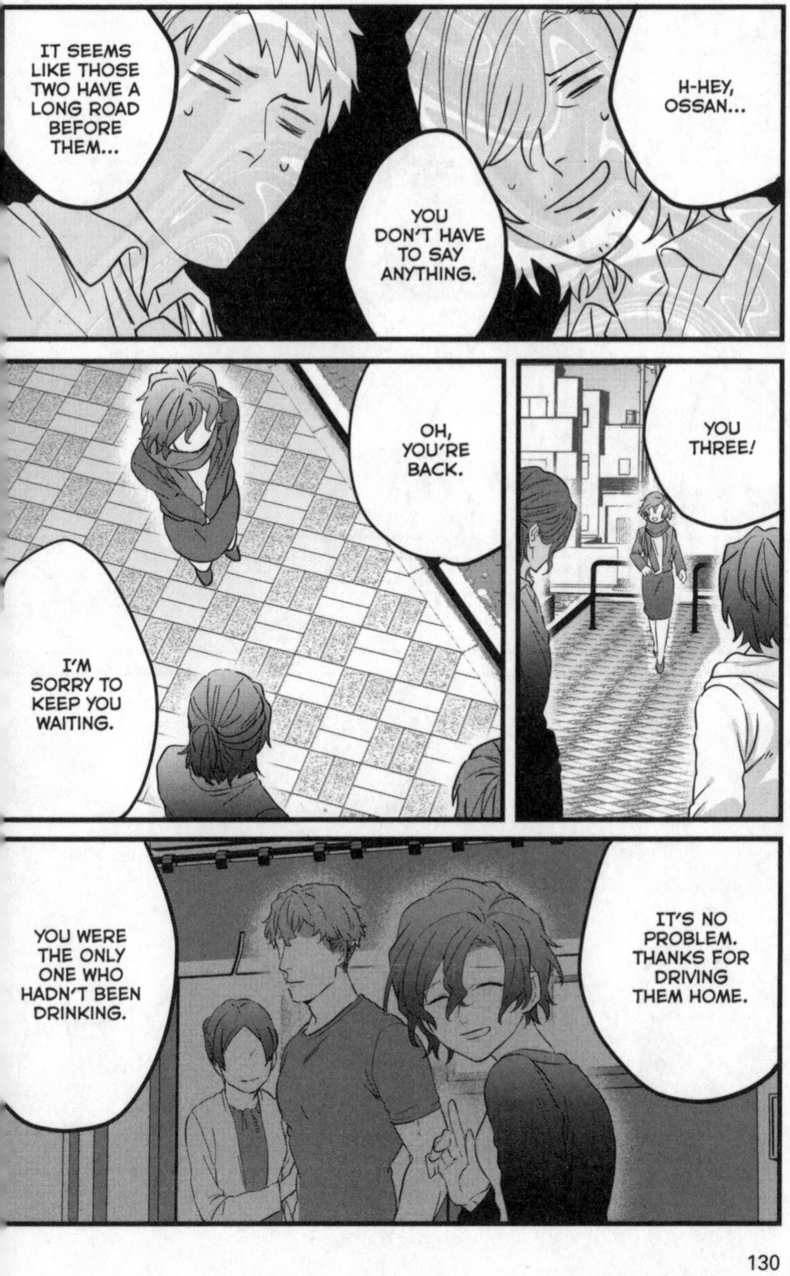
H-HEY, OSSAN...
YOU DON'T HAVE TO SAY ANYTHING.
IT SEEMS LIKE THOSE TWO HAVE A LONG ROAD BEFORE THEM...
YOU THREE!
OH, YOU'RE BACK.
I'M SORRY TO KEEP YOU WAITING.
IT'S NO PROBLEM. THANKS FOR DRIVING THEM HOME.
YOU WERE THE ONLY ONE WHO HADN'T BEEN DRINKING.

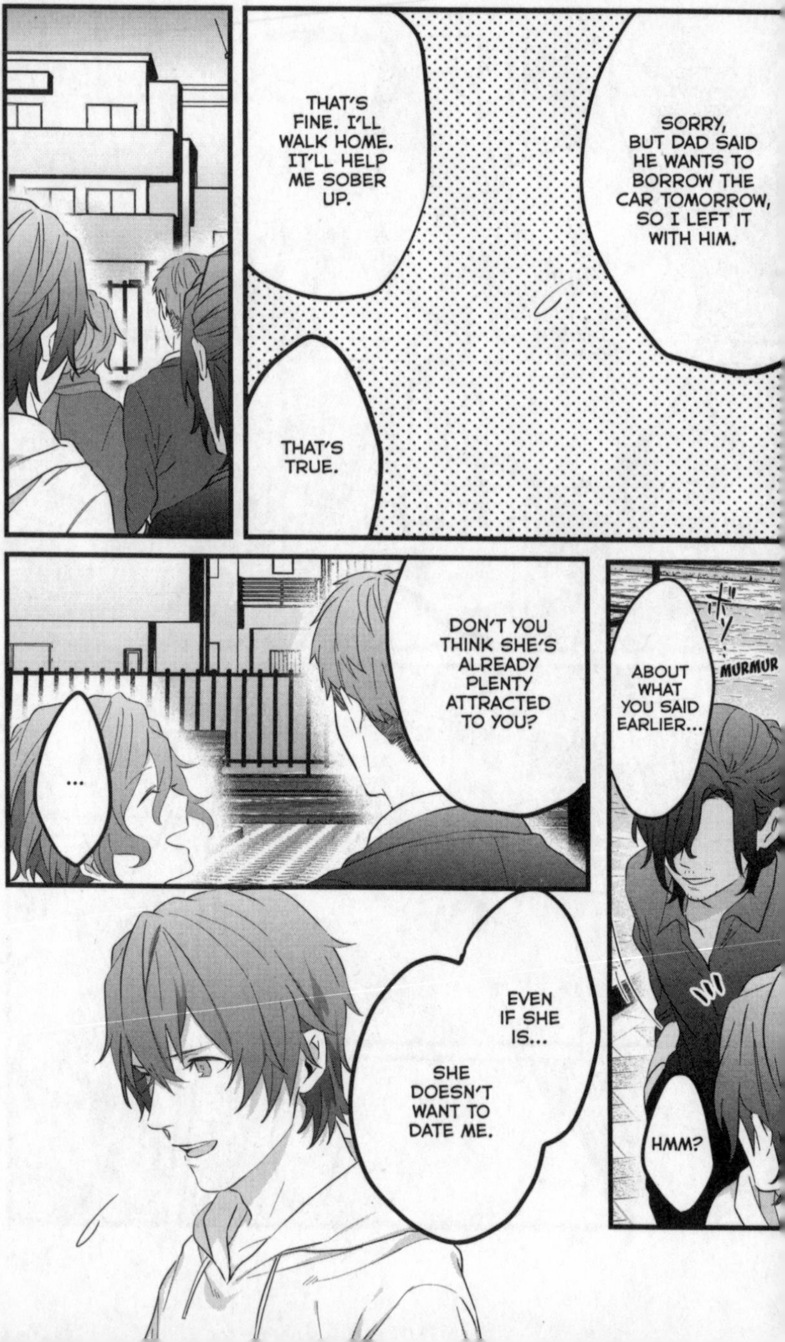
SORRY, BUT DAD SAID HE WANTS TO BORROW THE CAR TOMORROW, SO I LEFT IT WITH HIM.
THAT'S FINE. I'LL WALK HOME. IT'LL HELP ME SOBER UP.
THAT'S TRUE.
ABOUT WHAT YOU SAID EARLIER...
MURMUR
HMM?
DON'T YOU THINK SHE'S ALREADY PLENTY ATTRACTED TO YOU?
...
EVEN IF SHE IS...
SHE DOESN'T WANT TO DATE ME.

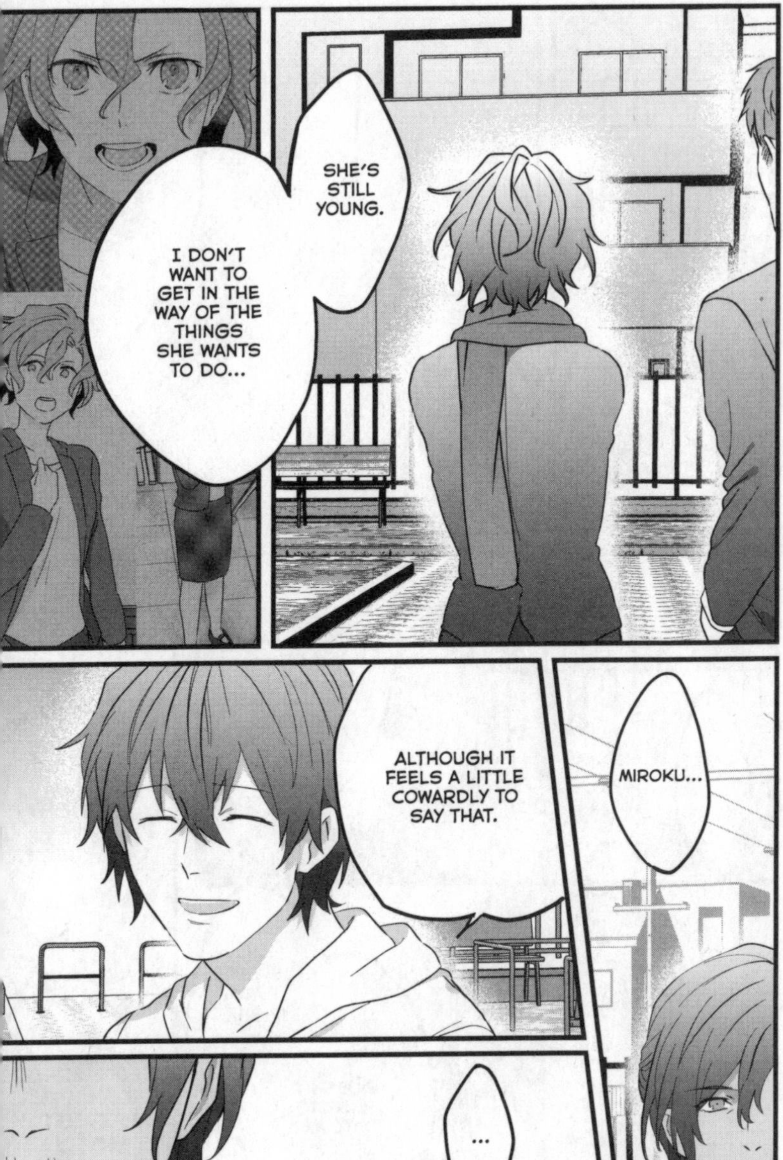
SHE'S STILL YOUNG.
I DON'T WANT TO GET IN THE WAY OF THE THINGS SHE WANTS TO DO...
MIROKU...
ALTHOUGH IT FEELS A LITTLE COWARDLY TO SAY THAT.
...

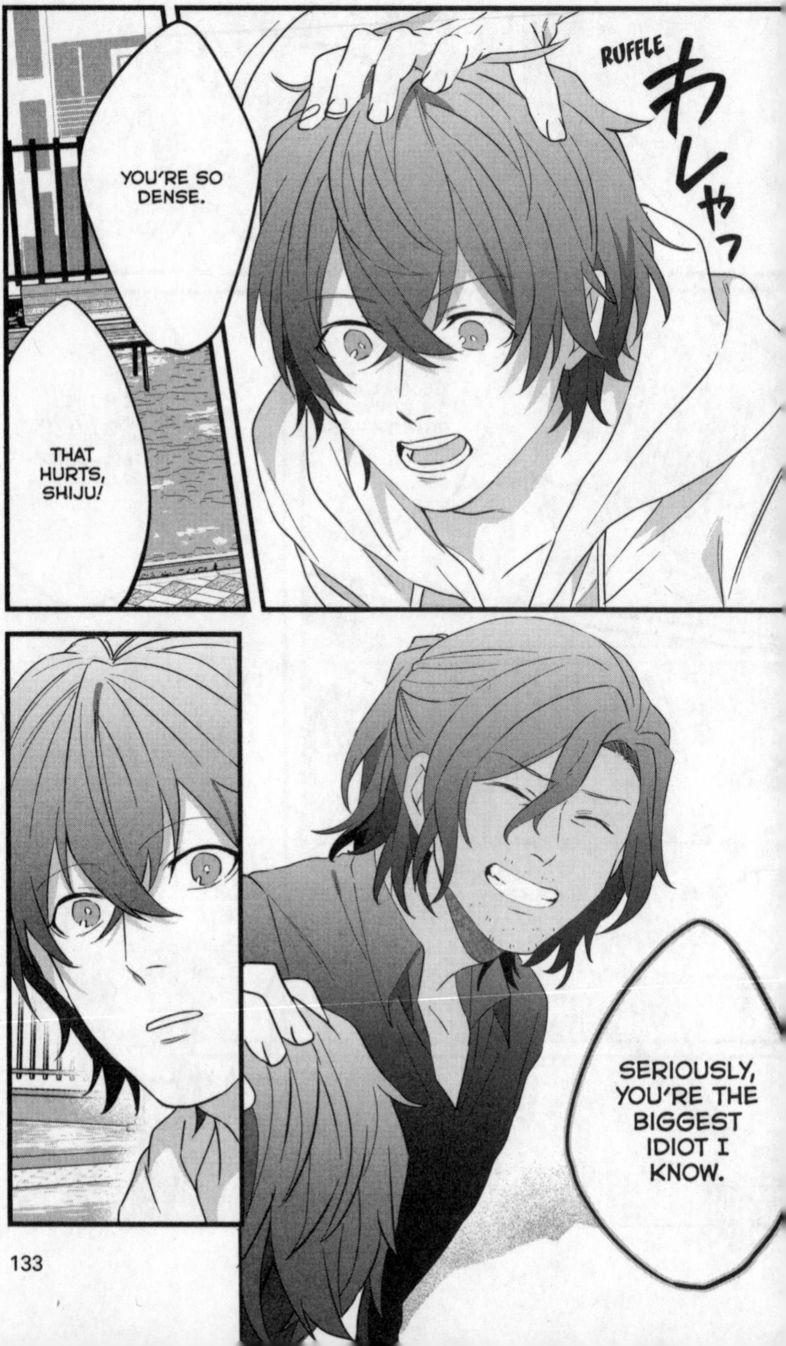
RUFFLE
わしゃっ
YOU'RE SO DENSE.
THAT HURTS, SHIJU!
SERIOUSLY, YOU'RE THE BIGGEST IDIOT I KNOW.

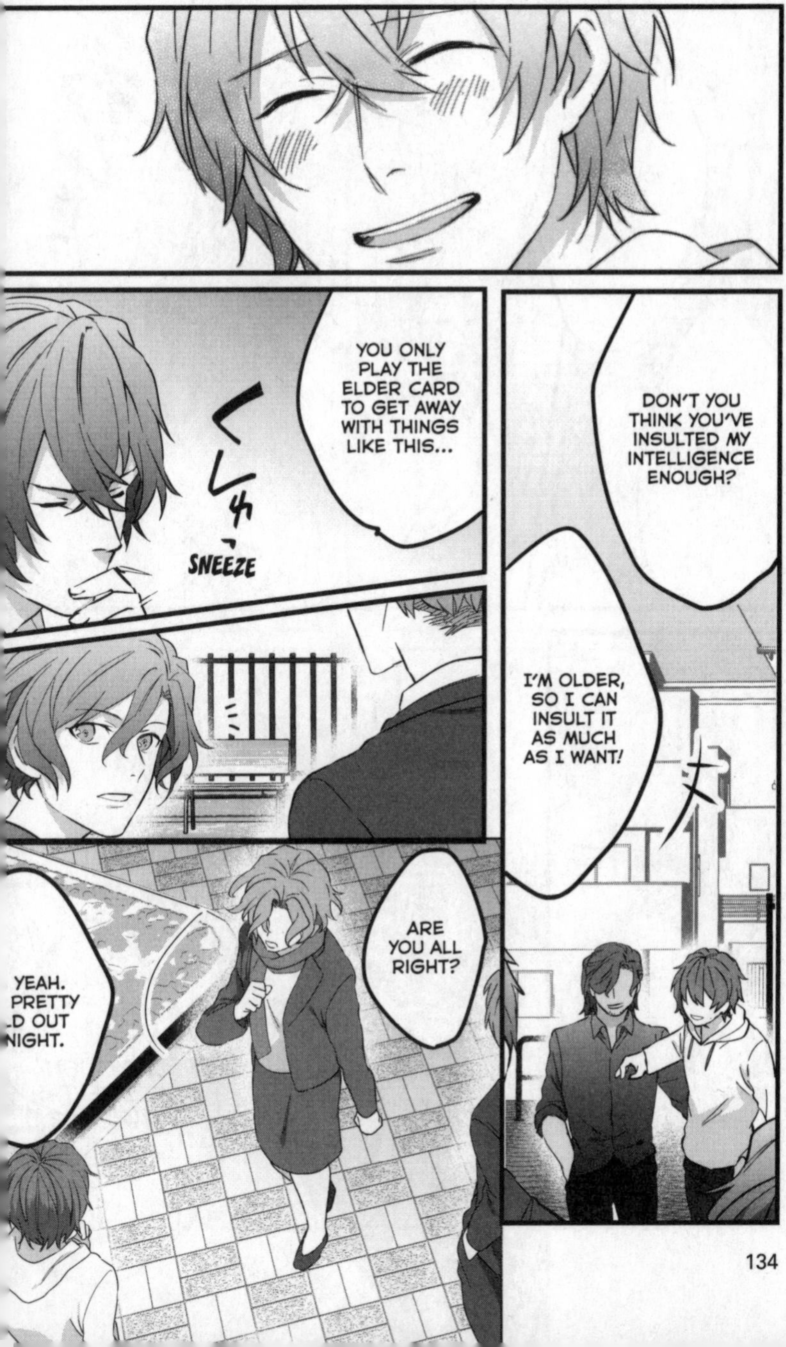
DON'T YOU THINK YOU'VE INSULTED MY INTELLIGENCE ENOUGH?
I'M OLDER, SO I CAN INSULT IT AS MUCH AS I WANT!
YOU ONLY PLAY THE ELDER CARD TO GET AWAY WITH THINGS LIKE THIS...
SNEEZE
ARE YOU ALL RIGHT?
YEAH. PRETTY LD OUT NIGHT.

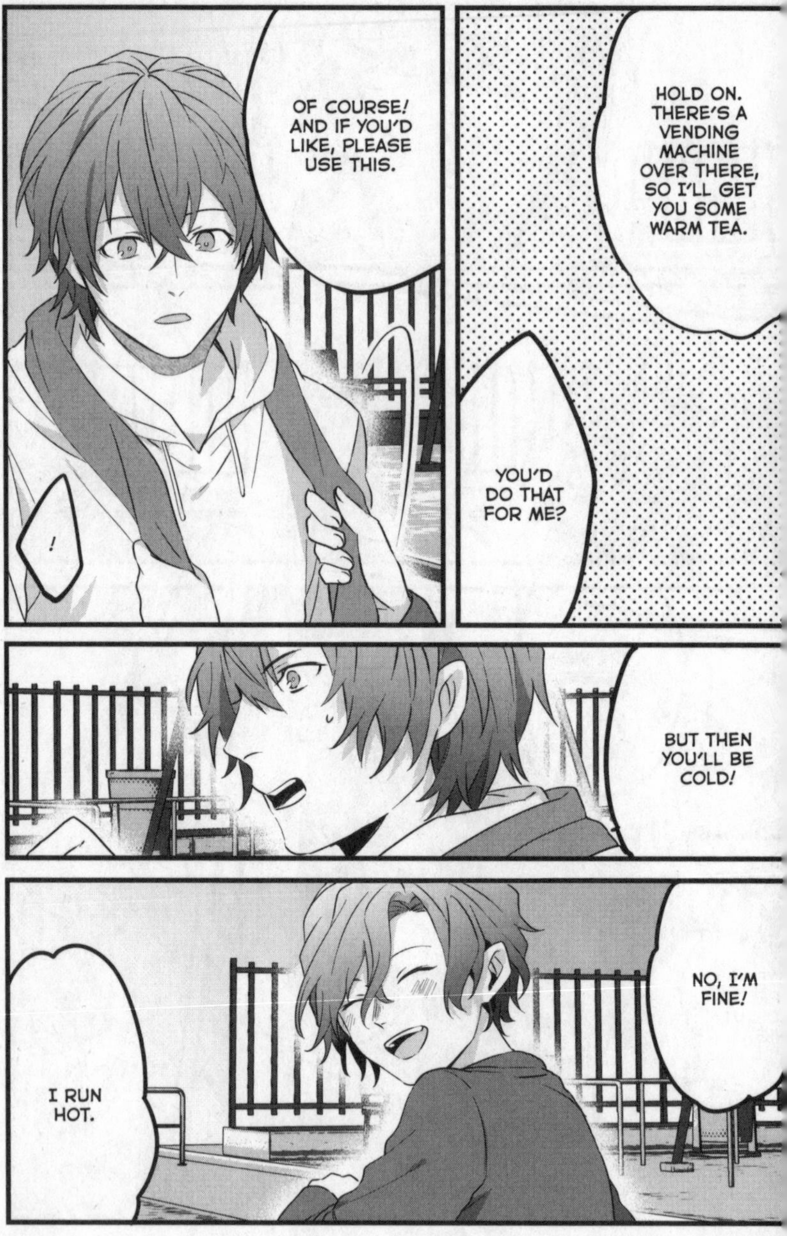
HOLD ON. THERE'S A VENDING MACHINE OVER THERE, SO I'LL GET YOU SOME WARM TEA.
YOU'D DO THAT FOR ME?
OF COURSE! AND IF YOU'D LIKE, PLEASE USE THIS.
!
BUT THEN YOU'LL BE COLD!
NO, I'M FINE!
I RUN HOT.

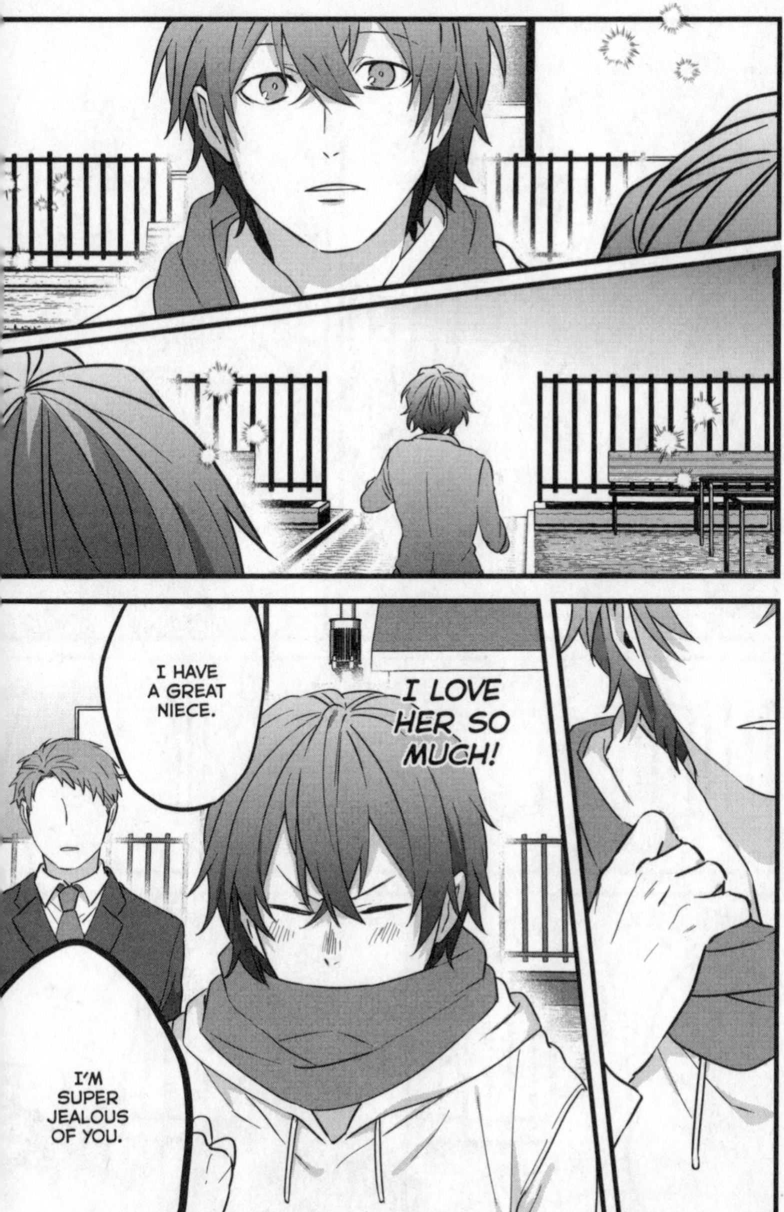
I HAVE A GREAT NIECE.
I LOVE HER SO MUCH!
I'M SUPER JEALOUS OF YOU.

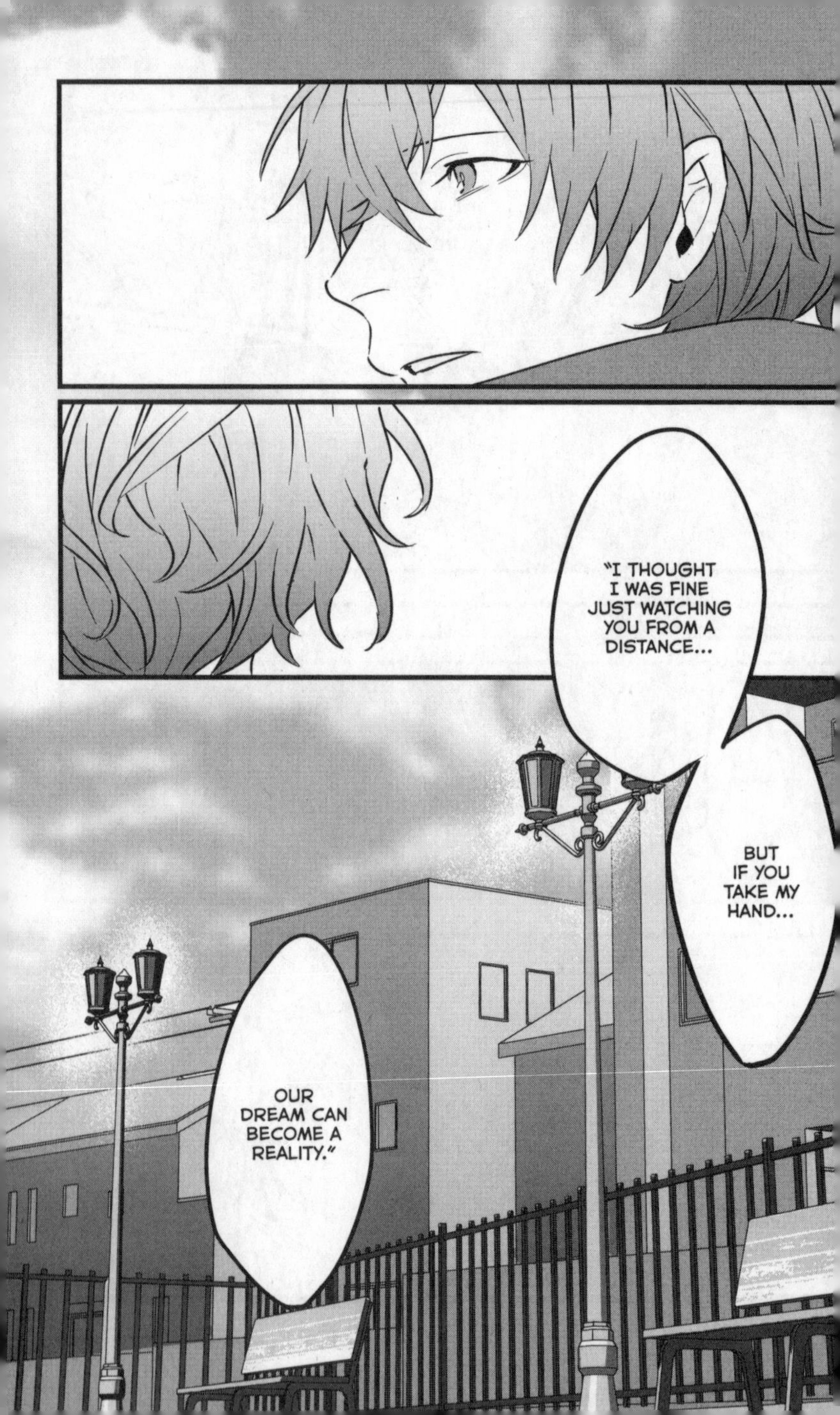
"I THOUGHT I WAS FINE JUST WATCHING YOU FROM A DISTANCE...
BUT IF YOU TAKE MY HAND...
OUR DREAM CAN BECOME A REALITY."

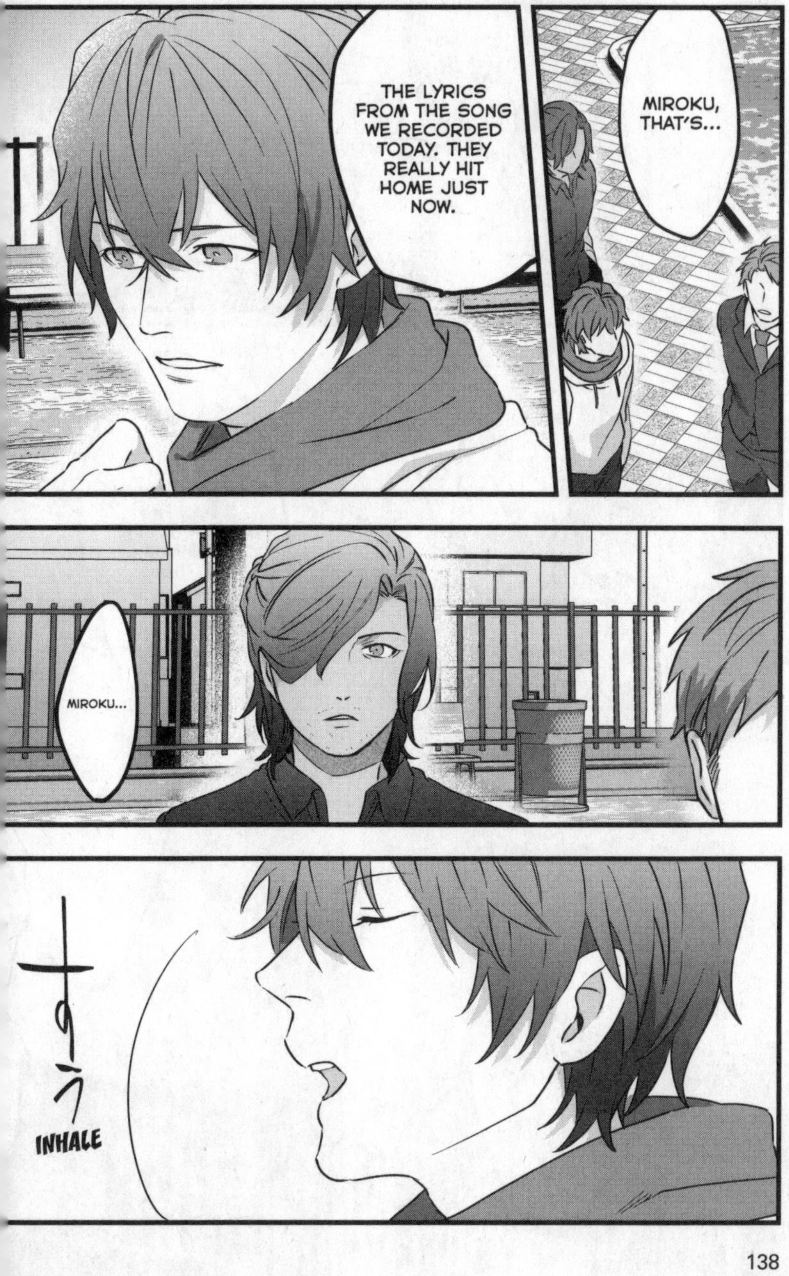
MIROKU, THAT'S...
THE LYRICS FROM THE SONG WE RECORDED TODAY. THEY REALLY HIT HOME JUST NOW.
MIROKU...
すう
INHALE

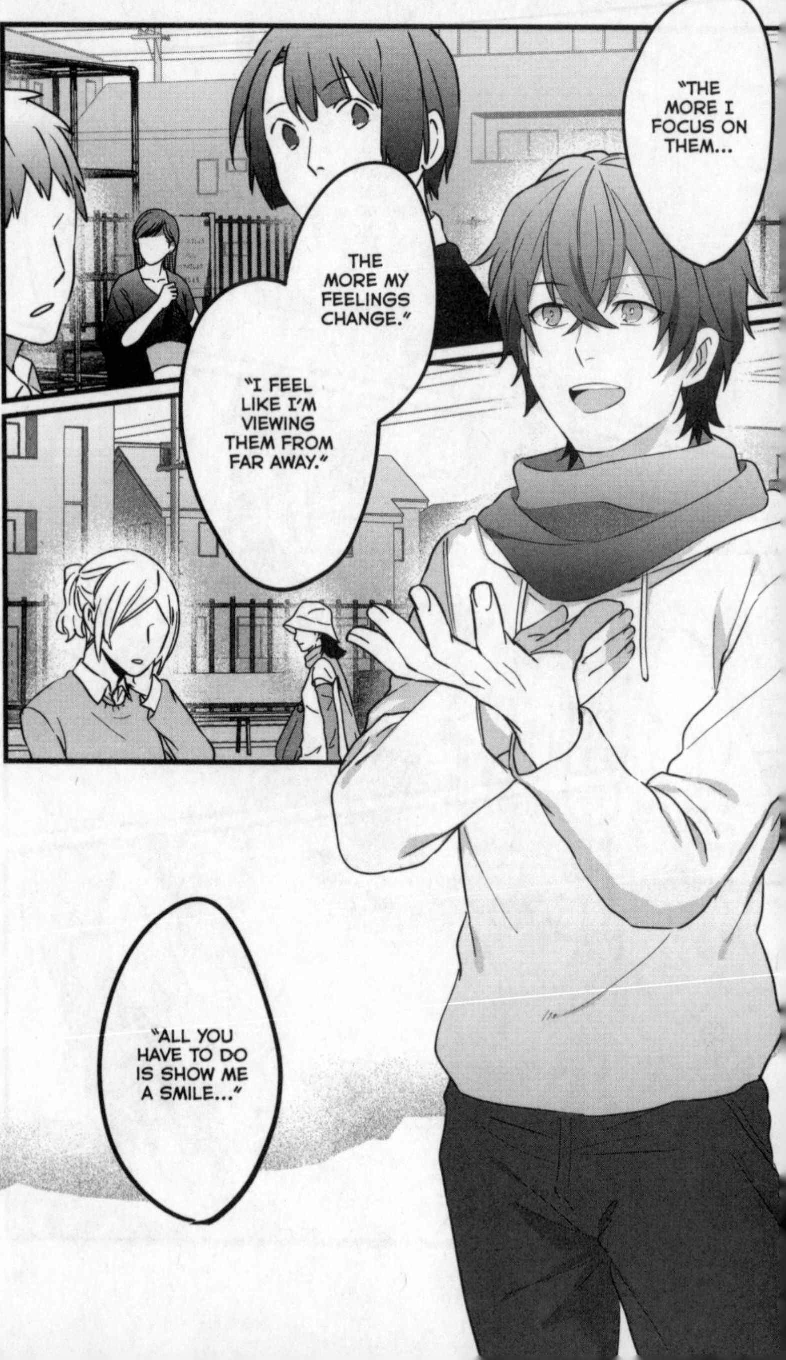
"THE MORE I FOCUS ON THEM...
THE MORE MY FEELINGS CHANGE."
"I FEEL LIKE I'M VIEWING THEM FROM FAR AWAY."
"ALL YOU HAVE TO DO IS SHOW ME A SMILE..."

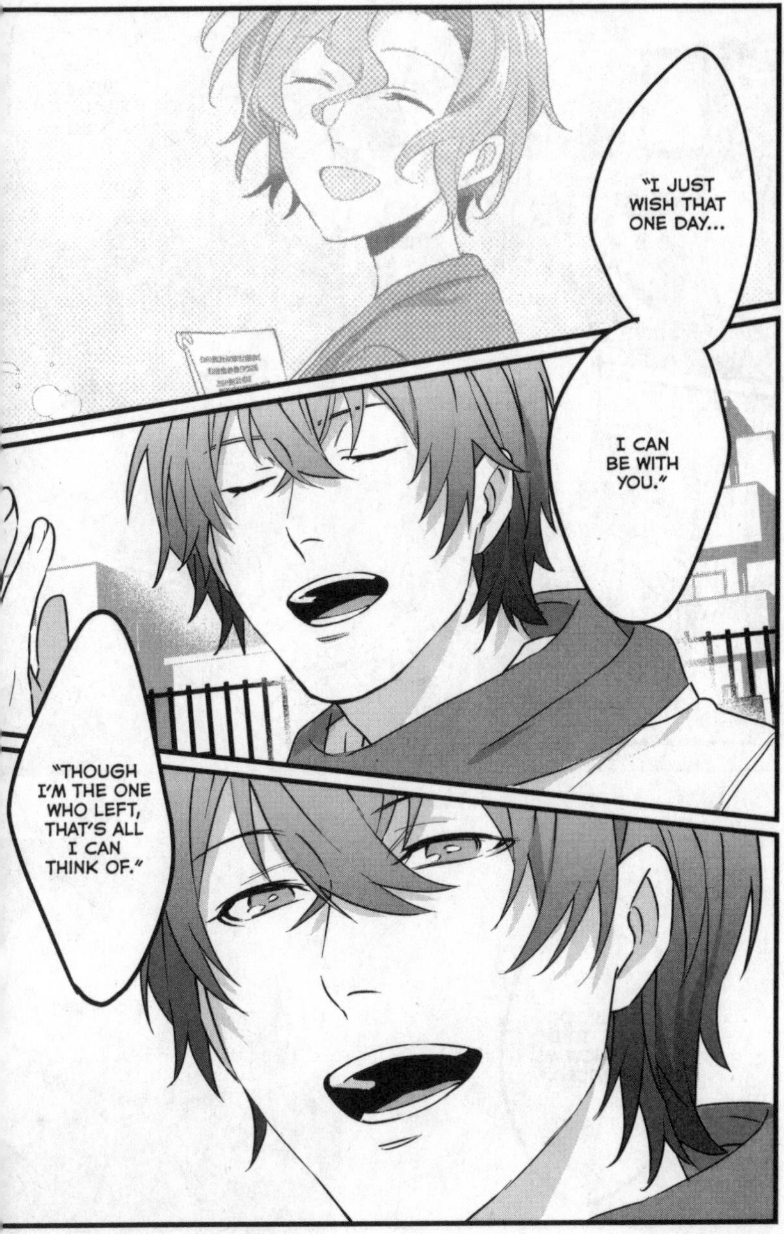
"I JUST WISH THAT ONE DAY...
I CAN BE WITH YOU."
"THOUGH I'M THE ONE WHO LEFT, THAT'S ALL I CAN THINK OF."

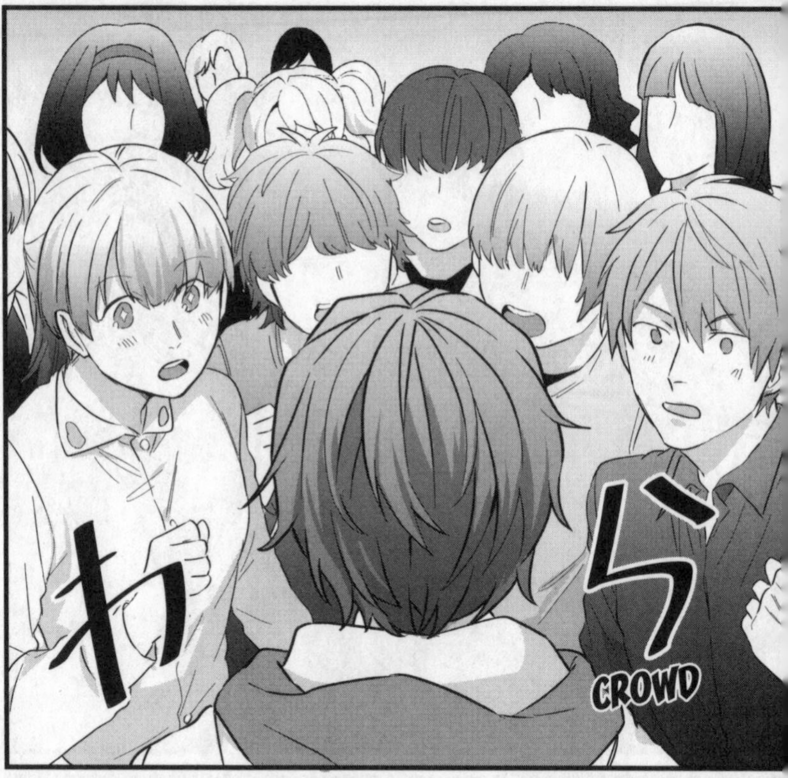
わら
CROWD
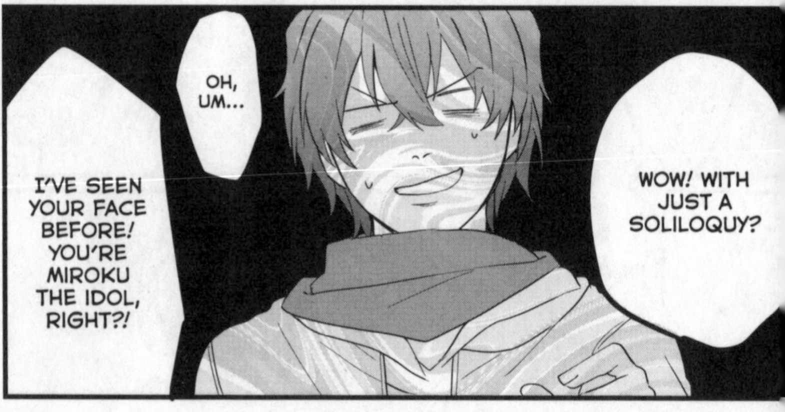
WOW! WITH JUST A SOLILOQUY?
OH, UM...
I'VE SEEN YOUR FACE BEFORE! YOU'RE MIROKU THE IDOL, RIGHT?!

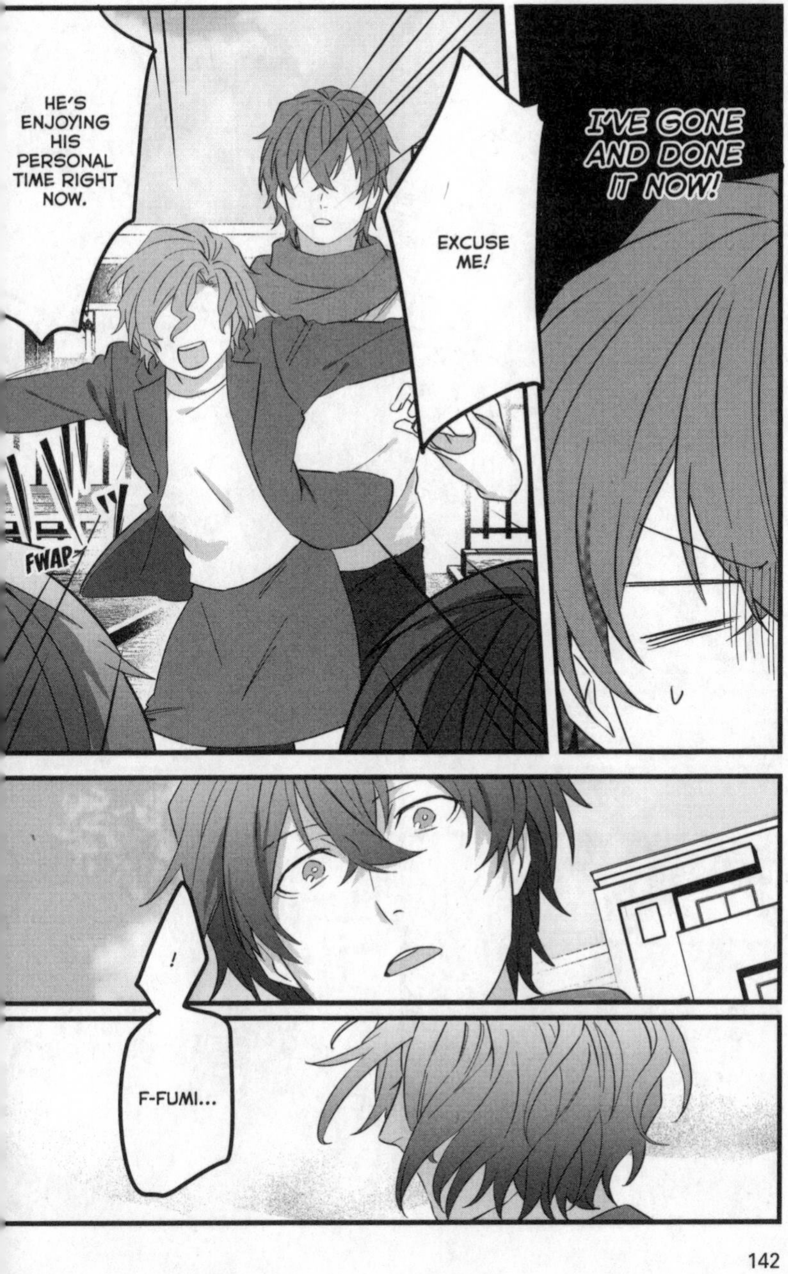
I'VE GONE AND DONE IT NOW!
EXCUSE ME!
HE'S ENJOYING HIS PERSONAL TIME RIGHT NOW.
FWAP
!
F-FUMI...

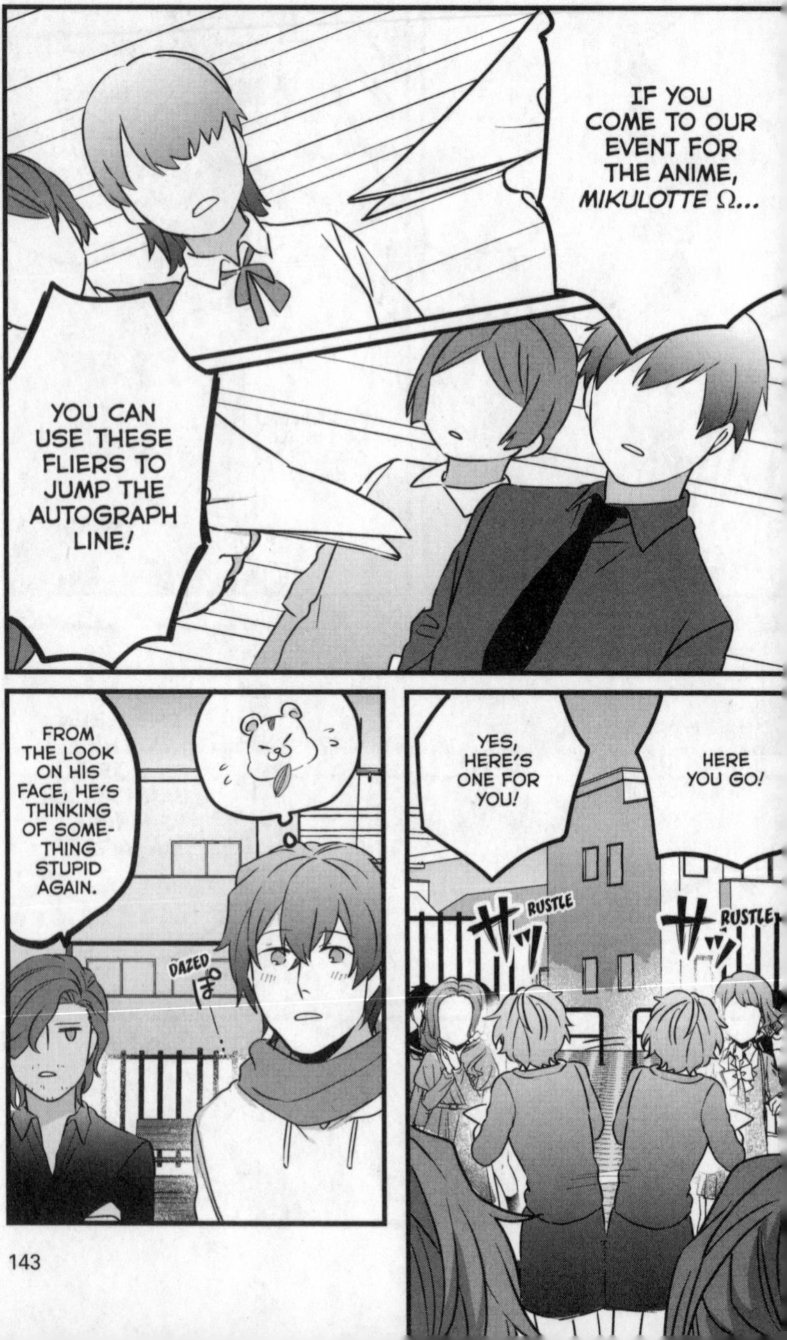
IF YOU COME TO OUR EVENT FOR THE ANIME, *MIKULOTTE Ω*...
YOU CAN USE THESE FLIERS TO JUMP THE AUTOGRAPH LINE!
HERE YOU GO!
YES, HERE'S ONE FOR YOU!
RUSTLE
RUSTLE
FROM THE LOOK ON HIS FACE, HE'S THINKING OF SOME-THING STUPID AGAIN.
DAZED

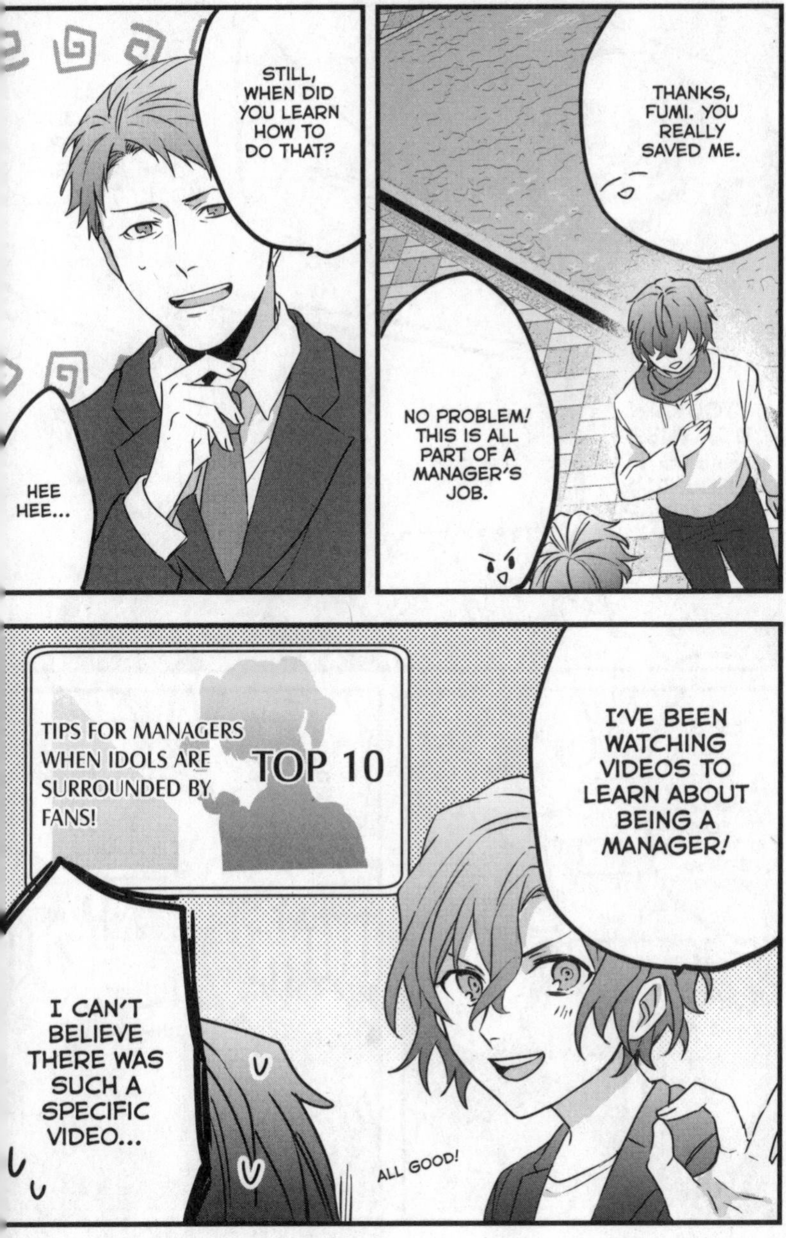
THANKS, FUMI. YOU REALLY SAVED ME.
NO PROBLEM! THIS IS ALL PART OF A MANAGER'S JOB.
STILL, WHEN DID YOU LEARN HOW TO DO THAT?
HEE HEE...
I'VE BEEN WATCHING VIDEOS TO LEARN ABOUT BEING A MANAGER!
TIPS FOR MANAGERS WHEN IDOLS ARE SURROUNDED BY FANS!
TOP 10
ALL GOOD!
I CAN'T BELIEVE THERE WAS SUCH A SPECIFIC VIDEO...

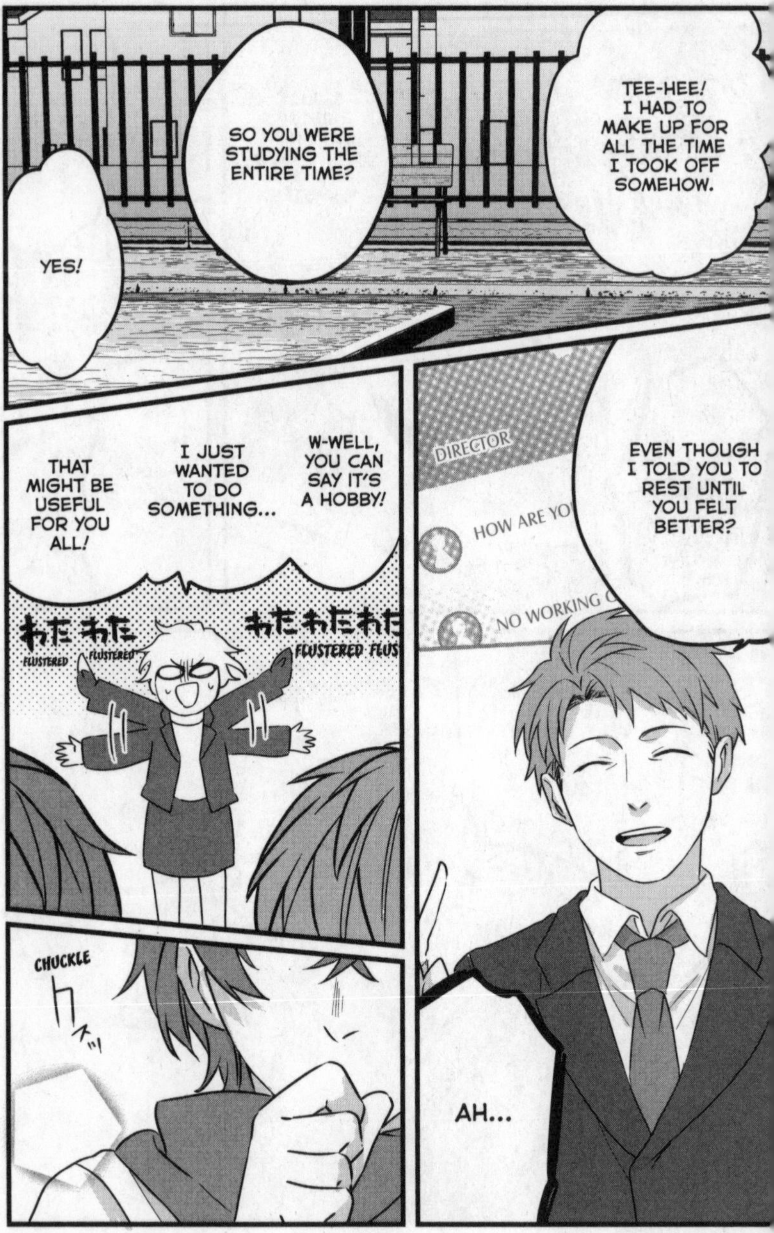
TEE-HEE! I HAD TO MAKE UP FOR ALL THE TIME I TOOK OFF SOMEHOW.
SO YOU WERE STUDYING THE ENTIRE TIME?
YES!
DIRECTOR
EVEN THOUGH I TOLD YOU TO REST UNTIL YOU FELT BETTER?
AH...
W-WELL, YOU CAN SAY IT'S A HOBBY!
I JUST WANTED TO DO SOMETHING...
THAT MIGHT BE USEFUL FOR YOU ALL!
わたわたわた
FLUSTERED FLUS
わた わた
FLUSTERED FLUSTERED
CHUCKLE
クスッ

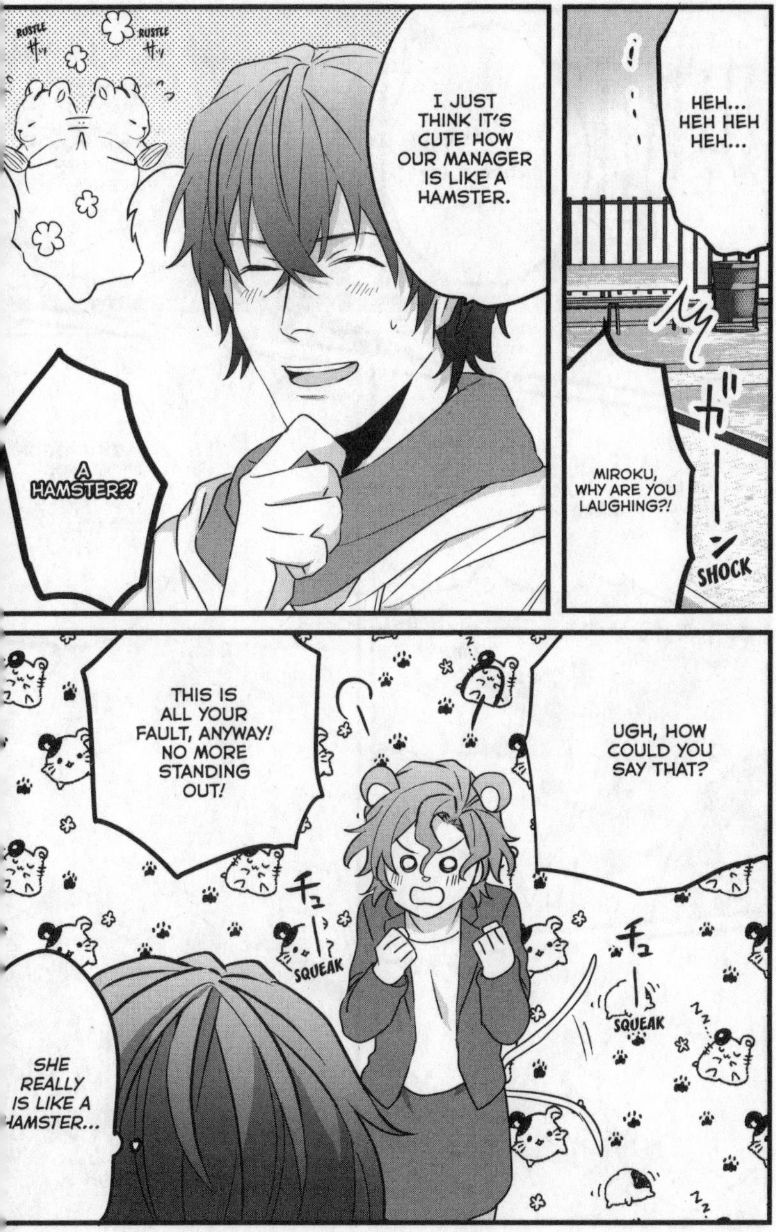
!
...
HEH... HEH HEH HEH...
MIROKU, WHY ARE YOU LAUGHING?!
SHOCK
RUSTLE
RUSTLE
I JUST THINK IT'S CUTE HOW OUR MANAGER IS LIKE A HAMSTER.
A HAMSTER?!
UGH, HOW COULD YOU SAY THAT?
SQUEAK
THIS IS ALL YOUR FAULT, ANYWAY! NO MORE STANDING OUT!
SQUEAK
SHE REALLY IS LIKE A HAMSTER...

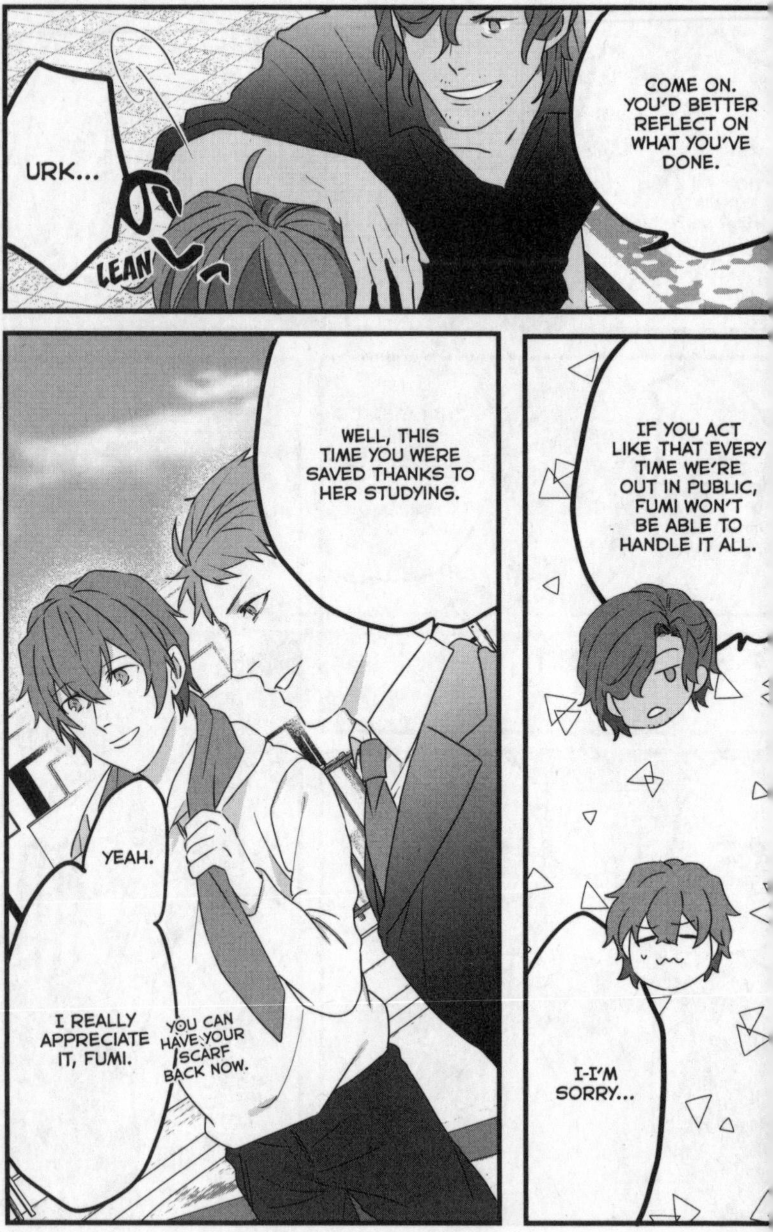
COME ON. YOU'D BETTER REFLECT ON WHAT YOU'VE DONE.
LEAN
URK...
IF YOU ACT LIKE THAT EVERY TIME WE'RE OUT IN PUBLIC, FUMI WON'T BE ABLE TO HANDLE IT ALL.
I-I'M SORRY...
WELL, THIS TIME YOU WERE SAVED THANKS TO HER STUDYING.
YEAH.
YOU CAN HAVE YOUR SCARF BACK NOW.
I REALLY APPRECIATE IT, FUMI.

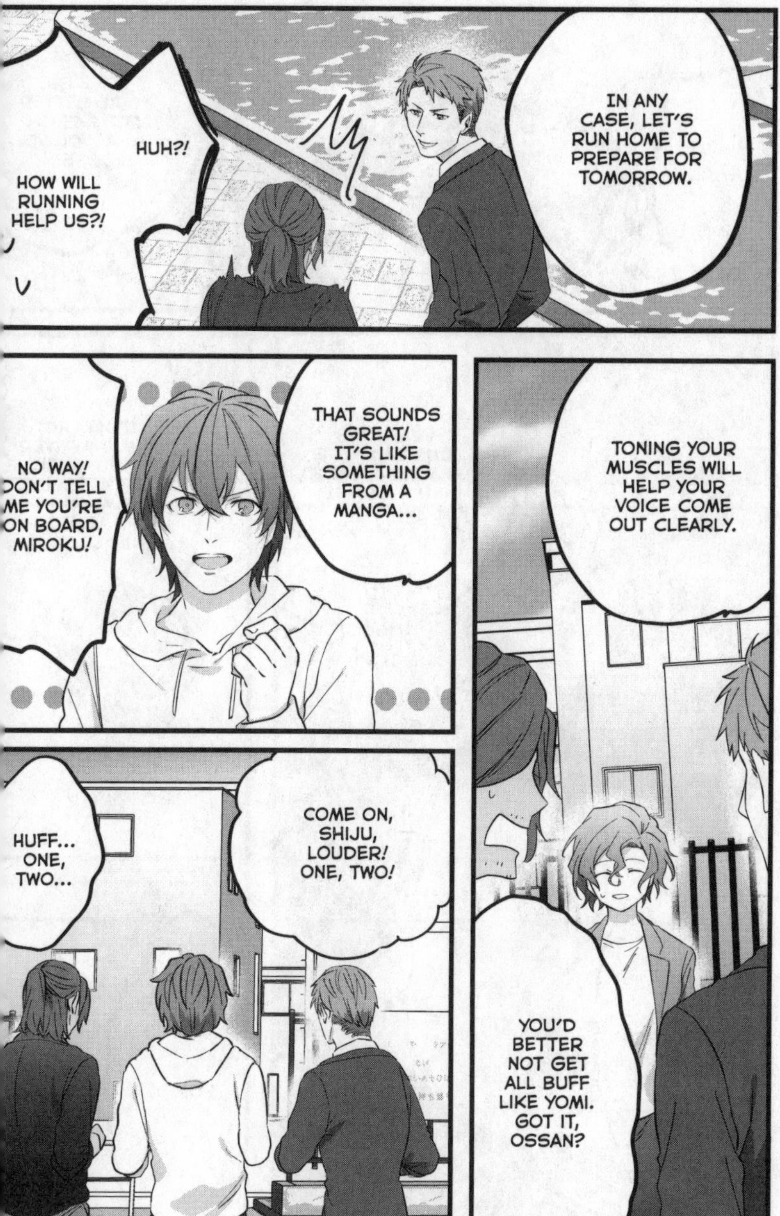
IN ANY CASE, LET'S RUN HOME TO PREPARE FOR TOMORROW.
HUH?!
HOW WILL RUNNING HELP US?!
TONING YOUR MUSCLES WILL HELP YOUR VOICE COME OUT CLEARLY.
YOU'D BETTER NOT GET ALL BUFF LIKE YOMI. GOT IT, OSSAN?
THAT SOUNDS GREAT! IT'S LIKE SOMETHING FROM A MANGA...
NO WAY! DON'T TELL ME YOU'RE ON BOARD, MIROKU!
COME ON, SHIJU, LOUDER! ONE, TWO!
HUFF... ONE, TWO...

Chapter 23

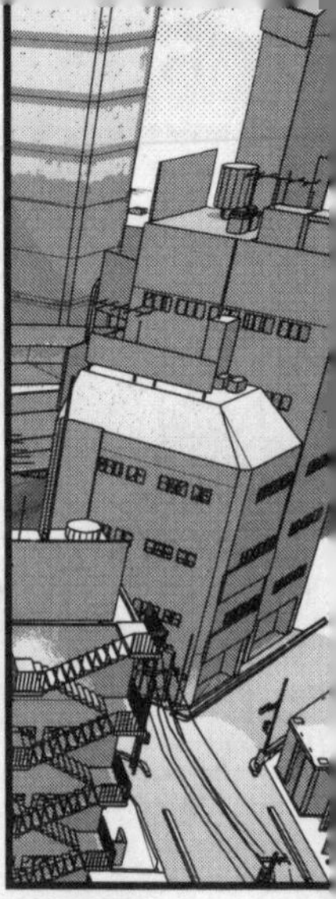

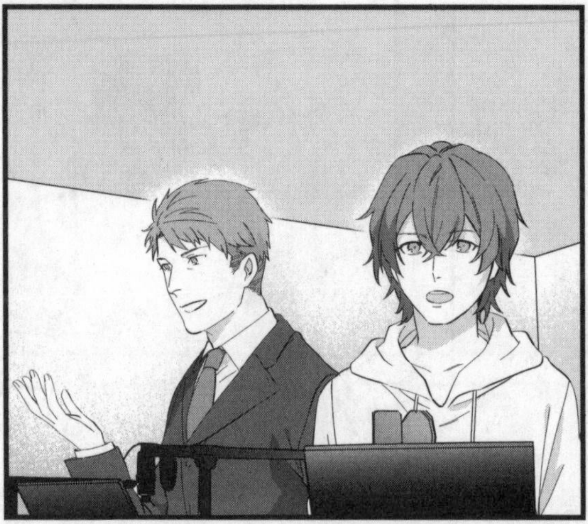

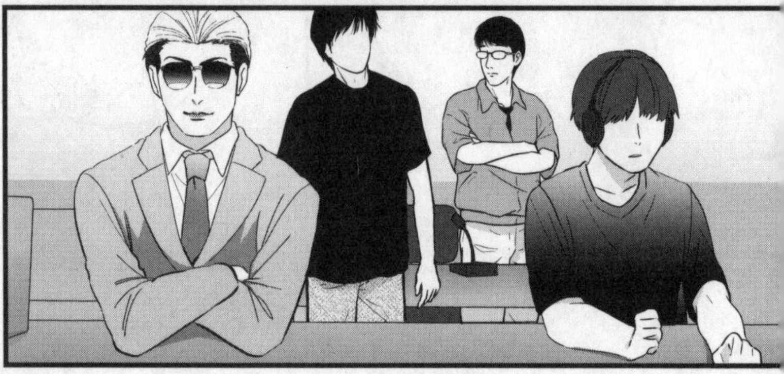

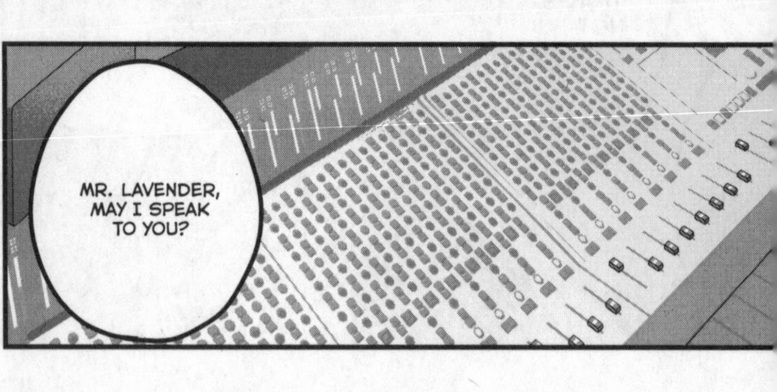
MR. LAVENDER, MAY I SPEAK TO YOU?

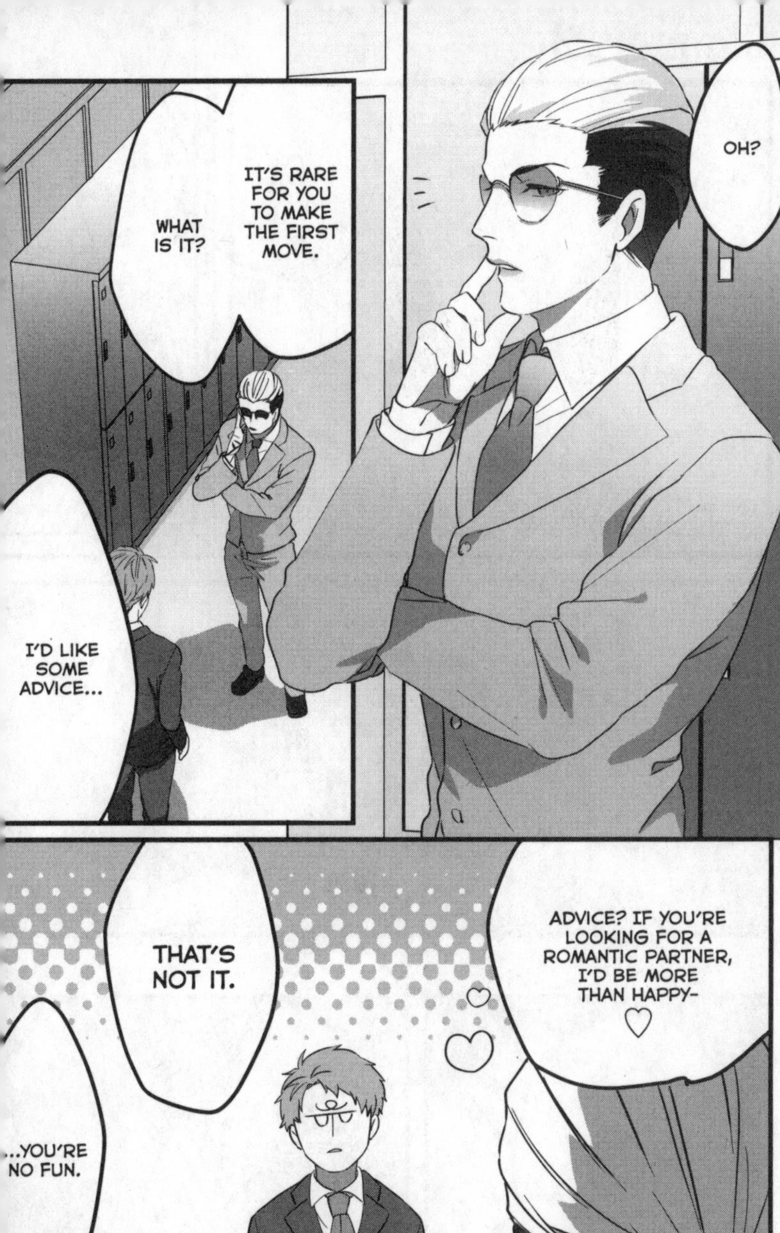
OH?
IT'S RARE FOR YOU TO MAKE THE FIRST MOVE.
WHAT IS IT?
I'D LIKE SOME ADVICE...
ADVICE? IF YOU'RE LOOKING FOR A ROMANTIC PARTNER, I'D BE MORE THAN HAPPY- ♡
THAT'S NOT IT.
...YOU'RE NO FUN.

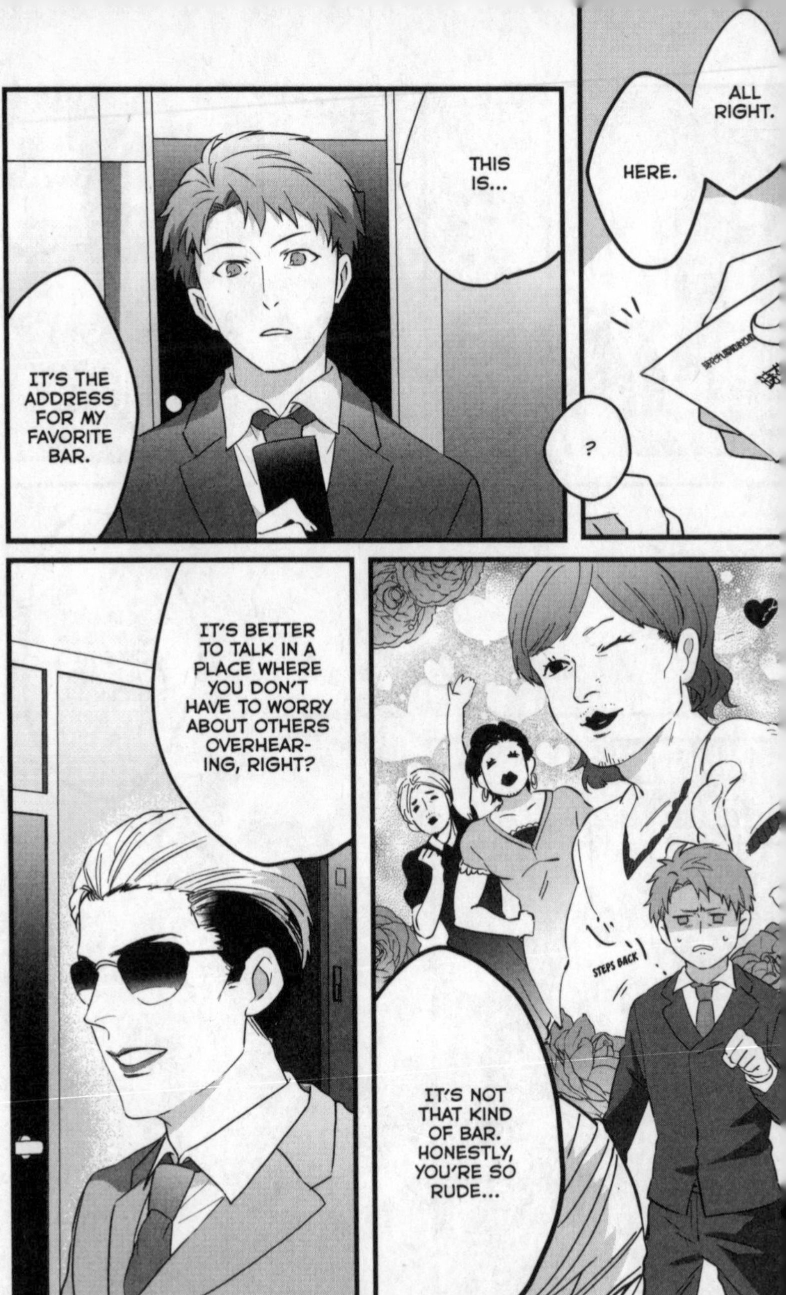
ALL RIGHT.
HERE.
?
THIS IS...
IT'S THE ADDRESS FOR MY FAVORITE BAR.
STEPS BACK
IT'S NOT THAT KIND OF BAR. HONESTLY, YOU'RE SO RUDE...
IT'S BETTER TO TALK IN A PLACE WHERE YOU DON'T HAVE TO WORRY ABOUT OTHERS OVERHEAR-ING, RIGHT?

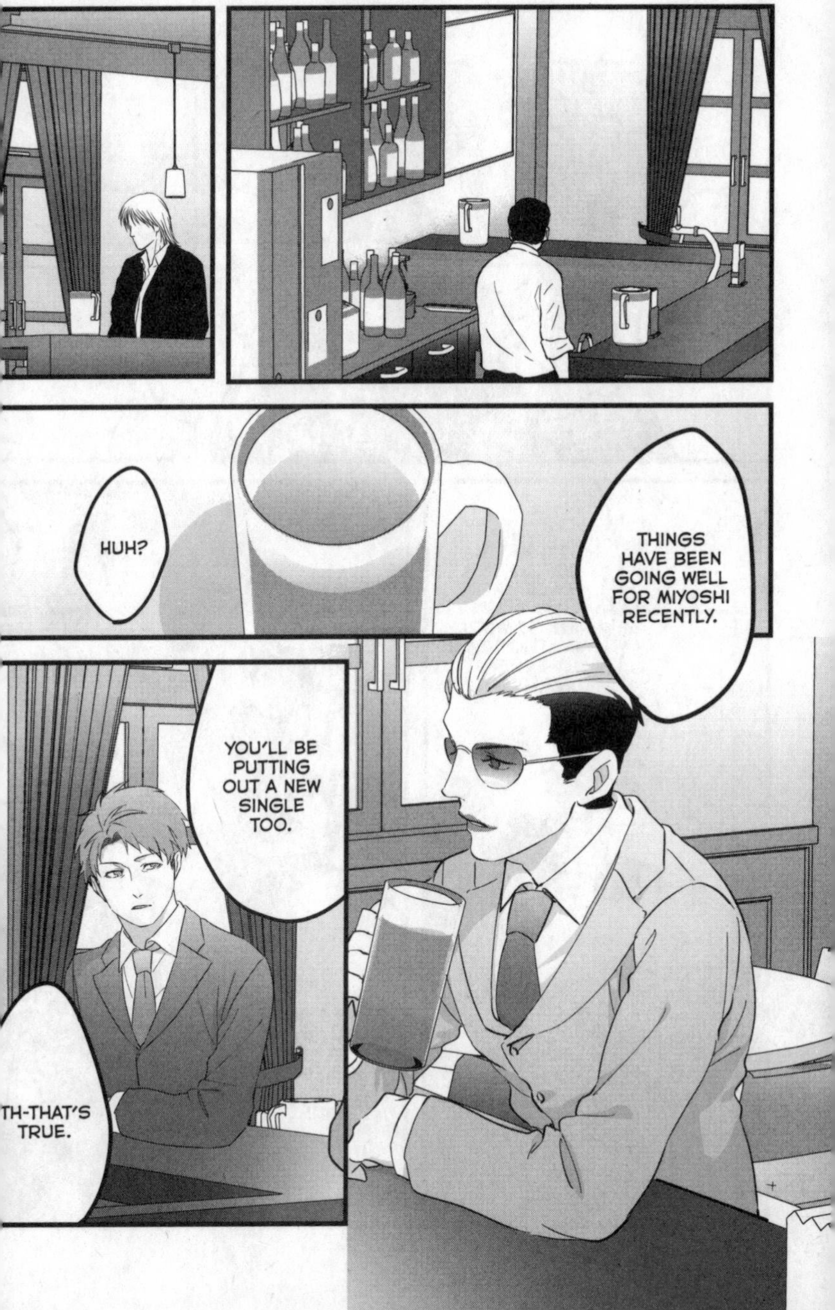
THINGS HAVE BEEN GOING WELL FOR MIYOSHI RECENTLY.
HUH?
YOU'LL BE PUTTING OUT A NEW SINGLE TOO.
TH-THAT'S TRUE.

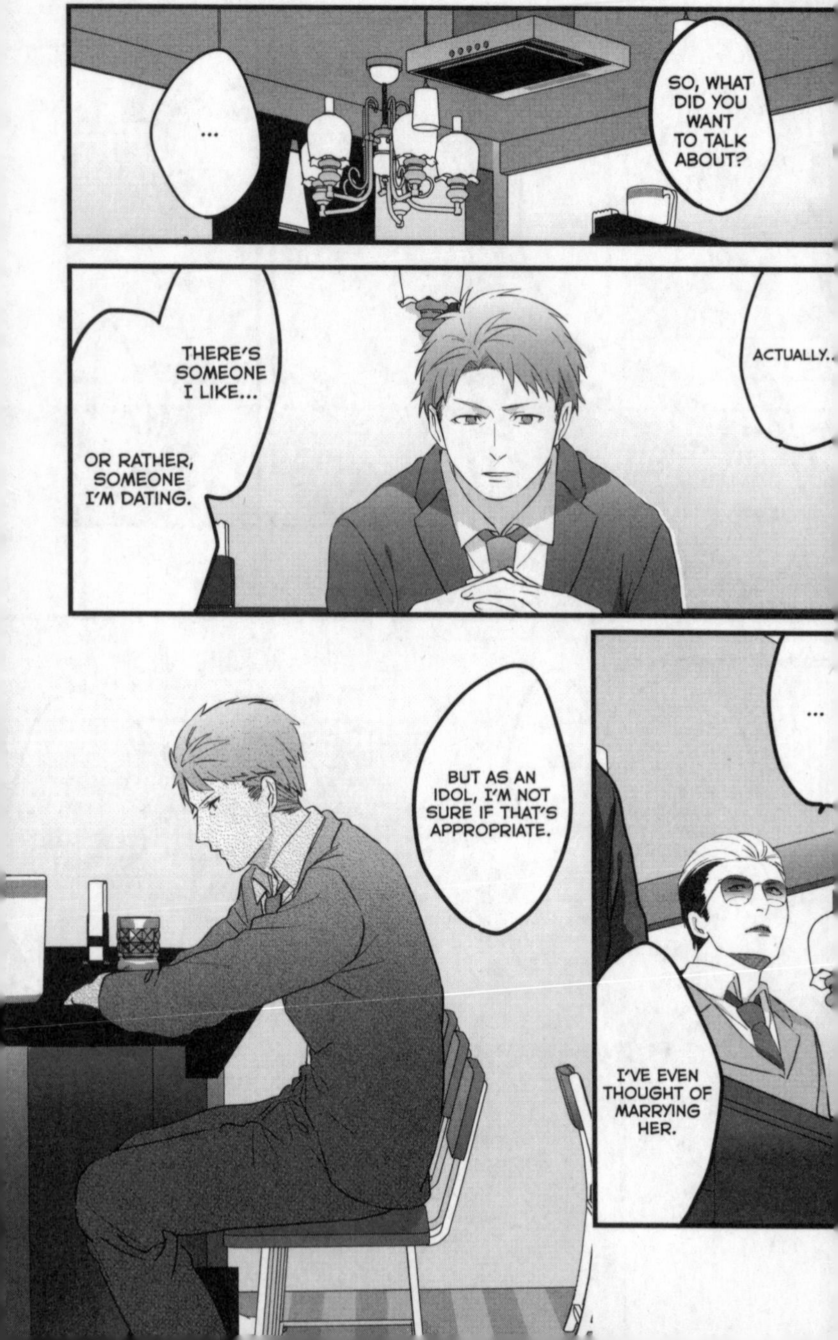
SO, WHAT DID YOU WANT TO TALK ABOUT?
...
ACTUALLY...
THERE'S SOMEONE I LIKE...
OR RATHER, SOMEONE I'M DATING.
...
I'VE EVEN THOUGHT OF MARRYING HER.
BUT AS AN IDOL, I'M NOT SURE IF THAT'S APPROPRIATE.

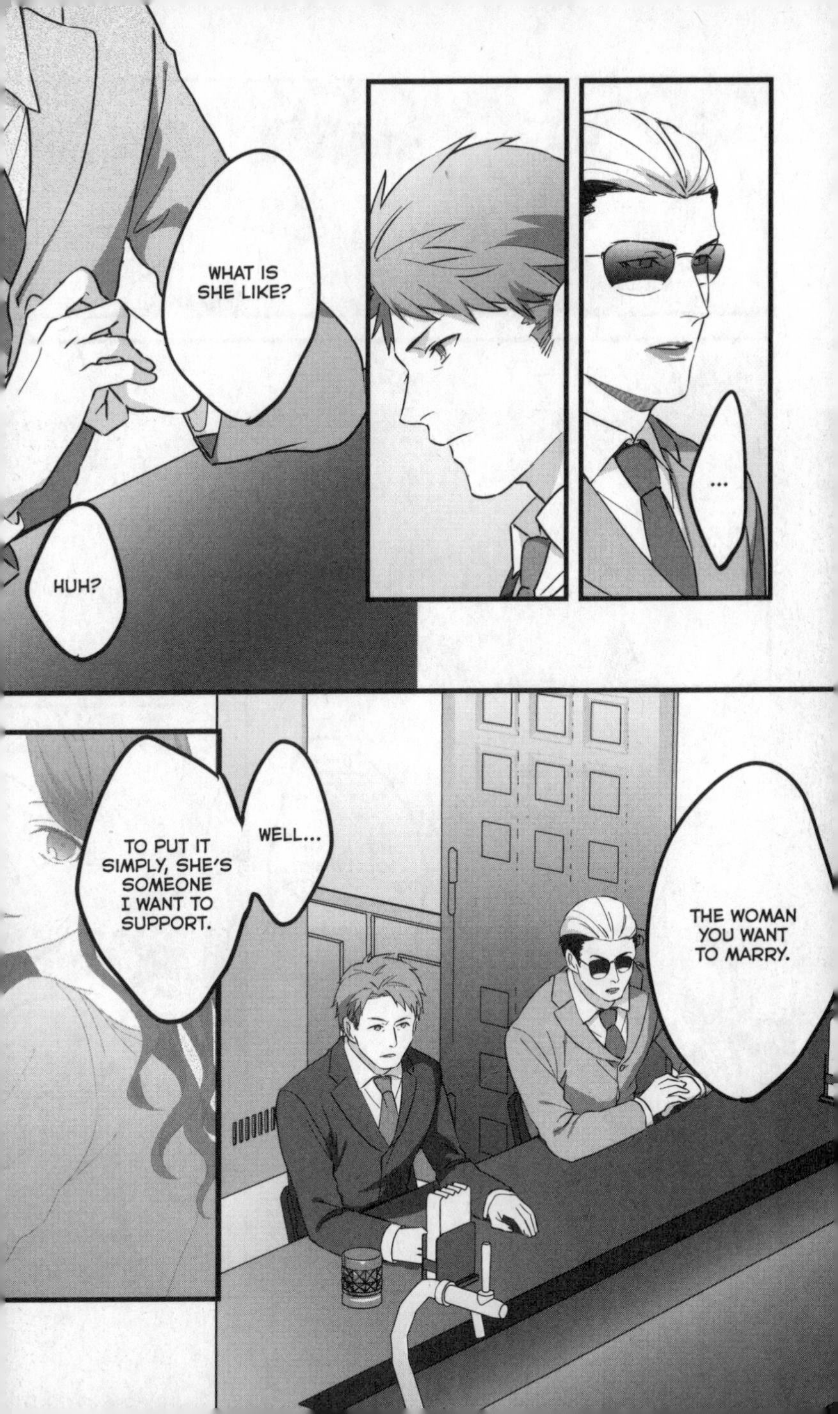
...
WHAT IS SHE LIKE?
HUH?
THE WOMAN YOU WANT TO MARRY.
WELL...
TO PUT IT SIMPLY, SHE'S SOMEONE I WANT TO SUPPORT.

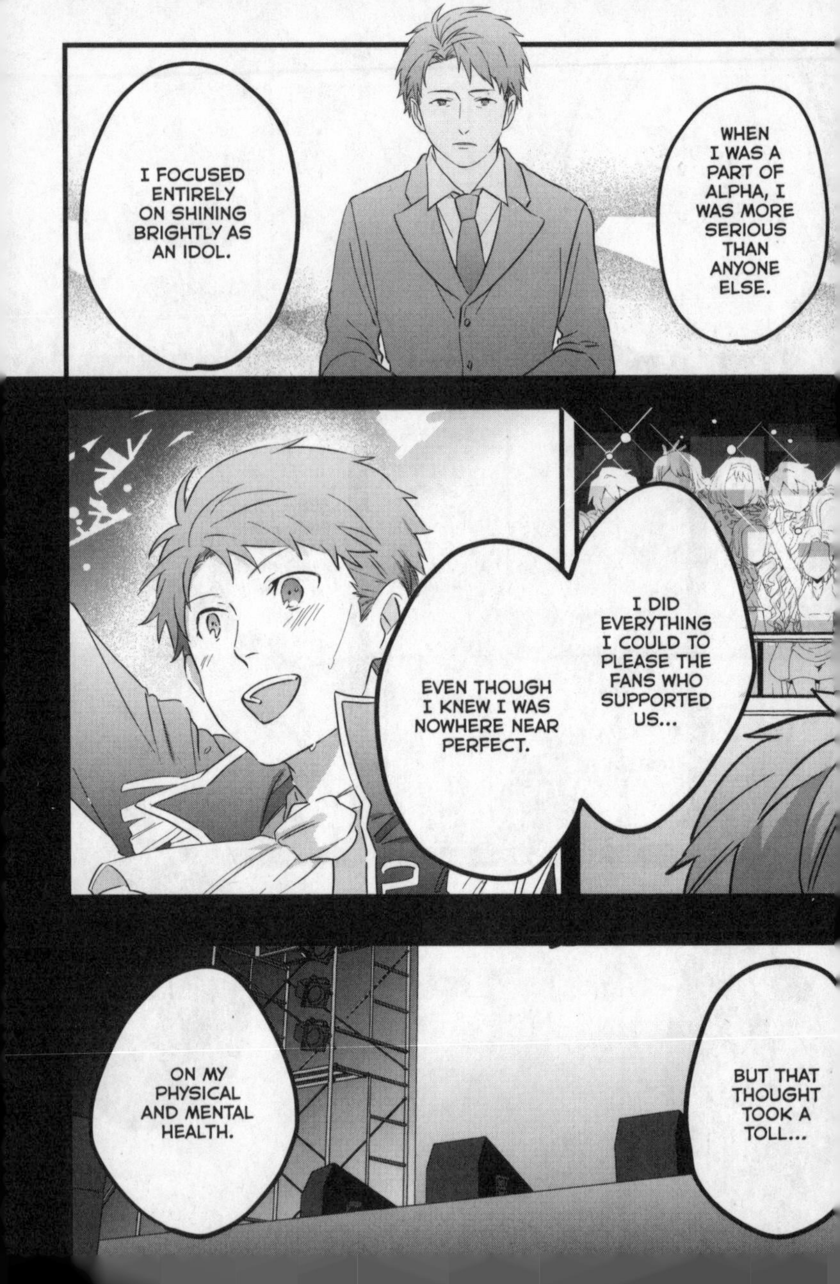
WHEN I WAS A PART OF ALPHA, I WAS MORE SERIOUS THAN ANYONE ELSE.
I FOCUSED ENTIRELY ON SHINING BRIGHTLY AS AN IDOL.
I DID EVERYTHING I COULD TO PLEASE THE FANS WHO SUPPORTED US...
EVEN THOUGH I KNEW I WAS NOWHERE NEAR PERFECT.
BUT THAT THOUGHT TOOK A TOLL...
ON MY PHYSICAL AND MENTAL HEALTH.

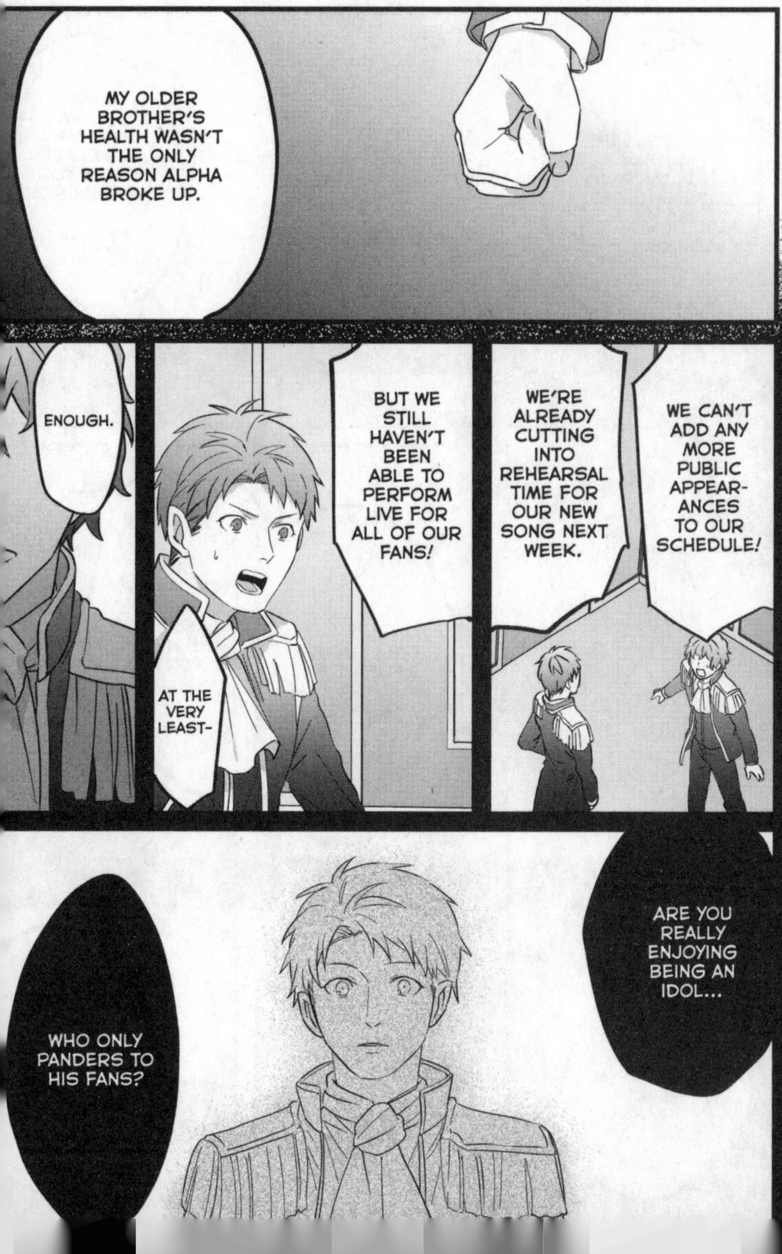
MY OLDER BROTHER'S HEALTH WASN'T THE ONLY REASON ALPHA BROKE UP.
WE CAN'T ADD ANY MORE PUBLIC APPEAR-ANCES TO OUR SCHEDULE!
WE'RE ALREADY CUTTING INTO REHEARSAL TIME FOR OUR NEW SONG NEXT WEEK.
BUT WE STILL HAVEN'T BEEN ABLE TO PERFORM LIVE FOR ALL OF OUR FANS!
AT THE VERY LEAST-
ENOUGH.
ARE YOU REALLY ENJOYING BEING AN IDOL...
WHO ONLY PANDERS TO HIS FANS?

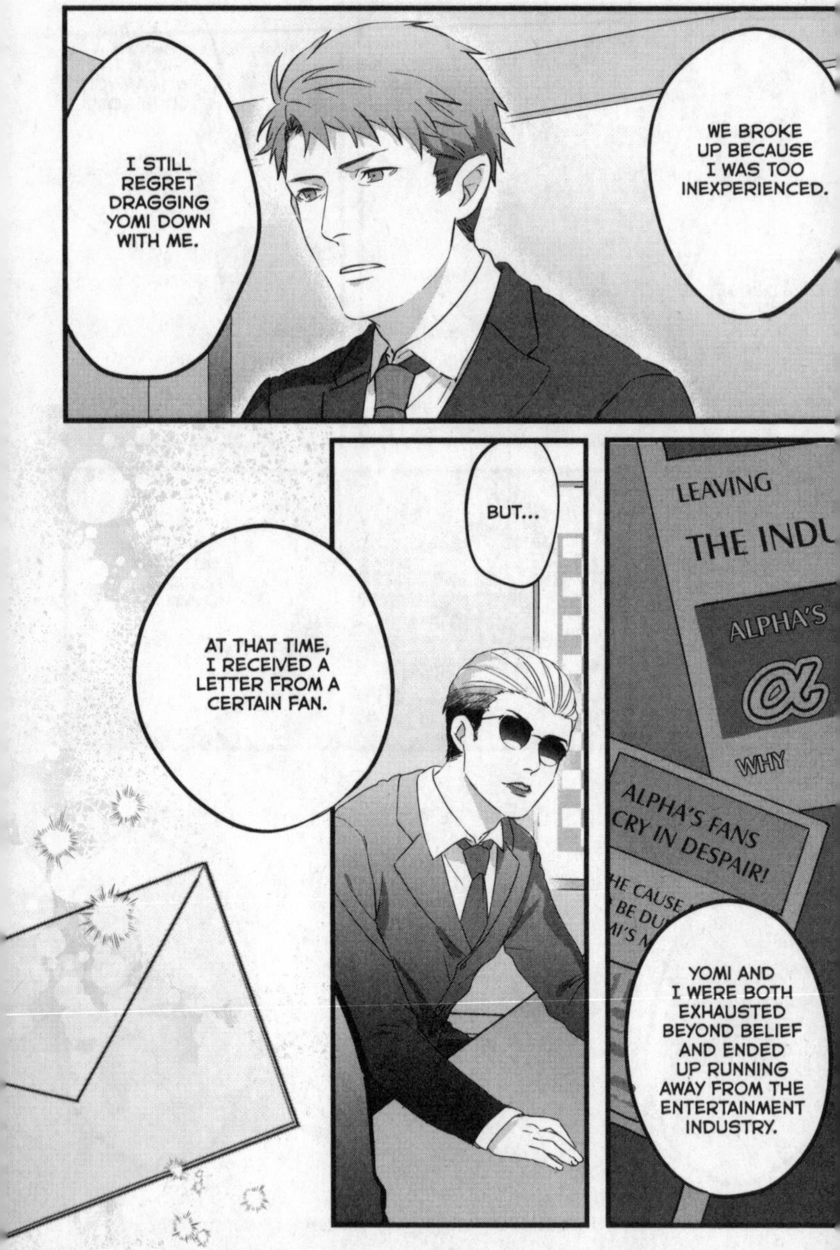

WE BROKE UP BECAUSE I WAS TOO INEXPERIENCED.
I STILL REGRET DRAGGING YOMI DOWN WITH ME.
LEAVING
ALPHA'S
WHY
ALPHA'S FANS CRY IN DESPAIR!
YOMI AND I WERE BOTH EXHAUSTED BEYOND BELIEF AND ENDED UP RUNNING AWAY FROM THE ENTERTAINMENT INDUSTRY.
BUT...
AT THAT TIME, I RECEIVED A LETTER FROM A CERTAIN FAN.

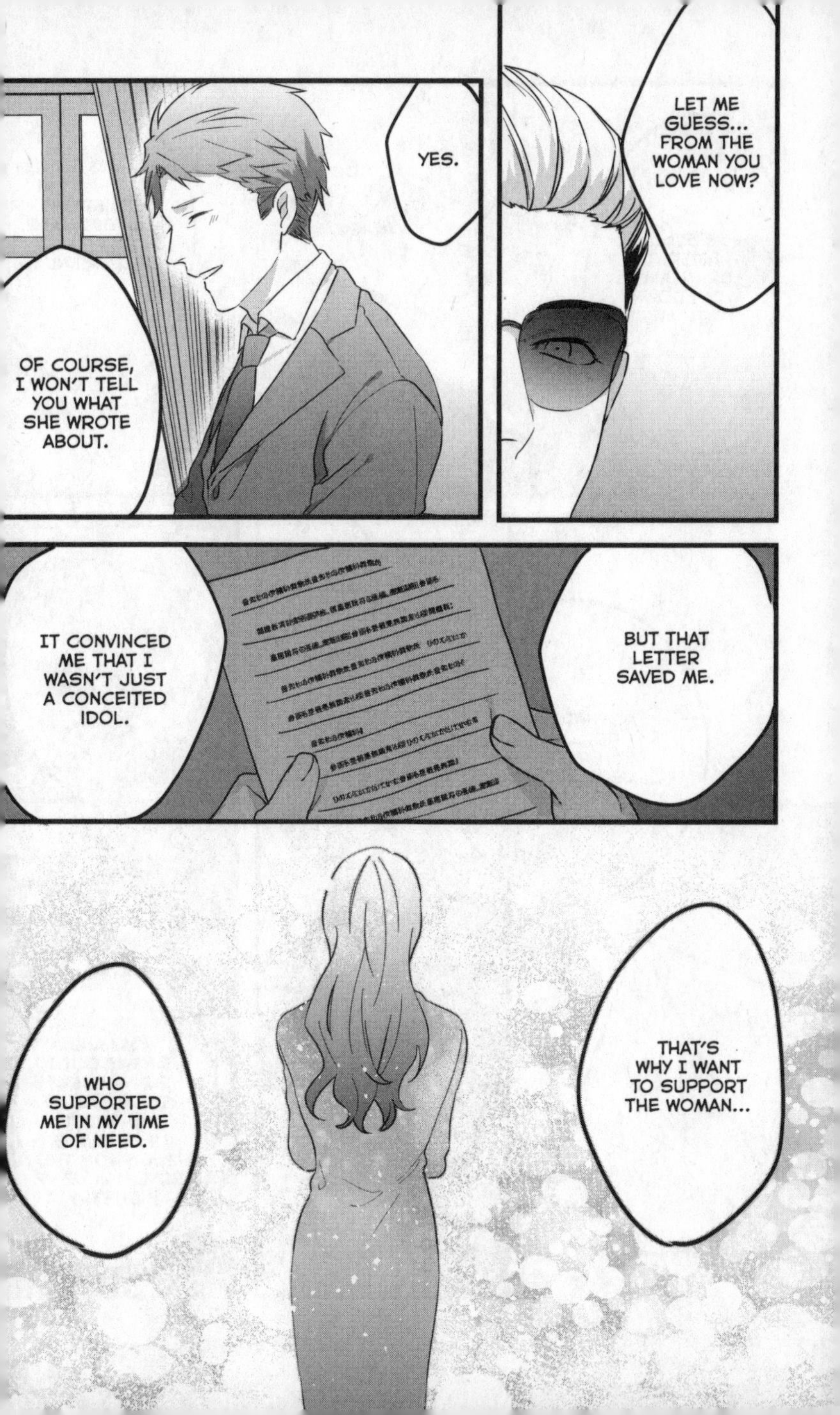
LET ME GUESS... FROM THE WOMAN YOU LOVE NOW?
YES.
OF COURSE, I WON'T TELL YOU WHAT SHE WROTE ABOUT.
BUT THAT LETTER SAVED ME.
IT CONVINCED ME THAT I WASN'T JUST A CONCEITED IDOL.
THAT'S WHY I WANT TO SUPPORT THE WOMAN...
WHO SUPPORTED ME IN MY TIME OF NEED.

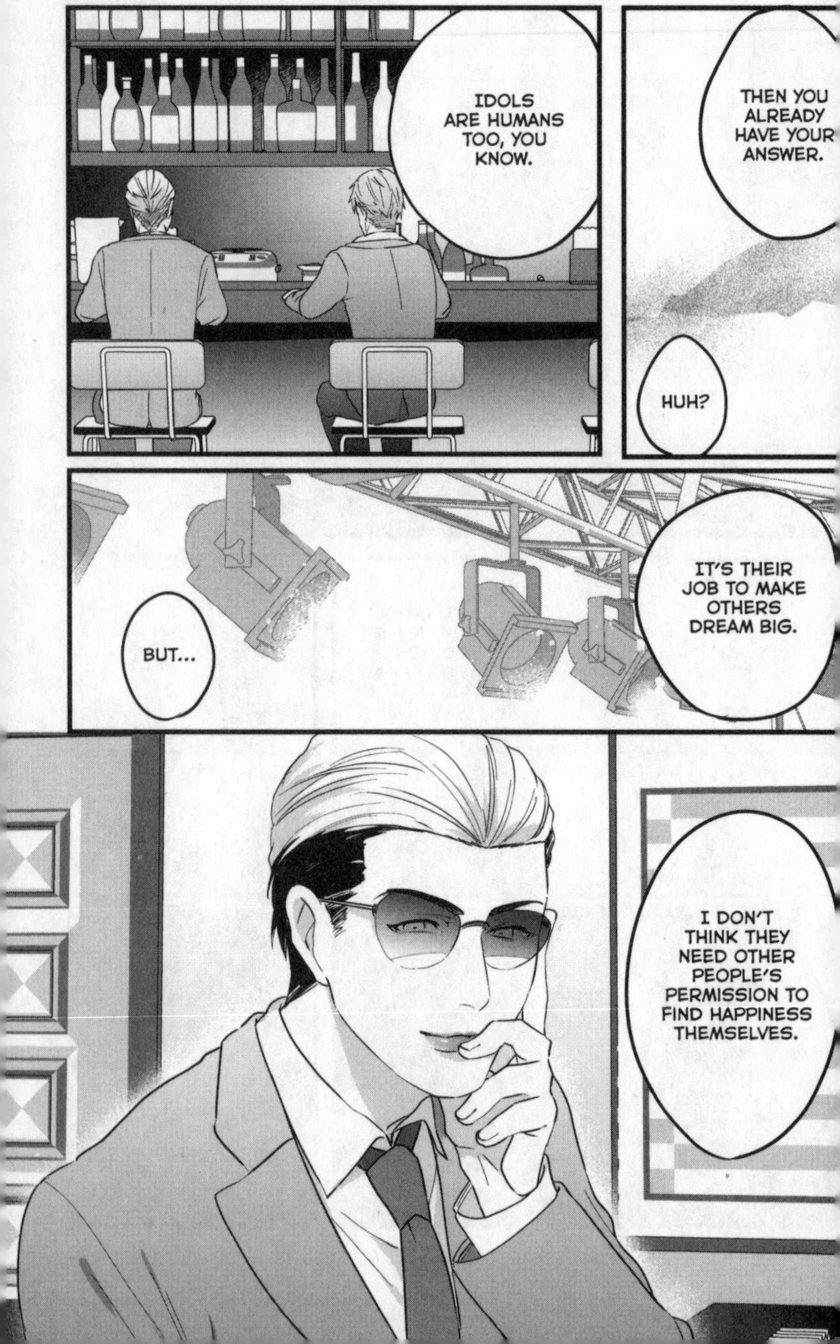
THEN YOU ALREADY HAVE YOUR ANSWER.
HUH?
IDOLS ARE HUMANS TOO, YOU KNOW.
IT'S THEIR JOB TO MAKE OTHERS DREAM BIG.
BUT...
I DON'T THINK THEY NEED OTHER PEOPLE'S PERMISSION TO FIND HAPPINESS THEMSELVES.

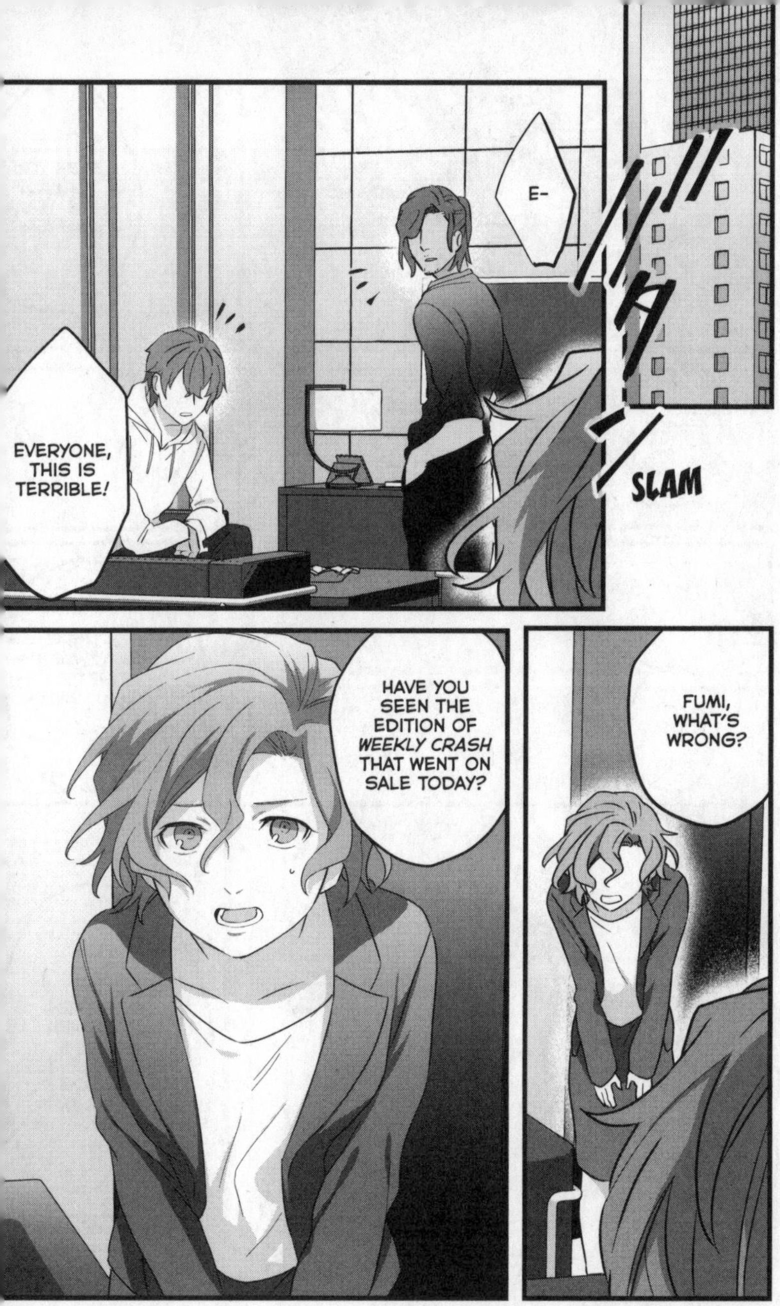
SLAM
E-
EVERYONE, THIS IS TERRIBLE!
FUMI, WHAT'S WRONG?
HAVE YOU SEEN THE EDITION OF *WEEKLY CRASH* THAT WENT ON SALE TODAY?

WEEKLY CRASH
IS FORMER ALPHA MEMBER YOICHI IN A PASSIONATE AFFAIR?
INCLUDES A SCAN-DALOUS PHOTO!
SH
YOICHI IN A PASSIONATE AFFAIR?
INCLUDES A SCAN-DALOUS PHOTO!
IT CAN'T BE...
DID THEY SEE ME WITH MIHACHI?
FLIP

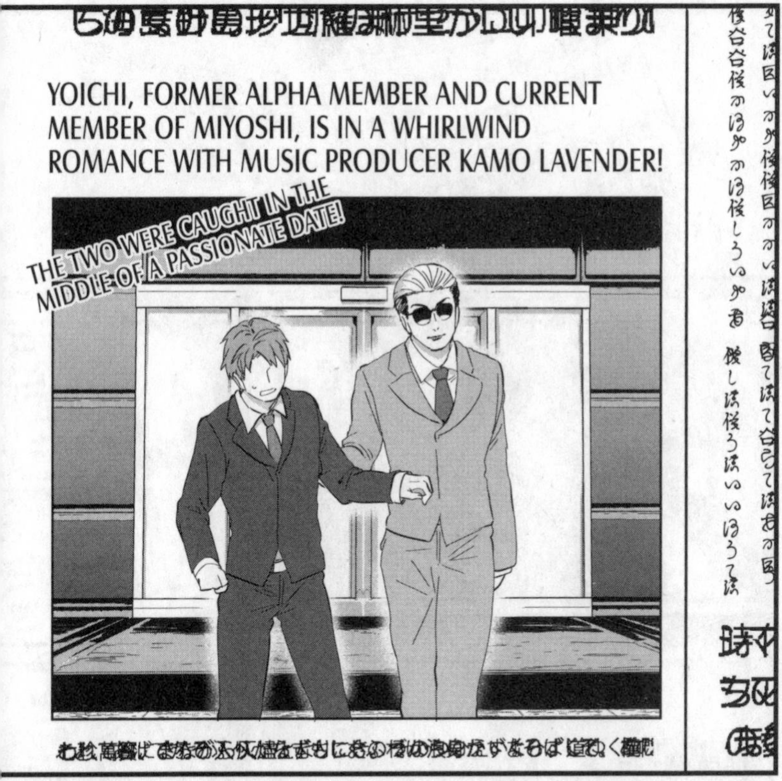
YOICHI, FORMER ALPHA MEMBER AND CURRENT MEMBER OF MIYOSHI, IS IN A WHIRLWIND ROMANCE WITH MUSIC PRODUCER KAMO LAVENDER!
THE TWO WERE CAUGHT IN THE MIDDLE OF A PASSIONATE DATE!

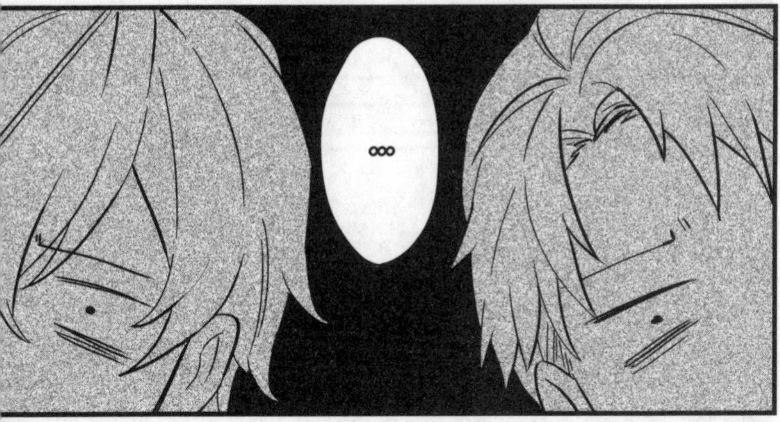
...

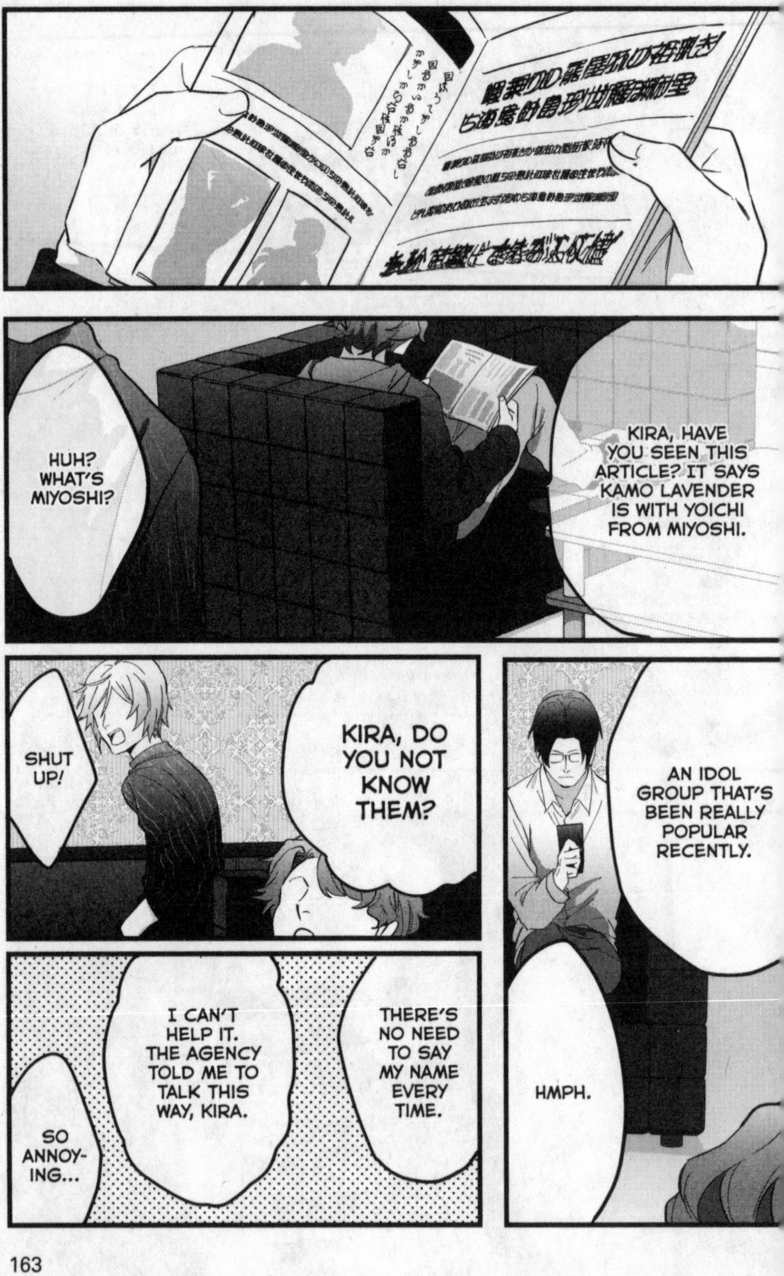
KIRA, HAVE YOU SEEN THIS ARTICLE? IT SAYS KAMO LAVENDER IS WITH YOICHI FROM MIYOSHI.
HUH? WHAT'S MIYOSHI?
AN IDOL GROUP THAT'S BEEN REALLY POPULAR RECENTLY.
HMPH.
KIRA, DO YOU NOT KNOW THEM?
SHUT UP!
THERE'S NO NEED TO SAY MY NAME EVERY TIME.
I CAN'T HELP IT. THE AGENCY TOLD ME TO TALK THIS WAY, KIRA.
SO ANNOY-ING...

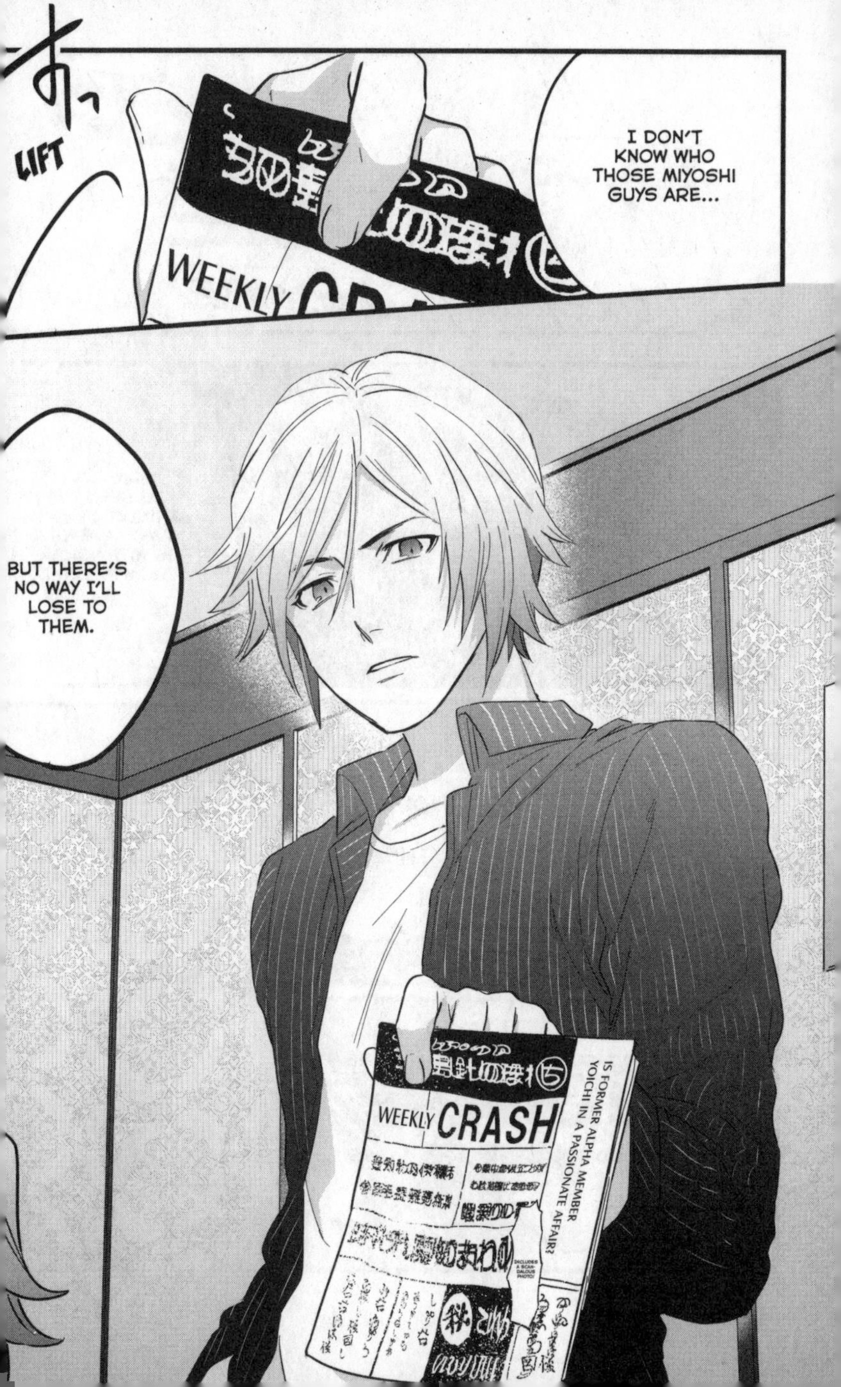
I DON'T KNOW WHO THOSE MIYOSHI GUYS ARE...
あっ
LIFT
BUT THERE'S NO WAY I'LL LOSE TO THEM.
WEEKLY CRASH
IS FORMER ALPHA MEMBER YOICHI IN A PASSIONATE AFFAIR?
INCLUDES A SCANDALOUS PHOTO!

OSSAN IDOL!

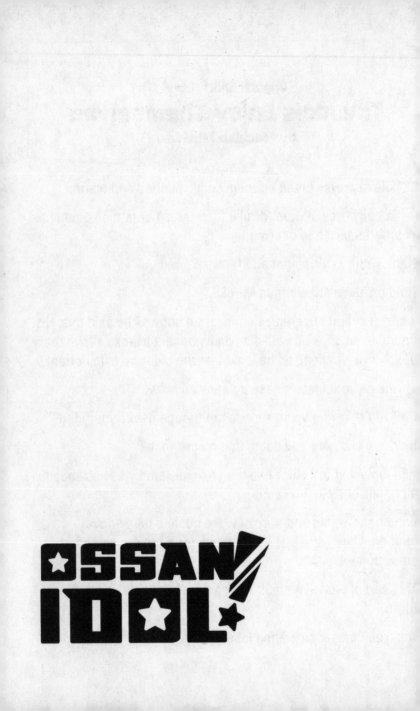

The Idols Enjoy Themselves
by Mochiko Mochida

His pale skin was tinted alluringly pink, flushed and warm.

As his body grew hotter, Miroku focused on breathing quietly as his breath started to get rough.

"Hah… Yoichi, it's so hot and feels so good…"

"Hold on just a little longer, Miroku."

Beads of sweat covered Yoichi's toned body as he said this. His almond eyes crinkled with a smile as he met Miroku's own teary eyes, Miroku panting as he looked at the older man imploringly.

"This is my first time. Please go easy on me…"

"Oh? You're giving up so soon, even though it was your idea?"

"Hey, you two. Are you doing that on purpose?"

Shiju looked at the other two men exasperatedly as he rubbed salt on his body in the sauna.

That's right. Yoichi and Miroku were not in a lovey-dovey situation. They were just there to film for a hot spring and sauna-themed show.

"This sort of work isn't bad. You can really cuddle up to others…"

"Yes, you can get nice and close…"

"Who exactly is that fan service for?"

You guessed it. They're acting like a couple for work.

The filming was for a TV program that shows exclusive features of popular spa facilities. The director decided to invite idols as special guests and MiYoShi received an offer.

They were likely given the offer because, despite being idols, they were not exactly young. The spa facility they were visiting had a number of different saunas, and everyone knows that ossans love saunas. At least, their sponsor seemed to think that way.

"I've never visited a sauna with other people before! And to think I get to enjoy it with Yoichi and Shiju… This is great!"

"Oh, Miroku…"

"Miroku…"

The two older ossans were touched to learn that the youngest member of the group was genuinely happy to spend time with them.

They almost accepted the offer without asking for details, but their talented manager stopped them, steering them back into safe waters. After many twists and turns, they found themselves in the present.

After the last take was okayed and the staff had dispersed in a state of exhaustion, the idols found themselves with free time.

"It's a shame that Fumi's off on her own. It's kind of lonely."

"Don't tell me you want to see our manager naked."

"Miroku…"

"That's not it!"

Their manager, Fumi, had previous engagements and would be meeting up with them later on. Since Yoichi was the director of the talent agency they didn't have any issues managing their schedule, but…

"Ugh, I get so lonely when Fumi's not around that I become completely useless. I'm like an alpaca."

"An alpaca? Don't you mean a rabbit?"

Yoichi tilted his head at Miroku, who seemed suspiciously knowledgeable about animals. After all, otaku aren't just obsessed with entertainment — they tend to be experts in a wide variety of fields.

Since the theme of the facility was "cutting yourself off from the outside world," there were not only magazines and books in the rest areas inside, but also comics and fiction novels for a total of over twenty thousand books. Miroku's eyes sparkled as he immediately set about perusing the shelves.

"Hey, there's a hammock over here."

"Shiju, you shouldn't underestimate hammocks…"

"Ossan, what have hammocks ever done to you?"

Apart from the hot springs and saunas, there were many areas where men and women could relax together. Though they were

ossans, their good looks were starting to attract attention.

Holding several books in hand, Miroku sank into a large cushion with a charming smile, causing several women in the room to let out shrill squeals. The collar of Yoichi's yukata was open wide, baring his chest to help him cool down after the hot sauna. Shiju was just as guilty as he lazily dried his hair, sending out waves of his own fragrance.

"Yoichi, Shiju, let's go in the open-air baths later!"

"Miroku, you're so energetic. But sure, I'll go with you."

"I'm going to get a drink at the bar, so you two can go without me." Shiju had been fighting the hammock for a long time and was finally stretching out on it, so he waved his hand and told the others, "Have fun."

"No, Shiju! One of my editor friends said that it's best to move as a group in these sorts of places."

"You mean the person who interviewed us for the anime magazine before?"

"Yes. You might find yourself caught up with a weirdo if you go off alone."

"They were probably just... Ah, never mind. We should go together."

"Yeah, I agree. Let's all go, Miroku."

"Okay!"

The two older men exchanged exasperated glances as the

...oungest member grinned eagerly.

A few days later, the group held a feedback session at the ...alent agency. They had been able to wear clothes in the sauna, ...ut wearing a towel in the open-air baths was against the spa's ...ules. So they had gone in naked, but their manager fainted ...when she arrived late and saw Miroku in all his naked glory.

"I was just following the rules."

"Be serious, Miroku. We're supposed to be giving each other ...eedback."

"Well... Since the program had a huge amount of viewers, ...guess it was all right in the end... right?"

RUSTLE
ザッ
RUSTLE
ザッ

OSSAN IDOL!

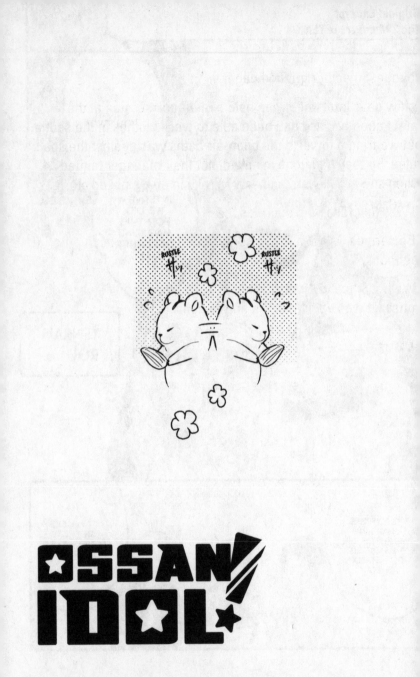

Original Excerpt
The 3 Members of TENKA

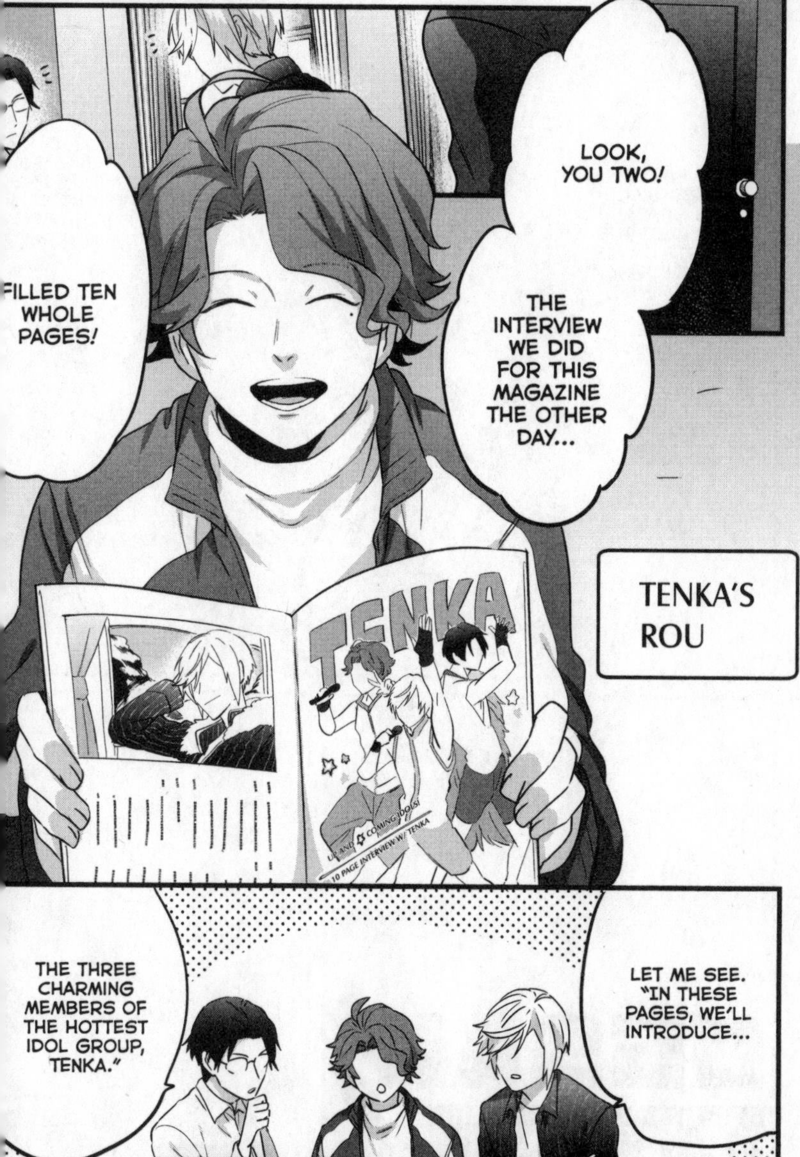
LOOK, YOU TWO!
THE INTERVIEW WE DID FOR THIS MAGAZINE THE OTHER DAY...
FILLED TEN WHOLE PAGES!
TENKA'S ROU
TENKA
UP AND COMING IDOLS!
10 PAGE INTERVIEW W/ TENKA
LET ME SEE. "IN THESE PAGES, WE'LL INTRODUCE...
THE THREE CHARMING MEMBERS OF THE HOTTEST IDOL GROUP, TENKA."

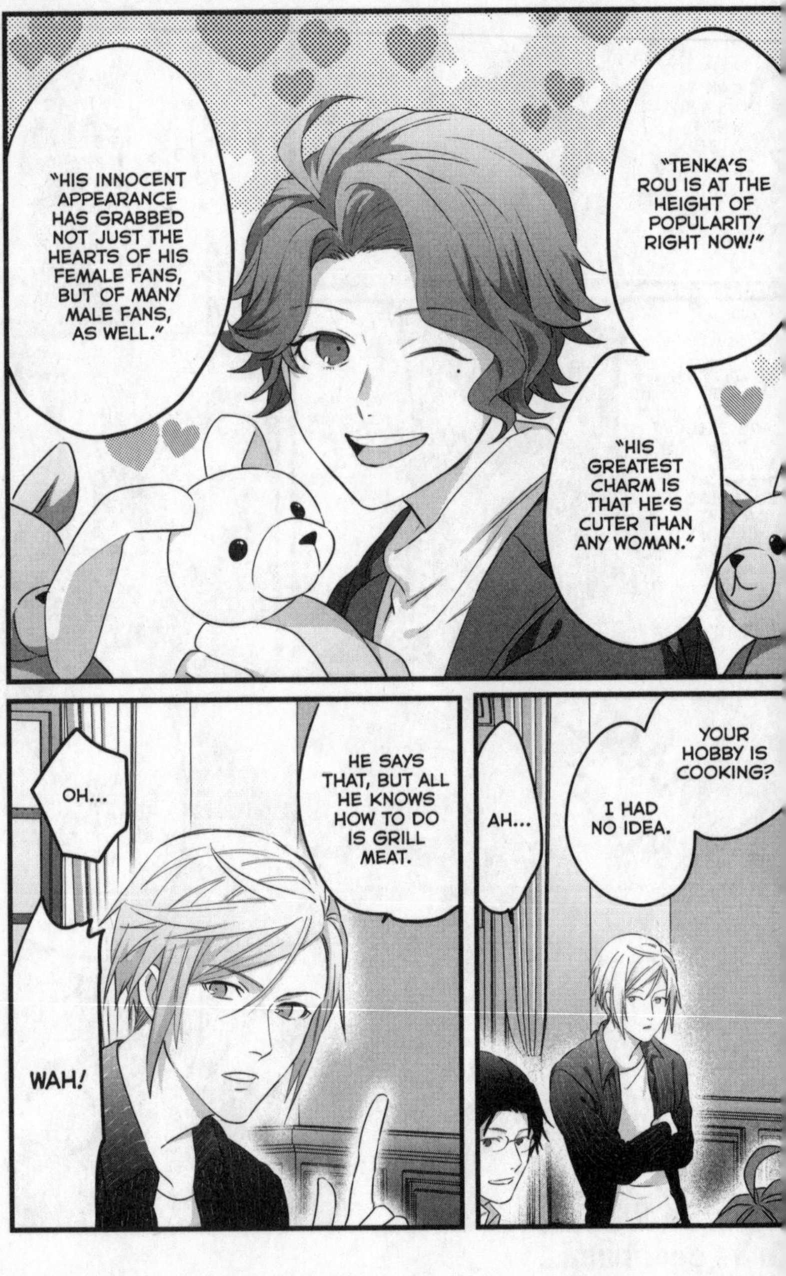
"TENKA'S ROU IS AT THE HEIGHT OF POPULARITY RIGHT NOW!"
"HIS GREATEST CHARM IS THAT HE'S CUTER THAN ANY WOMAN."
"HIS INNOCENT APPEARANCE HAS GRABBED NOT JUST THE HEARTS OF HIS FEMALE FANS, BUT OF MANY MALE FANS, AS WELL."
YOUR HOBBY IS COOKING?
I HAD NO IDEA.
AH...
HE SAYS THAT, BUT ALL HE KNOWS HOW TO DO IS GRILL MEAT.
OH...
WAH!

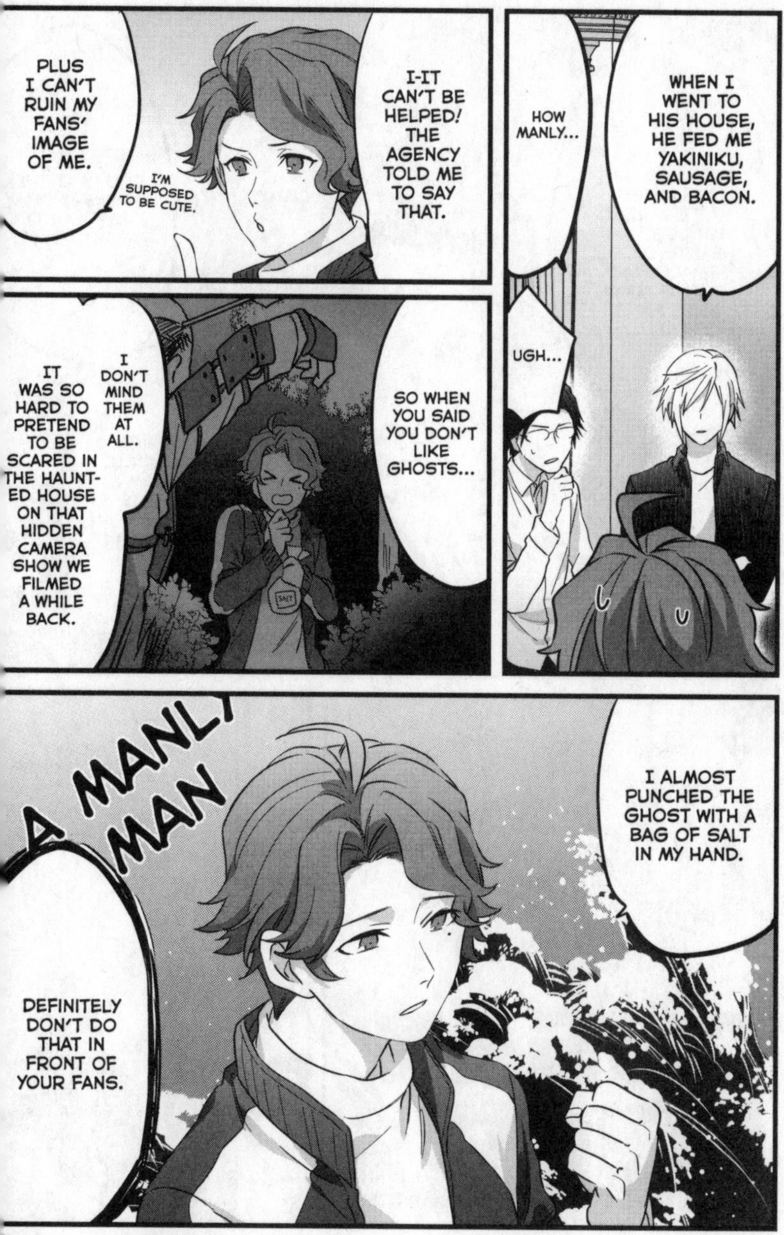

WHEN I WENT TO HIS HOUSE, HE FED ME YAKINIKU, SAUSAGE, AND BACON.
HOW MANLY...
UGH...
I-IT CAN'T BE HELPED! THE AGENCY TOLD ME TO SAY THAT.
PLUS I CAN'T RUIN MY FANS' IMAGE OF ME.
I'M SUPPOSED TO BE CUTE.
SO WHEN YOU SAID YOU DON'T LIKE GHOSTS...
I DON'T MIND THEM AT ALL.
IT WAS SO HARD TO PRETEND TO BE SCARED IN THE HAUNTED HOUSE ON THAT HIDDEN CAMERA SHOW WE FILMED A WHILE BACK.
SALT
I ALMOST PUNCHED THE GHOST WITH A BAG OF SALT IN MY HAND.
A MANLY MAN
DEFINITELY DON'T DO THAT IN FRONT OF YOUR FANS.

To be continued...

OSSAN IDOL!

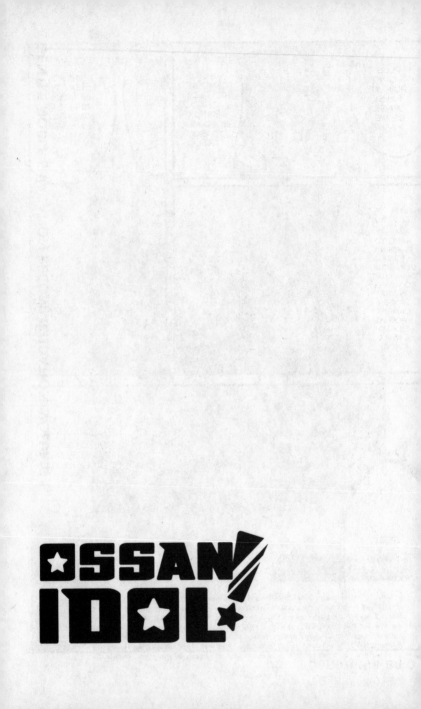

A GENTLE NOBLE'S VACATION RECOMMENDATION, VOLUME 1

Misaki, Momochi & Sando

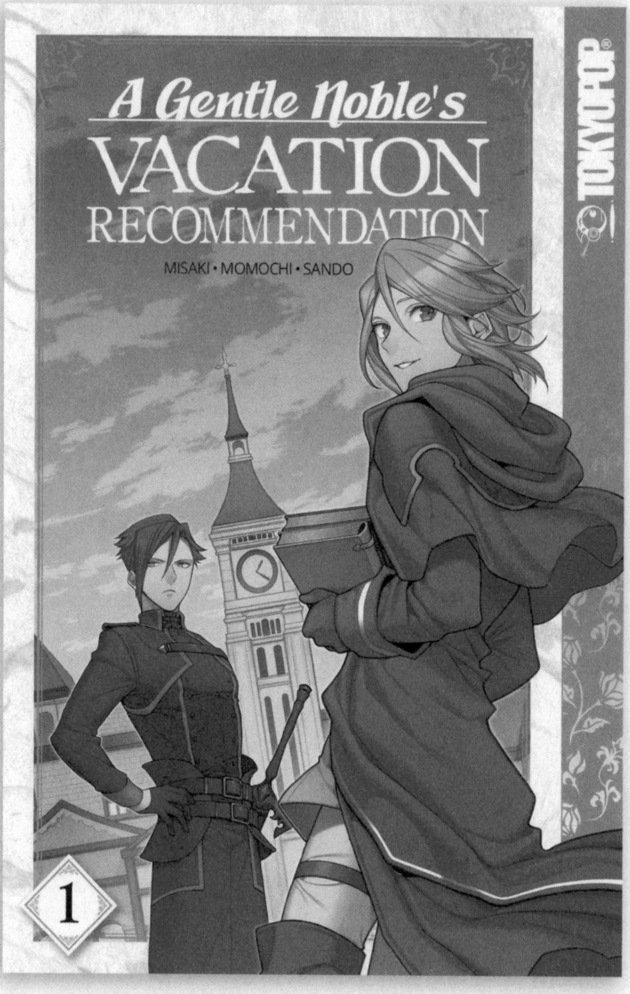
A Gentle Noble's
VACATION
RECOMMENDATION
MISAKI • MOMOCHI • SANDO
TOKYOPOP
1

ISEKAI

When Lizel mysteriously finds himself in a city that bears odd similarities to his own but clearly isn't, he quickly comes to terms with the unlikely truth: this is an entirely different world. Even so, laid-back Lizel isn't the type to panic. He immediately sets out to learn more about this strange place, and to help him do so, hires a seasoned adventurer named Gil as his tour guide and protector. Until he's able to find a way home, Lizel figures this is a perfect opportunity to explore a new way of life adventuring as part of a guild. After all, he's sure he'll go home eventually... might as well enjoy the otherworldly vacation for now!

TOKYOPOP

A GENTLE NOBLE'S VACATION RECOMMENDATION, VOLUME 2

Misaki, Momochi & Sando

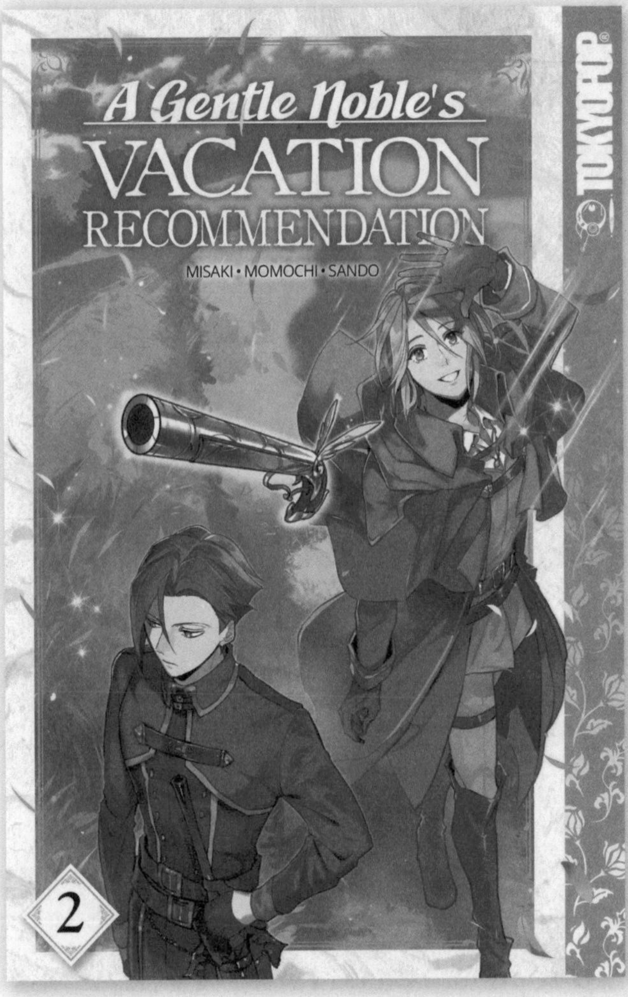
A Gentle Noble's
VACATION
RECOMMENDATION
MISAKI • MOMOCHI • SANDO
TOKYOPOP
2

ISEKAI

Lizel has officially formed a party with his guard and companion, the famous adventurer Gil, who has promised to protect Lizel as they become an official part of the adventurer's guild — and the two are already making waves! Lizel's charming personality has earned him a few friends by now, among them a young appraiser named Judge, the grandson of a rich merchant from the mercantile capital of Marcade. When he asks them to guard him on a trip to visit his grandfather, Lizel happily accepts the opportunity to sightsee and explore in such a famous country. Gil, on the other hand, is more excited to see if there are any super-strong monsters to fight in Marcade's Labyrinth. It's time for the newly-formed party to prove their mettle!

TOKYOPOP

TOKYOPOP
BanG Dream!
Girls Band Party!
Roselia Stage
1 DR PEPPERCO
Craft Egg / Bushiroad

BANG DREAM! GIRLS BAND PARTY! ROSELIA STAGE, VOLUME 1

Dr pepperco

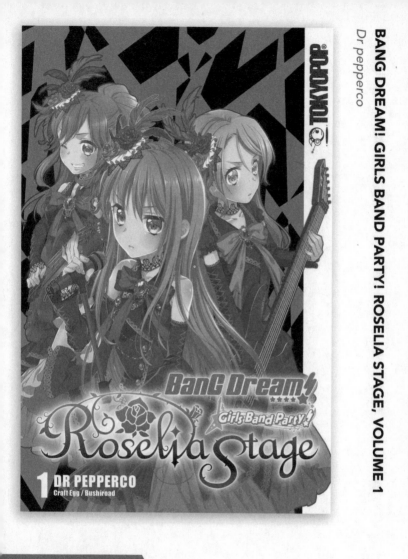

IDOL

After her father's dreams of making it big in the music industry crumble beneath the strain of trying to appease both his managers and his fans, singer Yukina Minato is determined to make him proud by forming the "perfect band" of her own. But first, she'll have to find all the right members. They'll need unparalleled skill, passion and drive if they're going to succeed as a J-rock band in such a crowded scene! Future World Fes is the biggest music event of the year, a world-famous spectacular that showcases only the best of the best. Do five high school girls have what it takes to rock their competition and secure a spot on the main stage?

BANG DREAM! GIRLS BAND PARTY! ROSELIA STAGE, VOLUME 2

Dr pepperco

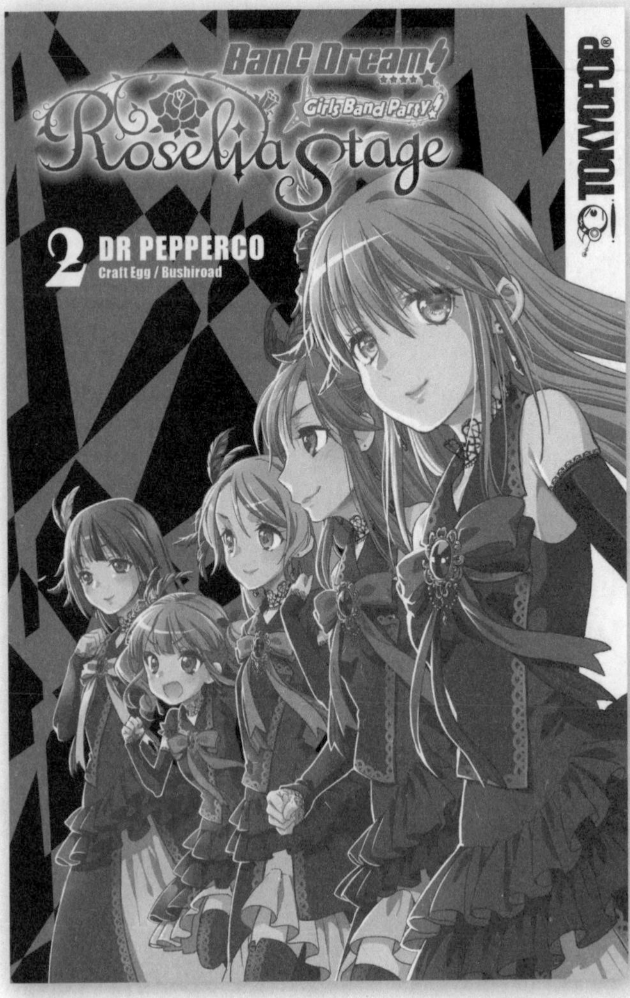
BanG Dream!
Girls Band Party!
Roselia Stage
2 DR PEPPERCO
Craft Egg / Bushiroad
TOKYOPOP

IDOL

As the contest to perform at Future World Fes draws near, pressure mounts from all sides for the members of Roselia — the rigorous practice they need to do every day to stay sharp, family tensions running high, and on top of everything else, a shocking development for Yukina.

When a professional record label approaches her to sign a solo deal, Yukina finds herself facing an impossibly heavy choice. Should she take the shortest path to achieving her dreams, even if it means leaving her band members in the dust? Or should she risk it all, staking her future on the ragtag group of amateur musicians she might actually be willing to call her friends?

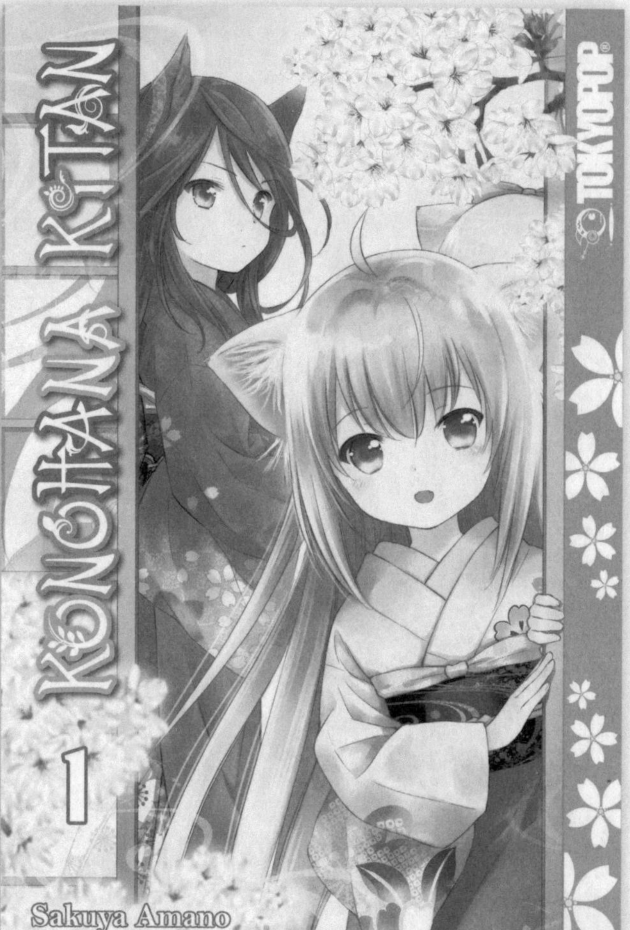
KONOHANA KITAN
1
Sakuya Amano
TOKYOPOP

KONOHANA KITAN, VOL 1

Sakuya Amano

FANTASY

Yuzu is a brand new employee at Konohanatei, the hot-springs inn that sits on the crossroads between worlds.

A simple, clumsy but charmingly earnest girl, Yuzu must now figure out her new life working alongside all the other fox-spirits who run the inn under one cardinal rule - at Konohanatei, every guest is a god!

TOKYOPOP

KONOHANA KITAN, VOL 2
Sakuya Amano

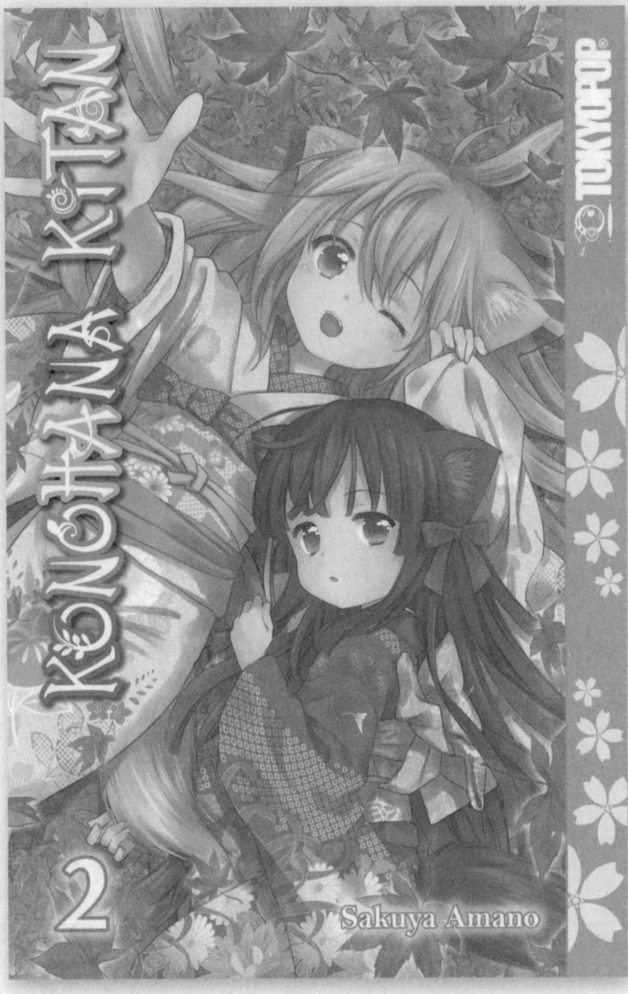

KONOHANA KITAN
2
Sakuya Amano
TOKYOPOP

FANTASY

At Konohanatei, every guest is considered a god — but when an actual deity, the Great Spirit of Bubbles, comes to the inn for a bath, Yuzu and her fox friends get (many) more of her than they bargained for!

Other guests stopping by the inn this time include a beautiful girl who weaves with the rain, a cursed Japanese doll, and... a mermaid?! Even Hiiragi, Satsuki's gorgeous older sister, drops in for a visit despite their rocky relationship. Perhaps the peaceful, otherworldly Konohanatei is just the right place to mend strained sibling bonds.

TOKYOPOP®

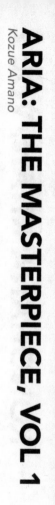

ARIA: THE MASTERPIECE, VOL 1

Kozue Amano

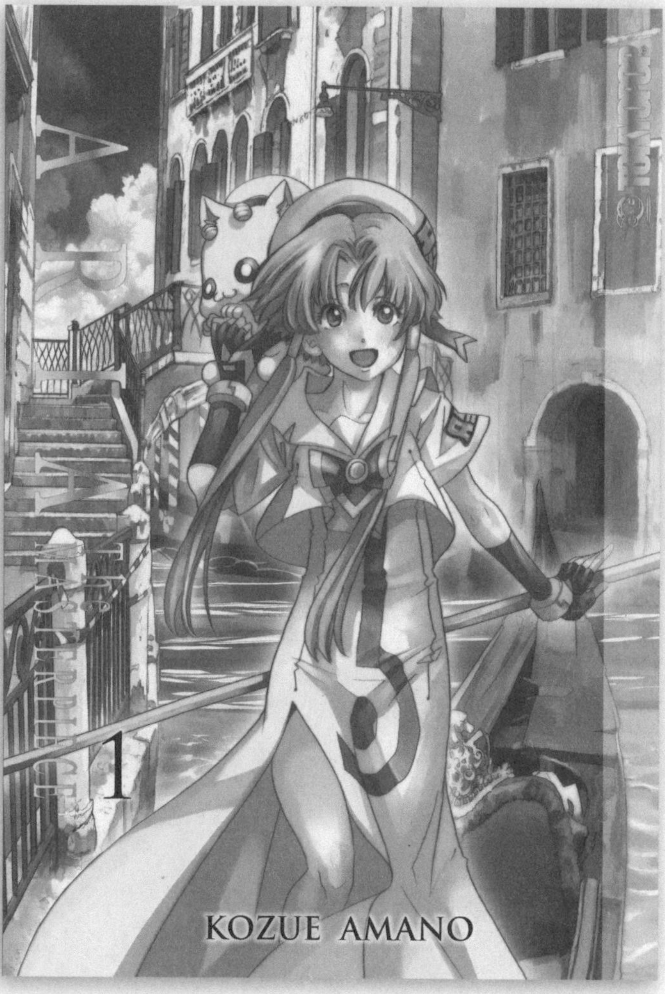
KOZUE AMANO

FANTASY

On the planet Aqua, a world once known as Mars, Akari Mizunashi has just made her home in the town of Neo-Venezia, a futuristic imitation of the ancient city of Venice. In pursuit of her dream to become an Undine — a gondolier who leads high-end tours around the city — Akari joins as a trainee with the Aria Company, one of the three most prestigious water-guide companies in Neo-Venezia.

ARIA: THE MASTERPIECE, VOL 2
Kozue Amano

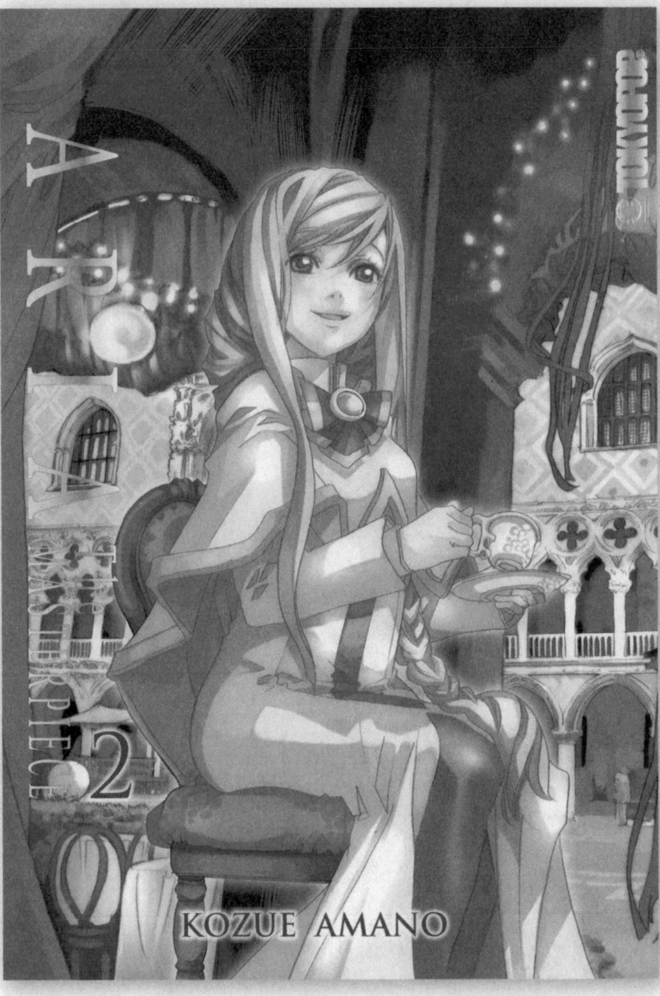
ARIA
THE MASTERPIECE
2
KOZUE AMANO
TOKYOPOP

FANTASY

On her journey to becoming an Undine, Akari works hard alongside trainees from the other prominent tour companies, Himeya and Orange Planet. Even though they'll be competitors one day, it doesn't mean they can't get along! Every day brings all sorts of new adventures, new friends, and new sights to see around the beautiful Neo-Venezia.

Experience the world of Aqua like never before with Kozue Amano's gorgeously detailed illustrations and full-color spreads in this deluxe collector's edition!

TOKYOPOP

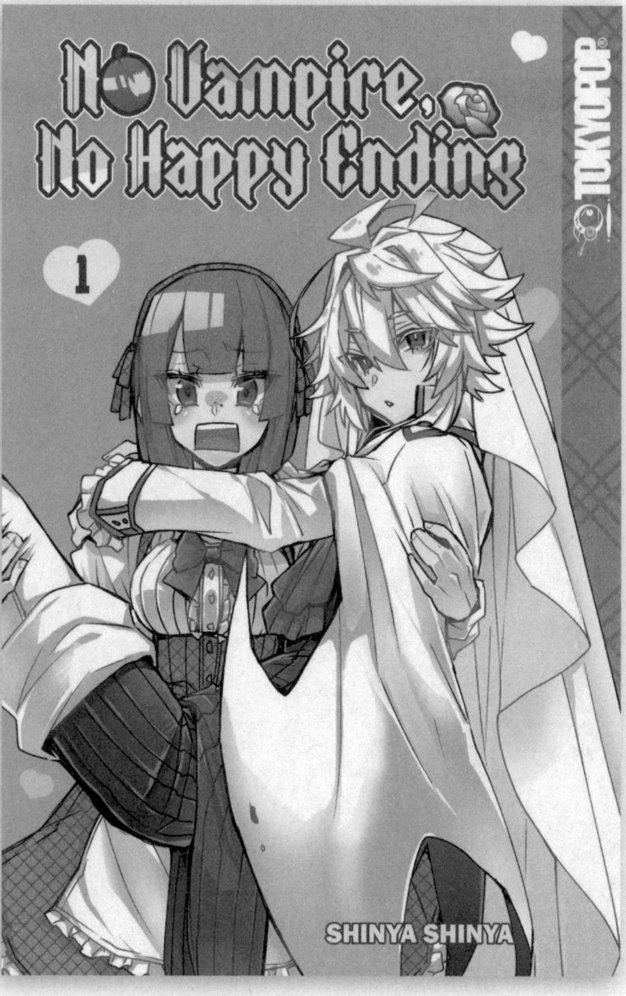

No Vampire, No Happy Ending
1
SHINYA SHINYA
TOKYOPOP

NO VAMPIRE, NO HAPPY ENDING, VOLUME 1

Shinya Shinya

LOVE x LOVE

Arika is what you could charitably call a vampire "enthusiast." When she stumbles across the beautiful and mysterious vampire Divo however, her excitement quickly turns to disappointment as she discovers he's not exactly like the seductive, manipulative villains in her stories. His looks win first place, but his head's a space case. Armed with her extensive knowledge of vampire lore, Arika downgrades Divo to a beta vampire and begins their long, long... long journey to educate him in the ways of the undead.

TOKYOPOP

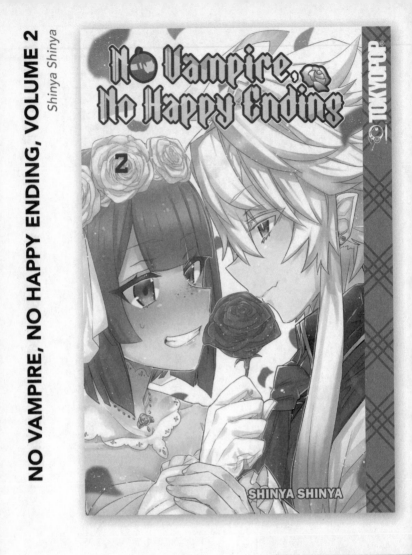

No Vampire, No Happy Ending

2

SHINYA SHINYA

TOKYOPOP

♀LOVE-x-LOVE♂

TOKYOPOP

When die-hard vampire enthusiast Arika comes across a mysterious young man named Divo, it seems she struck the jackpot-- she's found a drop-dead gorgeous vampire of her own! Unfortunately, she quickly finds out the disappointing truth: Divo is all beauty, no brains, and no vampire instincts whatsoever. What's a vampire-loving girl to do? Teach him, of course! The grand finale of the laugh-out-loud supernatural love comedy featuring a vampire in beta and the vampire fangirl determined to make him worth her time!

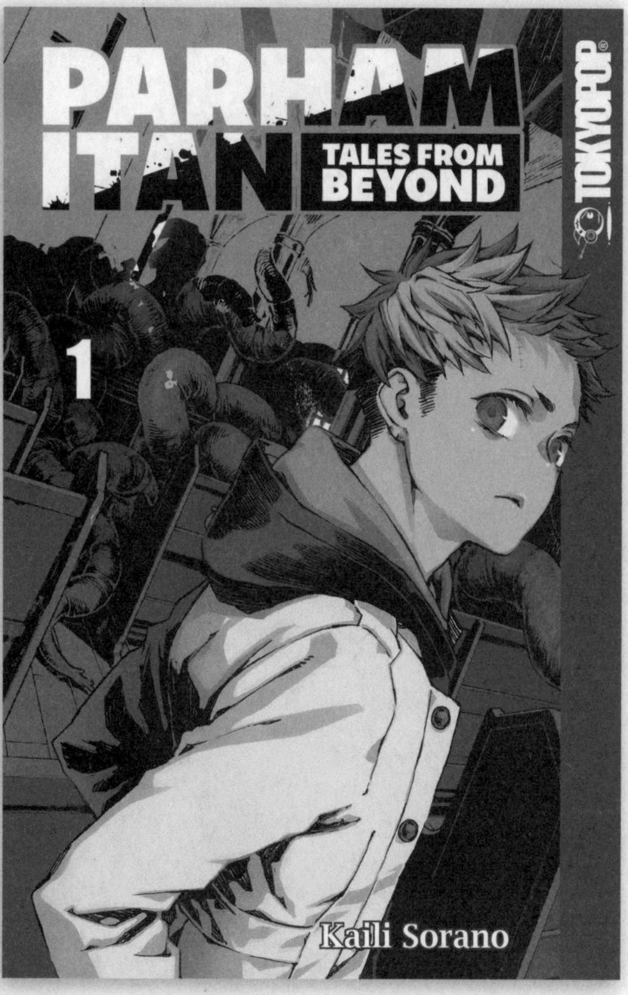
PARHAM ITAN
TALES FROM BEYOND
TOKYOPOP
1
Kaili Sorano

PARHAM ITAN: TALES FROM BEYOND, VOLUME 1

Kaili Sorano

SUPERNATURAL

Yamagishi and Sendo are schoolmates, but that's about as far as their similarities go: one is a short, no-nonsense boxer, while the other is a tall, bookish conspiracy nut. But when they find themselves embroiled in a paranormal phenomenon at school involving plant-faced monster people assimilating innocent victims, it seems they'll have to set aside their differences and work together as best as they can. Of course, it doesn't help that the only one with any answers to this bizarre situation is a mysterious "paranormal investigator" named Akisato, who insists they must find some sort of "key" to stop it all — before giant insects and other preternatural perils from the world "beyond" get to them first. Inspired by Lovecraftian horror and the Call of Cthulhu, this is a brand-new manga series from the creator of Monochrome Factor!

TOKYOPOP

PARHAM ITAN: TALES FROM BEYOND, VOLUME 2
Kaili Sorano

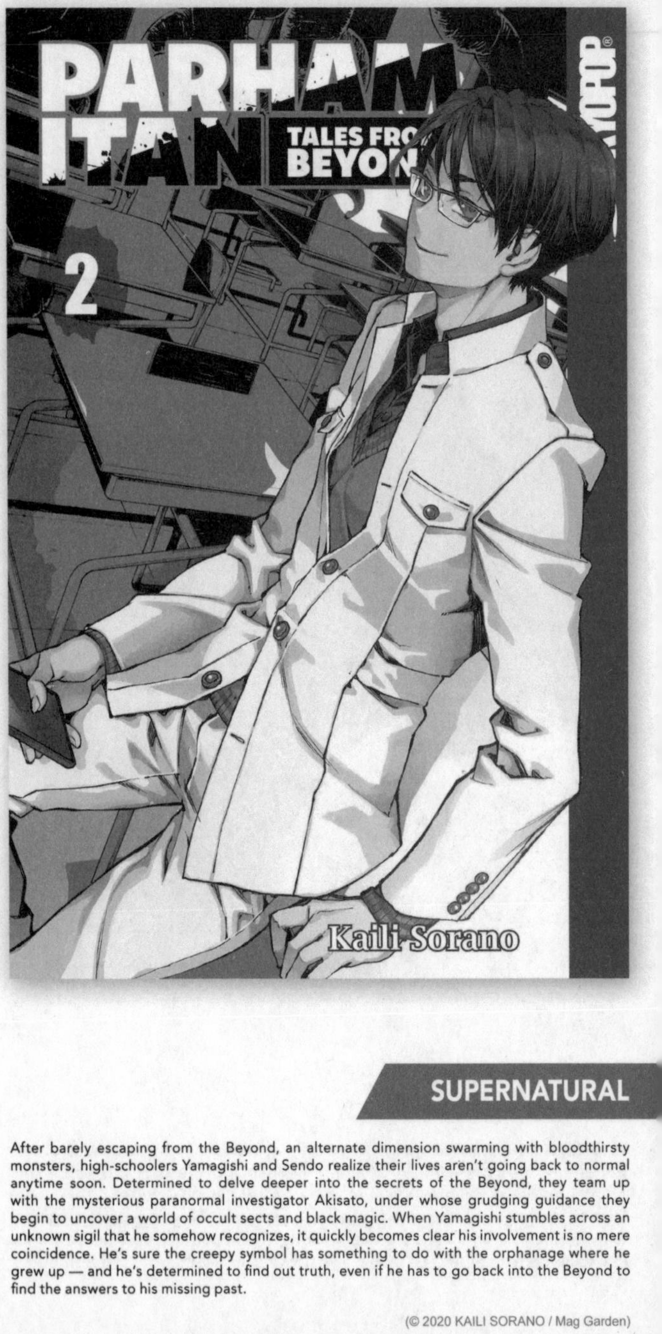
PARHAM
ITAN
TALES FRO
BEYON
2
TOKYOPOP
Kaili Sorano

SUPERNATURAL

After barely escaping from the Beyond, an alternate dimension swarming with bloodthirsty monsters, high-schoolers Yamagishi and Sendo realize their lives aren't going back to normal anytime soon. Determined to delve deeper into the secrets of the Beyond, they team up with the mysterious paranormal investigator Akisato, under whose grudging guidance they begin to uncover a world of occult sects and black magic. When Yamagishi stumbles across an unknown sigil that he somehow recognizes, it quickly becomes clear his involvement is no mere coincidence. He's sure the creepy symbol has something to do with the orphanage where he grew up — and he's determined to find out truth, even if he has to go back into the Beyond to find the answers to his missing past.

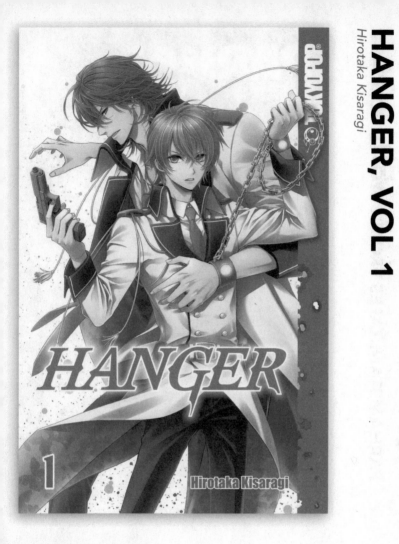

HANGER, VOL 1

Hirotaka Kisaragi

HANGER

1

Hirotaka Kisaragi

◊LOVE-x-LOVE◊

In a futuristic Neo-Tokyo, crime is rising rapidly in the wake of a new generation of super-drugs capable of enhancing the user's physical and mental abilities. Hajime Tsukumo is a new recruit on a federal task force trained to go after these powered-up criminals. Now he must team up with Zeroichi, a so-called Hanger looking to reduce his own jail sentence in exchange for helping to take down these chemically-boosted bad guys.

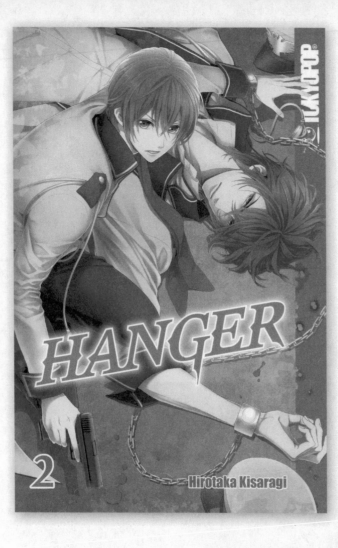

HANGER, VOL 2
Hirotaka Kisaragi

HANGER

2

Hirotaka Kisaragi

TOKYOPOP®

ᘒLOVE-x-LOVEᘒ

Afraid that Hajime could suffer the same tragic fate as his previous Keeper, Zeroichi intentionally widens the emotional distance between them for Hajime's own safety, leaving a frustrated and hurt Hajime doubting the kind of relationship they really have. Unfortunately, finding the time to sort out their feelings isn't a luxury either of them can afford— not with the mysterious group responsible for the death of Zeroichi's former Keeper suddenly terrorizing Neo-Tokyo once more.

TOKYOPOP®

Ossan Idol! Volume 4
Manga by Ichika Kino
Original story by Mochiko Mochida

Editor - Lena Atanassova
Copy Editor - M. Cara Carper
Marketing Associate - Kae Winters
Translator - Katie Kimura
Quality Check - Shingo Nemoto
Proofreader - Caroline Wong
Ediorial Associate - Janae Young
Licensing Specialist - Arika Yanaka
Cover Design - Sol DeLeo
Retouching and Lettering - Vibrraant Publishing Studio
Editor-in-Chief & Publisher - Stu Levy

A  Manga

TOKYOPOP inc.
5200 W Century Blvd
Suite 705
Los Angeles, CA 90045 USA

E-mail: info@TOKYOPOP.com
Come visit us online at www.TOKYOPOP.com

f www.facebook.com/TOKYOPOP
🐦 www.twitter.com/TOKYOPOP
📌 www.pinterest.com/TOKYOPOP
📷 www.instagram.com/TOKYOPOP

OSSAN 36 GA IDOL NI NARUHANASHI 4
©2020 Kino Ichika ©2020 Mochico Mochida

First published in Japan in 2020 by Shufu To Seikatsu Sha Co., Ltd.
English translation rights reserved by TOKYOPOP. under the license from Shufu To Seikatsu Sha Co., Ltd.

ISBN: 978-1-4278-6805-3
First TOKYOPOP Printing: May 2021
10 9 8 7 6 5 4 3 2 1
Printed in CANADA

STOP

THIS IS THE BACK OF THE BOOK!

How do you read manga-style? It's simple! Let's practice -- just start in the top right panel and follow the numbers below!

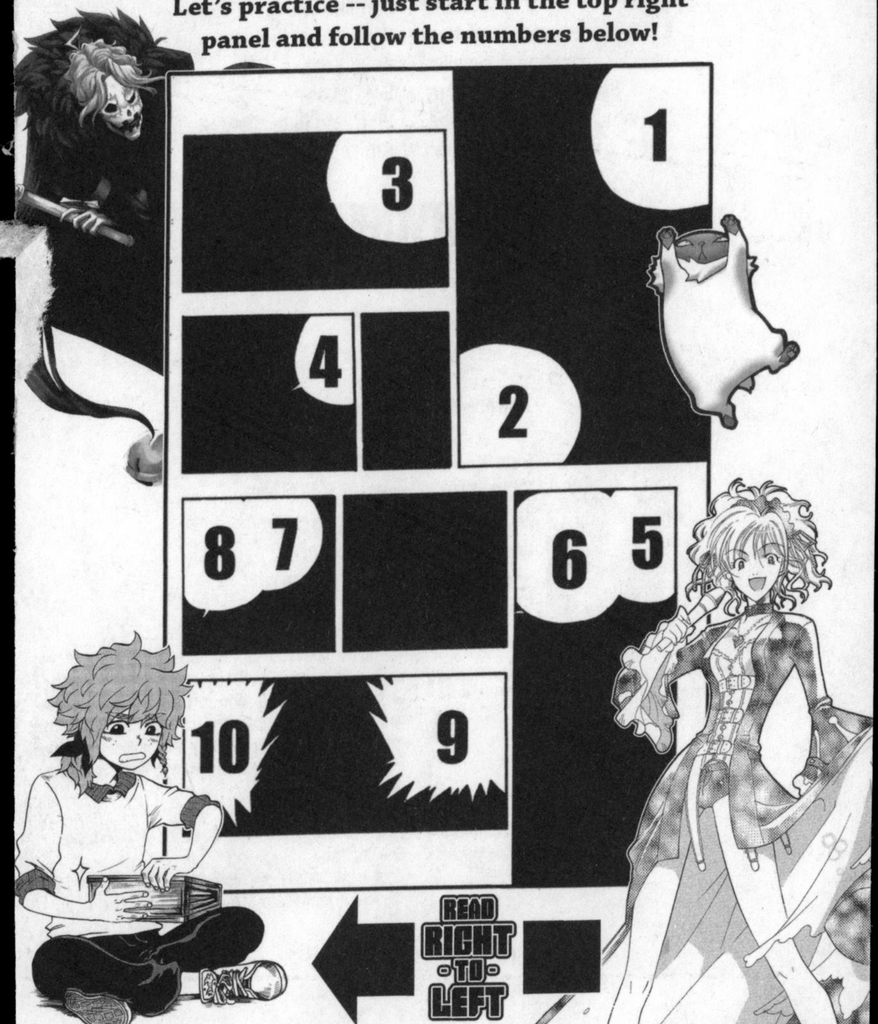
1
2
3
4
5
6
7
8
9
10
READ
RIGHT
-TO-
LEFT

Crimson from *Kamo* / Fairy Cat from *Grimms Manga Tales*
Morrey from *Goldfisch* / Princess Ai from *Princess Ai*